THE COMPLETE GUIDE TO
PAINTBALL

FOURTH EDITION

Hatherleigh Press
New York

THE
COMPLETE
PAINT

FOURTH EDITION

Jerry Braun • Rob Rubin • Dawn Allcot • Steve Davidson • Justin Owen • Mike Paxson • Pete "Robbo" Robinson • Stew Smith

Photographed by Peter Field Peck

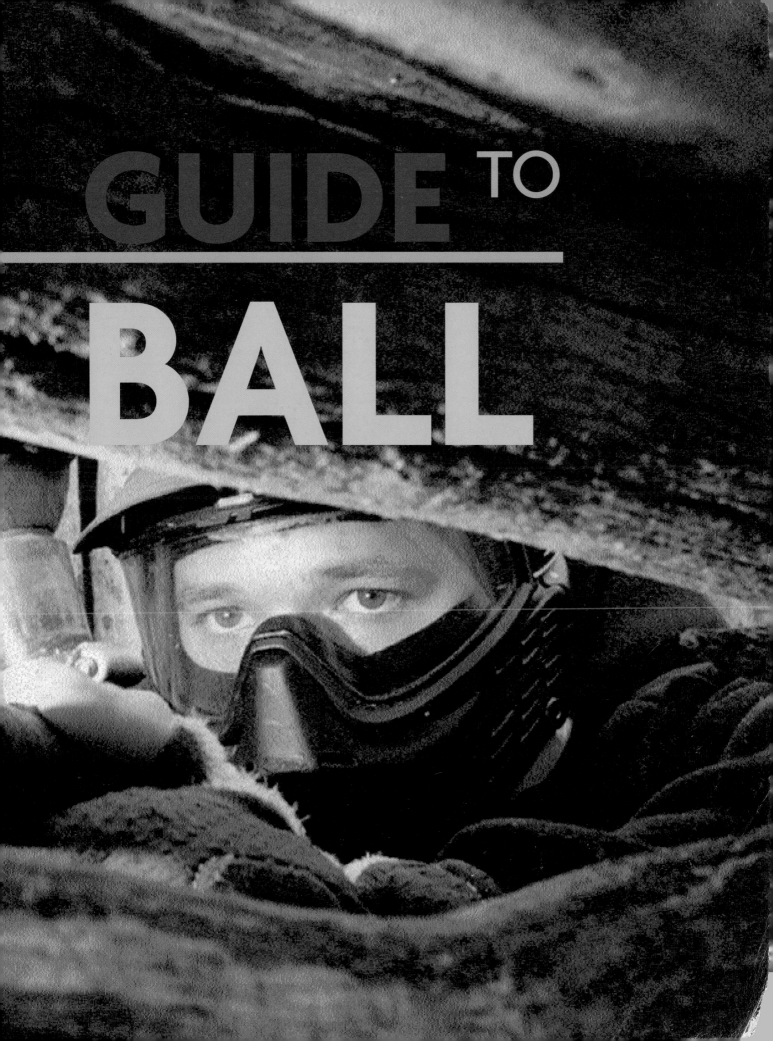

GUIDE TO
BALL

The Complete Guide to Paintball
Fourth Edition

ISBN: 978-1-57826-254-0

Adaptations of "Getting Started," "Rules to Play By," and "Common Mistakes," courtesy of splatterzone.com

The Complete Guide to Paintball
A GETFITNOW.com Book

Fourth edition © 2007 Hatherleigh Press/GETFITNOW.com
Third edition © 2004 Hatherleigh Press/GETFITNOW.com
Second edition © 2003 Hatherleigh Press/GETFITNOW.com
First edition © 1999 Hatherleigh Press/GETFITNOW.com

Hatherleigh Press/GETFITNOW.com Books
5-22 46th Avenue, Suite 200
Long Island City, NY 11101

Visit our website: paintball.getfitnow.com

All Hatherleigh Press titles are available for bulk purchase, special promotions, and premiums. For more information, please contact the manager of our Special Sales Department at 1-800-528-2550.

Photographed with Canon® cameras and lenses on Fuji® and Kodak® print and slide film
Text design and composition by edn Design
The text is set in Agenda
Cover photos by Michael Wise II © chrono300.com
Cover designed by Deborah Miller and Allison Furrer

Printed on acid-free paper
10 9 8 7 6 5 4 3 2 1
Printed in the United States

"A friend of ours found this gun in an agricultural catalogue that was used by cattlemen to mark cows. It wasn't long afterwards that we bought two of these things and had ourselves a little duel. After it was over, we just knew we had stumbled upon something great."

- Hayes Noel

Acknowledgments

The editors and publisher are grateful to the following individuals for their assistance and encouragement in the publication of this book.

Jerry Braun and Paintball Sports International, for their endless help and support.

Cousins Paintball, for the use of their field in Medford, NY for our photo shoots. Paul Sattler, Fred Dorski, and Elio Napolitano, for giving so generously of their time and knowledge.

Jay Tavitian, and everyone at Oceanside Paintball, for showing us the time of our lives.

Sarah Stevenson, Karen Barber, and the entire 2 Die 4 team for their knowledge, enthusiasm and determination.

Cleo and Paul Fogal, for sharing their home, their field, and their story with us.

Mike Henry, Jim Lively, and Colin Thompson, for always leading us in the right direction.

NY Dogs, a great bunch of guys and a terrific team of paintball players. It was an honor playing with them.

Glenn Palmer, for always lending his assistance and equipment so willingly to this project.

Graham Easton, for helping outfit us for this paintball adventure.

Bill Mills of warpig.com for all their guidance and assistance.

Guy Cooper of Pro Star Sports, for his informative "Paintball Field Operator's Guide."

Steve Dunn and Extreme Adventures Canada, for the use of their Flak Jacket. It helped make Peter's job a little less painful.

National Paintball Supply, for the use of Squeegee Man.

The entire Wild Geese team, and especially Ralph Torrell, for sharing with us his extensive paintball gun collection.

Jim Della Constanza, for making Skyball such an enjoyable tournament.

Matthew Howard, for all his assistance with our Australian paintball directory.

Rob "Tyger" Rubin, for his endless support, cheerful guidance, and invaluable advice.

Tom Kaye and Patrick and Diane McKinnon, who head Celebrity Paintball for no profit to benefit the charities and Paintball in general, for their assistance.

Dawn Allcot, Bea Youngs, and Mike Paxson, for the breath of fresh air and perspective that they brought to updating this project.

Andrew Mohebbi of pbreview.com, for generously lending us a print version of his fantastic field database and for maintaining such a great resource for paintball enthusiasts everywhere.

Michael Wise II of www.chrono300.com, for sharing his wonderful photo collection with us.

Jason "Muzikman" Beam, for his photos of Shatnerball and other scenario games.

Dawn Mills of Smart Parts, for her assistance in obtaining updated photos and graphics.

We would also like to thank the following companies for generously loaning us equipment.

ADCO, Brass Eagle, Diablo, Diggers, JT, Kingman International, Lapco, Palmer's Pursuit Shop, Pro-Team Products, R. P. Scherer, Sheridan, Smart Parts, Soft Boards & Barriers Co., Tippmann Pneumatics, WDP, and Zap.

To everyone in the paintball industry — the players, manufacturers, field owners, distributors, and fans. We couldn't have written this book without your help and support. Thank you!

Contents

WHO IS THIS BOOK FOR?

This book is for everyone who plays or is interested in playing paintball. Everyone will appreciate the scope of this edition; it is as much a tribute to the diversity within the game and its players as it is a guide. Regardless of your skill level, this book holds something for you.

We cover the fascinating history of the game (with firsthand accounts from its originators!), and the basic rules of the game (and descriptions of exciting variations on the paintball theme!). We offer in-depth equipment and gun information, and include essential tactical insights, as well as a thorough glossary and resource guide. Beginners and novices take note: Insights from the best players in the world make this book an ideal starting point for those of you serious about adding new dimensions of fun and excitement to your hobby and becoming great at this game.

For those of you who have played for a few years or are seasoned veterans, check out this book's authoritative analysis of guns and air systems, articles on advanced strategy, exclusive input on injury prevention stretches from former Navy SEAL, Stewart Smith, discussion of accessories, and comprehensive listing of international resources for both playing and purchasing equipment.

Our authoritative sections on the physics of paintball and guidelines for cleaning your gun correctly are among many gems in this book. We're sure that you'll find our interviews with great players both enlightening and useful in your search for competitive advantages. Motivated to elevate your game to the next level and beyond? Read on!

And then, of course, there are the pictures—visually arresting, dynamic shots taken by Peter Peck, who was himself "shot" innumerable times garnering these photographs as well as photos collected from all corners of the paintball world. If you just love the game and want a book that captures the action, look no further.

Although we have attempted to be comprehensive, we realize that this volume is not the last word on the sport. For example, such luminaries as Jerry Braun, Bob Long, Jim Lively, and Dawn and Bill Mills of warpig.com gave of their time and shared insights that made this book possible. We would have loved to include more from them. We did not cover scenario games, a paintball format that we learned early on truly merits its own book. That said, we believe that we're off to a strong start. In the interest of ensuring that future editions raise the bar, we encourage you to contact us with your feedback about aspects of the game we ought to cover for the first time or in greater depth.

WHO IS PAINTBALL FOR?

For those of us who play paintball and love it, the question is what are you looking for in a game?

The answers that lead directly to paintball are listed below

If these are your answers, welcome home! This game is for you. Otherwise, you should read on. You just may want to change your mind.

I want fast-paced, totally immersive action.

There isn't a single, true standstill in paintball play, nor is there a moment where you don't feel like something is at stake. You are on offense and defense constantly, and your objectives require you to be alert and decisive—not hyper, mind you, just in the flow of the game. Opponents lurk around every corner and paintballs travel at up to 300 feet per second. You need to survive, but be willing to make a coordinated sacrifice to win the game for your team. Your teammates count on you to act with caution and precisely controlled aggression from one moment to the next. You can hear your competition moving toward you. You see paintballs flying and hear them splat against trees or barriers. You slide forward on your knees, dive behind a tree, cover your teammates' advance, celebrate victory after a hard-fought contest. Guaranteed to render computer simulations a permanent second choice, paintball is the premiere action game.

I want a vigorous mental challenge as well as a rigorous physical one.

This is a thinking person's game. A lapse in concentration leads to elimination. If you're indoors, you may choose tactics based on speedy deployment with constant movement and firing in support of advances. If you're outdoors on a wide open field, you may want to split your force in two and converge on the enemy from opposite directions. To win at this game consistently, you and your team must use appropriate tactics while communicating (that means speaking and listening) coherently, and thinking quickly to adapt to the unexpected. It takes maturity to act as an individual without losing sight of your role in a team effort. It takes intelligence and quick decision making to prevail in the hair-raising scenarios that paintball presents.

I want a game I can play.

Except for the newborn, paintball is for everyone! The rules are straightforward, there are games and formats for every skill level, and the costs of playing are affordable. You can play the game with family and friends, with your church group, with corporate colleagues, or even go on your own simply to meet people who share your passion for intense, team-oriented sports. Whether things go well or not during your game, you will form a unique bond with whomever you play. And you can't make friends of strangers any faster than by playing paintball with them. It's safe to say that paintball is an unparalleled social experience, and open to all comers.

I want to be the best at whatever game I play.

If you put in the time and energy, form a great team, train together regularly, and have a little luck, you can become a professional paintball player, experience a tempo of game play that is unsurpassed, and vie for national and international championships against the best players in the world. For some, being a weekend warrior is enough. Others play for the thrill of victory, and seek out ever higher levels of competition. Paintball serves up plenty of opportunities for everyone. How far you go in this sport is largely up to you.

Whether you played tag or hide-and-seek when you were younger or yesterday, this game, in any of its manifestations, represents the most thrilling experience of competition you are likely ever to experience. Add to that the extraordinary comraderie you invariably develop with teammates, and you have one of the best games ever invented!

PAINTBALL IS FOR YOU!

Everybody wants to experience adventure—a highly intensified, dramatic realization of acting heroically and skillfully to attain a goal. We seek a sense of mission, of honoring our values, of taking advantage of opportunities that present themselves in our professional and romantic lives. Paintball is a microcosm of the adventure we experience each day. It crystallizes the sense of drama we seek to lend meaning to our choices and actions. Paintball taps into your imagination—what if my life hinges on what I choose to do in the next moment? Paintball provides a rapid succession of such moments that lead to an unparalleled gaming experience that is both universal and highly personal for every player. For those of you looking for a game that is more than the sum of its parts, here it is. Seize it!

WHO ARE WE?

The authors and interviewees are among the finest and most influential men and women ever involved with the game of paintball. For them, paintball is a passion of one sort or another. They share in common a singular devotion to the widespread enjoyment of this game, and that is why we sought their involvement with this endeavor. We think you'll be thrilled with the results.

The publisher of this book is a multifaceted multimedia company that perceived a unique opportunity to present an authoritative text on the subject of paintball to the game's growing base of enthusiastic participants, among whom we count ourselves.

GETFITNOW.com is an imprint of The Hatherleigh Company, Ltd. committed to developing multimedia health and fitness products for consumers of all ages. We believe that leading a healthy life-style can and should be a source of enjoyment and fulfillment. Paintball combines vigorous physical activity and tactical thinking in a way that we find irresistably fun.

You should go play this game as soon as possible.

—AWC

Genesis of the Game

Smart-thinking,
alert and precise action,
and good fortune
lead to victory

WHAT IS PAINTBALL REALLY ABOUT?

Paintball is an extraordinarily simple game in its basic form. A couple of people alternately hunt and evade one another, until one person or a team emerges triumphant over another. The victor is the first to achieve an objective or the last left standing. Yes, the game uses sophisticated technology, which is constantly evolving as people come up with new paintball accessories and gun mechanisms, and the specific objectives vary according to game designers' imaginations. But the basic game remains the same.

No matter what version of the game you find yourself most attracted to, its essence is constant. What is paintball's essence? The answer is two-fold.

Paintball is a Game

Paintball is, in the final analysis, one of many games people play with balls. In what is basically an advanced version of tag, the balls—gel-encased, water soluble goo—are propelled at up to 300 feet per second by a special, gas-powered gun. You eliminate (tag) opponents when paintballs you or your teammates shoot hit and break on them. Simple, right? And, as with any game, the whole point of it is to have a good time in a competitive context. Like football, basketball, and baseball, elements of paintball require players to acquire and practice certain skills. Like these other games, it has rules, some hard and fast and others that are subject to interpretation. It shares in common with more free form activities, like skateboarding and surfing, built-in enthusiasm for innovation, personal style, fast-thinking, and highly individualistic approaches. As the people who played the first game did, anyone can come up with their own version of the game. Once

with other people—family, friends, coworkers—who are our team members. There is no escaping the fact that however well we may do on our own, we lead more fulfilling lives when we spend time in meaningful pursuits with others who share our values and goals.

Especially in America, with our culture of "manifest destiny," and the "American Dream," we are hard-wired with an optimistic and moral sense that people should put forth their best effort, go for it, "just do it," when it comes to just about everything in life. We attach importance not only to our goals, but to how we achieve them.

Be honest. Don't lie.
Be considerate. Don't be violent.
Follow the rules. Don't cheat.
Be creative. Don't be predictable.
Have fun. Don't have a negative outlook.
Be a team player. Don't be egotistical.
Be resilient. Don't ever give up.

Of course, these are things all people value, not just Americans. They work for everybody in all situations.

Paintball captures the essence of the basic struggle of every living being. Staying in the game is the most obvious metaphor for staying alive. And winning is about being great at surviving while vanquishing foes in fair play.

The game of paintball creates a situation in which the only way to survive is to act in a manner that balances precise aggression with caution. You attain objectives by taking risks that you have a good chance of handling.

Being great at paintball requires you to learn how to take great risks and succeed.

you're equipped with the essential safety equipment, there is enormous room for having your own kind of fun with this game.

Paintball is About Survival

Paintball is also more than just a game. At its most exhilarating moments, it is an intensified version of what people do everyday. With varying degrees of success, we're all avoiding and confronting obstacles on our way to reaching goals. This is the case whether you're in school or pursuing a career, a man or a woman, regardless of your beliefs or ethnicity.

We're all survivors. We all have goals that we're in different stages of reaching. We take risks. We learn from our mistakes and get back into the fray. We improve at the skills necessary to meet daily objectives and lifelong dreams. We do all of this

It is also a very physical game, and to play it well means executing moves quickly and dynamically. The height of game play is achieved by mastering basic techniques and tactics, improvising effectively, working well with a team, and being fit.

The notion of paintball as a test of survival skills is what inspired its progenitors, Hayes Noel and Charles Gaines.

BIG QUESTIONS

A little less than 20 years ago, these two very close friends discovered a way to test ideas they had debated extensively during their relationship. Are we born with all the resources we need to survive, or do we learn how to survive in response to our environment? Are survival skills learned in one context portable to other contexts? How does a person's tolerance for risk affect his ability to prevail in

© Michael Wise II, chrono300.com

adverse conditions? What is the relationship between honesty and survival? To address these tremendous questions, Noel and Gaines devised a game they called, simply, "survival." Today, we know that game as paintball. When you play, give a moment's thought to the questions this game was first invented and played to resolve. What are your answers? You can learn more about what the founders were thinking in their interviews in this book.

FROM "THE NATIONAL SURVIVAL GAME" TO TODAY

Seizing a unique opportunity to turn the game into a profitable business model, Noel and Gaines teamed up with a friend, Bob Gurnsey, and started selling marking guns and paint, and access to fields where people could get together to play the survival game. The first guns—Nelspot 007s—were made by the Nelson Paint Company, which actually had the guns manufactured under contract by the Daisy Manufacturing Company Incorporated. They made up rules for simple games like Capture the Flag and Total Elimination. This was the birth of the first paintball franchise, The National Survival Game, and what would grow to a 3 billion dollar industry.

Soon other franchises emerged that started to experiment with new kinds of team games. New technologies and the development of unique paintball products dramatically accelerated the evolution of multiple paintball formats, from recreational play to scenario games, from amateur tournaments to professional, international championships.

The game has undergone dramatic changes over the years. If you look closely, however, you'll see that its essence has survived.

—AWC

In the Beginning

Hayes Noel

Walking through the woods one day . . .

The actual genesis of the game really started in my mind on a walk through the woods of Virginia with a friend of mine who lives in Charlottesville and has a farm there. We were walking through the farm and he was talking about hunting wild buffalo. I'm not a hunter myself, but I was enthralled by his story. He was talking about hunting buffalo in Africa and how he was in these bulrushes and couldn't see the beasts but could hear them, about having to be aware of wind direction, about the feelings he had experienced in this extreme scenario.

I was really caught up in the thrill and the excitement and the high that he clearly had felt doing that kind of thing. The severity of the situation he was describing, the notion of survival being boiled down to a few decisive moments, just blew me away. This was 1976 and I was 35 years old. I said, "Why don't we just stalk and hunt each other on the way back to the house?" I'd done this as a kid, playing cowboys and Indians and things. But somehow the context of his story made me feel like more was at stake, and I had this remarkable adrenaline rush. I didn't forget it when I returned to New York City where I lived for 15 years making my living trading the markets on the American Stock Exchange.

I used to go to New Hampshire about once every two months to see Charles Gaines, who's one of my best friends, as well as a big outdoorsman, hunter, writer . . . a guy just totally at home in the wilderness.

Charles said something like, "You know, if I ever got you in the woods you'd be dead meat in a second." So we began a conversation and then sort of a debate over almost a year and a half about surviving in the wilderness and what qualities it would take.

I told him that if I could survive in the Wall Street jungle, I would survive in any jungle. Charles thought this was nonsense, but I was convinced that survival skills were transportable across environments. For example, to my way of thinking tolerance for risk-taking, aggressive and defensive tendencies, a tempo of decision making and action are things that one masters in order to excel in any context. Charles believed that survival skills were inextricably linked to context, and could be learned or acquired in one environment without the benefits accruing to experiences in others. So I could be great on Wall Street, but would be devoured in the forest. Needless to say, this was a great debate.

We'd read Richard Connell's "The Most Dangerous Game" in high school and stuff like that always really turned us on. And then we were in the midst of this debate for over a year and half, and gradually over the course of our conversations we tried to devise good survival tests. And maybe with that story kicking around subconsciously somewhere in there, we developed a sense that we needed a hunting game to test our theories.

But we really never could come up with anything, until a friend of ours, George Butler, found this paintball gun in an agricultural catalogue that was used by cattlemen to mark cows. It wasn't long afterwards that we bought two of these things and had ourselves a little duel. After it was over, we just knew that we had stumbled upon something great. Almost right away we were talking about the potential for games based on survival using this kind of gun.

—Excerpt from interview with Adam W. Cohen

Hayes Noel currently trades the markets in Santa Cruz, CA, where he lives with his wife and two children.

Welcome to the Game of Paintball

PAINTBALL AT GROUND ZERO

Hayes Noel

ADAM COHEN: So who won that first duel?

HAYES NOEL: [Laughs] Charles did. He's a much better shot than I am. In fact, he shot me directly in the ass. [Laughs] I was wearing a bathing suit. We didn't have goggles or any protective gear, but what did we know? We were just thrilled to be doing this finally. I shot at him first and missed. Then he got me in the butt. His shot raised a little welt, which stung for a while. As far as I was concerned, that just made it more realistic.

We could see right then that we had the tool we needed to play this kind of hunting game that we wanted, because it wasn't like these tomato wars that they have in New Hampshire or Vermont. These guns were fairly accurate and could really tag you from quite a distance away. So they were sort of like guns without the danger of guns.

Not long after the duel, we played a little stalking game out in one of the wooded fields around his house. I was ecstatic because I knew that now we could play these awesome games whenever we wanted.

Photo courtesy of Hayes Noel

So then Bob Gurnsey got involved in it when we started to formulate the rules and an idea of the game. The three of us spent another six months arguing about the rules, and how a large-scale competitive version of the game would be structured.

We had decided to invite 9 different people that we knew to join us and play this game. The participants were from all over the country, people who were successful in whatever they had undertaken to accomplish. For example, we invited a guy from Alabama, who was one of the best wild turkey guides and hunters in the sport. We had two guys who had been long-range reconnaissance patrol leaders in Vietnam. Among the others were a lawyer or two, a doctor from Chicago, a movie producer from Los Angeles, and the outdoor writer for Sports Illustrated who had been cleared to do an article on the game.

The mix of people was exciting. Some were local New Hampshire friends of Charles. The man who eventually won, Richard White, was a local lumber man and deer hunter.

Anyway, we took this 80 acre cross-country ski area, filled with second growth woods. You could see through it. There were trails and it was clear enough that you could move pretty well through these woods. We marked off the boundaries of the space and appointed a responsible friend of ours to be head judge.

So we had these four flag stations. In each flag station there were 12 flags of the same color, one for each player. So there was one flag station with 12 blue flags just hanging out in the open and others with 12 green flags, 12 yellow flags, and 12 red flags. Each flag station had a judge with a whistle.

At 10 o'clock in the morning, we positioned

© Cleo Fogal

people at equal distances apart along the circumference of the area. Some guy fired a shotgun and it started.

The first person to go in and get one flag of each color and get back out without being shot won the game as soon as he reached the home base where the head judge was waiting. We didn't know how long it would take. Everybody had a different color paint, so you could tell who shot you by color. And if you got any paint on you at all, even splatter from a hit on a tree, you were out. That's not the way it's done now, but that was the way that we did it then. Everybody was cammoed up and looked really intense. I'm certain that observers would be simultaneously a little bothered and titillated by the militant look. We weren't striving for that. We were just wearing what made sense to wear when you're running around in the woods trying not to be seen.

At the beginning of the game, everybody had maps. And as I said, we had a judge with a whistle at each flag station. These judges blew their whistles every 15 minutes so that the non-woodsmen who couldn't read the map that well had a way of gauging their progress toward a given flag.

ADAM: What are some examples of strategies that you saw?

HAYES: One obvious strategy involved running full speed to the station you were closest to at the outset of the game, and then shooting every person who approached it. The idea was that once you shot 11 people you knew there was nobody else and you could just walk through the woods and get the other flags. This would be rational, but very risky.

Another strategy was just to wait. Remember, we didn't know how long it would take for everything to work out, and nobody wanted to get eliminated early. After waiting, you could move and feel relatively confident that your opponents weren't behind you. This was less risky.

Another strategy was to hunt everybody down,

play aggressive until there was nobody left—definitely the riskiest approach. There were a lot of different ways to play it.

ADAM: What was your strategy?

HAYES: Well, I was in really good shape. I knew that I would not get tired, no matter how long the game took. My strategy was to walk the perimeter, basically run around our field of 80 acres.

Since I was running along the boundary, I only had to worry about one side of me. When I got close to where a flag station was, I followed a straight line to it, and then returned along the same path. I knew I was unlikely to encounter someone where I had just been.

And it turns out there was not a lot of activity around the flag stations; the bottom line is that 80 acres was probably way too big for the game. But we didn't know that. I was doing well. I actually got three flags before anybody did. But then I couldn't find the fourth flag station [*laughs*], and

Welcome to the Game of Paintball

as I wandered around looking for it, I ended up getting in a fire fight with a doctor, Bob Carlson, who was this intensely aggressive guy. He was having fun trying to shoot everybody. I don't think he even got a single flag. In general, the more shooting fights you go into, the greater your chance of elimination. He eliminated me. Anyway, that was my strategy. And it was just totally exciting.

As it turned out, the illusion of danger was so real, it was the most exciting thing I had ever done. Every cell in my body was turned on. After the first 15 minutes, every breeze that blew something was like an alarm bell; you didn't know if it was somebody behind you, around you, above you. I mean it was a whole new level of excitement.

And it ended up that the game was over after about two and a half hours and I'd say at least nine or ten of the people were out of it at that point, or had been shot. The guy who ended up winning it had been in the woods all his life. Richard White never fired a shot at anybody, and he was never shot at the whole time. He just walked through the woods and kept himself out of trouble.

ADAM: How did this outcome inform your debate?

HAYES: The conclusion you can draw from the first game is essentially that the less aggressive you are, the better off you are. But that needs to be qualified. The guy who won was not taking a risk-less strategy. He went for the flags. He just avoided firefights.

ADAM: He was on offense, but cautious.

HAYES: Yeah, he was invisible. I don't think we really settled the debate. But we did know that this game was amazing. Bob and Charles and I knew that this was fun. Bob pushed this more than anybody, but we all knew that we were onto something that many people were going to want to do.

I mean, it would just turn people on when they read this Sports Illustrated article. We decided to start some type of operation, a company, to try and promote this game and make a business out of it, basically.

ADAM: So that's really how the first game went, and led directly to the formation of your company.

HAYES: That's pretty much the idea and origin of the first game and the experience playing it. It was unique for everybody, you know. Charles and everybody there had a different experience. For some people, like myself, I took it pretty seriously and I was really into it.

We played in June of 1981, and in November of '81, the Sports Illustrated article came out.

ADAM: Not soon after this experience, you started a paintball company.

HAYES: That's right.

ADAM: Tell us about how you made that happen.

HAYES: Sure. Bob and I flew out to the Nelson Paint Company that made the paintball gun and sought an exclusive contract with them to sell the guns to us and nobody else except cattlemen.

We knew there were people who wanted to play the National Survival Game. It wasn't called "paintball" back then. We named the company after the game as we'd named it, and we called the various scenarios we promoted survival games. Paintball is probably a better name, but that came later.

We flew out to their Michigan headquarters, and we asked them, "How many markers [paintball guns] did you sell last year?" Bob and I didn't have any idea of what their business was like. The paintballs were made by a company called R.P. Scherer that makes vitamins and gelatin capsules. They sold the paintballs to Nelson. Nelson just made the guns to try and sell paint. It was just a product they had.

So anyway, they responded, "Oh, we sold about 700 last year." And we said, "If you give us this price, we can guarantee sales of 2000." I literally just picked a number. It turned out in the first year we sold about seven or eight thousand. Nelson couldn't keep up with our orders. We didn't know whether we'd be a mail order firm or how it would work out. We ended up authorizing people to set up deals for fields and resell our merchandise.

Guys from Atlanta would call and say, "I'd like to start a paintball company. I'll buy 30 guns." So instead of selling guns to individuals, we'd sell 25 to a guy who was going to rent them out to people to play.

Eventually, areas around the country were covered by people who owned franchises, and we wouldn't sell guns to anybody else within their area. For the first two or three years, we were the only show in town.

Then, people found out about Nelson. Nelson began selling to them at the original retail price. We couldn't control that after a while.

ADAM: How was business?

HAYES: Incredible. Sales skyrocketed. We turned a profit after about six months. Most startup companies take two or three years to show a profit. These days you've got Internet companies that don't make anything but vaporware but are worth millions and billions. We were legitimately successful from the start.

We were never as confident as we probably should have been. We were preoccupied with the image thing, how the game was perceived.

ADAM: I've heard that the game's militant look was a publicity problem from the start.

HAYES: Unfortunately, yes. For instance, during the early going, I went to Chicago. The Donahue Show had called and wanted us to talk about what we were doing. Local news shows, anybody who had heard about it, they all wanted to come cover us, because it was kind of controversial and looked really violent. Of course, it really wasn't, but they were selling their story, and it made good copy and dramatic pictures.

I went out to Chicago for the Donahue Show, and then did a segment of Nightline with Ted Koppel in New York.

So, I talked a little bit to the Donahue producer about the game, and we sent them a gun. I really wanted Donahue to shoot me on the set, inside the studio, at point blank range. I figured that it would take something that dramatic, that looks cool and would make clear to people that paintball wasn't really dangerous, to soften people's impression of the game. Donahue wouldn't do it. Instead, he invited me and an "anti-violence" psychologist for a debate format. The psychologist thought any G.I. Joe toys and stuff like that were problematic. They

© Michael Wise II, chrono300.com

© Cleo Fogal

"Tonight we have the survival game. Is it a game or is it more than a game?"

Then he turned and shot this thing and it sounded like a cannon going off. [*Laughs*] And it went right through the paper target. [*Laughs*] It looked as though he could have shot it with a 38 caliber handgun. I mean, the hole looked just like what a bullet would make.

Then the paintball broke when it hit the curtain, and it was red paintball exploding on that white backdrop.

ADAM: So that was kind of bad. [*Laughs*]

HAYES: [*Laughing*] I said, "I know this looks really bad," to myself, and I got pretty uptight. Donahue went and rubbed his finger around the hole like it was a wound or something. He looked at me right in the face and said, "This scares the shit out of me." Just like that.

Well, I knew I was in trouble right there. At the opening of the show, Donahue said, "Well, we just shot the paintball, and I think I'd rather play this game in armor, than with goggles." The woman ended up shooting me on the show, and that was fine. But still, at the end of the show, the audience gets to ask questions, and some woman said, "I just don't even understand what this is all about."

ADAM: How did Nightline go?

HAYES: You wouldn't believe it. They had Ted Koppel doing a live interview with a guy named Frank Camper, who ran a mercenary school in Alabama. About four months earlier, a Pakistani airline flying into England had blown up and people had gotten killed. They had traced some of the terrorists back to this Frank Camper guy. So they presented this information, and then Koppel asked Camper if he ever killed anybody. Frank Camper looks right at the camera and says, "Yeah. Yeah, I have."

So they were saying, "Hey, look, this is what's going on in America. We've got terrorist training bases and now look what people are starting to do

also had a woman and her son who had played the game. There were four of us on the show.

Donahue came in and said, "Now listen, this is not like school, you don't have to raise your hands, it's going to be over in 15 minutes. If you guys have anything to say, you'd better say it." Then he said, "When I open the show, I'm going to shoot a police target." He didn't want to shoot me, so he planned to use a police target instead.

So we go into the studio and there's the live audience ready to go. I know there's a psychologist who's going to try and do me in, so I'm kind of nervous. Donahue's ready to fire away at this silhouette type target that you might see that police shoot at. It was a white, paper silhouette hanging on the back stage curtain.

I said, "Wait a minute. Hey! You can't do that. The paintball will go right through that paper target." And he said, "Oh yeah, you're right." So he got somebody behind the curtain to hold a blackboard up behind the thing. But then he said [*Laughs*], for recreation. Look at the games they're playing." They showed pictures of people playing the paintball game out in the woods, and they really tried to do a number on us. Anyway, that was on a Saturday night. Well, Monday morning in the office we got about 200 calls. [*Laughs*] "Where can I play this game. It looks great! It looks like fun."

After that we started to relax a little bit about the image. But we were always concerned about it. So anyway, the acceptance of it, it just really grew and it started evolving. And then other companies started making paintball guns and just like any business, rival manufacturers and stuff crept up and the industry took off.

ADAM: We've heard that the industry is up to 800 million dollars in total revenue. [Editor's Note: This was current in 1998, when this interview was conducted. Today, Paintball is a 3 billion dollar industry.]

HAYES: Yeah. So it's a really big business. And whether it's going to continue to grow and so forth will be interesting to see.

ADAM: To hear you talk about it sounds like it was a game that on some basic level everybody was playing. All kids play one form of tag or another, and hide-and-seek.

HAYES: Right.

ADAM: You guys sort of tapped into this whole idea of using the paintball gun instead of make-believe or fruit. You formalized the game, gave it a

© Michael Wise II, chrono300.com

new instrument and more mature format. But it's still a game that human beings just play, because they are naturally excited by the chase and the hunt.

HAYES: Yeah, I mean, you can ask any kid why he plays cops and robbers or cowboys and Indians. It's a raw, primal thing that never goes away.

In order to become a business, the game had to evolve from the individual game, which is far and away the most interesting in my opinion. The game we played where every individual was against every other individual was the ultimate. It became a game where teams played against other teams. When you play it that way in smaller fields, you shoot more paint.

So the name of the game is selling guns and selling paintballs. We were always against that. Let me clarify. We weren't against the idea of the team game, because from a business respect, that made more sense. But we opposed the virtual extinction of the individual game. Unfortunately, it just doesn't work as well from a business standpoint.

ADAM: What do you think about the game as it is played today?

HAYES: I was at this convention recently, they were debating whether they should have a rate of fire where the gun can't shoot more than 20 balls a second. Twenty balls per second? I think it's crazy, but if that's what the market demands.... It's still the same game underneath. It's just become something totally different on the surface.

The more you start to make it look like war, the more worried I get about the game's image.

I talked to Charles at length and we both agree. The industry needs to make the game visually pleasing. To make it viewer friendly for TV.

My opinion is that the flight of the ball is what's pleasing to see in any sport. If you watch people watching a tennis match, they don't watch the players, they watch the ball. And in football, you know you love to watch a pass spiraling through the air

and the receiver running under it. You would never watch a guy drive or putt a golf ball, if you couldn't see the ball.

So the challenge for paintball is to make the ball visible in a way that pleases the senses of the person watching it. I mean, it's totally uninteresting otherwise. Charles and I sort of both worked up this idea about how to make paintball visually pleasing. But it would involve slowing the game down, slowing the paintball down, making it bigger, playing an individual game rather than a team game.

And it wouldn't affect the game at the field level, they could still play the tournaments and have the 20 balls a second and these things that they do. They'd sell a lot of paintballs at the field level.

However, in order to get sponsorship and TV revenue and live gate revenue, in order to put asses in the seats, so to speak, you have to make it viewer friendly. Right now, it's not a viewer friendly sport. And so you look at the magazines that come out and this and that, and all the advertisers are basically people who are producing products that people

who play the game use and I think the only people that buy the magazines are people who play the game.

Whoever gets paintball on TV will make as much money as all the people selling all the paint and guns that exist today.

But, you know, that's not where they're at right now. They want to sit around and debate about whether to shoot 23 balls or ten balls. And to a certain extent they're not wrong to do so. 14-year-old boys want the best paintball gun money can buy for Christmas, and that's the market they're serving.

ADAM: Any final thoughts on the game, your sense of its essence, what you love about it?

HAYES: To me, this survival game is about whoever does well in the individual game. I'm not trying to be too heavy about it, but you know, a guy from the hills of Tennessee or a guy on Madison Avenue in New York is just as likely to have the qualities of a survivor as not.

So I wouldn't say a country or city boy is a better survivor than the other.

ADAM: It's the individual.

HAYES: Absolutely.

ADAM: Got it. Do you ever actually get together with these guys and just play the survival game, because just listening to you talk, it's hard to picture you enjoying the team approach much.

HAYES: No, I never did it in a recreational way. And honestly, to be on the floor of the American Stock exchange . . .

The thing is I used to love to play poker, and once I started trading the market by myself, I never played poker anymore. I know better than anybody who I know of what risk is. I get to take 50 risks a day if I want to. Or 20 risks or 10 or five. I get to practice what it feels like all the time. This is an important thing about survival games.

This wasn't initially why I wanted to start paintball, but it was very clear to me that because of the illusion of danger that you create in the game, it allows people to feel what it feels like to take risks.

ADAM: People don't usually like that feeling, but they're enticed by it.

HAYES: No, they don't like it at all. It's the same feeling whether you're falling in love or whether you're making a commitment, a real commitment to something or whether you're taking a financial risk. People don't really like that feeling.

At some point, you have to learn that on the other side of risk is growth and not death. It's one of T.S. Eliot's points in "The Wasteland." Between the thought and the action falls the shadow—between the conception and realization falls the shadow. The shadow is the personal fear that people feel, the anxiety they feel, and it's a physical feeling, in all of these things. I think it's an actual physical anxiety that people feel. You need to practice getting through that.

So I don't really play paintball anymore. Except for that first game, the survival game, which was so new. But I do "play" every day.

ADAM: Understood. Thank you for your time, Hayes.

HAYES: You bet.

© Cleo Fogal

From Backwoods to Big Channels:

The Explosion of Paintball

By Jerry Braun

[*Another version of this article appeared in the March 2004 issue of* Paintball Sports Magazine *entitled, "The History of Paintball."*]

THE GAME

The first paintball game was an individual effort of 12 men, each attempting to secure four different color flags located in four separate areas in a wooded field. That soon gave way to a standard two flag team game akin to the childhood game of capture the flag. Opposing teams started at their respective flag stations at opposite ends of a wooded field with the objective to make their way to their opponents' station, capture their opponents' flag and bring it back to their flag station for the win. That game, decades later, remains the staple of recreational paintball play to this day.

In the early to mid 80s, fields were large and games were long, generally a full two hours. Game operators had to devise ways to keep those customers happy who had the misfortune to get shot out early. With the adrenaline pumping, no one wanted to sit around for hours before the beginning of the next game. Game operators met this challenge by organizing "king of the hill" games where groups of players would be divided into attackers and defenders. The king of the hill type games were powerful, in your face, non-stop action affairs. A lot of players actually preferred this shorter, more aggressive style of play. A variation was to have both teams go after the same objective, usually one flag hung somewhere near the mid-field line. The winner had to secure the prize and drive it into their opponents' flag station. The very structure of this game promoted confrontation and power. It became the tournament staple from local to international competitions.

Imaginations ran wild in the mid 80s as new twists were added to old games and new games were devised. Game organizers started hiding objects in the woods, and players had to locate and secure these objects for the victory. Sometimes a win meant shooting the opposition captain, and so was born the concept of certain players being more valuable targets than others. As paintball became more popular, rec games got bigger. From just a few players on each team, pick-up games at major game sites would sport 20, 30, 40 or more on each side. Games became unmanageable at that level played the standard way, and either multiple pick up game fields would have to be organized to accommodate the ever larger influx of players, or games had to be concocted that would allow for play by large numbers of participants. Hence, the advent of the "Big Game."

Big games have been around since 1985. Many can boast of hundreds, even thousands of players organized into two teams. The standard two flag game was not able to accommodate such large numbers, so multiple objectives were presented, each worth a certain number of points. There could be a multiple number of bases, and teams would score points depending on the number of bases they held at one time and for how long. They could also score points on finding treasures hidden on the field or shooting the opposing general. The big game brought together many of the early innovations from the standard game.

Such large numbers of players required extended game times. If the games were forty-five minutes or even one hour in duration, they would virtually end before they had a chance to begin. Big games are generally day long affairs, which brings us back to one of the first challenges facing game organizers. What do you do with the payers eliminated early? These players had to be reinserted back into the game after a certain time had elapsed, and the "wounded player" rule was adopted. Players that were shot out of a big game were "wounded" and had to move to a "hospital" area, spend a relatively short time recuperating, generally 10 to 15 minutes, and then get back in the action by reinserting into the game at designated points of entry. Now everyone could play the entire day, no matter how often they got shot.

A natural evolution of the big game was to inject role playing into its structure. In the early 1990's Wayne Dollack from Ocala, Florida did just that and dubbed it the "scenario game". The scenario game can best be described as a big game on steroids. It has all the attributes of a big game, gaining and controlling objectives, big battles, the elimination of opposition officers, etc. But, there will now be a games master and role playing by the players, and the missions devised by the games master will take center stage. The games master will radio missions to the command center of a team, and if the team completes the mission successfully, they will earn points. Such missions can include classic ones such as controlling certain bases, finding valuable objects or eliminating opposing generals. But, they could also include others like assembling a "bomb" by securing various components on the field, finding gold on the field and using it to pay mercenaries (more role playing) to aid them in gaining key objectives or give them valuable information necessary to complete other missions. In scenario games, one is not restricted to just two teams; there can be one or two more. Scenario games can be, but don't necessarily have

© Cleo Fogal

Welcome to the Game of Paintball

to be, based on historic battles. Two of the most popular ones revolve around D-Day or science fiction tales like the popular movie "Star-Trek III, the Wrath of Khan."

Anyone who plays paintball for the first time has one overriding concern: survival. When children play "hide and seek," it is always more exciting to be the "hunted" rather than the "hunter," the prey rather than the predator. The scenario game capitalizes on this phenomenon. The scenario, the missions concocted by the games master and the point structure all emphasize surviving the mission to earn points and, hopefully, a victory for the team, not taking out and eliminating a massive amount of opponents. It is surviving as prey, not ruling as predators, that makes the games so thrilling and so popular.

THE SPORT

In 1983, NSG organized regional play of 20-man teams. The winners in each region were brought to the NSG field in New Hampshire to play for the first world title. The Unknown Rebels from London, Ontario, Canada were crowned World Champions and took home a purse of $5,000. In 1984, 20-man teams gave way to fifteen on a squad, and the championship went to a Georgia group called the Atlanta Blue Team. The game played was the standard two flag woods game, and remained the standard throughout the NSG tenure as the premier competition until 1989.

In July, 1987, our field, Survival New York hosted the first major open class, big prize money tournament called the Air Pistol Open. Any team was able to enter and play for the $22,000 in cash prizes by paying the requisite entry fee. Twenty-two teams answered the call from across the United States and Canada. This tournament revolutionized tournament play at

the top levels in that every major tournament from that point on, including the NSG championships, was open class, and the prize money purse kept getting larger.

Tournament games in the woods prior to 1987 were generally games of stealth. There was more sneaking around and pouncing on an opponent rather than a concentration of force used to overpower the opposition. This, too, changed in 1987 as Navarone, a team from Southern California, developed power shooting skills by using 12 gram CO_2 cartridges practicing against teams using constant air. They were the first to act as a team in firing at the opposition. While some players were changing their CO_2 cartridges, others were firing. When they had to install fresh CO_2, the first group was firing. Navarone dominated the 1987 Air Pistol Open decisively winning every game and turning the stealth game into a power game, literally overnight.

Tournaments flourished in the 1980s. They were all virtually paint centered where the paint had to be bought on site, and as such they were great money makers for the organizers. Teams were springing up all over Southern California. Across the pond, English paintballers got the fever, as well, and its big event, in which several American teams participated, was the Mayhem Masters. 5-man center

© Cleo Fogal

The Complete Guide to Paintball

flag tournaments were in vogue. $50,000 in prize money was not uncommon, and the first World Cups held in 1990 and 1991 at Survival New York gave away $80,000 in cash, $40,000 alone to the first place teams, the Piranhas from Buffalo, New York and the Ironmen from California, respectively.

Just as Navarone was the team to beat in the West, three teams dominated tournament paintball in the Northeast and Midwest: the Piranhas, the Master Blasters and the mighty Lords of Discipline. Among the three, they won nearly every major event in the middle 80's through early 90's, both five and 15-man. In fact, the Lords of Discipline, which became Aftershock in 1991, won more World Cups than any other team in the history of paintball. Other top teams from around the country dominating the competition during this period included the Terminators from Florida, the Wild Geese and Gang Green from New England and Swarm from Illinois. When all these teams got together at a major national event, the competition among these teams was as fierce and tough as the men who played the game.

In 1989, at the North American Championships won by the Master Blasters, Caleb Strong's Piranhas were judging. Play in the woods at Skirmish at that time was done in the rhododendrons, thick large leafed plants that made it difficult for judges to determine eliminations. In order to contain any playing on or wiping, Caleb instituted a new and unique policy of penalizing an offending player's team, the "one-for-one rule." A player caught playing on or wiping a hit was eliminated from the game, as was a teammate of his. Thus, the team not only lost the offending player, but lost an additional player, as well. The rule worked so well that it, and variations of it, is a standard rule of tournament play today.

The nineties were just as full of change and evolution. In 1991, some tournaments and series using the standard two flag format went from 15-man rosters to 10-man teams. By 1993, all major two flag tournaments were 10-man. By the end of 1992, the players and teams decided they wanted more say in the structure and management of tournament paintball. A meeting organized by the heads of 18 of the top teams took place in Chicago, and the National Professional Paintball League (NPPL) was born. The teams in the NPPL adopted a charter, formed a rules committee, elected officers and selected six venues for tournaments to be held in 1993. The only existing tournament that was placed on the NPPL schedule was the World Cup. All other events and venues were new.

Meanwhile in 1990, Debra Dion-Krischke, who handled and managed many of the early NSG tournaments, began one of her own in the Pittsburgh area catering strictly to the novice and amateur players. Her emphasis was on the new player and his introduction to tournament paintball in a festive atmosphere. It was the International Amateur Open, though as of 2007 the IAO seems to be moving towards less of a tournament and more of a paintball gathering under the moniker, "Pittsburg Paintball Festival and Industry Conference."

The World Cup left its New York home in 1994 and moved to Paintball World near Orlando. 5-man as well as 10-man became the staples of competition in the NPPL and at the Cup. By 1996, game fields at the Cup included arenas of well wooded areas, and by 1998, we were totally out of the woods. By 2003, the World Cup was hosting more than 350 teams from more than 20 countries and had found a new home at the Wide World of Sports complex at Disneyworld. The NPPL continued as the dominant series of competitive paintball, and in January of 2001, all the promoters of the individual events got together and formed Paintball Sports Promotions (PSP), a company in which they pooled their individual efforts and talents to collectively produce all the tournaments in the series, each of which hosted 5-man, 10-man and X-Ball competitions.

X-Ball is the brain child of Richmond Italia of

Procaps. It is an amalgamation of two sport structures, the 5-man center flag game and the scoring and penalty forms of hockey. A squad of five players from each team is sent out to play a center flag game. Hanging the flag in the opponents' station or the opposition conceding the inevitability of such a hang to save time results in a point scored. There is a two minute turnaround time period, and a new game begins. The teams continue to play such games until a predetermined time, usually 15 to 25 minutes, runs its course for the period. If a player commits an infraction, his team is penalized. A player has to serve a predetermined time, two minutes or five minutes depending on the severity of the infraction, in the penalty box and the team plays short for that time.

X-Ball has become the hottest form of competition paintball, and a professional league with each team representing a major city in the United States was formed in 2003. More than 200 teams played X-Ball at the 2006 World Cup. The rise of X-Ball sig-

naled the harbinger call for 10-man two flag competition at PSP events, and in 2005 tournaments stopped offering 10-man competition entirely.

The two flag tournament enthusiast was not without recourse, however. In 2002, a breakaway group from the PSP formed the "Super 7 Series," which offered the two flag game in a 7-man team format. Europe always favored the 7-man two flag format and, like PSP, evolved from the needs and desires of the paintball teams and industry on that continent to raise the bar and offer players more competition. Yet with the rising popularity of X-Ball in the States, Europe and the Millennium series eventually started moving in that direction as well.

THE MEDIA

When paintball first came on the scene in the early 80s, it was unique and controversial. There were those who said that it promoted, or at least desensitized, people to violent activity. Debate raged on

© Michael Wise II, chrono300.com

The Complete Guide to Paintball

news shows and talk shows about this new game and its effect on the people that played it. More press on paintball was generated in the first two years of its existence than in the next ten. But then, in the late 80s and early 90s, TV got more interested in the game itself. An independent production company, Gran Prix Productions, had the attention of Sports Channel, a major cable sports broadcaster of the time, and a match was organized and filmed at Survival New York among the Master Blasters, the Piranhas and the Lords of Discipline. Trees were shorn of small branches ten feet off the ground so that the cameras would be able to see deep into the woods and catch all the action. Four years later, another made-for-TV match was organized at Paintball World in Orlando, six episodes of which aired on both ESPN and ESPN2. Less than two years after that, another match for ESPN Networks was filmed at Disney World, but for the first time the game was filmed out of the woods. Color coded palettes were used on a field measuring 500 feet long by 200 feet wide. The ratings attained by these two series of matches were the best recorded for ESPN in the time slots shown.

The interest in broadcasting paintball games on television is hotter than ever. WGN, an independent broadcast channel centered in Chicago and a default channel on many cable television networks, broadcast a series of 3-man caged paintball matches in 2005. In 2006, ESPN2 broadcast the Super 7 playoffs and finals and the Smart Parts World Paintball Championships where eight of the top teams in the world, including the Russian Legion from Moscow, played a series of matches at the Mohegan Sun Resort and Casino's 10,000 seat arena in Connecticut.

From the beginning, there were also print publications. Soon after paintball hit California, the first paintball Magazine, Frontline, made its debut. Frontline stood alone for several years until late 1988 when Action Pursuit Games hit the streets. Soon after the advent of APG, Frontline closed its doors and went out of business. Like Frontline, APG also concentrated on the California scene, at least initially, since its editorial writers and staff hailed from that area. It also published prices and soon grew to be the place for paintball shoppers to go. Paintball Sports Magazine came out several months later in 1989. It covered the national and international paintball scene, both recreational and tournament play, and published articles of general interest to the readers, including those on strategy and tactics and news on gear. Today, there are at least seven publications in the United States and at least as many throughout the rest of the world.

As the 1990s came to a close, paintball chatrooms, message boards and forums began to flourish, and quickly following were actual sites devoted to providing its readers with news and happenings in the paintball world. The first such site was and still is Warpig.com run by Dawn and Bill Mills, but others soon followed. Today, there are many thousands of paintball internet sites consisting of companies in the industry promoting their goods and services, teams, individual players, fans, game sites and anything else that would possibly interest the paintball enthusiast.

TODAY

Today, paintball is played by more than 10 million people in the United States. According to the Sporting Goods Manufacturing Association, more people play paintball than play baseball. It is the fastest growing of all sports and leisure activities. You will find paintball in mainstream Hollywood movies such as "Failure to Launch," and in television series like "Las Vegas" and "Studio 60 on the Sunset Strip." There are movies out on DVD centered on paintball, like "The Court Jesters." There is a major Nintendo X-Box paintball game that has sold millions of copies. It has taken less than a generation for paintball to grow from an afternoon lark among 12 friends to a multibillion dollar industry. We can only imagine what the next 25 years will bring.

PAINTBALL EVOLUTION

ADAM COHEN: Steve, it's great to have a chance to sit down with someone who has been around the sport for as long as you have.

STEVE DAVIDSON: Thank you for having me.

ADAM: Let's jump right into the thick of things.

STEVE: Sure. Where would you like to begin?

ADAM: Everyone has their own take on the initial game. What do you make of it?

STEVE: Yeah, the story's kind of become the game's creation myth. A couple of guys had a debate about survival skills, and agreed on a way of settling it by playing a free-for-all version of capture the flag. The fact that a forester won without ever firing a shot is significant. It's a true story, and it's a simple one that tells you what the game is all about.

ADAM: The fact that being the last one standing isn't just about shooting loads of paint.

STEVE: Yes.

STEVE: I played a couple of games when the oil-based paint was still around, and boy are we all glad that was short-lived.

ADAM: Pretty disgusting, I take it?

STEVE: We're talking turpentine parties after every game, or just burning your clothes. But it was fun. I wouldn't change the way it was then, but I'm glad we're using water-soluble food dyes now.

Anyway, they started franchising the game across the country. Jerry Braun in upstate New York was one of the first franchises, as was Deborah Dion out in Pittsburgh.

Around that same time—it didn't take more than maybe about nine months—there were at least two other franchise corporations on the scene. One was based in Florida called the "Ultimate Game" and the other was Pursuit Marketing Incorporated (PMI), which remains one of the biggest and best distributors in the industry today.

National Survival Game (NSG) had a turnkey type of an operation: "We will supply you with

STEVE DAVIDSON'S PAINTBALL BIOGRAPHY

When Steve Davidson began playing paintball in 1983, he fell in love with the game.

1983   Began playing paintball

1984   Formed Muthers of Destruction team

1986   IPPA representative for NJ & Coordinator of Team Registration program

First article printed in APG magazine—10 Ways to Becoming a Better Team Captain

1989   Columnist for Paintball Sports International, PaintCheck & Paintball News; Forms Werewolves competition team

1990   Introduces team rankings & seedings; ranking & seeding services for World Cup, Lively Masters, ASO series, Paintcheck 5 Player & other events; Forms World Paintball Federation

1991   Authors MAXING: A Guide to Winning in Tournament Play

1992   Organizes National Professional Paintball League

1996   Secretary, NPPL

1997   Forms GTO tournament series

1999   Introduces United States Paintball League patented game format (visit getfitnow.com for more details!)

the paint, with the guns, with the goggles, the rules of play, the insurance, and show you how to set a game up."

ADAM: Let's talk about technology.

STEVE: Tech-wise, the mid-eighties were explosive. During 1981 through the first half of 1984, people were playing with paintball guns that were hand-cocked, single-shot, twelve gram deals. Nelson's Nelspot 007, NSG's Splatmaster, and Benjamin Sheridan's PGP were the three that you had available to you. They were all tilt-feed/gravity-feed types of things.

At the end of 1983, people started putting pumps on the Nelspots and PGPs. The plastic Spotmarker from NSG became basically a low-cost, field rental piece of equipment and the "Tech Wars" started to pick up steam. Very shortly after the pump was first introduced, and this is still 1983/1984, Constant Air (CA) came out. Some ingenious people figured that there had to be a way to hook a larger canister of air up to their gun. They found a way to do it and, bang, they were immediately banned from tournament play, which slowed things down tremendously for a good couple of years.

ADAM: Were they welcome at tournaments, or not even those?

STEVE: No, absolutely not. People, including me, fought it viciously. To us, the whole game, the nature of the competition, was about to change radically. If we allowed those guns in tournament play, everything would be different. The simple necessity of having to change those twelve grams after 10 or 20 shots maximum, the necessity of having to carry that stuff, of not being able to stand there for fifteen minutes, made the game a certain, special kind of experience.

ADAM: So you weren't opposed to the CA technology per se. You just

Courtesy of Steve Davidson

Werewolves, 1989. Steve Davidson sits third from left, front row.

wanted the competition to be driven by tactics rather than guns.

STEVE: That was the issue. There were people out in California in particular who had gone the Constant Air route.

Gravity Feeds came in right after the pump—again, the end of 1983, beginning of 1984—PVC pipe and a forty-five degree elbow. Then, around the middle of 1984, Gramps and Grizzly's started producing guns that came with those features standard.

ADAM: So the technology was driven by recreational play? It seems that way because the tournaments resisted these new tech features, but they were selling well to the rec players who were in the game for the fun of it.

STEVE: Sort of. It's interesting because you'd go to the tournament and you'd sit there and talk about all the nifty things that you could do to your gun, or that you were planning on doing to your gun, or that somebody else was thinking about doing to their gun.

We all recognized that there had to be some kind of a leveler at the tournaments. A bunch of people who were more into military simulation than they were paintball were trying to get things like smoke grenades and hand

The historic guns on the next few pages are identified by manufacturer, type and description, in this order.

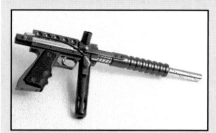

Carter; Buzzard; Top Level custom made tournament pump gun. Includes Smart Parts barrel.

Gotcha; Deuce; Double barrel stock gun with two-step trigger.

Palmer's Pursuit Shop; Nasty Typhoon; Customized double barrel semi with muzzle brake, double finger trigger, cosmetic trigger guard, bottleline with mounting brackets, and iodized blue.

Airgun Designs; Sydear.

grenades and walkie-talkies and heavier weaponry introduced into tournament play. In response to this, Fogal was the one who put it the best: "We can count on the fact that every paintball player is going to have a gun, but if we start asking everybody to have to bring forty smoke grenades and radios and all this other kind of stuff, we're just going to price ourselves right out of the market. So we have to make a conscious effort to cut it off somewhere. Where should that cutoff be?"

Things went back and forth for a while. There was a huge fuss over back check valves, these things that keep the pressure in the gun even when you remove the twelve gram or the bottle from it. It made it so you could remove your gas source and still have a few shots left in the gun. That was a big deal because we trained ourselves to listen for low air levels. You'd think to yourself: "He's about to change twelve grams, so we're going to rush him and take him out." Well, if I'm that guy running low and I've got a back check valve, baby am I ever waiting for you to come at me. I'm going to make the biggest, most obvious twelve gram change that I possibly can. Some cocky guy's going to charge me, hopefully with all

Courtesy of Cleo Fogal

Shot in the face at Skirmish, USA, 1985.

of his friends, and I'm going to take'm out. "Boink, boink, boink! See you all later. Thank you for listening!"

ADAM: Back checks sound very cool. Did they survive?

STEVE: No, those were banned. That little extra ability seemed to us like tinkering with the game, and we wanted to keep things very balanced and clear in terms of the mental and physical requirements.

ADAM: So the back check valve came along in 1984. 1984 seems like a big year for the game.

STEVE: It was a huge year for paintball technology. Absolutely. A lot of stuff was introduced in 1984. The back check valve came along with the CA.

Another big thing was a barrel extender. You take a piece of aluminum, stick it on the end of

Gun photos courtesy of Ralph Torrell

your barrel, and you have a longer barrel. Now, what that did for anybody? To this day, we still don't know. But somebody brought out the first barrel extender and they sold like hot cakes. So somebody else said, "Well, I'm going to come out with a field strip screw set for the gun," and people were beginning to realize that they could make serious money selling paintball equipment.

ADAM: Cleaning kits and harnesses emerge circa 1984?

STEVE: Everything, all kinds of stuff.

ADAM: Flak jackets and shin guards?

STEVE: You name it and it probably had its origins back somewhere between 1984 and 1985, right around in that period of time.

ADAM: Was there anyone keeping track of how many people were playing?

STEVE: No, it was really a very garage-type business. Somebody would order twenty guns from NSG and post business cards to resell the stuff at the local restaurant. Stuff like that.

[Paul] Fogal was actually marketing himself. He went on to teach a lot of people how to play. Jerry [Braun] and Deborah [Dion], too. Sat Cong Village out in California, Three Rivers Sur-

vival Game out in Pittsburgh, NSG, Skirmish USA, National Survival Game-New York, and then a little bit later on, Challenge Park in the Chicago area. Around Chicago you come upon the really big fields that pioneered how to market the game to people, how to set up the game for people, how to get folks to come in, what to charge, how to organize, how to train referees—all those kinds of things. Those five fields are really the major contributors to all that kind of stuff.

ADAM: And virtually all of these fields were playing the basic Total Elimination and Capture the Flag types of games.

STEVE: Yes, exclusively. The first scenario game was, I think, 1988.

ADAM: Actually the first game sounds like a scenario game.

STEVE: I guess you could probably put it like that.

ADAM: But it soon thereafter became a team-based game.

STEVE: That was probably the way NSG decided to package it. Somebody somewhere recognized that twelve individuals running around in the woods was not economically viable. So they probably figured, "We'll play 'Capture the Flag.'" I'm sure that those were the words used

Nelson Paintball Company; Nelspot 007; 12 gram pump gun.

Nelspot 007 with grip removed showing 12 gram C02 cartridge.

Sheridan; Piranha; Pump gun with 12 gram six pack from AirGun Designs, Inc.

Airgun Designs; Snyder.

Welcome to the Game of Paintball

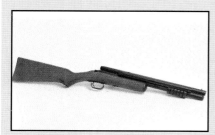

Sheridan; KP2; Stock gun with horizontal side mounted ammo tube.

Palmer's Pursuit Shop; Hurricane (serial #47); Originally a pellet gun, converted in 1992 to a constant air semiautomatic.

Palmer's Pursuit Shop; Squall (3rd one ever made); Semiautomatic spring feed, quicksilver, insta-pierce.

by somebody somewhere.

ADAM: And the other major game would have been just total elimination.

STEVE: The total elimination games were pretty funny. You have to understand, the games were initially two hours long, on about 50 acres in the woods. I played a couple of games where neither team saw anybody from the other team, and it lasted the full hour and a half. Of course, it was fun. You were crawling around in the dirt and leaves. You were scanning for opponents. But after a couple of games where you literally couldn't find the people you were supposed to be shooting at, it just seemed silly. And the field-owners were losing money, because they weren't selling paint.

Then again, the objectives were totally different then. Your goal was to get somebody to surrender to you, to psyche out the other team. Today, it's more about actually getting in their face and pumping them full of paintballs. The technology supported that kind of play because you could only get so many rounds out of the gun in a minute.

I loved it. If you could convince somebody that you could shoot, or if you could get somebody to fire and blow their wad before you had fired, then you could get them to surrender. There was a lot of sneaking around, a lot of finding the perfect ambush site. It was beautiful when they couldn't see you, had no idea you were going to be there, and you just know that plenty of them are going to come walking past that one particular spot. Knowing was as much fun as springing the trap.

ADAM: But then, somewhere along the line, they started to make the fields smaller.

STEVE: It started when some genius, somewhere, recognized that the more paint they got their customers to shoot, the more money they would make.

ADAM: The field owners made this happen?

Courtesy of Cleo Fogal

Member of the team, Lords of Discipline, at the 15-Man North American Championships at Skirmish, USA. That series ran from 1987–1990.

Gun photos courtesy of Ralph Torrell

STEVE: I would assume so. It kind of went hand in hand. The field-owners want to sell paint. That's their job, to sell paint. The players like to pull the trigger. And boy, do they. If you go to any field and you take a look at how much money they're spending at the target range just goofing off; it's incredible. But they're having a great time, and that's the bottom line.

ADAM: As the game has become more about splattering opponents with paint, are people spending more on paint now than they used to?

STEVE: Interestingly enough, the average usage per player has not changed significantly, in terms of the amount of money they're spending on their paint. For instance, back in 1983, 1984, 1985, if you were spending twenty cents a ball and carrying a hundred rounds onto the field, you were spending X for a day's worth of play. Now, the price has come way down, so you're carrying a case, case and a half out onto the field, literally thousands of balls. You're still spending the same amount of money, but you're shooting more paint.

ADAM: The player's perception is that they're getting more bang for their buck.

STEVE: Right. On top of that, some unsung hero recognized that when the games lasted more than fifteen minutes, customers end up sitting around while two or three people are running around in the woods trying to find each other. So fields started to get smaller. Smaller fields require fewer referees. Faster games, field owners gave people the feeling that they had played more frequently. I don't think anybody could tell you exactly who brought that concept into being.

ADAM: Sounds like a smart business move.

STEVE: Yeah. I don't think a lot of people realize that the concept of smaller tournament fields came from England. They were the ones that introduced the postage stamp size and everybody said, "Ding, ding, ding, it's a lot easier for four referees to cover two hundred feet by a hundred feet, than it is forty acres in the woods."

ADAM: Let's talk about the tournaments.

STEVE: The first tournament was in 1983—an NSG National Survival Game Championship. I believe it was the Unknown Rebels, a Canadian team, that won. I think NSG held a national tournament through 1989. NSG's structure of only allowing teams that came from the regional championships was cutting down on their attendance because there were

Line SI; Bushmaster; Sliding stock.

Line SI with stock extended.

Worr Games Products; '95 Autococker; ACI expansion chamber, hardline bottom line, copperhead sight, Lapco barrel.

Pro-Team Products; Retro-Valve Micromag with double trigger in Red Nights, with Millenium Series nitrogen system (gas-through foregrip).

Welcome to the Game of Paintball

Courtesy of Steve Davidson

Flag in hand, Steve Davidson sprints to victory.

fewer and fewer NSG fields. Fields realized they could thrive by going independent.

ADAM: So suddenly you have all these independent groups. How do they get together? How do they form a tournament? Spontaneously?

STEVE: Yes, pretty much. Jerry decided that he wanted to do his Air Pistol Open and Fogal got together the same year with PMI and started the North American Championship. That lasted four years and then faded.

Lively came along in 1989 and showed everybody how to do a trade show. He's definitely great at that. There's always been this disparity. The people who put on these major events know how to do one thing really well—put on a great trade show and lots of parties, or run the game on the field so that it's fair and quick. But they've never put the two together. That's the nut that still has to be cracked.

ADAM: And up to this point, it was virtually all outdoors?

STEVE: All outdoors.

ADAM: Let's back up from tournament play for a second. When did recreational indoors paintball start?

STEVE: The first person to open an indoor field was Caleb Strong up in Buffalo, New York. That was in November, 1984. That was pretty cool. I went up there with Paul Fogal to check it out, because he was thinking of opening up an indoor location in Philadelphia. They had this maze built, it was totally alien. Like no paintball we had ever seen before. Going through a door became an entirely new experience for me, let me tell you, because you had no idea what was happening on the other side. They played freaky music. There were places covered with black plastic so it was pitch black. You could not see anything in those areas. You were thinking somebody was in there. And if there was, they'd be able to see you well before you could see them. So I almost died a couple of times just because I was preoccupied with the dark sections. Then Paul and I would approach a door and we'd talk about who was going to go through it first. "Well, you're smaller, Steve." "Okay, Paul." [*Laughs*] That was just great fun.

ADAM: Let's get back to the tournaments.

STEVE: Okay. So Lively became the big thing on the tournament scene in 1989. We had Jerry with the Air Pistol Open, we had North American Championships and NSG still kind of all running simultaneously.

ADAM: Throughout the mid- to late-eighties.

STEVE: 1987, 1988, yes. Lively introduced his event in 1989. He got everybody in the industry to support it and that became the big thing. North American Championships went away quickly. Jerry was still there for another year or so and then he introduced the World Cup, which was supposed to be the first tournament that was going to have a hundred thousand dollar prize. Didn't quite make it, I think he gave away about eighty-two thousand dollars, which was still significant at the time. Nobody could compete with what Lively was able to do.

Eventually, Lively held five events a year, across the country in Tennessee, Texas, Chicago and San Francisco.

ADAM: No professional teams yet, right?

STEVE: Right. Everybody who played in tournaments was a professional team, literally. There were maybe five hundred people across the country who you could call professional tournament players, and everybody knew who everybody else was. We saw the same faces at every single tournament. The same rivalries were carried from one event to the next.

ADAM: Was there any emphasis on drawing people in to watch these things happen?

STEVE: No, none whatsoever. It was a very closed, tight-knit, insular community. We knew what we were doing and everybody else sucked. No offense, but you know how it goes. We were into our own cool thing.

I was big into science fiction

before I got into paintball and I was putting on science fiction conventions and stuff like that. Paintball was built on the same kind of insulated special kind of a community. We were more than happy to see each other in the city and then next month in another city.

ADAM: So nobody was in a rush to promote this game to the masses?

STEVE: The field owners were into getting new people to come out and play, but the person who made the transition from a recreational player to a regular member of a team had to be tough-skinned and talented. You had to be very motivated to get noticed and invited onto a team.

On the other hand, these teams throughout the '80s and early '90s were fifteen player teams. Organizing fifteen solid players who had the time to practice, the time to travel, and the money to afford everything . . . it wasn't easy. We wanted players who could think on the run, and there were so few. Every fifteen-man team from those days could have used another two or three or four players, but they just couldn't find bodies. It's amazing to me, looking back now, that I played with such a tremendous team.

ADAM: What happened to the 15-man team?

Gun photos courtesy of Ralph Torrell and Pro-Team PRoducts

Crossman 3357 Spotmarker; 50 caliber paintball gun.

Crossman 3357 open to show removable cylinder.

Pro-Team Products; Car 68; Police and military training semi-automatic. Can also come with 35 mm grenade launcher attachment.

Car 68 with stock extended.

Welcome to the Game of Paintball

Tippmann Pneumatics; SMG 60; Bulldog version, first full automatic, requires 62 caliber paintballs, first paintball gun banned.

Components Concepts Inc. (CCI); Phantom; Stock class with 45 grip frame and vertical 12 gram adapter.

Kingman; Spyder S.E.; Double trigger with expansion chamber, locking external velocity adjuster, and 45 grip.

STEVE: It's definitely history. A combination of factors just made it untenable. First of all, it wasn't easy to get 15-man teams together, so there really weren't that many of them. And as fewer of them were able to make the tournaments, the promoters started to raise their prices. The total effect of this was lower attendance at the tournaments. Around 1990, Jim Lively had the idea that making the teams smaller and reducing the entry fees slightly would get far more people to attend. Boy was he right. The team size requirement was reduced from 15 to 10. So if it cost $100 for a 15 member team, they dropped the price to $70 for a 10 player team. Attendance blasted off, so the promoters were making good money off of this move. But the game play suffered. It was far easier for teams to get into tournaments, but the level of competition really started to drop. Then the promoters wanted to move to 5-player teams.

NPPL was formed at the end of 1992. It was made up of 18 team captains. I was the coordinator for the first year, and I pretty much gave up playing so that everyone would view me as neutral. From the start, one of our central concerns was that diminishing team size require-ments were diluting skills. Just about anybody could put a team together, and just about everybody did.

NPPL wanted to preserve the highest possible level of competition, to set competitive standards that average paintball enthusiasts couldn't meet unless they put significant time and energy into training as a team. We were really pushing for the division that eventually arose at tournaments between professional and amateur game play. The NPPL tournaments in 1993 made this distinction for the first time. People registered themselves as pro or amateur according to their own sense of their level of play. What was really ingenious about this first year was that all of the teams competed against one another in the first round. The idea was that amateurs should experience the difference so that they could see what it takes to take their play to the next level. It was humbling for a lot of teams that thought they were good because they'd played several weekends together and done well against lame competition. For other teams it was eye-opening, because they were quite good, held their own, and saw possibilities for their team play that hadn't occurred to them. Based on their records in preliminary rounds, the top 8 pro teams went forward into exclusively professional play to determine the professional champions, and the top 8 amateur teams moved on to compete among themselves for the amateur title.

If an amateur team placed ahead of a pro team in the preliminary round, they had the choice of going pro, literally in the midst of the event! In fact, in that first year, Dallas 1993, a team did this and ended up taking 4th place!

In 1993 and 1994, there was a balance in the number of amateur and pro players. In 1995, however, there were almost 3 times as many amateur teams. Depending on their draw, some amateur teams had to play against pro teams whereas other amateur teams didn't. So this had awful consequences, and it still does today, because you get good amateur teams taken out of the running and ill feelings. They simply haven't reset the rules to reflect the reality that there are so many amateur teams.

Anyway, all of the tournaments pretty much adopted this pro/amateur distinction by the mid-1990s, or simply banned pro teams from certain tournaments.

ADAM: How do you feel about 15-man versus 5-man teams?

STEVE: 15 man teams are harder to put together, but you can do more with them. More is possible in terms of tactics. People don't account for the substantial role chance and dumb luck play in a 5-on-5 game. I mean really, you lose 1 guy and you've lost 20% of your force! On 15 player teams, you can adapt after losing 8 guys and go on to win the game. There's very little opportunity for true team play in today's 5-on-5 game. It was more rewarding and more competitive with 15-man teams. More about skills and training than it's become. That, at least, is my perspective on it.

The British had 12-on-12 for a while, but that

Courtesy of Cleo Fogal

These are two players at Skirmish, USA, 1984. They're using the Mark-4 guns, which were the first guns produced specifically for paintball and marketed by someone other than the National Survival Game. Note the shop goggles and lack of facial protection.

became 10-on-10. It's strictly 7- and 5-man teams now.

ADAM: You sound like you want to get back into the fray. Any chance that we'll see you in any tournaments?

STEVE: Truth be told, there's simply nothing like playing with people whose minds you can practically read.

Given the chance to play at that level again, and I mean with a truly fantastic team that could compete for a title, [grins] I would have to go for it.

The Attraction of Paintball

Jerry Braun

A Game for Children of All Ages

Stop and think about the very first games you ever played. There are two games most of us played as children. One of them was Follow the Leader. The other one was a primal hunt and chase game, such as tag or hide-and-seek. You can be Chinese, you can be Venezuelan, you can be American, you can be Aleutian, you can be anyone from anywhere in the world. These are games you have played, the ones you started with, the ones you associate with being a child bursting with energy.

Remember when you were a kid playing hide-and-seek? Your heart would be in your mouth because your friend was three feet away from you and was just about to find you out. You felt that the world was going to come to an end if you were discovered. Remember playing tag? There was always a safe spot, but you'd leave it and run as hard as you could in order not to get tagged. Sometimes you'd run behind an obstacle to gain time. The exhilaration of not being found or tagging another player is what you experience playing paintball. That is why it is so appealing.

Now, some of us pretend it isn't so, but human beings, like most animals, have predatory instincts. Look at the very first games played by kittens and puppies, they are primal hunt-and-chase games. They stalk each other, bat at and chew on each other. Basically, they playfully attack one another. Pure play is nature's way of teaching survival. Playing paintball triggers the same kinds of responses in humans, except that we don't have to learn how to "go for the jugular" to survive the way animals do. So our enjoyment of games like paintball is a little different than theirs.

People talk about the game being violent. No doubt the images of adults brandishing guns looks intimidating and suggests violence. The basic

Jerry Braun, 4th from left in back row, at Skyball 1999, Toronto, Canada.

characteristics of violence—the use of force to destroy or hurt others and a chaotic lack of structure that promotes reckless and dangerous behavior—are simply nowhere to be found in paintball. The objectives never involve hurting people, and the rules are clear and enforced.

When you first play the game, it elicits emotions in you that you may not have experienced since you were three years old. It's a sophisticated game of tag, except that it doesn't involve physical contact, incorporates teamwork, and frequently involves objectives beyond eliminating your opponent. And the pure joy you see on the faces of kids playing tag, that's what paintball provides. That's why people who play it once usually come back for more.

Charles Gaines

ADAM COHEN: Do you think the skills that you acquire and develop by playing paintball are applicable to everyday real-life experiences?

CHARLES GAINES: Absolutely! More to the point, I think the survival game, as it was played back when Hayes [Noel] and I played it, is illuminating for anyone who plays it. Unlike Hayes who held that people are born with certain survival skills, I think that for the most part, we learn them based on our will to immerse ourselves in an environment and discover it. And so the game is a way of finding out about yourself. . . if you want it to be. I can't say too much about the game as it's played today, because I haven't played it recently and it's definitely changed. But I imagine from what I read about it and hear about it, that at the very least, the game's essential experience still heightens your awareness of yourself as a survivor in a specific context. Your ability to win is related to your receptiveness to the details and the nuances of your surroundings and your response to the scenario you're in. So I do believe that it's true that you can take lessons learned in the midst of playing any version of paintball, and apply those to improving your everyday life.

ADAM: Knowledge is power, and what you learn in paintball is often very personal knowledge. In terms of risk-taking, in terms of learning about how you function under pressure, in terms of making quick decisions, in terms of communicating with others effectively. You agree?

CHARLES: It's true. The survival game is like a little paradigm for real life. You know, it's more this way with the original game. After all, we play life as individuals, not as a team, regardless of our social experience. I mean, you can be part of a team in a business or family, but we're all

Photo courtesy of Charles Gaines

individuals and we play life that way. Each of us has to make decisions and live with the consequences of acting on them.

I believe that the initial game, the every-man-for-himself format, was more paradigmatic of life than the team game. But, of course, both of them are nice paradigms. The point is always to succeed at what you're trying to do. And either alone or as part of a team, you have to act.

ADAM: The responsibility is still on each individual in the team game. Especially at the pace that the team game is played today, "teamwork" is really driven by individual actions that are more implicitly than explicitly coordinated.

CHARLES: That's how the initial paradigm plays out in today's game. Of course, in life, you're trying to make something of yourself. You're trying to succeed at making money or becoming happy or famous or all of these things. And accomplishing these things means taking steps. In the survival game, you're trying to succeed at a very limited task. You know, in the case of the team game, you go in and grab the other team's flag. In the case of the individual game, the way we played it, you grab all four flags and get out without being put out of the game. These are great metaphors for staying alive that are impossible to ignore, especially for first time players.

If you're smart about it, you bring to both the game and your life who you really are. You don't try to fake it. In other words, the people who got put out the quickest and the easiest in the game when I played it were people who were trying to be something other than what they were, the ones who pretended to have talents and skills that they didn't actually own. Being good at this game means being willing to play within yourself.

ADAM: Like a baseball pitcher in a clutch situation, you shouldn't throw a pitch you can't handle.

CHARLES: Exactly. But then you learn new pitches and start working them in as you get better at them. I think that may be the deepest and most piercing truth that overlaps playing paintball and playing at real life. All we know after a certain age in life is that the only way to achieve success is to be who we are, to rely on our real strengths, not our perceived or dreamed about strengths. And to play honestly. That was one of the things that we learned very early on about the game.

Now, I don't know if any of these things relate as profoundly anymore to the current game. I just literally don't know. I haven't played it and I don't even know how it's played. I hope it's the case. But the original game, the reason it was so resonant and the reason it was so much fun for us, was that it was so clear from the very beginning that we were doing something that really was alive with these metaphorical implications we're talking about now. You really teach yourself something about who you are, where you are, and something about the condition of life.

ADAM: Awesome. I completely understand what you mean. It's basically the kind of experience you have when you're faced with an extreme challenge and you have to rely on yourself to succeed.

CHARLES: That's it.

ADAM: And you know in that moment that whether or not you succeed is going to require you to keep your cool, keep focused, and simultaneously go for it. I mean it's a higher level of alertness. For me it comes in situations where I've been in sports competitions, or acting on stage, or speaking in public. Anytime I'm pushing myself.

CHARLES: Right. And so much of it has to do with timing, which is another thing that you learn in life. You can make the same choice at two different times and one time you'll be successful and the other time it'll cost you big time.

ADAM: Right. Having spoken with a number of people who are in the game now, I can say that it has lost this sort of philosophical edge. I wouldn't say the game itself isn't enjoyable as it's being presented now. It's just not what it was for you guys, an experiment, playing with ideas of survival. It's a business now, a diversion, recreation, entertainment. You have any comments on that?

CHARLES: Yeah. That's the way I perceive it to be. And it's one of the reasons for my sort of inattention to the game in its present version.

© Cleo Fogal

But I bet that the idea of surviving is still a factor, still part of the attraction of the game.

I mean, as far as I'm concerned, we who founded it had it at its very best. After we invented it, we started playing on a regular basis, both the individual game and more and more the team game. We had a field that we rented out, or borrowed. My kids played it, and my wife played it once and [Bob] Gurnsey's kids played it and we had our children out there acting as field judges. We'd make whole weekends out of this thing. And it was just joyous and wonderful. Good, simple fun with friends and family.

We'd have people come up from New York and out from Los Angeles to play the game. They would play it for the first time and immediately "grok" it and see how cool it was. I had my friend P.J. O'Rourke up to play it and he loved it.

It was great because it started as our little secret game. And then we introduced it to the world, which was like telling a very witty joke or some marvelously resonant parable for the first time. People could really see what we were talking about, especially after they played it. They'd say, "Ah, yes. Exactly. I get it. This is so cool!"

But then, we and the game were attacked by people who never played it but assumed that the presence of paintball guns somehow supported violence. Of course, in football and hockey, where they show highlights of people knocking each other's heads off, this criticism is virtually nonexistent. We had to fight this bad reputation that we really didn't deserve. And the business became somewhat difficult for me. The commercialization of the game, which literally turned it into what I perceive to be little more than shooting each other in the woods, cost me my entire interest in it.

ADAM: It turned into a team game when you started to turn it into a business, basically.

CHARLES: Yeah. That's right. But initially, we wanted it to be both a team and an individual game. But the individual game just sort of died out, out of lack of interest.

ADAM: That's mystifying.

CHARLES: Yeah, I thought so. I mean, to me it's a much more interesting version of the game. And would continue to be, I think. Maybe nobody even knows about it anymore. I don't know. But to me it would still be a more interesting version even given the high powered guns and the magazines that hold hundreds of paintballs. Given all of that it seems to me it would be more interesting than the team version.

ADAM: Well, you know, maybe it'll come back.

CHARLES: Maybe it will. That would be great.

Charles Gaines is an extraordinarily prolific and accomplished writer, published in magazines ranging from American Sportsman *and* Forbes F.Y.I. *to* Architectural Digest *and* Men's Journal. *He has also written various books, including* Survival Games *(1997). He was also author of the international bestseller,* Pumping Iron *(1974), and Associate Producer of the film based on the book, starring Arnold Schwarzenegger. He and his wife live in Nova Scotia.*

© Michael Wise II, chrono300.com

The Complete Guide to Paintball

The Paintball Necessities of Life

• **Goggles** • **Guns** • **Hoppers** • **Compressed Air** • **Paintballs**

GOGGLES

It's all fun and games until someone loses an eye

Without a doubt, protective eyewear is the most essential piece of paintball equipment you will ever purchase. A paintball travelling at 300 feet per second fired from 20 feet away can easily obliterate an eyeball, so safety must be your primary concern. As Rob Rubin is fond of saying to beginners before he takes them out for a game, "Your goggles must remain on at all times when you're on the field. If I see you even start to lift them, I'm going to tackle you, which may be unpleasant, but is infinitely better than losing an eye. Do yourselves a favor and follow this rule." Whether you are playing at a field or in your backyard, be sure to wear a paintball certified goggle system. Reliable goggle systems can be purchased for approximately $15, but the better ones cost $80–$90.

Most come with face armor and ear protection, which is required at every reputable field. The lens must be American Society for Testing and Materials (ASTM) tested, and approved for paintball. Other goggles are not acceptable, because they simply can't withstand the impact of a paintball.

Superior goggles come with features that maximize your field of vision, minimize glare, are well ventilated to prevent fogging, and have lenses that are easily and quickly replaced. They also use materials that increase the likelihood that paintballs will bounce rather than break.

There are many different kinds of goggles, and some are bound to fit you better than others, both physically and monetarily. We recommend trying on dif-

Firepower

The second most important piece of equipment is your paintball gun, sometimes referred to as a marker because it literally marks other players. For the purposes of this book, guns are used only to shoot paintballs (and wouldn't it be a better world if that were the case). As you'll see, guns come in all shapes and sizes, but employ very similar firing mechanisms.

Main Body

The main body or frame of the gun is the handle, trigger, and the chamber, which contains the cocking mechanism and the bolt.

Some guns give you the option of attaching your own barrels and different sized hoppers and compressed air. The chamber or breech is where the ball awaits the rush of air that fires it when you pull the trigger. Near the chamber is something called a ball detent. This mechanism holds the paintball in place so it doesn't roll out. It also stops more than one ball from feeding into the chamber. The paintball is fired out of the chamber and through the barrel. The barrel is a long tube that guides the paintball in a straight path as it leaves the gun. There are many styles available and they screw into the main body. Many say that brass barrels are the best because they have the least friction on the paintball (they are the cheapest). Others swear by heavier stainless steel barrels. Some only play with aluminum. A lot of designs have holes (called porting) drilled into them in different patterns.

Hopper or Loader

Basically a hopper is a plastic inverted bottle that holds your paintballs and allows them to feed into the chamber. Most hoppers rely on a gravity feed approach. Some, however, are motorized and ensure that another paintball will fall into place after one is shot. If rapid firing is key to your game, make sure you have one of these.

Hoppers come in all sorts of sizes; some hold only 40 balls, while others can hold up to 300. The range of sizes is as follows: 60, 80, 100, 130, 150, 200, 230, 300. Of course, by the time you read this, larger sizes may be available. Smaller hoppers are lighter, but carry fewer balls, creating that possibility of being caught short at the worst possible moment. The larger the hopper, the more balls you can fire before having to reload. Of course, this also makes the gun itself heavier. Most experienced players gravitate toward the large hoppers.

Air Power

The air tank is crucial. On most guns, it attaches horizontally off the back of the gun, and literally screws on. Some players prefer a vertical mount to keep liquid CO_2, which is an inevitable and potentially very annoying byproduct of firing, on the bottom of the tank away from the gun. The most common propellant used in paintball is CO_2. Almost all fields supply a tank with their rental guns. Other propellants include nitrogen and high pressure air (HPA). HPA is just regular air. The great thing about it is that it won't freeze or turn to liquid in the cold like CO_2 and nitrogen. HPA containers have very high pressures (as high as 4500 psi).

Most of the tanks are currently made of aluminum, which is preferred to steel because it is lighter. More expensive air tanks enable you to check the status of your air reserves. Some of the more elaborate models can even be worn on your back. This changes your experience of the game entirely; the gun no longer has weight, and you're not going to run out of air as quickly, but you're running around with air tanks strapped to your back, which some players find annoying.

Paintballs

By now it's probably clear that a big part of this game is about splattering paintballs on your opponents. Paintballs come in a variety of sizes: .50, .62 (which is often called .60), .63, .68, and .72 caliber. .68 caliber paintballs are spherical and dominate the market. The paint substance is composed of washable, nonflammable, food grade dye. In the early days it was oil based, and players held de facto turpentine parties at the end of the day. Not so anymore. Today, regular laundry detergents will do the trick!

Accessories

In most cases, you play a couple of 15 minute paintball games using 1 air tank and topping off your hopper in between sessions. But there will come a time when you'll be playing a significantly longer game, and will need to replenish your supplies on the field. Or, a ball may break in your gun, and you'll need to clean it with a squeegee on the fly. In those moments, you'll be glad you brought the following accessories.

Harness—Usually something worn around the waist that holds extra supplies—extra air, extra paint, maybe even smoke bombs. Typically they

are called 4-1 or 8-1 or 6-1. The "1" is usually a vertical receptacle for an air tank. The other numbers signify spaces for horizontal guppies (tubes for holding paintballs).

Squeegee—An instrument you'll find enormously useful if a paintball explodes in your barrel. This is also useful for the maintenance and upkeep of your gun.

Remote—An air supply separate from your gun carried on your harness. This tank is connected to your gun by a long, flexible hose. This is useful because it takes weight off your gun and makes it lighter and more maneuverable. It is a cheap addition, and you can even purchase good ones used.

Now let's take a look at the game of paintball, from the perspective of a new player.

—AWC

Welcome to the Game of Paintball

You're not a paint magnet, you're a newbie!

Rules to Play By

DON'T GET SPLATTERSHOCKED!

Here's a shocker. When you play paintball for the first time, you're going to make mistakes. We all did and we all still do. Knowing this going in will help you avoid splattershock: the distinct feeling that you are a paintball magnet who is hopelessly awful at this game. Bottom line: Don't get bent out of shape if things don't go well during your first couple of games. Mistakes early on are to be expected and present you with great learning opportunities.

In this section, you'll find the not-so-secret secrets of top-notch paintball players. You could study every word of these insights, memorize and recite them 3 times each before going to bed every night for many months, and still not improve your game. That's because you have to play the game to get good at it.

But, these 'secrets' are useful as guides. Store them in the back of your mind. Visualize yourself doing these things. They're worth being aware of, no doubt about it. They're even more effective when you're so accustomed to them that they become practically instinctual. To make that happen, there's absolutely no substitute for playing experience.

The key to becoming a player whose name strikes fear in the hearts of your opponents and commands respect among the elite is quite simple. Play the game. And then play it again. And then play it some more. Play with and against people who are better than you are. Stand back from the game and see it as a whole. Experiment with being aggressive and defensive, with taking different positions. Be creative. Above all, play the game for the fun of it. That is, after all, the main point, and, it just so happens that having fun will make you demand more of yourself every time.

You have to spill much paint before the wisdom in the following tidbits will become second nature.

STEVE DAVIDSON—BEING CAUGHT SHORT

"When I started playing in the early 1980s, fields were charging twenty to thirty cents a ball and fifty cents a twelve gram. You were considered a nut if you carried more than about fifty rounds onto the field. Well, I was a nut. I carried a hundred rounds. You see, I got caught short one time. But never again. I'm never going to be stuck out there without ammunition again."

Being a great paintball player is a path, not a destination. Enjoy every second of your journey!

- **The very first rule is never EVER take off your goggles!** This can't be stressed enough. Taking off your mask can be very detrimental to your vision's health. A paintball travelling at 10 feet per second would easily pop your eye out of your head. **Don't ever take your facial protection off.** Even in designated areas, look around yourself to make sure there isn't some doofus waving an uncorked gun.

- **Make sure you understand your gun and its limitations, whether it's a rental or your own.**

- **As soon as you get off the field of play, put a barrel plug in the end of your barrel and switch on the safety.** This is essential paintball etiquette and is only meant to save you from experiencing or causing excruciating pain or injury to others. If you see somebody waving a gun around that doesn't have a plug in it, remind them to put one in immediately.

- **Paintballs do not hurt when they hit.** Well, sometimes they hurt a little bit, but usually they just sting for a moment. You won't really feel sore until the day after. I have found that paintballs that hit you and don't break hurt a little more because they hit and bounce off. The time they are in contact with you is shorter and thus the force is greater (for all you wannabe nerds out there, the impulse equation from physics justifies this statement). When it does break, it is in contact with you longer and is cushioned by your skin, fat, etc.

- **Wear dark clothes; don't wear white.** White is just too bright, you will be too easy to spot and eliminate.

- **Wear some type of boots or comfortable hiking/running shoes.** Some people prefer football or soccer cleats. They are comfortable, light, quick, and provide excellent traction in grass and mud. A lot of paintball players are using cleats these days.

- **Always be honest.** If you get hit and see the splat on you, please raise your hand and exit the

Welcome to the Game of Paintball

game. Redeem yourself in the next game; there's always a next game. People who try to wipe their paint off and think they can get away with it are simply lame. Ask yourself if being perceived as a loser is worth staying in the game. When everybody knows you're a cheater, you'll find it increasingly hard to find anyone who wants to play with you. *If you cheat, you'll never truly win!*

- **Don't ever call an advanced paintball player a cheater.** They hate that and take their games really seriously. No matter what happens, don't do this. That is how seriously some people take their game. They are mostly very honest, down to earth people. But, sometimes they'll respond less than graciously. And you know what? It just isn't worth it. If an advanced player (or any player!) cheats on a regular basis, talk discreetly about it to the referee and your friends between games.

- **Don't be afraid to ask or learn.** Even with the amount of information technology available these days, broadband connections to web sites like splatterzone.com or warpig.com are no substitute for asking questions on the field between games. There are certain basic things that more experienced players can clarify for the beginner (e.g., tactical stuff, tidbits of advice) that may make a difference in your play.

- **Always appoint a team captain and follow his orders no matter what.** The team captain does not have to be the most experienced or the wildest or the most intelligent person in your group. But there has to be one captain. Follow orders even if you think you have a better plan. Don't be a gloryhound. When a team commits to a plan, it's able to do things that individuals acting alone can't do. Obey your captain even if it does

not conform to your method of play. If you think you have a great plan, ask to be captain for a game. You have nothing to lose.

- **Be alert and never focus too much on one thing.** Don't keep shooting at the same guy behind the same bunker over and over again. Move on and surprise him from the side or another angle.

- **Don't stay in the same spot too long.** If you are

in a fort, don't keep shooting from the same side forever. It's not productive. Go to the other end; go to the second level. Move away from the bunker, walk out unprotected and hold people down. Don't stay put!

- **Never give up.** Whether you run out of air, paint or energy, don't ever just stop or quit. You are still useful. No one has to know that you are on your last leg.

That's just for starters!

- **Never call yourself dead if you are unsure.** If you question whether a shot hit you and splatted, call a paintcheck and the referee will find out if you've been eliminated. Don't just call yourself out because you felt a hit. Wait for the referee to confirm.

—AWC

Mistakes New Players Make

WHERE THE HECK AM I?

Beginners are so pumped up with adrenaline that they aren't able to focus on the game as a whole. They tend to lose track of their position in relation to their teammates and foes. Because they feel like they're all alone in the game, they tend to be overly concerned with protecting themselves. Rather than engaging their opponents aggressively, they crouch behind the thickest bush or in the deepest hole available. Effectively, they take themselves out of the action: they can't see anything, are unable to provide information or cover fire, and are basically squatting on the spot where they'll be eliminated. They may tell themselves that they're in a great ambush position. The problem is that most beginners who think this way end up getting themselves ambushed. Take a few deep breaths and look from side to side every once in a while. Stretching your neck out before playing is a helpful way of reminding yourself to look from side to side.

CHARGE!

Some beginners are so pumped up that they run headlong into the fray only to find themselves pinned down by copious hostile paint without support or a good escape option. Their initial eliminations can be fantastic to watch as they squirm under a barrage of paint, but they probably don't feel so great. So listen up! It's always a good idea to choose your first

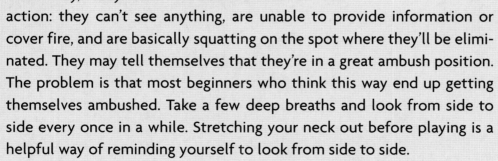

shelter before the game starts. A good shelter is one that will provide you with reasonable cover, while allowing you good opportunities to see the field, shoot, and advance. You must be within range of your opponents, but not so close that you can't use trees or barricades for cover. If the shelter you're behind is so small that you can't stick your head out, make sure you have a teammate behind you and can call for him to keep your opponents busy while you reach a better position.

ARE YOU MY MOTHER?

It's going to sound simplistic, but you should really take a moment to meet the people on your team. You don't have to swear blood oaths, but it's definitely in your interests to talk to them a little and briefly study their appearance. The last thing you want to do is shoot your own teammates, and they'll be more likely to respond to your pleas for help if you call them by name.

HEY, THAT HURT . . . WHOA, THAT ONE REALLY . . . OUCH!!!

To watch the way they go out, you'd think newbies are masochists. When hit, they'll wait for the incoming paint to stop pouring before they stand up and walk away. This means they'll get out wearing two or three layers of bright colors. The best policy is to get out of the way of incoming paint and stand up right away. Remember, if you surrender and your opponents keep pumping you full of

paint, referees will take them out of the game! So if you're shot, and know it, get up and out of the way quickly.

EYES WIDE SHUT!

Usually, if you see your opponent before he spots you, you've won. Of course, although this fact is probably self-evident to most beginners, they tend to be averse to sticking their heads out for a look-see at the action. So they never look around. Then, the newbies who do use their eyes tend to get tunnel vision, focusing so intensely on one single direction that they they close their ears to all noises, especially those coming from their sides. Don't be afraid to look around. You need as much information as you can get. Of course, your head will be a target, so look by the side of your barricade rather than above the top of it. If you decide to look above the top, don't do it for more than one or two seconds. It'll take that long for your opponents to spot you, take aim, shoot, and hit you.

FOR OUR MAIN COURSE, WE'LL BE SERVING A SITTING DUCK . . .

Newbies don't move enough. If you're not useful where you are, don't stay there.

The game is about moving, sighting, and shooting. It is dynamic. There may be situations in which you will be playing defense or setting up an ambush, and staying put is appropriate for a set amount of time. But for the most part, responding

to the game as it evolves requires you to stay in motion. If the rest of your team breaks through the enemy's defenses, it means they would have done better with you among them; additionally, there are no opponents left to protect your station against. If the rest of your team is beaten, they may have done better with you among them, and when your opponents arrive at your base, boy will you feel alone! Another example: Look at a newbie under fire. He's trying to make himself as flat as possible. As flat and useless as a flat tire. When you're in a position where you are easily pinned down, with no close help at hand, there are only three things you should think of doing:

1. Get away as fast as possible
2. Shoot back
3. Yell for help and indicate your opponent's location. If they're shooting at you, it means they've spotted you, so don't be afraid to give your position away.

Finally, when you are spotted (when you shoot at someone, you almost always are), be prepared to move to a new location so your opponent won't know where you are or from where your next shot will come.

HELP ME . . . HELP YOU

Beginners very seldom communicate well. A beginner keeps his problems to himself (he doesn't ask for help when needed) and doesn't brag about his knowledge (he doesn't tell you about the opponents he's spotted).

The only good reason to be quiet is to remain stealthy. Once you're spotted, there's no reason not to yell, scream, and shout if you have something useful to say. You'll get the help you need, and give your teammates the information they need to kick in.

I LOVE THE SMELL OF PAINTBALLS IN THE MORNING . . .

Usually, beginners are very accurate and seldom miss a player who's 10 feet away, especially if he is on the same team. They imagine that their gun has the power to nail targets over a hundred yards away. They also shoot too soon, and at everything that moves. Of course, all this does is give away their position and waste paint. If you haven't been spotted, your first shot must take your target out. Wait until the flight path is clear, or until the opponent sees you. Be patient, especially when you're on defense. The price of paint being what it is, they think that a ball that doesn't end on an opponent's camouflage is lost, so they never provide cover or intimidating fire. Sometimes, you have to shoot at opponents you can't see:

- **To help a teammate out of a dire situation!**
- **To make an opponent nervous behind his tree!**
- **To keep his head down while one of your teammates is closing in on him.**
- **To make noise to distract opponents' attention.**

THESE LADIES ARE 2DIE4

Editor's Note: Since this interview was conducted in 1999, several all-women and co-ed teams have emerged in the U.S. and abroad, with women players obtaining corporate sponsorships becoming increasingly integral to the sport. The team 2Die4 is no longer in existence.

ANDREW FLACH: We were just at Skyball (Toronto, 1999), and your team, 2Die4, was there, and The Iron Maidens were there. Both are all-women teams playing at a semi-professional tournament level.

There are some co-ed teams, but the vast majority of the paintball teams that regularly compete are all male teams. Tell me about your experience as women in such a male dominated sport. Are you treated with equal consideration? Are you considered an equal competitor?

SARAH STEVENSON: It's getting there. The first time that I played with Maidens, the guys had the attitude, "Oh, we're just playing a bunch of girls. Big deal! We'll smoke 'em." And they were pretty much right. They did, but not because we were women.

We stayed with it. We plugged away, trained ourselves, and now we're kind of a wild card. They don't know what to do with us. They don't know how to predict what we're going to do. Most teams are very predictable. You can read the field and know generally where they're going to go. As you saw at Skyball 1999, our team pulled off things that the other players never expected.

It's been nice to see that we register on the men's respect meter. All it took was a year and a half, hard work, practice, and execution, and now the other teams can't take us for granted. Attitudes changed pretty quickly once we started to win.

ANDREW: So the two of you first played together on The Iron Maidens?

From Left: Karen Barber and Sarah Stevenson

two polar ends.

KAREN: The men are definitely more competitive and more aggressive than the women. Probably all that testosterone. I did become accustomed to that style of play. The guys I played with are all like brothers to me. They always took care of me and made sure I was okay.

The men didn't treat me any differently, which I respected, and they knew that's what I wanted. I always worried that they were just keeping me around because my husband was on the team. We had this talk many a time, and that wasn't the case.

In fact, for a couple of years, my husband stayed with the All Americans and I went to the

KAREN BARBER: We met each other at World Cup '96.

SARAH: We had known each other before, and then I went and talked with the team and the team captain, Tracy Roberts. Tracy was just absolutely crazy about Karen, and for good reason. Tracy had been in the sport for a long time and knew about Karen and had watched her career as a paintball player evolve. We discussed things and decided to let Karen and a few other All Americans play with us at a tournament in San Antonio.

We contacted Karen and a couple of the other All Americans and they agreed to come down and play with us. This was a big coup. Our team was legitimized overnight.

ANDREW: When did you start playing with The Iron Maidens.

SARAH: Around the middle of 1995.

ANDREW: Having played on co-ed teams, and having played on all-women teams, have you noticed any difference in the way the team works.

SARAH: Completely. Yeah, you're looking at

All Americans 2. I decided to see what it was like to step down a level and play the amateur league. We eventually went pro because we kept working at it.

I definitely think that women, individually and

as a team, are more level headed, more patient. And some of them are better shots. Women are few and far between in this sport, but if you find the right ones and put them together, I believe women's teams would be very dangerous.

SARAH: I agree with Karen. Women are a notch more level-headed than men on the field. They have their mind set on where they want to go as a team, and they're a little more deliberate and less erratic than their male counterparts.

The men's teams that I've played on—probably the most serious being a team called Texas Shock Force—were tremendous. But they couldn't quite set their egos aside and play the game as an entire team with one unifying goal. They couldn't knit it together.

Whereas, when 2Die4 went to Skyball, I had no problems with egos on the team. No particular team member felt a need to be the star of the show. And I went up and told one of my players: "You're going to sit this game. I'm going to put so and so in." "Sure, no problem," was the response.

In my experience, men hear this kind of statement as, "You're just not good enough for this game, so I'm going to put somebody else in." So they can tend to get a little disenchanted, to put it mildly.

KAREN: Women tend to reason it out and deal with things. That's been very refreshing with this group. I haven't had to deal with any of that. Our team members are very supportive. Like a family.

ANDREW: What is your goal with 2Die4? As captain, where are you taking the team?

SARAH: Pro status. I've always wanted to go further, I've always wanted to go higher, but I don't want to get onto a team that's already pro, I want to build a team that can do well in any competition.

ANDREW: So you got on the telephone and called Karen at some point. Karen, what did you think when the idea was broached?

KAREN: At first I didn't grasp the seriousness of her proposal. I knew she had asked me to play and that she was going to organize this team. And I said, "Okay, yeah. That'll be fine." And then

I realized that all the girls involved were very serious and very talented. I saw right away that we had a good group of people that could probably go further.

ANDREW: Do you think we'll see separate women's paintball leagues, the way they have segregated basketball?

KAREN: Not for a long time, if ever. We're far from having enough players.

SARAH: I don't think the women would really want that. I like the competitive level we have now in a co-ed environment. We compete effectively as it is.

ANDREW: Paintball is a sport where skill, technique, and decision making take precedence. Just the fact that you have testosterone coursing through your body, doesn't mean you will win more games, does it?

KAREN: Well, I've always thought the All Americans are where they are today because they're the most competitive group of people I've ever met in my life. For instance, we'll be waiting at the airport because a plane is delayed. They find something to do and make a game out of it until each person wins. Everyone has to win.

I've never met women like that before, that competitive. I think that's one thing that the men have that we don't. Innate competitiveness.

Maybe professional women volleyball or softball players have it, but most women simply aren't like that.

ANDREW: How about in terms of strength issues. Would you say that paintball is a fairly accessible game for both men and women?

KAREN: Yes.

ANDREW: In terms of competition?

KAREN: Hmm. I don't know about that. In one way the sport's changing now, at least in the NPPL. You need to be fast and aggressive. Running quickly is becoming important. Unfortunately, speed is one thing I lack.

ANDREW: I'm sure if you had a couple of fast running players, sprinters, on the team . . .

SARAH: And a lot of teams do . . .

ANDREW: . . .that might even things out, don't you think?

KAREN: Yes. You need key bunkers and they are always the front ones that you have to hit. You need to get people into those quickly. We used to play with three or four "backup" players. Now there's only one or two. The rest of the team is forward. You have to be aggressive, because the only way to get the other team out is to keep moving or just go "bunker" them. That's the trend in competitions today.

ANDREW: What words of encouragement would you have for women interested in playing paintball?

SARAH: Stick with it. Don't let the things guys say get in your head. Somebody's always going to give you a hard time. I've found that in a lot of situations—being a Mom, I'm able to see this—men at the fields will test a woman the same way a kid would test a Mom. They see how far they can push her and see what they can do, maybe to get her to leave.

These guys think: "Paintball is our world, stay out of it." And, maybe four years ago, that would have been the case, for the most part. And so they would test and they'd push and they'd do the "Hey baby, hey honey," thing. That's gotten better, but they still will push on the women to see if they really want to stick around. Maybe they're a little intimidated by the presence of women, since there's a ton of baggage attached to being eliminated by a girl. I say stick it out.

ANDREW: Is paintball as a sport arriving at a time when it can develop as its own unique co-ed activity? Is it poised for that?

KAREN: I think it's always going to be co-ed. I don't think there will ever be enough women interested in playing the sport continually. Women get married, or pregnant. And, today, if you ask a girl, "Would you rather run around in the woods, where you may break a nail or get paint in your hair, or go swimming or play volleyball?" . . .

ANDREW: She'd choose the other sports?

KAREN: I think she would, without ever having tried paintball. You find very few women who absolutely love it and are willing to make a seri-

Member of 2Die4 discusses a call with a referee at Skyball in Toronto, 1999.

ous commitment to playing the game regularly.

Some women are also very intimidated by the fact that it hurts when you get hit. They don't like pain. I think women, even though they give birth, don't enjoy that kind of pain.

SARAH: And I just want to say—it's a different breed of women that wants to do this.

ANDREW: So women are concerned about getting hit by a paintball?

KAREN: Oh, yeah. I mean, when I used to work in an office and wore a dress and nylons, people would see the bruises left from paintballs and say, "You are absolutely a mess."

SARAH: It's always a good idea to wear protection—cups for the men, padded bras for the women. They're available. Use them. You're a little silly if you don't.

ANDREW: It's been great meeting with you. Are

there are any last thoughts you'd like to share with our readers?

SARAH: We appreciate the support that we do get from people. At Skyball, men and women came up to me, shook my hand, and said, "Your team is a good example of how teams should be at these events."

And that means a great deal to us. We don't want half compliments. Don't say, "Well, I've got to go back home with my tail between my legs because a girl shot me." Don't give me that. Give me, "You play well. You're a good player." Not as a woman. Just as a player. Period.

If more men in this game would adopt that way of thinking, that would be tremendous. In paintball, the men have all kinds of support. They have oodles of support. Verbal support from the crowds. Financial support in the form of sponsorships from the manufacturers. We're starting to get the sponsorship and we are starting to get the verbal support, too. We greatly appreciate that.

All we ask is to be treated like equals on the playing field. Give us your game, and we'll give you ours. May the best players win. It's as simple as that.

Welcome to the Game of Paintball

A Pretty (Tough) Face

Dawn Allcot

© Mike Paxson

BEA YOUNGS TALKS ABOUT HER EXPERIENCES AS ONE OF THE MOST INFLUENTIAL WOMEN IN THE SPORT

The first paintball game in the woods of New Hampshire didn't include any women at all. Although the sport has grown to include nearly 11 million players across the United States, only 20 percent of all participants today are female. And while the list of top female players may not be long, it is impressive. Debra Dion Krischke and Jessica Sparks, two of the first women in the industry, blazed a trail to be followed by talented players like Keely Watson, Tami Adamson and Bea Youngs.

Bea started her career as a founding member of the first all-girls tournament team, the Femme Fatales, immediately building a name for herself in the industry and on the field. The Femme Fatales appeared in Stuff and Maxim magazines, catapulting the team to immediate fame and garnering them many sponsorships. The young women appealed to the male market with their good looks and athletic bodies, but the team members also proved they could back up their beauty with skill on the field.

In 2004, Bea joined Destiny, a team launched by former Valkyries player Mona Hejazi. Destiny captured second place in the NPPL Division 2 in 2006, also winning the San Diego event. With Bea's fiancé, Mike Paxson, as owner and coach, Destiny moves toward the future in Division 1 with an eye on the championship.

In addition to playing on Destiny, Bea works as an announcer at PSP and NPPL tournaments, teaches clinics, writes for paintball publications, promotes products for sponsors such as Zap/Archon, and is one of the most influential players—male or female—in the sport. Here, she talks about the future of women in paintball and the challenges they face.

DAWN: How did you get started in paintball?

BEA: It was with Tami—Pickering at the time—Tami Adamson now. To make a long story short, she was dating Todd [Adamson]. He was big-time into paintball and she hated paintball. I was like, "Why don't you play, too?" So she came up with this bright idea to get an all-female team together. She said, "Well, you have some athleticism, why don't you play for my team?"

DAWN: So you actually started out playing competitively, rather than rec-ball?

BEA: Yeah, the only reason I started playing was to play tournament paintball. It was never recreationally.

DAWN: How has the role of women in paintball changed since you started?

BEA: My story's very different because I was very outgoing and really pushed to get my name known. I started playing in 2000, and I entered the industry in 2001. I started writing a column for Paintball.com within months of getting a job at JT USA. Next thing you know, I'm on TLC Junkyard Wars on their paintball tanks episode. Then Women's Entertainment called me to do a half-hour show on what I do for a living. But for females in general, I think our opinion is being considered a lot more than it was before. Debra Dion Krischke was really the only female doing it in the beginning. Because of how successful she's been, it's really opened the door for other females to have that opportunity.

DAWN: Who did you admire when you first started playing?

BEA: It's always been Tami. Todd Adamson also took the time, gave us some advice to get things started. I really give props to Chuck Hendsch, because he opened the door for me at JT, which in turn opened up a lot more doors. Nowadays, it's all about Mike Paxson, and not just from the paintball side of things, but on a personal level too. He's been amazing. Most of my knowledge of the sport comes from Mike.

DAWN: In its first year, Destiny added men to the roster. Why?

BEA: Destiny initially started out as an all-female team and we were struggling. We just didn't have the speed to make the tapes off the break, and even our secondary movements were difficult because once we got pinned in, it was hard for our front girls to battle out of that and get in to the snake or to a 50 position.

I can sometimes be a little tough. I try to be as nice as I can, but if someone's not performing, I'll get a little upset. If they don't show the commitment and dedication, I'm not going to be easy on them. I was losing girls, because I guess they weren't having any fun. For me, playing on a paintball team is more than just the fun aspect of it. We're definitely friends, but I play paintball to win and to have fun winning. And I think it wasn't like that for some of the girls that left the team. If you just want to have fun with your friends, then play rec-ball. When you're playing competitively and you've got sponsors that you've got to appeal to, we really don't have time to just rotate players and have fun. Now I think everybody on the team understands that.

DAWN: Are you going to keep Destiny co-ed?

BEA: I will. I kind of hold fast to that. And it's becoming increasingly more difficult to find females that can continue their performance. We've had a lot of girls come and go on the team since its inception in 2004.

DAWN: Why is that?

BEA: A lot of things, I guess, come up in a female's life that are more important.

Men sometimes have a one-track mind. If they're going to do a sport, they're going to stick to it 100 percent. Women are responsible for so

many other things in life. Sometimes they have to make that choice of giving something up in order to get pregnant or get married or whatever.

DAWN: Why do you think more women don't start playing to begin with?

BEA: I think a lot of it is because of their perception of how they're being treated on the field. I get a lot of e-mails from girls who say, "I'm getting a hard time from these guys that I play with because they're saying I'm not going to be able to make it." A lot of it is perception. Because of our sensitivity as women, we have a tendency to take things to heart a little too much.

DAWN: What can we do about that?

BEA: I think we just have to be stronger. We have to realize that even though we believe it's such an equal world nowadays, and women can be on top, there are still obstacles. On the field, if somebody says something rude to me, I never bite back. I always try to analyze it. Then I go up to that person and ask for constructive criticism. I just have to be the stronger, better person. Usually they're impressed by my strength and they're impressed that I have the guts to ask them for that help.

DAWN: How soon before we see a woman in one of the pro leagues?

BEA: There are two girls that I'm really praying and hoping I can push in that direction. I believe that Katie Kelly and Kat Secor both have a big chance of making it in the pro scene, at least within the next five years. They're both so young.

DAWN: Do you think the television networks and corporate sponsors will be open to seeing co-ed teams? No other professional sports have co-ed teams.

BEA: Yeah, it's going to be difficult. They're going to have to do a lot of work on the athletic side, train every weekend and maybe even a little bit during the week. It's not a usual thing to see a girl catapult right into the pro division. It's hap-

pened in the past but it hasn't lasted for very long. And I think longevity is a lot more important than just being there for a game or two. I'm hoping that I have a hand in making it happen, with my being a mentor to Kat and Katie both.

DAWN: Do you think we'll ever see an all-female pro league?

BEA: I don't know. I kind of like the fact that we're a one-of-a-kind sport, where we see females playing on a national level on co-ed teams, and I think that really sets us apart.

I think having balance makes the team a lot more fun to be on. Even when you do social things together, it makes it more intriguing when you can interact with the opposite sex and have the same interests in mind. What guy wouldn't enjoy that?

DAWN: What are some of the strengths and talents that women bring to the field?

BEA: Oh, definitely communication. It's easier for a guy to pick out a girl's voice.

And multi-tasking, too. It's been proven in studies that women can multi-task a lot better than men can. I think on the field, on an analytical level, women have a better handle on who's on the field, and where they're placed, and what needs to take place in order to make things happen. Flexibility, for sure, too. The thing that we're lacking is definitely speed, and also diving head first. It's not something that women grow up knowing how to do. It's kind of ingrained since the day we were born to be girlie.

DAWN: What about shooting ability? I've heard that women have better aim.

BEA: I think we're at the same level, as far as keying in on something and aiming and shooting. That's something both genders can do equally well.

DAWN: What can the industry do to try and recruit more female players?

BEA: Some of the advertising that I see can be a bit on the raunchy side, and it gives the wrong impression to women. They don't want to get involved in the sport because they feel like that's the way women are viewed. The industry can probably show more of the athletic side of women. I guess that's where it would start. I don't want to say give them sponsorship, but just show encouragement.

DAWN: Make the women feel welcome as players, not just as eye candy?

BEA: Right!

DAWN: With more teams and more women getting involved in the sport, is it still as easy for women to get sponsorship?

BEA: I think it's harder now. Six years ago, there weren't a whole lot of women playing, so we stood out more. But now there are so many, like Keely Watson, Lisa Harvey, Tami Adamson, and even myself—we've done the whole eye candy thing.

What sets us apart, though, is that we backed it up and we're still in the mix. We're still playing or in the industry. Keely is doing great things in the PSP, and Tami is doing great things with the Femme Fatales still, to this day. I'm still trying to promote the sport and I'm very much involved in the marketing aspects, as well as playing. It's going to be a lot harder for a good-looking woman to come in and do what we've already done and still get sponsors' attention.

DAWN: What advice would you give girls getting into the game?

BEA: Take it seriously. I always take a lot of pride in women that take the sport seriously, that do it for more than just the attention, but because they really and truly do love the sport. Somebody gave me this advice a long time ago. I forget who said it, but they told me: whenever you're in a position where so many people are trying to make it, the moment you think, "I'm going to give up," somebody else has already given up. So you may as well just keep going because you're one step closer to success.

Dawn Allcot *is Editor-in-Chief of* Paintball Sports Magazine. *Her articles have also appeared in* RECON, Paintball News, Paintball 2Xtremes, *and on Paintball.com. A diverse freelance writer, Dawn covers topics such as audiovisual technology, wellness, music and the arts for a variety of magazines and websites. Dawn's husband, T.J., introduced her to paintball in 2001. In 2004, he built the Armored Fist Panther tank, and Dawn secured a position as turret gunner. The AF Panther has participated in scenario games from New York to Tennessee, and appeared on a trading card in RECON Magazine. Dawn is also a Reserve Member of the Tippinators Paintball Team, known for their exemplary sportsmanship and for using Tippmann A-5s in speedball tournaments.*

Dawn, T.J. and their nephews, core members of the Armored Fist Panther crew, play at fields across the U.S., including Cousins Paintball, N.Y., and E.M.R. Paintball, PA.

Team Destiny: Back row: David Hogan, 14; Steve Conner, 20; Bea Youngs, 26; Mike Fairall, 19; Dustin Guidry, 19, Middle: Katie Kelley, 20, Front: Kaarin Schroepfer, 17; Kat Secor, 18; and Evelyn Choi, 26

Welcome to the Game of Paintball

Celebrity Spotting

Ally E. Peltier

One of the more interesting developments in the paintball world is the increasing likelihood of spotting celebrities on the field. What began as a handful of celebs occasionally picking up markers has erupted into the new mode of fundraising for charity events. Many of Hollywood's premiere stars not only play, but play competitively.

Before he died, Maurice Gibb was an avid paintball player. He even owned a series of paintball shops named Commander Mo's in Florida. The NPPL renamed one of its events the Commander's Cup in his honor.

In 2003, the National Professional Paintball League (NPPL) circuit welcomed a team named the Stoned Assassins featuring musical artists B-Real (Cypress Hill) and Everlast (formerly of House of Pain). The team still plays in tournaments and has even played against other celebrities, like their 2003 game against a team led by then-newbie actor Will Smith (the Assassins won, and rumor has it that Smith has been drilling and playing hard ever since). In 2005, B-Real wrote the song Play it for Real about the sport of paintball. He has also contributed to the Greg Hastings series of Paintball Games.

In June of 2006, more than twenty NBA and NFL athletes flew to Hawaii to participate in a charity fundraising event called "Celebrity Paintball Hawaii," which made newspaper headlines and which organizers hope to turn into an annual happening. Similar events at locations in California have garnered television coverage and are increasing in popularity as people grow accustomed to viewing tournament paintball as an extreme sport on channels like ESPN and FOX.

If that's not enough, high profile movie stars have been seen on the fields, not the least of whom is William Shatner. In the last few years, Shatner, "SPPLAT," nationally broadcast morning radio personality Eric "Mancow" Muller, and Airgun Design's president Tom Kaye, have been the force behind a scenario game series nick-

(© Jason "Muzikman" Beam)

Tom Kaye and Bill Shatner at Shatnerball 2004

named "Shatnerball." Each game in the series has its own name and promoter, with themes varying widely, from "Mobster Mash" to Star Trek-based adventures. Shatnerball has produced scenario games for crowds as large as 1,000 to benefit charities such as Ahead with Horses, the 100 Club of Cook County, and the Nerine Shatner Charity Fund. You can find out more about the next Shatnerball event via its primary promoter, www.celebritypaintball.com

So don't be surprised if the next time you play paintball, you suddenly realize that you're sharing a bunker with someone famous. You may find yourself hunting your very own high-profile target!

© Jason "Muzikman" Beam

Spplat Attack!

PART 2

GUNS

The Evolution of the Marker

Paintball is a technology-driven sport. If it weren't, we couldn't shoot paintballs at each other in the first place. But when you consider that the same paintgun used in the first game of paintball could still be used on a modern field, it says something for the longevity of the gear we use. Many of the basics haven't changed. We use a paintball that is .68 inches across. We shoot to mark an opponent, and we're still playing capture the flag for the most part. But a lot has changed since twelve guys stepped into the woods of New Hampshire.

If you read the first part of the book, you know that the first game was played with pistols powered by a small 12-gram CO_2 powerlet. Today's high-end paintguns don't look anything like the original "Nellies." And the history is very interesting.

Paintball markers evolved from two basic designs. The "Nelson" design, which is the Nelspot 007 pistol, and the Sheridan design, seen in the PGP pistol. Both are good designs, and both spawned a lot of clones. For years, players used these pistols exclusively. Players would often work on customizing these paintguns in the tool shed—the original 007 didn't even have a pump arm! If you ever meet an old timer, check his left index finger. If there's a scar on it, it probably came from working the cocking knob of an old Nelspot 007.

One of the hybrid designs was the "Splatmaster." To be fair, the Splatmaster launched paintball into popularity and made it fairly easy for fields to open up. The pistol was made of mostly plastic parts and worked by pushing a "plunger" in the back to cock it. The fact that it was inexpensive, and that more players could realistically afford them, led to a popularity explosion of what was then still called the "Survival Game."

As time went on, paintguns became a little more sophisticated. Players

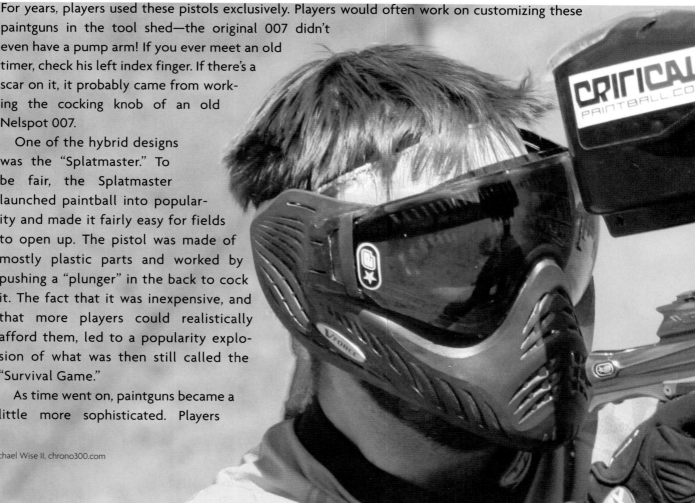

began to use "constant air," a seven ounce CO_2 tank, instead of the 12 gram powerlets. The first tanks had large valves that had to be physically opened, but they were replaced with a more user-friendly pin-valve. The larger air tanks allowed players to shoot more paint before needing more air, and actually lead to even more innovations.

The concept of a semi-automatic paintgun was always toyed with. The first attempts at this were in the Splatmaster camp. The "Rapide" was a double action, meaning that the action was reliant on the pull of the trigger and not like modern styles of air-assisted cocking. It also had a primitive clip/hopper system, a rectangular block that held 40 rounds in 10 round "tube" sections. It was a fun paintgun to play with, but it wasn't a true semi-auto.

The first real semi-automatic began to show up in the late 80s based on the existing Sheridan pump system. There are many debates about who "invented" it first, and the truth may never be known as the first prototypes are scattered to the winds. There was once even a fully automatic marker available, but since it shot a .62 ball it fell out of popularity. That and its rate of fire, 9 balls per second, was just too much for the time. But when the semi-automatic paintgun really came into its own, the game became very different.

Modern semi-automatic paintguns are of two basic types: mechanical and electronic. Mechanical semi-autos are what most people use, simply because they're easier to maintain and cheaper to purchase. The mechanics work in several ways, but the action is generally based in the parts' working together physically.

Electronic semi-autos, however, are usually run by a circuit board in the paintgun itself. The advantage to this is that the rates of fire increase dramatically when you use electronics. You can adjust the trigger to be shorter and lighter, meaning that you can shoot balls at a higher rate than with a mechanical. By customizing the circuit board, you can give a paintgun performance tweaks, have multiple modes of fire (burst, full auto, ramping) without changing your actual paintgun.

So why hasn't everyone switched to electronics? Many reasons, but cost is the biggest. Speed costs money, not to mention you can triple your paint bill if you're not careful. The next is that the electronics package isn't necessary if you only play a few times each summer. So why spend money on something you don't really need? In the end, the right marker for you is simply the one that meets your needs.

Mechanical or electronic, both styles have seen massive evolutions in both functionality and style. Paintguns have gotten a lot lighter. The EXC-68, for example, was six POUNDS of metal, without an air tank or a hopper on it. It was a massive paintgun, to say the least. Not to mention the "68 Special," which was one of the only paintguns with a significant kick to it.

The reason they were so large was that the parts inside were massive! They needed to be large to get enough air to push back the bolts, but this made them heavy. Within a few years, the paintguns became significantly lighter and smaller. The F-1 Illustrator, for example, was light and thin compared to the EXC-68. Other models followed, like the Spyder and Alley Cat. All of these paintguns share a common heritage with the Sheridan pump guns. If you look at the over/under design of most blowbacks, and the over/under design of a Sheridan pump gun, the similarities are still there.

Other semi-automatics abandoned the Sheridan design all together. The Automag, for example, uses

Guns

a "blow forward" design that's unlike any pump gun ever made. And yes, it's also significantly lighter than the EXC-68 Specials.

There are still throwbacks, however! Pump paintball is very much alive and well. Sheridan stopped producing, but the Nelson design is still around in such brands as the Phantom and in custom houses like Carter Machine. Pump has two flavors: normal direct feed pump and "stock class," which is a nod to the old days. A lot of players use pump games to sharpen their skills for when they play semi-auto games. And a lot of players play pump all the time, just for the extra challenge.

A LOT OF PLAYERS PLAY PUMP ALL THE TIME, JUST FOR THE EXTRA CHALLENGE

It's also possible for the end user to customize paintguns. You can get aftermarket parts to change everything from the color of the body to the placement of the air tank. There's simply not enough room in this section to discuss every possible customization. But, here are some of the highlights from the last few decades.

Colors are nothing new; some of the old style paintguns came in red or green, but most came in any color you wanted as long as it was black. Now players can get paintguns airbrushed, powder-coated, anodized or otherwise colored to meet any need or desire. You can even get a matching hopper.

A "drop" is a method of putting the air tank lower on the paintgun, and push it forward a few inches. It may not seem like much, but it offers a player the chance to customize the length of the tank in reference to the trigger and grip. So no longer are you forced to deal with a paintgun that feels two inches too long. Now you can simply get a 2" drop, and make it more comfortable. Since they're made of metals that can be colored, shaped, milled or otherwise customized, they can be matched to an individual's personal style.

Grips, rails, body kits . . . almost everything that can be yanked off a paintgun can be modified! Many players have the body of the paintgun milled into organic shapes or with intricate designs. Some just want to make it lighter, and replace everything they can with lighter parts. Some want more comfort, so they replace the grips. There's no "right" way to customize a paintgun, only the way that's right for you.

When you talk paintball markers, you can't just talk about the marker itself. Barrel technology has jumped as well over the years. Originally, paintguns had a "fixed" barrel, meaning it was part of the main body of the paintgun. You couldn't remove it, short of taking a hacksaw to the thing. But shortly after the first paintgun with a removable barrel was on the market, someone decided they could do better and made their own.

All sorts of materials have been used, and everything from porting to rifling has been tried to make the paintgun more accurate. The problem is the ball, not the barrel. Paintballs vary in size from ball to ball on a small scale. We'll cover this a little later in the book in detail, but most serious players carry a variety of barrel sizes when they play. Unfortunately, this can be bulky in a gear bag.

Smart Parts was the first company to make an insert kit to address the problem. You got a front, a back, and a kit filled with individual inserts. You could then match the insert to the ball size at the field before playing. Soon companies like J&J, LAPCO, Empire and every other major company created a barrel "kit" with several backs and a single front. These smaller kits make it easier for players to match the barrel to the paint they're using that day. Plus you can buy a kit to match your style, like carbon fiber or aluminum.

Then there's the power source. All paintguns work on compressed gasses. The first paintguns used 12 gram carbon-dioxide filled powerlets, which were good for 20 or 30 shots. Larger canisters that held seven ounces of air not only changed the paintguns, but it also changed the game as players remained on the field longer with a single air fill, and the tanks were cheaper to fill than the equal number of shots per 12 gram. Canisters started coming in several sizes; 7, 9, 10, 12, 16 and 20 ounce tanks are now commonplace.

Nitrogen, or "compressed air," was introduced to paintball by Tom Kaye in the early 90s. He brought it to a tournament and turned more than a few heads with it. Nitrogen had clear advantages over CO_2 for paintball use, and players scrambled to get their hands on it. As with CO_2 tanks, several sizes and configurations were tried. Things finally settled on tanks that are either steel or fiber-wrapped. They are labeled with an internal "cubic feet" capacity, and note how much pressure you can put in them. So a "88/4500" holds 88 cubic feet of air and can hold that air at 4500 pounds per square inch (PSI). The regulator controls the output pressure of the tank. And this is where it gets fun.

Most players can get a "high pressure" output system for their paintgun. Normally these tanks just screw into the air adapter for the marker. Most paintguns on the market are ready for this, as these tanks basically emulate the same pressure as compressed CO_2 (800-900 PSI output). For most players, this is the best, and least expensive, bet.

Some players have their setup dialed for "low pressure," meaning that the ball is launched at a lower output pressure but with a higher volume of air. The debate of which is better, low vs. high pressure, is one best suited for internet forums. If you can't tell the difference, go with a high pressure setup.

The biggest difference between paintball now and paintball then is the versatility. A player can easily get markers and related parts from the manufacturer that not only fits their style of play, but also their personal style. A player who wants to make something more comfortable doesn't have to tool in the shed for a day to get it; they can simply add it on. And trust me, when your gear is comfortable for you to use, your game becomes much better.

—RR

Guns

The Science of Paintball

PAINTBALL 101

Required reading for hard core paintball enthusiasts!

At its inception, paintball borrowed its technology and science from other sources out of sheer necessity. There was no such thing as a 'paintball gun', a paintball designed to be shot at 300 feet per second, paintball specific goggles, or any other piece of specialized equipment, simply because the game did not yet exist. But there was precedent for the development and production of these things, so paintball really hit the ground running.

During paintball's formative years, enterprising individuals and companies developed products using a trial-and-error, cut-and-paste, tinkering-in-the-garage approach. In scientific circles this is known as an 'empirical' method. You come up with an idea, build something based on the idea, identify its flaws and errors by using it, make corrections, add refinements, and continue on to a finished product.

Science, in the form of highly educated and degreed individuals working out complex formulas on blackboards, was not necessary. That work had already been done. The art of creating paintball products and equipment was simple and straightforward. If you could understand how a paintball gun worked, if you could cut PVC tubing with a hacksaw, work a mill or a lathe, or sew a few pieces of material together, you were in business.

Just as scientific disciplines underly the paintball industry's growth, unique technologies that have emerged from paintball have found applications beyond the game. At present, gas regulators developed for paintball guns are used by a major manufacturer of computer chips (for clean room regulation), a tire manufacturer is investigating the use of pressure gauges designed for paintball (for use with self-inflating tires for military vehicles) and aerospace technicians are investigating paintball gun electropneumatic systems as possible maneuver control systems for small spacecraft.

Paintballs in Space!

This is only a brief sampling of how far and wide paintball science has already spread.

HOW PAINTBALL WORKS

Integrating scientific disciplines in the name of paintball fun!

The art of designing a paintball gun (or a gun barrel, goggles, or propellant system), is an interdisciplinary one. You can't work with electronics to the exclusion of ballistics; paintball technology requires an understanding of how these and other scientific disciplines interact.

You also have to appreciate the fact that no one knows everything yet. There are still some very interesting puzzles to be solved.

Newtonian Basics

To understand the science of paintball, you need to start with Isaac Newton. Newton discovered the law of gravity (he's the guy the apple fell on) and several related laws of motion and energy that affect everybody and everything.

Newton's laws can be found in any basic physics text. A summary is provided here.

Things have changed dramatically over the past few decades and, while it is not yet possible to earn a degree in paintball science (something which is not all that far from happening), a firm grounding in such things as physics, ballistics, pneumatics and hydraulics, chemistry, materials science and related disciplines will come in very handy when attempting to work with today's paintball technologies. And paintball players may even find all of this interesting, too!

One of the most interesting aspects of paintball is the wide range of sciences, both hard and soft, that it touches upon. The fact that equipment designers use the laws of physics is no surprise, but the use of the 'soft' science of ergonomics (fitting tools to the human body) might be. The use of ballistics is another obvious match for paintball. Psychology's relationship to paintball, on the other hand, is less intuitive; nevertheless several well-respected psychologists have studied paintball in relation to risk-taking behavior, stress, and a variety of other aspects of human behavior.

- Two objects with mass attract each other; the force of attraction is proportional to their mass and depends upon how far apart they are. This is gravity.

- An stationary object will remain stationary unless something acts upon it. Likewise, an object in motion will remain in motion unless something acts on it. These are laws of motion.

- Energy is never lost, though it may take different forms. Now you know the conservation of energy principle.

How do these laws affect paintball? It should be obvious to anyone that a paintball fired from a gun is not going to keep on going forever. Gravity will eventually pull it to the ground. You need something to get a stationary paintball started; how expanding gases propel a paintball down the barrel of a gun is partially a result of the effects of the laws of motion and conservation of energy.

These are fundamental laws of the natural universe. Only by taking them into account can you truly understand how and why a paintball gun works the way that it does, or why a paintball behaves as it does after being fired.

Fluid Dynamics

An understanding of fluid dynamics also comes in handy; this is the study of how fluids (in this case, gases) operate in varying conditions, as well as how to manipulate them. This particular science is one that is still not completely understood, not even by NASA. However, the laws of fluid dynamics tell us certain essential things, such as the fact that the faster a fluid is moving, the lower the pressure will be (and consequently the temperature). These laws explain to some degree what happens when a stream of moving gas interacts with a stationary mass of gas, or why a golf ball with dimples travels farther than one without dimples—or, for that matter, why a paintball with dimples does not travel as far as a paintball without them.

Fluid dynamics can be used to understand and manipulate the way in which the gas propels the paintball, how it flows down the barrel, how to get faster or greater flow of gas through a regulator and related uses.

Ballistics

Ballistics is the science (and art) of the motion of projectiles. How and why does a rock shot from a catapult, a bullet from a gun, a man from a cannon or a paintball from a paintball gun behave the way they do? Ballistics attempts to answer these and other questions. It is also used to predict what might happen to a projectile given a particular set of circumstances (e.g., the shape and density of the projectile, its mass, the speed at which it is fired, the air density, gravity, the angle of the shot).

Some specialized equations, formulas, factors, and laws have been developed specifically for the understanding of ballistics. Among these are:

- The **ballistic coefficient**—a constant relating to the mass and shape of the projectile

- The **form factor**—another number which mathematically represents the shape or surface area of the projectile.

Because (1) the ballistic coefficient is essential to any equation which seeks to explain how a paintball in flight will act, (2) the form factor is critical to establishing a ballistic coefficient, and (3) developing an accurate form factor for the paintball has proven elusive (given its large size, small mass and inconsistencies of its surface features), the ballistic properties of the paintball have yet to be accurately modeled or understood.

So how does all of this relate to paintball?

Is a paintball a solid mass, at least for the purposes of resolving an equation? Does the fluid (paint) inside the shell move? If it moves, does it move enough to affect anything? Does the shell rotate around the fluid when the ball is in flight or does the fluid move?

Fluid dynamics quickly gives way to aerodynamics—the study of the forces acting upon an object which is moving through a gas. The most common application of aerodynamics is the airplane. The forces that aerodynamics studies are the same ones which make an airplane fly. A law of fluid dynamics, Bernoulli's Law, states that the faster a fluid (or gas) moves, the lower its pressure will be. An airplane's wing takes advantage of this force by causing the air which travels over the top to go faster than the air passing under the wing: since the pressure above the wing is lower, the air below the wing wants to move in that direction, creating lift and allowing airplanes to fly.

If a paintball were perfectly spherical in shape (which it isn't) the airflow around, over and under the paintball would be the same. Does the additional friction caused by the seam of the paintball create any lift? Does it cause the paintball to rotate so that it presents the surface area with the least resistance to the air? Would a spinning paintball behave differently from a stationary one? Would the direction of spin affect its flight?

These questions are being asked today by paintball researchers and designers. A huge debate currently centers on what effect (if any) forward and back spin has and if the 'Magnus Effect' is operating. The Magnus Effect says that a spinning object will have regions of higher and lower pressure around it, which will create lift. Theoretically, if a paintball is backspinning, the air moving over the top of the ball is moving faster than the air below the ball, creating lift, while frontspin causes the air below the ball to move faster, which might actually cause the ball to drop towards the ground faster than if it weren't spinning. Musket balls are a pretty good analogy for paintballs (they even have seams from molding); perhaps the mass of the musketball has more influence.

> If you could see the ball as it flew from your barrel, the ball would either be spinning towards you—backspin, or away from you—frontspin.

Might controlling this spin allow paintballs to travel further? Will a ball that is spinning rapidly be more stable than one which isn't? Bullets are spun by their barrels, so that they are spinning around their long axis. This gives them stability in flight. Do the same forces act in the same way on paintballs? Most of the evidence seems to say, "No," because paintballs are not spun anywhere near fast enough to gain any benefit from this effect. Furthermore, testing seems to indicate its spin will probably have negative effects on performance.

PRINCIPLES OF GAS PROPULSION

Chemistry and Paintball

Chemistry should not be overlooked either. Imagine the precision needed to create a gelatin shell that is elastic enough to withstand being accelerated to speeds in excess of 300 feet per second in a few milliseconds, yet also remains brittle enough to break against a relatively soft and yielding surface after it has given up most of its momentum.

However, there are several things which are much better understood than the flight characteristics of paintballs. The 'Gas Laws', for instance, were formulated in the 1700s and remain fairly predictable to this day. Among other things, the gas laws state:

- A gas will expand to equilibrium. In other words, gas in a closed volume will be at the same pressure everywhere in that volume.

- Gas pressure increases proportionally to temperature. This means that pressure in a given volume increases when it is heated and decreases when it is chilled.

- Gas pressure also increases proportionally with a decrease in volume. This means that if you compress gas in a volume to half its original size, the pressure of the gas in the volume will double. If you increase the available volume by doubling it, the pressure will decrease to half of its original pressure.

Taking advantage of the action of gases according to these laws is what allows a paintball gun to fire a paintball. Gas (carbon dioxide, nitrogen, or air) is compressed into a tank, such that the pressure of the gas inside the tank is many hundreds of times greater than the surrounding air. This gas stored under pressure is an energy source, better known as 'potential' energy.

POTENTIAL ENERGY IS ENERGY THAT IS WAITING TO BE USED. ENERGY THAT IS BEING USED IS REFERRED TO AS KINETIC ENERGY.

When you open the valve of the tank, the gas contained inside wants to achieve equilibrium with the surrounding volume, which in this case happens to be the Earth's atmosphere; 14.7 pounds per square inch is the generally accepted air pressure at sea level.

When we use compressed gases in a paintball gun, we are turning potential energy into kinetic energy, or transferring the energy we get from the gas to the paintball. This occurs by briefly opening the valve to the propellant tank, which allows some high pressure gas to escape into the barrel of the gun. This gas enters a volume in the barrel which is behind a loaded paintball. The energy in the expanding gas is sufficient to overcome the balls' inertia (its tendency to remain motionless and its tight fit against the wall of the barrel), which pushes the ball down the barrel. Energy continues to be imparted to the paintball so long as the gas behind the ball, seeking equilibrium, continues to expand.

Understanding the gas laws allows us to 'regulate' (i.e., finely control the duration and volume of a gas flow) gases, to use gas as both a mechanism for firing the paintball and re-cocking a semi-automatic gun, and for a variety of other applications.

Electronics, and even computer science, have recently been rearing their heads in paintball as well. The latest technological buzzword in the sport is **electropneumatic.** This is simply another name for using electronics in place of mechanical systems in some semi-automatic paintball guns. Initial attempts at marrying the space age to the steam era have proven quite successful. There is no doubt that many more advances will come in this area.

There are many other scientific disciplines pushing the paintball we know and love today toward an even more amazing tomorrow. So many, in fact, that it is impossible to cover them all adequately. It is amazing how rapidly the science of paintball has progressed from a garage-tinkering hobby to the cutting edge of various scientific endeavors.

—SD

© Cleo Fogal

© Michael Wise II, chrono300.com

JOHN RICE ON SAFETY

Paintball has developed extraordinarily fast over a very short period of time. We've come a long way from the traditional little pistol that used to fire one shot and then required a reload. And everyone used to wear a completely unsafe goggle system. Nowadays you're going up eighteen shots plus, and the goggles are designed to withstand the impact of balls traveling 200 miles per hour in rapid succession. It's a whole new standard of safety for a whole new kind of game. As an industry, we've agreed to hold back on firing rates. My technology could take us up to thirty shots per second, but is the player ready for that? Is the safety equipment ready for that intensity? No matter what, safety needs to set the limit for the implementation of new technologies. On that, we should all agree.

Guns

PRINCIPLES OF WORR

Bud Orr

"My dad always said, 'If some guy built it, then you can fix it.'"

In 1953, Bud Orr learned about engine conversions from his father. In 1960, he worked for the U.S. Air Force as a jet fighter mechanic. In 1969, he started working for the Navy overhauling ships (literally, entire ships!). He took up scuba diving, and soon began learning about air flow, gas pressure, and soon began redesigning regulators and compressors. Then, in the mid-1980s, Bud fell in love with paintball. Much of what makes paintball what it is today is directly attributable to innovations pioneered by Bud Orr, founder of Worr Games Products. *Editor's Note: This interview was conducted for the first edition of this book in 1999. Some information may be outdated. Budd Orr's Autococker, one of the earliest paintball markers manufactured, is still one of the most popular guns on the market. You can find out more at www.worr.com.*

ADAM COHEN: So how did you discover paintball?

BUD ORR: Well, one day I came back from vacation and my family wanted to go play paintball. My son wouldn't go unless I went. So, we all went, and basically, I think I rented a PGP at the time and I got shot up pretty bad. And, of course, I loved it.

ADAM: This is back in 1985?

BUD: Yes. And from that point on, we went ahead and went back the next weekend and I thought I could do better because I had thought about the game. The same thing happened, but I figured out why they were shooting at me. Every time I released a CO_2 to change it, they'd run up on me. They were listening carefully and knew when my gun was dead.

So, I went home that week and developed a little device that enabled me to vent CO_2. The following weekend I had more success. I'd vent it, they'd run up, and I'd shoot them. Then, I started modifying guns because I didn't have enough CO_2's. So, I made a manifold so I could actually bolt more CO_2's on it. I was into scuba diving at the time and designed some stuff for the scuba diving industry, so I had access to these little quick release devices. I used them to make it so that you didn't have to expend CO_2 until you pulled a lever.

So, I made a manifold, I bolted two of those on there, and I went out and played all day with two 2.5 ounce CO_2 cylinders.

ADAM: Up to this point, you were doing this primarily because you just loved the game?

BUD: That's right. I just loved it. It was an adrenaline rush. Up to that point . . . well, I've been a racer all my life. I'm real competitive as far as racing is concerned—drag car racing, sports car racing, boat racing, motorcycles, you name it, I've done it.

The adrenaline rush was just about like it was in racing, only it lasted longer. Just the thrill of the hunt and of being hunted. There's nothing like it, not to this day. Two hours of pure adrenaline rush.

I just started improving the guns. We went to stick feed and then I went over to Sat Cong village and I was a gunsmith there. And in late '86, I

Autococker, in all its glory!

The Complete Guide to Paintball

was shooting Annihilators. I was actually buying and selling them, and I couldn't really get them from the guy that was making them. He sort of laughed at my ideas for improving the gun. So I went home that week, designed in my head what I wanted to build, and prepared to put it together myself.

I'd been thinking about it for a long time because of all the problems that people had, and different types of play and different atmospheres of play.

ADAM: What were the central problems you wanted to solve?

BUD: I thought it was important to have a feed system on the gun, as well as a constant air system attached directly to the gun. I thought the gun should be closed so that you couldn't get sand in it. Stuff like that. I wanted to build a pretty accurate gun. I didn't like the idea that you couldn't change barrels.

I really didn't like the idea that you had a hose going to the gun from a remote CO_2 system. But, before that, I started to use what they call Ansel bottles; they're for CO_2 cylinders that are made out of steel. I'd mount those on the Sheridan rifles. A guy could play all day on a single bottle of CO_2.

Then I started refilling the cylinders at that point, and I designed an apparatus that we could transverse fill. I don't know that anybody came up with that before I did. Basically, I actually had the first commercial transverse filling.

And from that point on, I was building guns with all kinds of bottles hanging on them. Then I went home one night and I was watching "Miami Vice." Before I watched it, I went out and had a body and frame made in about two hours. After the show, I spent most of the rest of that night building the gun, which became the Sniper.

The next morning I finished it. I went to the Sat Cong village at Battondoon and shot the guy who had laughed at me in the butt. [*Laughs*]

ADAM: When was this, now?

BUD: That was late 1986.

ADAM: Wow. So in essence your first year of involvement with paintball was just one innovation after another.

BUD: Oh yeah, I never quit. It was just one thing after another for a couple of years. It was neat. The technology was so young; there weren't very many innovative products available. A few people had some really cool stuff, but I wanted it to be more. I pushed the technology a few logical steps further. That's what the Sniper was. It was the first actual paintball gun, the first that was manufactured explicitly for paintball, as opposed to being modified for paintball.

Most of the guys took pellet guns from Sheridan, and they took paint markers . . . 007's that were made for marking cows . . . and I think there were a couple of other guns out on the market at that point. Players would take the top barrel off and put a barrel on it and use it for paintball.

I built that first gun. It was the first paintball gun with a direct feed; the first gun out with a closed bolt system that you could field strip. You could actually adjust the velocity without having to tear the gun apart to clip springs.

It was also the first gun to offer a removable barrel. It was one of the leaders in the pumps and stocks, where you had a stock come with it standard.

ADAM: So, within your first year of playing the game, you had started up a company for manufacturing and selling these guns.

BUD: Yeah, I founded Worr Games Products in 1987. It was Thanksgiving of 1987 when I actually incorporated the company, bought my first trailer, and started a business.

Then a year later, in 1988, my Dad was sick. I put in for a leave of absence, so I could spend some time with him. And then he passed away before I even got the time off. That was a bad break. So, I just took the leave the absence.

Now I had worked for the United States government for 22 years, overhauling navy ships in private shipyards. Got kind of tired of that. My wife made pretty good money, so we sat down and figured out that we could live off her paycheck if we needed to. So I just started manufacturing guns in 1988.

I had four months. Four months to make it or break it, you know? And it took off from that point. My daughter, a friend of mine, and my wife and I committed to it.

ADAM: So, you never turned back.

BUD: Our growth was amazing. It was just one innovation after another until 1991. Our company came up with the first speed limit. And we invented the first barrel plug, the first constant air gun, the first screw-in barrel. We had the first ammo box. Actually, we were neck and neck with another company, but when we started making them, we were the only one in the market addressing this need. Russell Maynard, who was the editor of APG at the time, and I made the 45 round ammo box happen.

We spent hours making this ammo box, so it would feed well. We figured it out and it was a huge hit. We sold over 500,000 ammo boxes. From there, we went on to speed ball.

ADAM: How did you come up with the idea for the barrel plug?

BUD: Out of necessity. Guys would come up to the window of our retail store, which we ran for about 5 years. My wife would take a gun from a guy and it would go off and just miss her. She's nice looking, blonde, blue-eyed, and I just didn't want to see her get hit in the face with a paintball. So we actually came up with a barrel plug.

ADAM: So you invented it to protect your wife?

BUD: [Laughs] Yeah, but we knew it would be good for the market.

The original barrel plug was designed so that if you were shooting at 350 feet per second or under with a nine-inch barrel, the ball would not make it to the end of the barrel because of the air pressure. It would just cushion and stop the ball.

And then, in 1988, I was flying back to see a gentleman named Ray Gong. This man was spearheading a drive to legalize paintball in New Jersey. In 1988, if you owned a paintball gun in New Jersey and got caught with it, you'd go to jail. [EDITOR'S NOTE: At the time, paintball was legal in 48 states. Only New Jersey and Massachusetts made it illegal. Currently, paintball is legal in all 50 states.]

So, Ray Gong, myself, Jessica Sparks, and Russell Maynard went to the Supreme Court in New Jersey, and it took us two sessions to get an old law overturned so it was actually legal to play paintball in New Jersey.

ADAM: Cool.

BUD: Yeah, it was a battle, but we won. Anyway, I was flying back to meet with Ray, and I met some women and children whose fingers broke when they were hit with paintballs. Like I said, there wasn't a chronograph at the time. Very few people used chronos. The way they adjusted a gun's velocity was pretty crude. If the gun shot bark off a pine tree, it was shooting too hot. So, you turned it down and cut the spring until you shot and the bark didn't come off. That was supposed to be a safe level. Of course, people were still getting their fingers broken, which was intolerable.

I went to an orthopedic surgeon and asked him what were the average pressure level and types of pressures that fingers could withstand in terms of the impact of a paintball. He told me that the average would be about 12 pounds of energy.

I calculated the weight of the paintball and all that stuff and came up with 300 feet per second. Not that the gun shot very well at that speed. It was simply a rational safety factor; guns wouldn't break bones at that level. So, I was the one to come up with 300 feet per second, which is the paintball velocity at virtually every outdoor field. They turn it down even more for indoor fields, to about 270 feet per second or lower.

ADAM: From that point forward, the key challenge was developing guns that fire reliably and accurately at that speed.

BUD: You bet it was. And we even accounted for variations that might make the gun fire hotter all on its own. You know, people make mistakes, like setting their gun out in the sun. My gun, if it got up over 1100 pounds of pressure in a chamber area, would fire at about 320 feet per second. But after 1100 pounds, the gun simply won't fire.

The weight of the hammer and the chamber pressure, the spring pressure, and the speed of the hammer are all designed to prevent the valve chamber from opening until the pressure reaches the level that fires at 300 feet per second.

We didn't have regulators at that point. Around 1990, Tom Kaye, inventor of the AutoMag, and I solved that problem. Tom Kaye and I are extremely good friends. We actually met in '87 or '88, and I flew back to meet him, and we were going to do some projects together. I had the ammo project and he and I were both independently plugging away on the semiautomatic at the time. When I walked into his facility and sat down and talked to him, I was shocked. Right there on his desk was almost an identical copy of what I was working on.

He and I thought the same way. As a matter of fact, the only difference was in the hammer. He used rubber bands to adjust the pressure, as far as pulling the hammer back into place, whereas I used an old beat up spring. That was it.

And, so we made a deal. I'd go off on ammo box, he went off on the semi. Eventually, I actually made my semi and sold it to PMI.

None of us had a lot of money back then. I helped him out and he helped me out. Tom still comes out once a year and we go over old times. There's nothing that we hide from each other. We're fierce competitors on the open market, but we're still really good friends. And I think we'll remain that way the rest of our lives.

ADAM: Tell us about the origins of the Autococker.

BUD: Well, in the early 1990s, semiautomatics were coming and, to be perfectly frank with you, I really didn't like that. Back then, I was trying to push on people what I liked about paintball. I thought the idea of semiautomatics would subtract from the development of paintball as a highly competitive, skills-oriented game.

Paintball was originally designed to highlight individual skills. The point was never what a player had in his hand. It's great that Hayes [Noel] came up with the paintball gun, but even he thought of the gun as a means, not an end. The game was originally about survival, and that's the way I

always looked at it. The way the game forces you to improvise is so unique. I've actually thrown paintballs at people and got them out because I was out of CO_2. That's the thrill of it. Not firing tons of paint. Anyone can pull a trigger, but knowing how to do it so that you prevail is the real thrill.

ADAM: Suddenly it looked to you like the technology was going to upstage the skills.

BUD: Yes. And it has. The game I loved is hard to find. Whenever you can sit back and just hose paint at somebody, it takes away from the sport.

So, at that point, I didn't want to be a semi-guy. But Tom had brought out the automatic and, from a business perspective, I was just forced into it.

I had a bunch of ideas. I ran across a gentleman named Jamell, out of Sacramento. We put our ideas together and came up with the Autococker.

Jamell got out of paintball and I continued on with the Autococker. We're talking 1990, because I

sponsored the Ironmen team that year. It was one of the first teams I ever sponsored, and they used the Autococker.

Up until a few years ago, some of the guys on the Ironmen team still played with pump guns. There are actually point men who play with a pump gun. Some of them hated the semis, couldn't get used to them. And we're talking about amazing point men, guys who are doing a ton of shooting in every game.

The Autococker is actually a pneumatic system that I bolted on to a pump. If you take the pneumatic cocking system off, you have a top of the line pump on the market. The closed bolt system, which is a design of the Autococker, seems to have good range and consistency. Too many gun manufacturers fall short of that, even today.

Then we came up with regulators and regulating systems. That's the first one. Unique Sporting Goods brought out a design for an on-off valve that goes into cylinders. And it would be a nightmare to make any of those valves in quantity, so we came up with another design, and that's the on-off valve that's on the market right now. That's probably one of the last, really influential projects that we were responsible for.

ADAM: So, how would you describe the state of the Autococker today?

BUD: Great. If you look back at the history of paintball, this gun's back in all the magazines. It came out in the second or third issue of APG, and it's been in there ever since. It's outlasted all other guns on the market. I don't know of any gun right now—with the exception of the PGP—that was on the market 10 years ago.

ADAM: Have there been any modifications to it? Significant modifications in that time?

BUD: Every day. And all of the modifications that we've made on the Autococker will fit on the original gun. So, no matter what year's model you own, even if you bought one of the first ones, ten of which had no serial numbers, all of my modifications to date will fit on that gun.

That's what makes the Autococker like a 1911 Colt .45. It's a standard that ages quite well. And many people make a living off of making accessories for the Autococker. Modifications on it are unlimited. Every time I think I've seen them all, along comes something new.

ADAM: Is there anything you can share with us about the future of Worr Games paintball guns?

BUD: Sure. We're heading into electronics. We're already working on them. We're actually working on retro-fit kits for the Autococker so that it can become an electrically operated pneumatic system. Like everything else in this world, the gun is going to be computer-operated.

ADAM: Like the Angel.

BUD: Yes. If you really look at the Angel, it's basically an open bolt 'cocker, because they use a three-way. As a matter fact, the valve system in the Angel is identical to mine, just scaled down a little bit, which we talked about. I mean, they didn't copy it; what they've done is pretty great. They made it work.

ADAM: Do you still play the game, Bud?

BUD: Oh, yeah!

ADAM: And when you do, what are some of the accessories that you use with your Autococker? Are there any you can't go without at this point?

BUD: Not really. When I go out to play, I usually pull a new Autococker off the shelf, one that's ready to ship.

That's how I know whether my stuff is good enough for the public. If I see somebody who would like what I have, and I know he can't afford it, I usually give it to him when I'm done for the day. I haven't done that lately because most of the people out there that play nowadays can afford to buy my stuff, I guess.

It costs a lot of money to play nowadays, and that's annoying. When I first started, it would cost me $25 bucks a day, because when I started, paintballs were anywhere from 12 to 15 cents a piece, and we were shooting enamel paint.

So, when we went out and got hit with enamel paint, we had to have turpentine with us to get it off our skin. And the safety equipment that we used back then? We wore sunglasses.

ADAM: Anybody lose an eye?

BUD: [*Laughs*] How we didn't blast our eyes out of our heads, I don't know.

ADAM: What do you think about the state of the game?

BUD: The survival part of it is just a great mind trip. I hunted animals for quite a few years, and I was pretty good. I never got skunked in all the years I hunted. I went to areas where they said there were no deer or antelope, and brought out my animal.

So, I classified myself as a pretty good hunter. And I often wondered what it would feel like . . . you know, I was in the military, so I've been hunted, but that's quite different. The sides were rarely equal, and if you got caught, you might die. Paintball provides an altogether different feeling.

When you're the hunter as well as the one being hunted, and it's not your actual life so much as your pride as a survivor that's on the line, it's just a great experiment. The experience is a test of survival skills and instincts. A bunch of people put themselves in this context where only one can emerge a victor. I haven't been able to duplicate it in any of the things I've ever done in my life. And I've taken my life in my own hands in many ways. I've jumped out of planes, scuba-dived, participated in every type of extreme sport except bungee jumping. Paintball is just a greater thrill than any of those things.

ADAM: Do you believe that the game today is very different from the game you're describing?

BUD: Today's game can get a little weird. Referees blow a whistle to start the game, and people who don't even see anybody start shooting paint. It's literally impossible that they could hit anybody, but that's irrelevant to them. They are there to shoot.

Right now, there's no adrenaline rush for me unless I play with some of the veterans of the game. They don't shoot unless they have a clear shot and the time is right. These people who just start shooting at anything, who think the ability to shoot, not to hunt, makes them good, they're the ones who've taken over the contemporary game.

ADAM: You ever talk to kids about your way of playing?

BUD: Actually, yes. I was with some kids in New Jersey, and I taught them how to hunt. They took a whole new look at paintball; they felt the adrenaline rush I get from the game. They were turned on by the idea of a guy who doesn't even know they're there stepping over them.

ADAM: Is there any effort currently underway to promote paintball as a survival game?

BUD: I would love to change it back. You know, I love kids; kids are the backbone of our lives. And if I had my druthers, I'd like to take kids out and spend about five or six hours teaching them survival skills in the woods. Then you test those skills by putting them up against another group of kids that are equally trained and go play paintball the way it used to be played.

And if they want to use a full automatic, they would get only 200 rounds. I used to go out with 20 rounds on me, and take out four or five people.

The game was quieter, but no less active. It was more intense.

We used to crawl on our hands and belly over rocks. I'd be crawling . . . I could crawl right underneath someone . . . and before they even knew I was there, I got 'em all! And I'm a big guy. That's the thrill!

Other times, I'd walk in on a group of people that thought I was on their side, which you accomplish by keeping your armband away from their eyes, so they can't see it. I'd take out 10 of them before getting hosed, but it was worth it.

ADAM: Are there plans to resuscitate this style of play on a widespread basis?

BUD: Yeah. I talked to Hayes Noel about it. Yes, I would say there are plans. Somewhere along the line, when I slow down a little bit from what I'm doing now, I'd like to be involved in that.

There are people that I know who do play this way now. They're renegade players. They take 30 people out in the forest with two cases of paint and play paintball the way it was meant to be played.

ADAM: This is "outlaw" paintball?

BUD: Yeah, 'outlaw,' 'renegade,' it's all the same thing. It's just about a bunch of people who are sick of going to a field where everybody just wants to hose everybody else. Sometimes it gets pretty bad. On some fields, you shoot a guy 15 times in the goggles and he says he's not hit. Some people can't deal with the most basic rule: if you're hit, you're out. Hold up your hand and walk off the field.

I've gone to seminars, talked to people and some of the older groups that used to play paintball, and they would love to see the old game mainstreamed. Some of us set up some games with pump guns that are played on an individual basis. We've offered a $10,000 purse for first, second, and third place.

There's 10 people playing, and you're against all of them. That's the way to play paintball.

ADAM: That's definitely old-school paintball.

BUD: Yup. That puts a whole new aspect on it. We used to play one on one. We used to play "hare and hound" at Easter time. They'd send a 'hare' running, and then release a 'hound' every 15 seconds. They were all against each other, but the goal was to eliminate the hare. So they're hunting someone who can shoot back at them, and they have to look over their shoulders, because every hunter has incentive to take out the other hunters as well. It was awesome. And I think they still do it like that in some places. But those are just scenarios.

We'd take Easter Day, get 30, 40, 50 people out there, and run two or three games, with everyone fending for himself. There's just not a rush like that. It's unreal.

ADAM: You and Hayes Noel are birds of a feather on this view of the game.

BUD: That guy is incredible.

ADAM: Have you played with him?

BUD: Never played with him, but have you ever met him? That guy is just absolutely top of the line. He's just a really neat, fun, individual. I don't know of anybody that could say anything bad about him. He's put me where I am, and I appreciate that. He just started paintball. I'm one of the people that followed in his footsteps when he backed out of it.

ADAM: If he hadn't played that first survival game . . .

BUD: . . .I wouldn't be in business today.

You know, I had often thought about what he thought about, but I didn't know what to use. I was going to use blow guns or darts or slingshots. I always wanted to see if I could survive in the woods, with people chasing me around.

ADAM: Looks like you got your wish.

BUD: Sure did.

ADAM: I really appreciate your sharing your insights with us.

BUD: No problem.

How the Angel Got Its Name and Everything Else You've Always Wanted to Ask This Man

John Rice graduated college with a degree in metallurgy and spent 12 years at TI research laboratories in Cambridge, England, and another 5 years at GE/GEC joint ventures based in England. He specialized in materials technology, high vacuum and surface coating technologies for Joint European Toruss at Harwell Atomic Research. He joined WDP in 1994, working in their new product developments division, and signed on full time as Technical Director in 1995. At 35 years-old, John has been married for 13 years and has a 9 year-old child. His first gun was a Bushmaster, his favorite pump gun is the Sterling, and his first semi-automatic was the Automag.

John Rice and his gun, The Angel, are legendary in the paintball industry. One of the most coveted guns around, the Angel is the first electropneumatic gun to arrive on the scene.

ANDREW FLACH: Where did the idea for the Angel originate?

JOHN RICE: There are certain stars in paintball, players who are very skilled and fast on the trigger. Joe Public wants to be a star. So, I think, how can I make "Joe" a star? The first question in my mind was "how easy is it for 'Joe' to pull a trigger?"

I thought that if I could make it possible for anyone to pull a trigger real fast, as fast as someone who's super fit, it's going to appeal to that player because achieving something awesome will feel "easy."

Now, if you have something that's mechanical and there's a certain timing sequence to maximize the rate of fire, you have to be quite skilled in coordination to achieve the desired result. That's a disadvantage to some players, whereas it might be an advantage to others. So I wanted a leveler, I wanted everybody to have their 15 minutes of fame. That's where electronics come in.

ANDREW: Did you wake up one morning and say 'Eureka'?

JOHN: No, it wasn't as easy as that. If you could have seen the prototype you'd know what I mean. It was spread over about a 5 foot table—bits of valve over here, some electronics over there. Have you ever heard the term "Heath Robinson?"

ANDREW: Heath Robinson is a term? No, I haven't.

JOHN: "Heath Robinson" is English terminology. He was a famous artist who used to draw crazy machines to solve simple problems. Like America's Rube Goldberg. Our first products were like that.

ANDREW: In other words, it did its thing, but you couldn't fit it into a gun.

JOHN: Exactly. But we were thinking about how we were going to make this work. Some of the technology simply wasn't available at the time. That was a major hurdle. I was quite fortunate that, with my background in the industry, I could apply certain industrial technologies to paintball. My former research and engineering experience exposed me to a wide range of possibilities.

New types of materials and different ways of doing things. I realized early on that what I wanted to achieve with a paintball gun could only be achieved with electronics.

I had to take a lot of what the individual did out of their control. I just wanted them to point the gun and pull the trigger, I didn't want them to have to apply any further skill to that process. Basically, that's what the electronics do.

The Angel was born out of my desire, my frustration, my blood, sweat, and tears. And also out of the faith of people like Gerard Green. He believed that we could come up with a product that would work.

We targeted a niche market; the Angel is aimed squarely at the top pro player. It's made in England, and, as I'm sure you've heard, it's very expensive.

That's the first thing people say: "It's expensive. Why should I pay that much money?" The answer is that making things in England is expensive. Our labor costs are very high. Machine costs and raw materials are more expensive. These facts, in conjunction with our commitment to R&D and next generation products, plus the level of customer support we offer, lead to an expensive product, but one with a great deal of value built into it. The consumer is receiving the most technically advanced paintball gun in existence.

Europe nowadays cannot rely on a mass market. I don't know if you're aware of how the European market works, but mass marketing in Europe is dead. We can't compete with Poland or Taiwan. So, we specialize. In Europe, everything's moving towards specialization.

ANDREW: Craftsmanship is a way of adding value.

JOHN: Exactly. So we set up the Angel, developed it, launched it, aimed at a very small niche, low production numbers, at the top end player. Due to it's success, it's actually cascaded down, which has surprised us. We're amazed at how many Angels we've sold. And we're actually seeing young kids buying them. 12-year-olds are hassling their parents to buy them. And yes, we'll build a rapport with the parents, offer them support. But that's amazed us.

Our product was not targeted at them. And you know, when you see a young lad come up to you, 12 years old, and he's holding his Angel up, it does knock you for six a bit. [*Laughs*]

One thing we recognized very quickly was that our product was moving across the pond, and to support customers we had to come to America on a regular basis. Because if you're asking someone to part with a lot of money and they say, "I've got a problem, where do I go?", you better be able to answer them.

ANDREW: So, what year marked the origin of the Angel?

JOHN: The first working prototypes that you could actually hold in your hand and play with appeared in 1995. That's when you could actually say "this gun looks like an Angel."

ANDREW: Who named it?

JOHN: Dave Poxon, our Marketing Director. Have you ever heard of a rock group called Saxon? It's a heavy metal group, early 80s, and he used to be its manager. He was into marketing, and he knew which way the music industry was going. He said "Angel is going to be a big word on the music scene," and he chose it as the name of our gun, too. Sure enough, records come out with "angel" themes and lyrics, and it became this new happening thing. That's his skill.

That's how the Angel name came about. It was called the Angel V6. We chose V6 because it sounds gutsy, earthy. In America they like V6. It was V6 because it's 6 volt, no other reason. Amazingly, we dropped the V6, but people over here still say, "Oh, I've got a V6."

Also, the Angel had another appeal. It's a little mysterious. A little sinister. A little dangerous. You could turn a dark side to it. That's where the Dark Angel was born.

ANDREW: Double entendre.

JOHN: That's it. And it worked very

well for us. So that's how the Angel got its name.

Another interesting bit of Angel trivia is the fact that on the packaging, the gun depicted is a left-handed model. The reason it is photographed this way is because I'm left-handed. It wasn't until very late into the design and production of the Angel that we spotted the oversight.

Andrew: So the early production models, the design models . . .

JOHN: . . . are all left handed.

ANDREW: What is it that makes the Angel a unique paintball gun for the player?

JOHN: First of all, the shape works well. It's very sleek, very modern looking. That's come out of European styling more than American styling. In America, space is so free. Everything in the U.S.A. is big. Look at your appliances, look at your cars, look at your houses. You've got space, and you like to fill it. The Americans also like to bolt things on and add things because of this perception that there is no space restriction. In Europe, everything's got to be small. We made everything small deliberately.

People buy instant prestige when they buy an Angel. They're buying something that is European, that is new, that is unique.

ANDREW: Tell us about the Angel's technical features.

JOHN: With the Angel, you can have a very short trigger pull. In fact, the first prototype triggers were so soft you could literally blow on them and they would go bang. People shot themselves a good deal. [*Laughs*]

So the trigger is very easy to use, everybody can pick up an Angel and achieve a very high rate of fire. They don't need the skill to do it.

ANDREW: Now, when you pull the trigger you're activating a circuit?

JOHN: You're basically starting a sequence of events.

Manufacturer: Warped Sports Type: Dark Angel Description: Customized and modified Angel with double trigger. *Courtesy of Rocky Cagnoni.*

ANDREW: What is the sequence?

JOHN: The sequence of events is basically as follows. When I pull the trigger, I start an elaborate clock which now needs to drive electro-pneumatic valves and solenoid valves. And what we've actually got is a Japanese valve. We call it a "fourteen way valve."

It's called that because it has fourteen gas galleries. It's a very reliable valve. The Japanese have done an excellent job in miniaturizing it for me. What that then drives is a traditional mechanism, and although there are several unique features that we've patented in that mechanism, it's still using gas to fire a paintball.

Gas comes into the fourteen way valve and it drives a servo. A servo is how to get some movement using less force, like your brake servo on a car. If you didn't have a servo, you'd be pressing on that brake with all your strength to get an effect. The servo translates a mild force into a heavier force.

For example, if I have a very small piston, I could lift a 300 ton weight with my thumb. I'd only move it very slightly, but I could do it, because I could apply force over a very small area, the way a car jack works. It's mechanical advantage. That's what a servo does. A servo actually drives what we call the spool.

The spool changes gas direction, which drives a hammer forward, and that hammer will strike a valve. Just how long that valve is open for is controlled electronically. Controlling it electronically is extraordinarily efficient. This is all happening in sixteen milliseconds. Sixteen thousandths of a second! This eliminates the "chopping of paint."

ANDREW: And chopping paint is?

JOHN: It's where your bolt or your mechanism comes forward, and it literally chops the paintball in half, before it's properly positioned for firing. You can make guns shoot incredibly fast, but you haven't got a hope in hell of shooting paint. Because if a gun's shooting faster than you can feed it paintballs, it turns into an emulsion gun.

ANDREW: You're blasting out broken paintballs.

JOHN: So with the Angel what you can do is actually adjust the timing. Now, because I can control the timing of the firing mechanism through electronics, I can achieve a very high rate of fire. The Angel has the fastest rate of fire of any paintball gun available.

ANDREW: Which is?

JOHN: In addition to having an adjustable range from 10 bps to 31 bps, the Angel offers an unlimited MROF (maximum rate of fire) setting. The new Angel 1's 30+ bps performance is unmatched by any other paintball marker available.

ANDREW: Semi-auto or full auto?

JOHN: Either. There's a set of dip switches on a chip inside the gun that changes the mode of firing. You have semi-auto, full auto, three shot burst, and a "zipper burst."

ANDREW: What is a zipper burst?

JOHN: Zipper burst was developed in reaction to what they called the "Turbo Trigger." Essentially, it's an eight round burst. It's purpose was to show the farcical nature of some of the current definitions of a trigger action. But that's another story altogether.

ANDREW: Would you have specific loader systems that are recommended for use with this or do

Wire synchronizes electronic loader with firing rate of the gun.

people widely use whatever they desire?

JOHN: The most popular system is made by Viewloader. It's a motorized system. However, the paintball industry is on the verge of the next big step, which is force feed.

The limiting factor with any of the current loader systems is gravity. Once you take gravity out of it, rate of fire can go sky high. Way above 30, even hundreds of paintballs a second. It's virtually unlimited, in theory.

THE AIR SYSTEM

ANDREW: The Angel is a compressed air gun, right?

JOHN: Correct. Carbon dioxide is a very harsh gas, and the trouble is it's stored in its liquid state. As it turns into gas, its temperature drops. The colder it gets, the less it wants to give off gas. I call CO_2 a "dirty" gas because it's slow to fill up, it freezes, it's not very temperature stable, and it's very abrasive. The ice crystals that form in it are actually physically abrasive to gun parts.

For running a paintball field, CO_2 is attractive. It's cheap, it's simple, because all you're buying are cylinders of CO_2, you don't have to have a high pressure air regulation system.

With the classic 12 ounce cylinder, you can get

2000 shots off under perfect conditions. Such are the thermodynamics of CO_2. That means you fire one shot, you allow the gas pressure and the temperature to recover, and then fire your next shot. Paintball guns aren't used that way, of course. Paintball guns are shooting faster and faster.

ANDREW: So, in other words, the CO_2 has a lag time between shots caused by the nature of the gas.

JOHN: Yes.

ANDREW: Because each shot costs pressure, and it takes time to get back up to pressure.

JOHN: Up to pressure and temperature. So you can take a CO_2 gun and fire it. The number of shots you get out is phenomenal initially, but things go downhill from there.

ANDREW: So compressed air was your vision from the start.

JOHN: Yes. That was the only choice, in my view. I wanted air, nitrogen. I did not want CO_2.

ANDREW: Now, I heard you use a term earlier, low pressure regulator? The LPR. That sounds like a scuba diving term.

JOHN: Because the Angel is pneumatically driven, I need a lower pressure to drive my pneumatics. My servo valve will not survive high pressure, so I needed a lower pressure to do that.

ANDREW: So you need something to stage it down.

JOHN: Correct. The LPR.

THE INFINITY BARREL

ANDREW: What kind of barrel systems do you use? Do you develop your own?

JOHN: We make our own barrels, which we call the Infinity Series. Barrels are such a personal choice. I could sit here and say Infinity barrels are the best barrel in the world and believe it. But in the end, it's very personal.

ANDREW: What are the unique features of the Infinity barrel?

JOHN: It's a step bore. Have you heard of step boring barrels?

ANDREW: No, tell me what that means.

JOHN: Step boring a barrel is an old system in the manufacture of real firearms for many years. Basically it's a barrel with two bores, each with a separate diameter. The smaller bore provides the acceleration and the wider bore provides guidance. The holes in the side provide a silencing effect.

Now, previously everybody's accomplished this step bore manufacturing process in a two part design. Our two bores are achieved with one tool. Traditionally, step boring required people to hone a bore of one diameter in the first tube, and another diameter in a second tube. Then the two tubes would have to be mechanically joined.

We actually achieve two bores with the same equipment. If you look down the barrel, you can actually see the two bores. Hold it at a distance, and you'll see something like a ring. That's where the two bore diameters meet. No seam is visible.

We don't hone. Some people hone barrels out, we don't. We use a technology that was developed in Germany, using special types of tools and special high pressure coolants. It gives us an edge that no one else has. I believed it was the best way to go. I don't have any misalignment problems involved with joining two points together.

THE LED DISPLAY AND THE FUTURE OF ELECTROPNEUMATIC GUNS

ANDREW: I notice there's a LED on the back of the Angel. What information does that give the player?

JOHN: Looks good, doesn't it?

ANDREW: Yeah.

JOHN: A cosmetic thing. Seriously, though, it's a safety feature. Somebody can see it from a distance and know the gun is on and capable of firing. It's a visual indication, too. When you pull the trigger, the LED changes color. The gun makes a bang sound, but it allows you to see that information.

ANDREW: Have you ever thought of putting a counter on the Angel?

JOHN: No comment. But, if you're asking me where paintball's going, I'll tell you where I think it's going. Electronics are here to stay. You're going to be hooking them up to your computers, you're going to have digital displays. You're going to have RS232 ports, infrared links. You're going to have user interfaces, you're going to have head up displays. That's where the sport's going.

ANDREW: High tech all the way.

JOHN: Technology is being applied to everything. People are timid about electronics initially. When we first launched the Angel, people said "Oh, it's going to be unreliable," or, "It's not going to work." There was a lot of negative speech about electronics. Electronics are used in every walk of life. Anything you do counts on electronics. That's a trend that's only going to get bigger. And soon, any competitive paintball gun will be electronic as well.

ANDREW: What's the next step for WDP? How long is this version of the Angel going to be around?

JOHN: No comment. *[Smiling]*

ANDREW: Why are you smiling?

JOHN: I could tell you, but then I'd have to kill you.

ANDREW: *[Laughs]*

JOHN: Just wait and see.

Editor's Note: Since this interview was conducted in 1999, the Angel has gone through a major reinvention. To learn more about the latest technology and specs available on the Angel 1 and other WDP products, visit their website at www.wdp.tv.

The Complete Guide to Paintball

F/A THE DAY AWAY

Single-Action. Auto-Trigger. Pump-Action. Double-Action. Semiautomatic. Full-Automatic.

Paintball guns have evolved radically since its inception, driven by players' fervent desire for ever increasing rates of fire. This has become a source of contention, concern, and debate among members of the paintball community.

Back in 1981 and 1982, when this great game was just getting started, there were really only two gun choices: the side-cocking Nelspot, remembered by its users for the calluses it left on their fingers, and the rear-cocking Sheridan PGP. Both guns had to be recocked between shots using a rather complicated procedure. For the Sheridan, you had to turn the bolt a quarter turn, pull it back until it clicked, tilt the gun back, so the ball could roll into the chamber, tilt the gun forward, push the bolt back in, and then turn it back a quarter turn. For the Nelspot, you had to raise the cocking lever, pull it back, tilt the gun forward, tilt it back, push the lever forward, and then lock it in place.

It's hard to remember the procedures in correct order, let alone retain the mindset necessary to shoot someone two or three times using it! It's no wonder that players were considered to be paint hogs when they carried more than 50 or 60 rounds per game.

Rate of fire was not something that concerned those who played the game in its infancy. Waiting an hour for a single elimination was common. Forcing opponents to surrender was considered the highlight of the game. But then, what more can you hope for when you can only fire about three rounds per minute?

Missed shots, chopped balls, empty firing chambers, and general frustration led many players to concoct their own solutions to the problem, beginning with the pump. A relatively simple modification, the pump did away with the need to pull and turn the bolt. Shortly after, someone came up with the idea of the 'gravity feed,' which

meant that it was no longer necessary to roll the ball into the chamber. Both ideas were combined and the paintball technological revolution was underway.

The new ideas caught on quickly; less complicated guns meant more people could play the game. More paint being fired meant that game site owners were making bigger profits. Start-up manufacturers now had hundreds of potential products and a new audience waiting for them.

Players quickly became obsessed with how many balls they could fire per second. With the invention of the auto-trigger, a device that eliminated the need to pull the trigger when firing,

your average player could now pump out four to five rounds per second. Legendary players were clocked at seven rounds per second!

The quest for a user-friendly gun now turned into a mania for increasing rates of fire. Before anyone could figure out how to make a semi-automatic, at least two companies marketed a double- action, the first pumpless paintball gun.

Unfortunately, the mechanics of a double-action (releasing the sear and resetting the bolt in one pull of the trigger) created a slower rate of fire, relegating these guns to the backwater of paintball technology. However, the first generation of semi- automatics was not long in coming.

First introduced around 1990, most new semi-automatics were technological disasters. They were prone to breakdowns and leaks, in addition to being poorly designed and sensitive to weather conditions. Manufacturers were rushing to supply a new demand.

The first protest against this increasing rate of fire made itself heard around this time. Probably due more to the bad performance of the new guns than to anything else, many tournament teams refused to use semi-automatics and lobbied tournament promoters to ban their use also.

This protest was short-lived with the arrival of the second generation of semi-automatics. They were more reliable, less complicated, and backed by some of the most respected companies in the industry. Seeing a trend in the making, many event producers offered 'open class' competition where any gun was welcome. High profile teams began endorsing them and semi-automatics quickly became the guns of choice.

Gun designers and experienced players had learned something over the intervening years; paintballs are only accurate within a very limited range. Beyond that range, luck plays a huge role. The only way to increase the chance of a hit is through volume and persistence. Once players realized this, the quest for increasing rates of fire swept all other priorities aside. The need for a fully automatic paintball gun had arrived.

The late 1990s ushered in the second introduction of the fully automatic. In 1985, Tippmann Pneumatics introduced the SMG-60 (later converted to the SMG-68), which could fire up to twenty balls with a single pull of the trigger. It met with mixed reviews from the players; some feared it and felt that it represented a safety hazard, particularly at close range, leading it to be banned from many playing fields and events. Other players had nothing but contempt for its users, after having learned that once the clip was emptied the user was vulnerable as the SMG could take well over a minute to reload. The gun itself was a good performer, accurate and very robust, but just a little ahead of its time.

Other companies, like Palmer's Pursuit Shop and Pro-Team Products, introduced novelty full-automatics around the same time. These were extremely expensive show guns that were designed more to demonstrate technical prowess than to create a marketable product.

It took over a decade for development to come full circle with the introduction of the electropneumatic paintball marker. Once you start running a gun with a microchip just about anything is possible.

In 1995, Tippmann Pneumatics introduced the F/A, a spring actuated full-automatic. It's only real drawback was that after reloading, the user had to crank the spring by hand. Later that same year, Smart Parts introduced the Shocker, an electropneumatic paintball gun with three modes of fire: single shot, three round burst, and full automatic. At the same time, Airgun Designs unveiled the Reactive-Trigger Automag (RT) and WDP from England introduced the Angel, another electropneumatic equipped with multiple modes of fire. Shortly after the introduction of these new guns, the rate of fire debate began and has been going strong ever since.

Smart Parts engineered an after-market upgrade for their gun called the 'Turbo Board,' which was able to anticipate the user's highest firing rate and then reproduce that rate, even if the user was pulling the trigger at a slower rate.

Although not truly fully automatic, the RT was dragged into the same category of 'super-semi' because of its ability to fire at very high rates with little intervention by the user. The Angel was also classed as a 'super-semi' because it had the ability to replicate the performance of the Shocker and RT.

The electropneumatic paintball guns are amazing performers. In fully automatic mode, they can put out a total blanket of fire. Two or more of these guns used by experience players can virtually shut down an entire field of opponents.

Yet while at first enthusiastic about the ability to shoot more paint—half the fun in paintball is pulling the trigger—players have begun to complain about getting hit. Field owners have become concerned over their insurance liability and the loss of customers due to the perception that, "playing at that field will get you lit up." Goggle manufacturers are asked if their lenses and frames can withstand "multiple impacts in a short period of time." Paintball technology has, in a way, become a victim of its own success. The gun manufacturers give the players exactly what they are looking for, but maybe not exactly what

Getting ready for a game

Guns

is needed for the game to thrive.

Is it safe to subject players to a situation in which they can be hit by up to sixteen rounds per second? Does paintball need to limit its technological growth? Is there such a thing as a reasonable limit for high rates of fire?

Some members of the paintball community advocate a self-imposed rate of fire limit of thirteen and a half rounds per second (the current high without electronic assistance). Some also recommend such artificial fixes as a three round limit, which means that players must stop and check on their opponents' condition after firing three rounds. Others are making suggestions for new rules such as an engagement range limit, the separation of players into classes based on their guns, or limiting the amount of paint that an individual can carry.

Players will continually seek to enhance their technological edge. The bottom line is that if they can't do it on the commercial paintball fields, they'll do it on private fields. Players, regardless of their stripe or 'the truth', love to boast that their rate of fire is better and faster than everyone else's. Silly? Yes. A reality not likely to change anytime soon? You bet.

A three round shot limit is completely impractical; new players can barely remember how to pull the trigger, let alone stop themselves after three counts to inquire about the status of the person who is shooting paint at them. All it takes is one player to decide that he/she will fire four shots before checking. Furthermore, there is absolutely no way that a referee can keep track of how many rounds different players have fired at any given time.

Any rule that does not take into account the natural way that players participate is bound to fail. Players do not carry signs saying, "I surrender," which automatically deploy whenever an opponent gets within a certain distance. New

players, who are the most likely to order the guns with the highest firing rate, and then complain strenuously about getting hit too much, resort to instinctive responses during the game (e.g., holding the trigger down and firing as fast as they can at anything and everything that moves, or just hiding when they get hit and getting bunkered for their choice). Such responses do not follow rules.

Fields can try to organize games based on technology, but the reality is that few fields ever have enough players in each category or class to make this economically viable. You can't ask paying customers to play with two or three other people based on the type of gun they purchased. After a few days without much competition, they'll find somewhere else to go.

As time progresses, the industry will come to realize the truth: paintball companies are firmly in the business of giving customers what they want. It is a field's business to provide a fun and safe experience, without the customer having to be confused by artificial rules and restrictions whose use and enforcement are dependent upon them. If pain and multiple hits are customer concerns, products which reduce the impact should be introduced, or a lower velocity limit should be imposed.

The irony of this situation is that lots of paint being fired translates into industry success. Because of that incentive, the rate of fire will be difficult to limit. If it's possible to create a paintball gun that can shoot one thousand rounds per second, someone is going to build it, someone is going to buy it, and someone is going to get shot by it. The demand underlying this trend pretty much obliterates all other considerations, unless safety issues are not properly addressed.

The only real question concerns how the industry is going to respond responsibly and effectively to emerging technologies. Will the new super guns be embraced by commercial fields, where their use can be controlled and supervised, or will they thrive in the riskier, uncontrollable private field arena?

No matter how the industry responds, paintball players need to consider that the game is really not about the paintball gun. Yes, obviously, the gun is a key tool, and there's nothing wrong with wanting the latest and greatest semi-automatic. But using any paintball gun prudently is a responsibility that ultimately falls to the players of this game. If you love the game, hopefully you'll take that responsibility seriously and insist that your fellow players do so as well.

—SD

EDITOR'S NOTE: Today, many of the major gun manufacturers have agreed to establish a voluntary moratorium on the manufacture of full-automatic paintball guns, and further agreed to limit the upper rate of fire of all semiautomatic paintball guns to a maximum of 15 rounds per second.

RATES OF FIRE

Rob "Tyger" Rubin

Paintball has been slowly creeping up in technology levels. The boom of the electronic semi has pretty much taken over the industry, and become the "must have" on every paintball marker. If you're serious about the game, you probably own an electronic paintball gun, or at least one with an electronic trigger.

Using Electronic Triggers

The main advantage to electronic triggers is the rates of fire you can produce. This is from the light trigger pull that, in some cases, feels like clicking a mouse button. If you can imagine being able to launch one paintball with the click of the mouse, you can begin to imagine what these triggers feel like. Since most of the electronic paintguns have two-finger or extended length triggers, the players have come up with several techniques to allow you to utilize this technology in ways that are a radical departure form normal shooting mechanics.

The Complete Guide to Paintball

First we'll talk about walking a trigger. In this, you alternate the pull of a trigger between your index and middle finger. It's similar to rapidly typing the numbers 1 and 2 on a keyboard with two fingers. The result with a light trigger is that you tap it faster, and your rate of fire increases.

Second is a technique called Raking. To perform this, you rub your index finger up and down the front of a two-finger trigger, tapping all the bumps on the trigger. With practice, each rake can produce multiple shots. With a properly set-up electronic semi-auto paintgun, you can easily achieve over 15 shots per second, sustained.

As of this writing, electronic semi-autos can easily reach 20 shots per second. With loaders like the Halo and the Evolution 2 being made faster, and the electronic interface of the Warp feeder to electronic triggers, the limit of how fast the rates of fire can go is regulated only by physics. And why do we need such radical rates of fire? The new speedball.

Smaller fields and faster players add up to the need to shoot streams of paint into a specific area in an attempt to lock out opponents from reaching the position.

Electronic Trigger (© JT USA 2004)

Photo by Rigo Ramirez, © JT USA 2004

This is usually called lane shooting or sweet spotting.

To do this effectively, you have to fill an area with paintballs. It refers to the Running Man Drill mentioned later in the book (page 166) and Shooting Lanes (page 190), but the paintballs are in a much tighter grouping as they fly through the air.

One key to winning on smaller, more open fields is dominating the mother team. Once they are effectively shut down, your teammates can move up on them and eliminate them with better angles. High rates of fire allow your team to dominate shooting lanes.

Do you absolutely need the highest rate of fire semi-auto out there? Probably not. If you play in the woods most of the time, or you play only occasionally, you won't need something that can throw a one-person-volley-of-balls. And even if you play on arena-style courses on an occasional basis, you won't absolutely need anything that fast. But if you're playing high-level competition, it can't hurt to go with the "big guns".

Equipment Counts

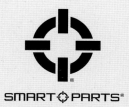

SMART PARTS' ADAM GARDNER TALKS ABOUT INNOVATION IN THE PAINTBALL INDUSTRY.

Interview by Dawn Allcot

Smart Parts launched out of Adam and Bill Gardner's desire to design better markers and barrels for their team, the All-Americans. Smart Parts is now a household name in paintball. The Philadelphia Americans (successor to the All-Americans) and a host of other teams compete using the company's gear. "For the past three years, five out of the six national championship teams won with Shockers," Gardner said.

From the high-performance Shocker to the industry-changing Ion, Smart Parts stands at the forefront of equipment innovation. Adam Gardner shares the details behind the company's top products.

DAWN: What was your first paintball experience?

ADAM: Billy and I were down in Florida over Spring Break, 1986, when we first played. When we got home, we ordered Splatmasters and played in the woods. We played for a couple of hours and ran out of paint. We looked for a store so we could buy more paintballs, and that's how we found out there were [organized] fields. We showed up in blue jeans, while everyone else had camo. We felt out of place, but we were instantly hooked and fell in love with it!

Our first tournament, 20-man, was at Wolf's Lair in Pennsylvania, which is now EMR Paintball. We wound up taking second place and won $15,000 cash. Shortly after that we formed the All-Americans. We had a lot of success at those tournaments. They were just a lot of fun.

DAWN: I recall hearing a story of how Smart

Courtesy of Smart Parts

Parts began with you and Bill making barrels in your garage. Is that correct?

ADAM: Before we were even making barrels, we started modifying barrels. Billy started polishing and spiral porting barrels for our first customers in his garage. People would send barrels in to us and we drilled ports in them that allowed the gas pressure to equalize with the outside air before the ball left the muzzle. This eliminates the "pop" that can make paintballs spin and hook randomly and also makes the shot quieter. The Smart Parts name started growing fast and before we knew it we were making our own barrels. The All-American [barrel] gained international popularity, and at the same time we were using it ourselves and winning. It just snowballed from there.

DAWN: Smart Parts introduced the first electropneumatic paintball gun, the Shocker. How was it developed?

ADAM: Before the Shocker, we were shooting Automags. We had modified them to operate at lower pressures than their stock valve allowed, giving us the ability to shoot more fragile paint and do it more quietly. Back then, the major tournaments were all in the woods, so stealth was an advantage.

We were after lower pressures and higher rates of fire, but there was only so far we could go with the Automag design.

We worked with a group of electrical and pneumatics engineers to produce the first Shocker. Going to an electronic trigger meant we could make the trigger pull incredibly light and crisp. We use the term "electro-pneumatic" because the electronics control compact solenoid valves that re-direct low-pressure air flow which, in turn, moves the larger parts that fire the paintball. The difference in how fast you could shoot the Shocker compared to a purely mechanical blowback paintgun was like night and day. We were stepping into a whole new world.

DAWN: What happened next?

ADAM: Fast forward a year, and we started designing in-house, taking the operating principles of the original Shocker and mixing in lessons learned with it on the field to produce the Shocker Sport.

As ground breaking as these early electros were, times changed, the industry evolved and so did the Shocker. The Sport used a pair of solenoid valves: one to control the opening and closing of the bolt, and one to control the exhaust valve that releases the gas that fires the paintball. While we liked the ability to fire the Sport from a closed bolt, ensuring high efficiency, there were some limits we were facing as to how fast the two separate systems could cycle.

As anyone who has stepped onto a paintball field knows, speed matters. If I can shoot five paintballs at the guy on the other end of the field in the time he can shoot two, I stand a much better chance of getting him before he gets me. That's why we introduced the Impulse. The Impulse tied together the bolt and hammer, driving them both with air from a single solenoid valve. That gave us more speed, and we were winning tournaments with it, as were the other teams shooting our guns. We also introduced Vision for the Shocker and Impulse. Infrared sensors let the marker's

microprocessor see if there is a paintball loaded into the breech yet. By waiting until the ball is loaded before it fires, the chance of a chopped or broken paintball shrinks to almost nothing.

Then, in 2003, we brought out the Shocker SFT. Compared to the Sport, the Shocker SFT is much smaller, lighter and faster. The SFT shares the name of the earlier Shocker models, but it really was a new design. We integrated the exhaust valve into the bolt. This meant the body of the Shocker SFT was a single tube structure, not a stacked tube like the earlier models.

DAWN: Where did the name SFT come from?

ADAM: In order to seal the breech, we put an o-ring in the breech itself, rather than on the bolt. The bolt only has to press against it at the very end of its stroke, instead of facing friction through its entire range of motion, but it seals completely before the ball is fired. We called this Seal Forward Technology, leading to the name Shocker SFT.

DAWN: The newest model is the Shocker NXT. What new features does it incorporate?

ADAM: We had been building custom team editions of the Shocker SFT for some of the more

The Shocker NXT in black

The Shocker NXT in red (Courtesy of Smart Parts)

prominent Smart Parts teams, building in the features they wanted, and styling the bodies to their aesthetics. This guided the Shocker NXT design. It has a sleek look, with curved lines that make the body and grip frame look more blended. The bolt assembly is our High Efficiency Shocker bolt—one of the most popular upgrades for the Shocker SFT. The NXT regulator is our highest flow design to date, to keep consistent velocity even at high ramping rates of fire. Break-Beam Vision is a standard feature. It's more reliable than the reflective Vision in the Shocker SFT.

We have basically packed more features, longer component life and better efficiency into the Shocker and given it a new look. At the same time, most of the NXT components are backwards-compatible for Shocker SFT owners.

DAWN: In Spring 2004, you changed paintball once again with the Ion, the first affordable marker with high-end features. How did the Ion evolve?

ADAM: If you look at the history of our markers you will find that even though we keep introducing new technology, we also keep refining and simplifying our existing concepts. Look at the number of parts and difficulty of maintenance on an original Shocker compared to the NXT. The Ion is further refined, and a big part of that was making a marker that had high-level performance, but wasn't so expensive that only the top players could afford it.

DAWN: How did you keep the price so low?

ADAM: We reduced the number of parts needed in the Ion and designed those parts with production efficiency in mind. For example, the fire chamber—the inner receiver of the Ion—is radially symmetrical. That means the machining is less complex, and can be done on a single machine. The more fire chambers we can produce in an hour, the less they cost to make and the lower the final cost of the Ion.

Another factor is sheer volume. The more you make of anything, the less expensive it is to make,

because design and production start-up costs have been amortized. The trick is you have to be willing to commit the resources to produce in large numbers from the start, and we were. The Ion blew people away when we released it because nobody else was making a true electro-pneumatic marker in that price range. Its performance has enabled younger players who couldn't afford high-priced electros to compete.

DAWN: Smart Parts has been one of the driving forces to get X-Ball televised. What were some of the major challenges to getting World Cup on ESPN 2 in 2004?

ADAM: Television has always been a major goal for most of the paintball industry. In order to achieve that goal, you need to have an industry work together. After a few years of effort and a lot of money, we got the ball rolling with Dick Clark and ESPN. The Super 7 kept it going with the US Paintball Championships last year. Smart Parts continued that process this year with the Smart Parts World Paintball Championships. As far as I am concerned, anyone who is willing to step up to the plate and put forth their effort and money to get paintball on TV is helping the industry grow.

DAWN: The World Paintball Championship looked great. How were the ratings?

ADAM: The ratings were very good. We had an average of 200,000 to 300,000 viewers for each

The Gardners played on the field before they became players behind the scenes: Adam (left) and Bill (right)

© Courtesy of Smart Parts

airing of the show. We hope that we have introduced one million new players to the sport.

DAWN: Although Smart Parts is still heavily focused on the tournament market, you recently introduced the SP-8, a woodsball-specific marker, and launched Smart Corps, the web site, and the Smart Parts factory scenario team. Why the increased emphasis on woodsball?

ADAM: We started playing paintball in the woods. We have played and won national tournaments in the woods, we still love playing in the woods, and all of our markers work as well in the woods as they do on a mowed lawn with inflatable bunkers. In the past, so much of our marketing efforts focused on the tournament scene, and that makes sense, because the players that use our gear are winning; we thought it was time to draw attention to other aspects of the game as well, to let people know our equipment excels there too.

DAWN: Tell us about the SP-8.

ADAM: With the SP-8, we wanted to provide a marker that addressed some of the specialty features that players in scenario games look for—modularity and lots of accessory rails. We built the SP-8 around the core of the Ion. People get wowed by the looks, but when they shoot it and find out how quiet, fast and accurate it is, that is when they get hooked.

DAWN: Smart Parts also began sponsoring scenario teams in 2006. Are the criteria the same as they are for pro teams?

ADAM: With all sponsorships, we need to look not only at the team we are helping to thrive and advance, but also how that relationship will reflect back on us and help spread the word about our products. With tournaments, a team's record of wins is often a good indicator of the direction they are going.

We call the sponsored scenario teams our Smart Corps Special Forces. For them, we don't have the same type of rankings. You don't have a

Courtesy of Smart Parts

The Gardners take their business seriously: Bill (left) and Adam (right)

first place team walking away at the end of a weekend long scenario game. Instead, we look at the team's visibility on the field and in magazines, how often they are recognized as most valuable team, and what sort of presence they have online helping other teams and players.

DAWN: What would you like to tell new players about Smart Parts, your products, your mission?

ADAM: We have been a leader in innovation and technology for the past 18 years and plan to continue to lead our industry. We started as players and have never forgotten where we came from. Our general philosophy is: Life is a Game. Live to play. Equipment Counts.

Dawn Allcot is Editor-in-Chief of Paintball Sports Magazine. *Her articles have also appeared in* RECON, Paintball News, Paintball 2Xtremes, *and on Paintball.com.*

Choosing a Barrel

In order to avoid any confusion when it comes to purchasing a barrel for your gun, we'll get this said right up front:

Buying a barrel is a highly personal, non-scientific activity that you could spend a lifetime mastering.

By this we mean that there is no tried-and-true method for purchasing the 'perfect barrel.' Most paintball players are absolutely convinced that they already have the perfect barrel—namely, the one screwed into their gun when they buy it. If this were true, if each gun came packaged with the perfect barrel, then there would be no need to purchase an aftermarket one. That brings us to the critical question:

Is there a need to purchase an aftermarket barrel?
The answer is yes . . . and no.

Most guns are purchased with a 'stock' barrel. Originally, the 'stock' barrel was all you could get. Most gun manufacturers made and continue to make fine barrels. However, once removable barrels arrived on the scene, which not only promised superior performance but were definitely far easier to clean, somebody was bound to make an aftermarket barrel that actually was 'better.' Major growth of demand for aftermarket barrels soon followed. As a result, most gun manufacturers have stopped making expensive stock barrels and instead provide a basic one for you to use until you can go out and purchase a 'perfect' one. Today, there are many different barrel brands.

But it doesn't stop there. Each brand of barrel has to have a different model for each different gun on the market. Add to this the fact that there is no industry standard when it comes to the manner in which a barrel is attached to a gun, and you have a huge number of barrels available across a wide range of prices. Most are threaded (like a screw), but there are several models which use a 'twist-lock', and several which use a pressure fit.

Barrel Length Counts

Most everyone agrees that you need at least 8 inches of barrel to make the most effective use of the gas and to give the ball some accuracy over decent ranges. After that there is virtually no agreement. Barrels come in lengths ranging from 8 to 18 inches. The length of a barrel also affects the issues of gas volume and pressure: guns with very low operating pressures will require a longer barrel.

Barrels are also made out of several different materials. Aluminum, brass and stainless steel are the most common, but you also can find carbon-fiber barrels and mixed-material barrels. Different inner-coatings also have been added (teflon, for instance), as have various forms of rifling. Barrels can come with 'muzzle breaks,' spiral rifling, gas porting, and a whole museum's worth of external patterns, sculpturing, and colors.

The barrel's inner diameter also varies. This might not seem to make sense. After all, a paintball is .68 caliber, right? Well, in fact, that's not entirely true. The ideal paintball is perfectly round and exactly .68 inches in diameter, no matter where you measure it. A real paintball is anywhere from .65 to .70 inches in diameter, sometimes oblong in shape, with a seam around it. In other words, it's far from a true sphere. Paintballs are commonly referred to as small-bore (.65 to .67) and big bore (.68 to .70). Be-

cause of this, the inner diameter (or ID) of a barrel can vary from as small as .685 to .692. Admittedly, this is a relatively small difference—but when it comes to performance, it's a critical one.

Every paintball barrel manufacturer out there will say that the most important factor in choosing a good barrel is picking the right paint. After that, they'll say that the 'fit' between your barrel and the paint you are shooting is the next most important thing. They're right.

Of course, there are the ambient or 'local' conditions, things such as temperature, humidity and air pressure, that also affect performance: the barrel you use today with such amazing results may

belong in the bottom of your gear bag tomorrow, even if you are shooting the same gun, with the same paint at the same velocities as the previous day. The differences in performance may be due entirely to the changing play conditions, and they aren't necessarily your barrel's fault.

No one who plays paintball for any length of time always shoots exactly the same paint each and every game. Paint varies from brand to brand (and from batch to batch). In order to counter this, most serious rec players have adopted the strategy of collecting a variety of barrels, in different lengths, with different IDs, made out of different materials, so that no matter what paint they are shooting, they will always have a barrel that makes a good match.

The general rules of thumb when buying a barrel relate to the ID, the length, the material it is made from, the presence or absence of rifling, porting and breaking, and the barrel's aesthetics.

Fortunately, you can be a little more discriminating (although you will probably end up with your own barrel bag eventually). When it comes to ID, most companies tend to make one to three different 'bores' (the tube inside the barrel is the bore).

These bores generally correspond to a 'tight', a 'medium,' and a 'loose' fit. Tight bores are for small bore paint, loose bores are for big-bore paints and medium bores are for everything in between. Brands that only offer one or two bore sizes usually make a tight and a medium, since most paint tends to be small these days.

Try and settle on a particular brand of paint to use most of the time. This might be a brand offered by a local retailer, the brand of paint sold at your local field, or the paint recommended by local experts. Find out what 'size' this paint is (call the supplier if you have to). Your general-purpose barrel should have an ID which matches this brand of paint, since this is what you will be shooting most frequently.

Material really has only one determining factor,

© Michael Wise II, chrono300.com

and that is its weight. The lightest barrels are generally 'composites' (carbon fiber) and aluminum, although some companies are doing amazing things with stainless steel. Brass is next in weight, followed by most stainless steel barrels. (Don't forget that the length of a barrel also contributes to its weight.) The smoothness of a barrel's bore is an important factor. The smoother it is, the less friction will be experienced by the ball as it travels through the barrel. All of the materials mentioned have roughly the same smoothness factor, so this is not a huge consideration. Sometimes smoother surfaces actually create greater drag. This is exactly why choosing a barrel is an art, rather than a science.

When it comes to porting, breaking and rifling, it's probably anybody's guess as to which implementation creates the best range or accuracy. Rifling is a technique borrowed from firearms technology. A helix of ridges and grooves is cut down the length of the inner surface of the barrel. These are used to grab the soft body of a bullet and cause it to spin. This gives the bullet greater stability in flight. Unfortunately, paintballs are not solid, aerodynamically shaped objects, and conventional rifling can't be used because it

would rip and shatter the paintball. Nevertheless, barrel makers have come up with at least three paintball versions of the same thing, none of which work by 'spinning' the ball, but which can aid it in other ways. Polygonal Progressive Rifling (Armson) barrels have twenty-eight blunt-edged lands (the ridges of rifling) which curve down the inner surface of the barrel. These provide a greater surface area for the ball to seal against and help stabilize the ball as it leaves the barrel. Spiral Porting (Smart Parts) uses a patented external version of rifling. Two lines of 'ports' (holes drilled through the body of the barrel) are created down the length of the barrel in a spiral. This relieves pressure behind and in front of the ball and allows the ball to make a smooth transition to the air. Straight Rifling (J&J) uses four straight lands cut down the length of the bore to provide greater stability and better control of the ball as it moves through the barrel.

Most barrels, however, are 'smoothbore' barrels; they have no rifling of any kind. By the way, players have had tremendous success with all bore styles.

Muzzle Breaks are another adaptation from 'real guns.' They are typically used to suppress noise, reduce pressure at the muzzle (when the gun is fired), and suppress the 'flash' coming from a barrel. In paintball guns, it is generally believed that a muzzle break will aid the ball when it makes the transition from the barrel to still air. Muzzle breaks can be found on a wide variety of barrels.

Porting is generally used for its sound-suppressing qualities. Small holes (of varying number and size) are drilled down the length, or a portion of the length, of a barrel. These are not cut in a spiral (like the external rifling), but in straight lines. Sometimes slots are used instead of round holes.

And now we come to length. Determining the ideal length for a barrel is the biggest source of controversy when it comes to barrels. Some people swear by long barrels, some by short ones. Some are convinced that thirteen inches is what you need, while others think that sixteen inches is the mandatory minimum. The truth is that only a gun's manufacturer (or someone who works closely with a particular model) knows what the 'best' barrel length for that gun is. In general, you need the length of a barrel for two things.

- First, it needs to be long enough so that an optimal amount of gas will get the ball up to the desired velocity.

- Second, it should be long enough to give the ball some accuracy in its flight. However, if a barrel is too long, it will slow the ball back down again.

Unfortunately, these factors vary from gun to gun. The most efficient barrel, in terms of gas use, is one that is exactly long enough, and no longer. This may not be the same length as is required for the desired degree of accuracy, so choosing a length becomes the art of balancing these two goals within a range that is good for that particular gun. Usually, an inch or two in either direction won't make a tremendous difference: if your gun 'needs' a twelve inch barrel, you'll still get good performance out of a ten inch barrel or a fourteen inch one.

The basic rule of thumb regarding length seems to be that if you are planning on playing up-front and personal (close to the other team), you want a shorter barrel so that you can 'tuck in'; and it will give you the kind of accuracy you are looking for with short to medium ranges. If you are planning on longballing (shooting long distance), you'll want a longer barrel to increase your sight radius and achieve greater accuracy. Remember to keep in mind that these are relative lengths, based on the kind of gun you are shooting.

A barrel's look is nearly as important as everything that has gone before. If your barrel looks cool, then you look cool, and it hardly matters whether you're hitting anything or not! WOOO-HOOO! (Just kidding.)

Most barrel manufacturers have developed distinctive styles for the outer surface of their barrels. Grooves, cuts, slashes, stippling, bumps and ridges have all been cut into barrels. Then there's color; you can get a barrel in just about any color you can imagine. Other manufacturers have begun to add graphics to their barrels and feature things like flames and skulls. Your typical macho-stuff can be found in virtually infinite variety from the tasteful to the tasteless. Chances are, whatever look you want, you'll be able to find a barrel to match it.

When you finally do go to purchase a barrel, remember to take along the information you've gathered about the kind of gun you are using and the paint you'll be shooting; remember that no barrel lasts forever. Think of your first barrel purchase as the beginning of a long and rewarding learning process, and save up your money so that you can afford to buy the next best thing.

—SD

Tippman, Then and Now

Editor's Note: This interview is the combined text of interviews conducted for previous editions of this book, each updated to reflect current product and company information. Most importantly, the Model 98, hailed as the most customizable marker available, has been replaced by the 98 Custom— only slightly modified, the 98 Custom continues to hold Tippman's place as the number one customizable and universally appealing paintball gun for beginners and pros alike. With over twenty years in the business, Dennis Tippman, Jr. and his company have been integral to the growth of the game as a sport and as an industry.

STEWART SMITH: Tippmann is the first name we heard of when we started out to make this book. How long have you been in the paintball business?

DENNIS TIPPMANN, JR: I've been doing this since 1986. I don't know of any bigger companies in this industry that are older than we are.

STEW: As an established leader in the paintball industry, how do you explain your success?

DENNIS: We keep improving the quality and the price point of our products. The mass market volume sales we do enable us to do this, and our commitment to improving upon our guns in ways that are cost-effective for us and our customers keeps us ahead of the game. We make valuable guns that simply perform reliably and consistently over time. They're easy to maintain and we support our products very aggressively.

STEW: Your guns are also unique in that you diecast them in aluminum.

DENNIS: That's right. It definitely saves us money because we can avoid the more expensive class of machining.

STEW: Do you find the diecasting durable?

DENNIS: Oh, yes. Basically, it's the same material. Diecast aluminum is very tough.

STEW: How do you explain the popularity of your guns with field owners?

DENNIS: Rental places need our expertise. They need good, reliable, affordable guns, and they want the best CO_2 system guns they can buy. One thing we've always been good at is making great CO_2 guns. The rental guys need parts and service, too. That's another thing we do well. We get parts to them quickly. We offer one-year warranty on all our equipment. Because renters are more abusive and the gun gets used everyday, our support of fields is critical to their success. They need a gun that's extremely durable, and a company to back it up. That's why they use our equipment.

STEW: Tell us about your Tippmann Model 98.

DENNIS: Sure. Our guns have always been solid, but we wanted to start introducing some of the high end advances to the mass market. Model 98 brought an advanced trigger system to the masses. Real high end guns go out of their way to build really good trigger systems, so that's where we started. We made the trigger really light on this gun, and it shoots very fast.

STEW: It's a reactive trigger?

DENNIS: Yeah, we call it the hyper-shot trigger. A light trigger with great response pressure. You see, on some guns with light triggers, the trigger doesn't swing back after you fire. We don't have that problem. The Model 98's return pressure gives you "lightness," speed and control.

STEW: So can you take the stock 98 out of the box, and add on bit by bit until you're up to a tournament level?

DENNIS: Yes. Absolutely. In fact, there are companies right now that are buying these receivers off us raw and doing stuff like this to them because we diecast that receiver. We don't have much money invested in the receiver anymore. So they're buying the receivers and making a number of little jazzy modifications to them. Double triggers and stuff like that. As we're doing a lower-priced gun, we have the volumes real high. We can afford to diecast it. And then they can take that same diecasting, go and modify it, whatever they want.

STEW: Are you in any retail stores?

DENNIS: We're in everything from Wal-Mart and K-mart to sporting goods stores like Dicks, Bass Pro, and Sports Authority. You can even find our goods in some department stores now, like Sears and Boscov's.

STEW: What is an expansion chamber?

DENNIS: This is the first upgrade you would perform on a Tippmann Model 98 [*Ed Note: it also works with the 98 Custom, Custom Pro, and A-5*]. A lot of players put a barrel on right away and expansion chamber kit next. Because CO_2 pressures go up and down, sometimes you'll get liquid CO_2 in your gun. You point your gun down, the liquid enters your gun and it responds by shooting really hard and erratic. The expansion chamber helps eliminate this effect. It makes it harder for liquid CO_2 to form and get into the valve of the gun, and the absence of the CO_2 drip maintains a more consistent velocity, which in turn maintains accuracy.

STEW: Tell us about how your guns work.

DENNIS: When you pull the trigger on the gun, you release the bolt, and the rear bolt is connected to the front bolt. That'll shuttle a ball into the barrel. Now when the rear bolt gets clear forward, it hits the valve. When the valve is opened, pressure goes two directions. A very little bit goes to recock the gun, maybe 10%. The rest of it goes around the valve and shoots your ball. A little bit of pressure comes to the rear bolt, and recocks the gun. Normally, you wouldn't even be able to let off the trigger by the time the gun's recocked. The sear hits the back of the trigger, and then you let out the trigger and it reengages the top of the trigger for the next shot. There's a latch to hold the ball in place so it doesn't roll out of your barrel until the trigger is pulled.

STEW: This latch is a piece of rubber?

DENNIS: Yeah. So, it's really a pretty simple system. This is what they call a blow-back system. The bolt's blown back. There are two other systems. The blow-forward system, like your automatics, and the closed-bolt system, which is like a pump gun with an automatic pump. What they mean by "closed bolt" is that the bolt's forward, ready to fire. When you pull a trigger on a closed-bolt system, the bolt's closed. That means the bolt has already shut the chamber off. When you set the gun off, the ball's already in the barrel. So the closed-bolt is like a pump gun, with an automatic pumper on it, like your Autocockers.

STEW: Autocockers are closed-bolt?

DENNIS: Yeah. Automags are blow-forward, and mine are blow-back. Tippmann actually invented the blow-back system. We've got the patents on it.

STEW: The most efficient use of air would be the blow-back system?

DENNIS: They all run pretty neck and neck. But right now, I'd say probably the most efficient system besides ours would be your closed-bolt system, which is found in Worr Games' Autocockers. They're extremely efficient because of the way they use the exact amount of air needed to cock the gun, and the exact amount of air needed to shoot the gun. Since the systems are all compartmentalized, it's easier for them to achieve high levels of efficiency. It took us a lot of tuning to get to that level. Bud Orr's (Worr Games) guns have been efficient for a long time. And the next level we'd step up to is the CVX valve. It's our high performance valving system, and we're sure players will notice its advantages, particularly its reliability.

STEW: And this is something that you developed?

DENNIS: Yes. I do all the drawings. I make the prototypes. My father and I sit down and go over the designs before they're made. I'll draw a 3D model of the gun on my computer, which then actually talks to a milling machine. It writes a tool path that'll cut that shape out of a block of aluminum. So those prototypes are made out of solid aluminum. And that same software can be used to make a mold.

STEW: You have a family business. That's wonderful.

DENNIS: Yes, as far as design and conception. Yes, it really is.

UPDATE, 2ND EDITION

ANDREW: Dennis, several years have passed since you spoke with Stew Smith for *The Complete Guide to Paintball*. How has paintball changed since then?

DENNIS: The entire industry has grown quite a bit. The technology in the guns helps grow the industry, make it bigger, keep it exciting. Some of the big changes would probably be the electronics. There used to be very, very high-end guns offering these electronics. But the price has come down quite a bit and it's a lot more reasonable for the average consumer to afford some of the electronic equipment that they're offering now. Tippmann Pneumatics is also offering some of these electronics options.

ANDREW: In terms of the game itself, the electronics have obviously made the play faster.

DENNIS: Very true. The game actually is being played quite a bit quicker, which makes it more fun to watch. Paintball is becoming more of a traditional sport in a sense—probably a lot closer to an extreme sport.

ANDREW: With the increased speed and the rate of velocity of feeders and the number of paintballs per minute, is the sport becoming a little more expensive for most people? Are they basically shooting more paint?

DENNIS: Well, no matter what happens, the customer demands more firepower. And I do believe they are spending a little bit more when they go out to play. But it also seems, because the industry

© Cleo Fogal

is growing, that volumes are going up on everything: the volume of markers that we make, the volume of paint that's being made, everything. And the prices are actually coming down. The more markers we make, the cheaper we can make them, and the customer is saving in the long run. The same with the paintballs themselves.

ANDREW: Is there any movement toward bigger games or smaller games?

DENNIS: Two things seem to be happening. Ever since the beginning, it seems like the size of the teams has been getting smaller. It used be twenty-man teams, and now you see a lot of tournaments with clear down to three-man teams. Even something like a ten-man team seems to be getting less popular, and three-man and five-man teams are becoming more popular. And I think a big part of that is just the logistics of trying to get that many guys together at once.

ANDREW: What about the players? Do you see a younger demographic, an older demographic?

DENNIS: We've seen the age groups drop since the beginning. The average playing age ten years ago was

mid- to upper twenties. And I believe the average age is closer to sixteen now. I think the reason for that is the price of the equipment has come down quite a bit. And it's becoming more of a mainstream extreme sport, which is very popular with the younger group. That's one of the reasons the industry has grown: because that age group has got a lot more free time. They can get out every weekend and go play, where some of the older guys can get out once a month maybe.

ON THE TIPPMANN A-5 AND THE CYCLONE FEED SYSTEM

ANDREW: Let me ask you about the A-5, one of your state-of-the-art paintball markers. What's so special about it?

DENNIS: The biggest feature on the A-5 is the Cyclone Feed System. Basically it's a forced feed system. It eliminates the traditional problem of chopping balls, where a ball falls halfway into the gun when the gun's going off and gets cut in two inside your gun. Once that happens, your gun isn't

going to work correctly; it's going to be inaccurate. So this feed system pretty much eliminated that problem by feeding quite a bit faster and more reliably.

The balls fall down into what we call a sprocket, and the feed paddles rotate with every shot. So as you pull the trigger, these things constantly index. And they index at a top speed of about sixteen times a second, far faster than any traditional feed system or any gravity feed system. Most of those have a reliable maximum of around ten. And even at ten, gravity isn't really reliable, so you run into this problem of chopping balls. We're very reliable up to sixteen, which is a huge advantage.

Feed paddle technology has been around for a little while, with one of our previous guns, the Tippmann F/A. But we weren't real happy with the way it worked on the F/A because it was a spring-loaded system; you had to wind it up all the time. So we took the opportunity with the A-5 to put this feed system back on. We redesigned it so it's air-powered; there are no headaches. It works

just like the traditional gun where you pour your balls into your ammo box and it's ready to go.

ANDREW: What's the hopper capacity on it?

DENNIS: Two hundred.

ANDREW: Do you have any kind of agitation working as well, or is it just gravity feeding into the paddles which are timed with the action of the gun?

DENNIS: The paddles do two things. They act like agitation, and they feed balls into the gun. So you get the benefits of both. Traditional feeders agitate the balls in order to try to get them into a single-file line to be gravity-fed into your gun. This system has a very large feed neck, so several balls fall down onto the paddles, and as those paddles agitate, the balls fall into the teeth or "socket" of the paddles. That loads those balls into the gun directly.

ANDREW: Can you upgrade a variety of guns to include the Cyclone Feed System, or is it only on the A-5?

DENNIS: Originally, it was only for the A-5. We looked at possibly making a universal feed system, but

to get the best results, we had to design the gun around the feed system. Until that point, most of the feed systems available on the market were battery powered. The Cyclone Feed System is an intricate part of the gun and is air powered, so batteries are not needed. It works off of waste air, so the gun is just as efficient. As of July 2005, the Cyclone Feed System is available as an accessory upgrade for the 98 Custom and Custom Pro markers as well.

There's one other feature of the A-5, which is kind of overlooked because the feed system was such a huge step forward. But one of the other features that doesn't get talked about a lot is how easy the gun is to field strip. We've put a lot of effort into that, because with most paintball guns you need a few Allen wrenches to get the gun apart. And with the A-5 you can disassemble the gun by pulling the four push-pins out; it pretty much comes all the way apart from there.

© Cleo Fogal

THE FLATLINE BARREL

ANDREW: Let's talk about the Flatline barrel. I think that's one of the real revolutionary innovations since *The Complete Guide to Paintball* was first published.

DENNIS: I believe the idea came from jai alai, where they've got the curved basket where you put the ball in and throw it, and it puts a spin on the ball. And that's where the original idea came from to put a curve in the barrel itself. Just like a golf ball: when the ball has back-spin on it and it's flying through the air, it gets some lift. Putting this backspin on the paintball actually takes the arch out of the ball.

We worked on developing that barrel for over two years. There are so many variables there: once you put that spin on, it's easy to put on a little too much or too little. We eventually came up with a happy medium where the ball flies as flat as possible. So the big advantage of the Flatline barrel is that it shoots farther. Maybe an even bigger advantage than that is

that it shoots extremely flat. When you aim at a target, you don't have to compensate by aiming high if the target is a hundred feet out there. Instead, you aim right at your target. That's especially useful in the woods, where a lot of times you get trees up above. If you try to arch a ball through the trees and it's not going to make it there, it's going to hit something. When you can actually look down the line of sight and see a clear target, and you can aim right at it, that's a huge advantage.

ON THE PROSHOP

ANDREW: Dennis, tell me about the Proshop. Why did you set it up?

DENNIS: It used to be that a lot of our customers were doing upgrades to their guns, and there were always a lot of questions and our service guys weren't always on top of the latest technology coming from the different parts of the industry. A lot of companies make accessories for our guns now, and we offer some accessories. We set up the Proshop to help the customer with all the accessories that are available on the market. And we do sell quite a few of those accessories through the Proshop.

ANDREW: So these are not necessarily Tippmann manufactured products, but there are other parties involved in manufacturing approved products that can be upgraded to the Tippmann line.

DENNIS: Exactly. What we call our GTA Parts—the GTA stands for Genuine Tippmann Accessories—are parts that we make ourselves. But we do offer quite a few of the other accessories that are made by other companies for Tippmann products. There are electronic kits that you can put on your marker. Then there's the Flatline barrel system, there are some other barrels made by us, and there are some of the more popular barrels that are on the market. Plus the real velocity adjustment kits, double trigger kits, low pressure kits, drop forward kits. Just about anything you could imagine that you could put on your paintball marker we offer through the Proshop, and we also install it. We give the customer peace of mind and get the equipment working properly.

A lot of times with these accessories, there are gray areas that the customer gets confused with. You can use this adjuster with this trigger, but you can't necessarily put the low-pressure kit on now. Or say for example a customer wants to know if he should have an expansion chamber on his gun with a compressed air kit. Well, our Proshop guys would tell him no, there's no need to do that, the expansion changer is designed for CO_2 and it's not necessary if you've advanced to the compressed air kit. All these things are available through the Proshop, and this helps our customers do whatever they want to their paintball marker.

ANDREW: What's the average turnaround? Can you deliver most upgrades within a certain number of days?

DENNIS: We try to turn everything around, service and Proshop, in twenty-four hours. We feel that the customer needs his paintball marker for the weekend. It takes a couple of days to get it here, it's going to take a couple of days to get it back, so we try to turn it around as fast as possible.

THE HELLHOUND

ANDREW: Now let me ask you, what's the story with the Hellhound? Everybody wants to know.

DENNIS: The Hellhound was originally made for a trade show in Atlanta, Georgia. It was mostly made to be a booth attraction, with the intention of taking it to some of the different paintball shows also. We pretty much sat down and designed the thing from scratch. More than anything it's an attention grabber.

ANDREW: Do you ever put that thing on a paintball field and demonstrate it?

DENNIS: We demonstrate it once in a while, but we never take it on a paintball field. If you took it in a big game, the game would be over. Too much of an advantage.

ANDREW: I think so. What is the quick rundown on the features on the Hellhound?

DENNIS: The number one feature is the Vulcan ten-barrel Gatling gun on the front of the Hellhound. The Vulcan gun is fed by a 600-round capacity ammo box up above the driver's head. So the roof of the vehicle is essentially a large container for paintballs. The Hellhound does have the Cyclone Feed: it has two Cyclone Feeders, one on each side. And two large tubes—they look like vacuum cleaner tubes—come down to each side of the Vulcan gun. The gun itself is run by a cordless electric drill. And it shoots extremely fast. Top speed is around 50 rounds a second.

THE FUTURE OF TIPPMANN PAINTBALL

ANDREW: Let's talk about the future of paintball and Tippmann. In 1998, the Tippman 98 was the hot item, and it was replaced by the popular 98 Custom. Then we were looking at the A-5. Where do you

Guns

see paintball going next?

DENNIS: It's hard to predict what's going to happen with the industry. It always surprises us; it keeps growing and growing. The sport will probably be quite a bit bigger if it keeps growing at the same rate. The other thing we notice is that it seems like the technology has definitely slowed down since the beginning. In the beginning you couldn't design things fast enough. Now it's getting harder and harder to come up with new and better gun designs. So I could see a lot of fine-tuning of the current equipment that's on the market. But I don't think there's a need for a lot more firepower. A lot of the tournaments are starting to limit, and obviously they don't allow full auto in most tournaments. Pretty much everyone is putting on a rule that semi-auto is the limit.

But they are allowing the electric triggers, which allow you to shoot very quickly in semi-auto. So I don't see a lot happening on the firepower side of it. But the Cyclone Feed System, for example, makes the firepower that is available more reliable. And I see a lot of gun makers, including Tippman, concentrating on more reliable, more consistent, more efficient equipment.

I also see some room for more reliability in the paint ball itself. It seems like that's one area of the industry that hasn't developed a lot. The balls can be damaged by moisture, or humidity, or if it gets too cold. I see some room for improvement and some new materials, maybe a tighter tolerance on the ball so you get more accuracy.

ANDREW: You've also been developing a line of pistols.

DENNIS: We saw a need for sidearms for the guys who just play the big games. Big games are not super-strict on the rules, whereas in a tournament you wouldn't necessarily even be allowed to carry a sidearm. I think they're pretty strict on the one gun per player rule there. But the big games, they just want you to have fun. And if you want to take a pistol or something similar out there on the field with you, they're very happy to let you do that.

We also see some demand for a pistol on the law enforcement side for training. And also—this number is debated a little bit—around seventy percent of players play what we call outlaw. Which means they don't play in an organized field setting; they're just a bunch of buddies getting together in the woods somewhere. And we see a demand for the sidearm in that application also.

ANDREW: Sort of like the original days of paintball, going back to the roots, with fewer shots and more hunting.

DENNIS: Yeah, plus the guys that play outlaw paintball make up their own rules. And if they want to carry an extra gun with them and no one else cares, like I said, they make up their own rules.

You can find out more about Tippman and their products by visiting their website, www.tippman.com

PART 3

GEAR

Is It Safe?

PAINTBALL—THE SAFEST SPORT IN THE WORLD

The latest insurance information on paintball rates it safer than football, bowling, and statistically safer than staying in your house.

SO WHAT ARE YOU WAITING FOR?

Paintball is an exceptionally safe sport. The reason paintball is so safe is that the safety precautions have been evolving as fast as the game has been evolving. Safety equipment is vital to paintball, and should never be ignored no matter where you play.

AGOG ABOUT GOGGLES

Paintball goggles are highly specialized for the sport and must pass strict ASTM standards for paintball lenses. For example, paintball goggles must be able to absorb the impact of a paintball moving at over 400 feet per second (that's over 270 mph!) fired from less than one meter away. Many new players assume they can wear ski goggles, tank goggles, shop glasses, sunglasses, or shooting glasses. This assumption is completely erroneous, and therefore extremely dangerous! Paintball goggles are designed to absorb impacts that would shatter other goggles or dislodge them from the wearer's eyes. Your eyes are the only bodyparts that you rely on and regularly expose during the game that can be catastrophically injured by a paintball; whenever you're around paintball guns, don't trust anything other than paintball goggles to protect your eyes.

Paintball goggles are also designed with the game in mind. They have a wider peripheral vision than other styles of goggles. Many styles can be worn over glasses. There are "thermal" systems available to help prevent goggles from fogging up. You can even get fans to blow in fresh air to help prevent fogging. Goggles also have attached face shields and ear armor, which you are required to wear at most fields. There are several styles and colors to choose from.

You must wear your goggles at all times when you're on the playing field or on the target range. Even when you're eliminated, you don't want to remove your goggles until you're in the staging area and off the fields.

Plug It Up

After goggles, barrel plugs are the most critical safety equipment you'll need to be in the habit of using. A barrel plug is a device you stick onto or into the open end of the paintgun's barrel when you are off the field. This device prevents a paintball from coming out the end of the paintgun's barrel. *When used with the mechanical trigger safety switched on, the barrel plug makes it safe to remove your goggles in a "goggles off" area.* Just having the safety on is not as "safe" as it appears. Using a barrel plug is a visual way to show your paintgun won't hurt anyone, and if anyone forgets to put one in their gun, you should tell them to plug it up immediately.

Every player must use paintball goggles and a barrel plug for their paintgun. More than any others, these two pieces of safety equipment make paintball safe for players.

There is one more vital piece of safety equipment that every good field uses regularly, and will make available for your use when you bring your own

equipment. A "Chronograph" measures the speed of a paintball as it comes out of the barrel of a paint-gun. In the early nineties, the IPPA (International Paintball Players Association, now disbanded) helped create a standard of 300 feet per second (300 fps) as the safest maximum speed for paint-balls coming out of the barrel. This has held ever since. For indoor paintball, the top limit is usually lowered to 270 fps or less, depending on the field size. Higher velocities are unnecessary with smaller fields. If you have your own equipment, you will need to adjust it to get under the field speed limit.

Know where your gun's safety is and always use it. But don't stop there. Insert your barrel plug to ensure maximum accident prevention.

Safety—Above and Beyond

There is more safety equipment you can use as well, but it is not mandatory. (Read: common sense indicates that using additional equipment goes above and beyond the essential safety require-ments.) This is effectively the point at which you can exercise your personal preference to acces-sorize for further safety. Some items make good sense to use. Men should wear a cup. Women should wear fem-guards to protect "soft spots." If you have bad ankles, wear shoes with ankle support or wear a brace if necessary.

If you have bad joints, or you don't like the idea of crawling on rocks and twigs, you can wear knee and elbow pads. Many styles are available, and many are paintball specific. If you slide a lot you may want knee/shin guards. If you crawl a lot, then elbow pads would be a good idea. It's all about wearing what you are comfortable moving around in. Wearing loose clothing will also help absorb some of the impact of a paintball. You don't want to go overboard, however. If your clothes are too baggy, you'll have a hard time moving around.

Other products are available for personal safety, such as neck protectors, hard or soft armored vests, gloves, head wraps and protective caps. Some people think you can't be too safe; others feel like they sacrifice agility and actually become more vulnerable to getting hit when they wear these extras. You'll have to make up your own mind about these items.

But, if I ever catch you not wearing your goggles on a paintball field, I'll tackle you.

—RR

The Complete Guide to Paintball

The Gear Revolution

Rob Rubin

One of the things that has defined paintball from the first game to modern day is the technology. When you compare how the first game was played to what we play now, the gear we used "back in the day" seems archaic. When the game first began, anything that you wanted to play paintball with that wasn't either the paintball or the paintgun had to be found or made by yourself. That lead to a lot of player ingenuity.

The first players had some basic problems to solve. They wanted to protect their eyes, carry more paint, be protected from incoming paintballs, and have fun without really hurting themselves. Most players raided their local army/navy surplus store to buy supplies, and many players still do. But as time went on, many people decided they could do better, and so they did.

For example, when you look at the goggles we used to play paintball in, it's a minor miracle we didn't all go blind. Many players used chemical goggle, sunglasses, or ski goggles thinking they'd be safe. We know now that this just isn't true, and the goggles today are infinitely better than what we had back then. Some of the original innovations came from Motocross companies like JT and Scott. JT adapted one of their popular motorcycle goggles and made it tougher for paintball players. The "whipper snapper" was a popular brand for a long time. Then Scott introduced goggles with more

peripheral vision, and players started demanding more from their eye protection. Goggle companies have come and gone, and a lot of innovations were tried. Straps that buckle in the back to allow players with glasses an easier time putting them on. A technology from motocross was borrowed, and "tear aways" became popular for a while. Some innovations have survived, like gradient tint lenses and chin straps.

Modern goggles not only have more peripheral visibility, but also more up and down as well. They give full face protection, the masks having become integrated with the goggle frame to protect your ears from impacts. They've gotten lighter, more comfortable, and to top it all off they protect you better. The evolution of the true paintball goggle has been one of the main reasons paintball is as safe as it is today.

Other cornerstones of safety that we take for granted today were born in the early days. Chronographs were adopted to regulate the velocity of a paintball. Original chronographs are still used to this day, but new chronographs are lightweight and small enough to be carried in your pocket.

Barrel blocking devices were slower to catch on. Many of the original BBDs were knurled plugs you'd insert into the paintgun. These tended to get lost eas-

ily, and they scratched the insides of the barrels. Several companies made various kinds of plastic plugs as the years went on, most with a large "bat-wing" end for easy gripping. The down side to these plugs was that they either worked too well and were impossible to remove, or didn't work well enough and ejected from the paintgun when hit with a ball.

To remedy this, in the late 90s several companies manufactured "barrel caps," or "socks," to place on the end of the paintgun. This sleeve stopped a paintball, and if used right wouldn't eject from the barrel if a ball hit it. It had an added bonus in that it could be carried in a pocket without being a large protruding target. Now, most fields require barrel socks on the ends of all paintguns in safe areas.

Safety features aren't the only area of improvement. The first paintball pistols could only carry 10 balls at a time. Obviously, this wasn't enough, so players invented ways to increase the capacity of their paintguns using PVC pipe and sock holders. Many players would place a "stick feed" into the 10-round tube and wing it out to one side to carry 20 balls. Then there was the "cheese wedge" hopper that held 40. The "Whaler" held a massive 150 paintballs, an incredible development at the time.

As the loaders got larger, the problem of feeding paintballs became apparent. 200 paintballs stacked on top of each other have problems dropping into a single hole unless they get moved somehow. Players would physically shake their paintguns to get the balls to load while shooting! This was solved in the mid 90's when Viewloader came out with the best working solution to moving paintballs in a hopper. They placed a paddle into the hopper, and a motor would activate and spin the paddle when a beam wasn't broken in the feed neck.

Several other companies have made several other designs, but they all work on the same concept. If you move the balls around while someone is shooting, the paintballs will fall into the single feed hole easier. In the last several years, this concept has been taken even further with force-feed systems. Airgun Designs invented a "warp feed," which actually pushed paintballs into the paintgun from underneath. The idea was to take the hopper off the top, but in doing so they also took the technology to another level.

Now, most high-end players use a "Halo" hopper, which can push paintballs into the gun at a rate of 25+ per second. This is actually faster than gravity can let the balls fall, allowing players to keep a blistering rate of fire going as they play. The downside is that if the power source goes out, the hopper is completely useless--unless you have a hand crank on it. It's a last resort, but it's better than nothing.

Another driving force of the game is the paintball itself. Players want to carry more on them, and why not? When players started raiding the surplus stores for gear, the game was played with oil based paint that came in "cigar tubes." You could buy pouches that would perfectly hold 15 of these tubes, but it was a struggle to open it while under fire. Players also used shotgun shell belts to hold the tubes, but it wasn't easy to carry these and everything else you needed to.

As time went on, companies like ICS developed vests that could carry more paint more easily. But these designs had limitations for size. When the hoppers got larger, so did the pods. Players found it was easier, and more compact, to carry 50 paintballs in one canister instead of five cigar tubes. And as pods got larger, the vests and packs we used to hold them had to adapt as well.

The first "guppy" pods were solid pieces of PVC pipe with flip-caps on the ends. The flip cap made all the difference, as 10 round tubes only have a retaining cap. Players didn't lose flip lids, and they became wildly popular. Other experiments were attempted, including PVC pipe that would snap into a retaining clip so you wouldn't need lids, and a hopper that would interface with the pod, doubling your effective hopper size. They didn't work because the open pods would gather a lot of water in the rain, and water on paintballs isn't good.

As bulk pods became more popular, companies made gear to haul them around in. ICS developed one of the first "bulk loader" packs, as opposed to the vests most players used. The idea was that you carried them around your waist, and the pods were placed in individual, specially-built compartments rather than large "generic" pouches. Someone got the brilliant idea that instead of wearing the pack around the front, it would be better to spin it around and wear the pods on your back. That way, paintballs were less likely to hit the pods and break. And the first modern harness system was truly born.

It would be almost impossible to follow the pack genesis in a few paragraphs. In fact, if we took a whole chapter and dedicated it to the pack evolution, we'd not only take up a lot of space but we'd surely miss more than a few innovations. Smart Parts invented a Velcro pack you'd attach to your jersey to prevent it from rolling around. Unique Sporting came up with a pack that held six pods, three on each side, and a large tank to keep it off your paintgun. The old idea of "stacking" was rediscovered by JT and ICS, and companies made packs that held more pods over the base layer on your back. So now when you talk about a 3x4 pack, you're talking about one with four pods against your back, and three stacked between the cracks of them.

Harnesses have so many styles now that you can easily find anything that fits what you're looking for. Everything from the small 2x1 for players moving light to the massive 5x4 that carries over 1250 paintballs are easily available. Vests and hybrid harnesses are great for scenario players who need to carry more than just paint. On a Special Ops vest, for example, a scenario player can carry a radio, several forms of ID, paint grenades, "nerf" rocket rounds and even their air tank.

Some things have changed in ways that the innovators could not have imagined. You may not think anything of the clothing you wear when you play paintball, but it makes a difference in how you play. When the game first began, players wore surplus

Gear

camouflage. Many players still do—it's versatile, wears like iron, and it's pretty cheap to get. But it has limitations. If you have to fit into a weird position behind a bunker, the clothing has no give to it and it can rip. Plus BDUs have buttons and other hard surfaces on them that can break paintballs.

"Tiger Stripe" pullovers were the rage in the early to mid 90's, along with other camouflage patterns. Companies like Tiger Stripe Products and Renegade supplied all the serious players with their camouflage. The pullover was a good design for paintball, and a lot of long-time players still wear them. Pullovers also allowed players to place their names and a team number on the back, just like other sports teams did. The first team to do this was the New Jersey Devil Dogs in the early 90's on their "Realtree" pullovers, and many teams quickly followed suit.

Many companies picked up on pullovers, and crossed the jerseys from other sports into it. JT and Scott both encouraged their sponsored teams to wear motocross style jerseys. The original jerseys were made of cloth and faded after several washings. It took several years, but the paintball-specific jersey eventually became a reality.

Today's jerseys are made of materials designed to wick sweat and to keep a player cool on the field. You may not think of it, but in mid summer these things are a blessing. Plus they come in colors we just didn't use way back when, which makes team designation a lot easier. Many companies like CSG or Animal Paintball will custom-create jerseys for your whole team, giving you a unique look. It cuts down a lot on "friendly fire" when you see your team's jersey on the other side of the field.

Even pants have been reworked specifically for paintball. As I mentioned before, clothing can rip

The Complete Guide to Paintball

when you're in strange positions. Much like the jerseys, motocross pants were used for a while. But they simply weren't designed for the strains we put on them, and the designs were changed. Modern paintball pants have built in knee padding, stretch panels to avoid ripping, venting to keep you cool, and even a panel on the back to grab your harness to keep it from shifting when you play! Most importantly, a lot of them also have padding over your . . . most sensitive areas. And the nicest part is that these styles come in many designs, including some for the scenario players!

Other developments for paintball have also been adapted from outside of the sport, such as the use of radios. Players have been using these for a long time, but in order to get any power out of them we had to get large, bulky systems. Portable radios (often times incorrectly called "walkie-talkies") have

gotten smaller and more powerful with each generation. Companies like Firefox make throat-microphones and hands free systems that let you simply talk without having to reach for your radio every time. Plus, with the use of "sidebands," there are hundreds of channels to talk on, so the odds that your signals will be discovered are minimal.

Compared to when we first played, modern gear makes the game more enjoyable to play and a lot safer, too. As the game changes, so does the gear we use for it-new innovations constantly come along. But a word of advice for all you new guys: if you see some old guy using a paintball gun that looks like it has parts made in his garage, and he's wearing an old army style pouch with tubes, don't laugh at him. He may have been playing longer than you've been alive.

© Michael Wise II, chrono300.com

It Ain't Just Paint

Have you ever eaten a bowl of jello? Maybe it had whipped cream on top, or fruit buried in it. Did you ever watch it wiggle and shake? It's not possible that there is anyone in the world who hasn't at least *seen* jello.

Well, if you haven't then you must be the only person on the face of this planet who hasn't seen the substance paintball shells are made of.

It's called gelatin and it was invented circa 1900 as a 'neutral' food that could be added to just about everything and flavored to taste like just about anything. For a brief period, it was a popular delicacy, reserved for kings and queens and aristocrats.

Today, of course, gelatin no longer holds such a lofty position—definitely not in its capacity as the shell of the humble paintball. It's no longer a privilege to eat gelatin—although doing so won't harm you. Gelatin has been run through some pretty high-tech processes that make it just strong enough to be shot from a gun, yet brittle enough to break when hitting cammo'ed paintballers more than 100 feet away. Nonetheless, gelatin is quite digestible. (As any newbie will attest!)

Gelatin is created by 'rendering' the soft tissues, hooves, bones, and other unmentionables left over after a pig or cow has been prepared for market. During manufacture, sorbitol (a preservative), some glycerine, and starch (to give the shell 'body') are added to the mix. At the end of this process you get long, thin, sticky sheets of gelatin. Using a process originally developed for the pharmaceutical industry, these sheets are then used to mold the shell of the paintball. As the sheets of gelatin are fed through an encapsulating machine, they pass through a reservoir of fill or paint. The two halves of the ball seal together and the entire paintball is left to dry.

The inside of the paintball is what really counts, though. Because gelatin wants to absorb water (just drop one in a glass of water and watch it swell), the 'paint' inside can't be water-based. In fact, during paintball's formative years, the paintball fill was oil-based.

Over the years a 'water-soluble' paintball was developed that replaced the petroleum-based oils with mineral, vegetable, and fish based oils. The most commonly used natural oil is polyethylene glycol. Added to this is starch, which serves as a thickener, and water. Artificial, non-toxic dyes are used to provide color.

—SD

Everything that goes into a paintball is edible, non-toxic, and completely biodegradable.

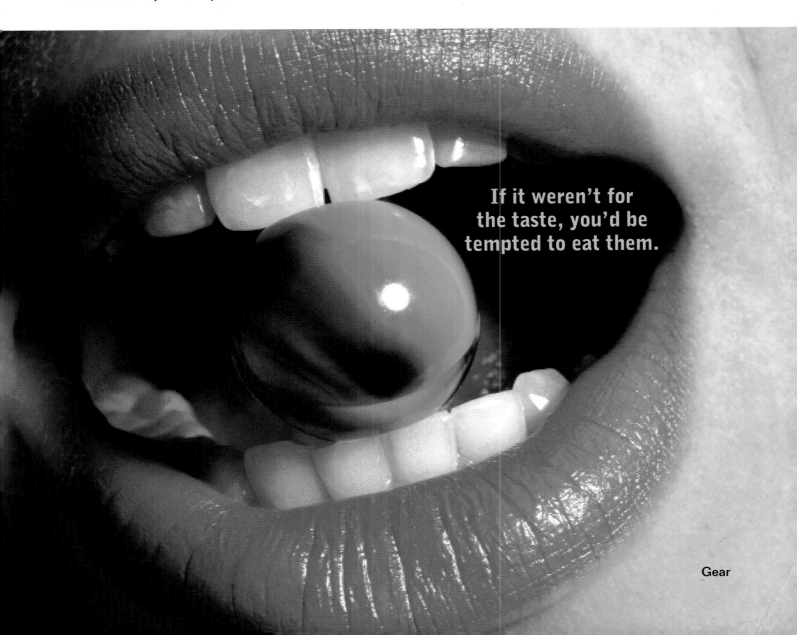

If it weren't for the taste, you'd be tempted to eat them.

Gear

RON OLKO, TECH REP FOR AIR AMERICA, SPEAKS WITH STEW SMITH AT THE 1998 WORLD CUP ABOUT HIS COMPANY'S AIR SYSTEM:

STEWART SMITH: To start, what are you cleaning the regulator with and what are you lubricating it with?

RON OLKO: Just wipe it off with a rag or paper towel.

STEW: No solvent?

RON: The only solvent that you'd want to use at all is maybe a little bit of rubbing alcohol. Rubbing alcohol works really well because it doesn't promote rust. It cleans up the paint and it evaporates. You don't want to use too much alcohol on the regulator though, because it can ruin the o-rings. But generally, you just wipe it off. You very rarely need any type of cleaning fluids.

You get all the paint off, any broken shells that may be in there, and then you lubricate it. Really, one of the best lubricants to use is automatic transmission fluid. It's readily available, and it's not corrosive on the o-rings. You want to avoid most real firearm solvents. Those are terrible, because they're meant to break out carbon deposits in guns, and there are no carbon deposits in here. What ends up happening, if you put that on a paintball gun, is it attacks the o-rings, causing them to swell and break down. When the o-rings get damaged, you get leaks, and they're a problem. You want to avoid that.

You also do not want to lubricate with any type of aerosol, WD-40, or something like that. That's very bad. WD-40 is so thin, the o-rings will absorb it and swell up and cause the gun to jam.

BASIC FIELD STRIP

RON: As far as basic service and trouble-shooting goes, if there's a problem, check out the whole valving. It's either dirty pins, springs getting compressed over time, or dirt where it shouldn't be.

STEW: What are some indicators that those items are dirty or something's wrong with them?

RON: You'll have erratic output. High or low pressure swings. You have two gauges on the system. You have your bottle pressure, your high pressure gauge. This tells you your unregulated pressure. Then you have a low-pressure gauge that shows you when there's a load on the system, what your output pressure is. As you pull the trigger, and cycle the weapon, you'll see the needle deflect or bounce. If there's a slow recovery from that deflection, that means there is a problem. If you see the needle swing past your set pressure, and it keeps climbing, that's another indicator that the valve pin is not seated properly. The system is not regulating the pressure correctly. Any kind of leak, however small, will affect your pressure. When I take the regulator apart, I'll show you the piston. There's an o-ring on it that can get dirty or worn or harden over time and cause a breakdown. It's a little thing

© Cleo Fogal

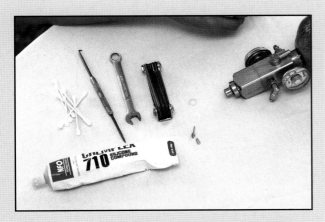

that can make a big difference, and it's easily consumer replaceable. We've made this a very simple and user-friendly system.

STEW: Looks like it's no more complicated than regular scuba gear. It might be a little more difficult.

RON: No, actually, for the average paintball player, this is probably easier to maintain and troubleshoot than a scuba system. It's best, though, especially in situations like this tournament, to leave repair to technical representatives, which is why we're always out here. We come out early. We stay late. Make sure players get quality service, make sure things get done right. A lot of consumers outside the tournament circuit don't have direct access to tech support, and don't have the knowledge base. So, you'll see them putting black rubber o-rings in there which may last for one cycling of the gun and then blow apart, or they wrap teflon tape around internal portions of the regulator. They're thinking, "Hey, it stopped leaking, so it must work, right? Wrong. That's why a step-by-step process like this is really important. Our air system is very easy to maintain. We try to educate our customers. They get an operator's manual that outlines these same procedures, how to troubleshoot.

STEW: For the basic servicing of the Air America system here, what tools do you need to have?

RON: The main tools you need to do any consumer level maintenance would be a set of hex keys, a main set of 16ths, 5/32nds, a pick or o-ring tool, and a 7/16ths open-end wrench. That'll perform 99% of the maintenance. Q-tip swabs and some rubbing alcohol to clean out dirt and debris, and a lubricating oil or grease.

STEW: Any one in particular for lubrication that you recommend?

RON: What shouldn't you use? A lot of players use vaseline, or auto grease on the piston. Any kind of grease other than this silicone lube I'm using collects dirt. Lightweight motor oil will work fine, as well as gun oil. Any of these can be used to perform routine maintenance and lubrication. In addition to the piston, we also put oil on the mainspring, also called the spring pack. It's a series of stacked concave disks that doesn't look much like a spring, but the concave disks working against each other provides a spring action. If you don't keep it lubricated, and the disks become corroded, it increases friction and the spring becomes less effective or erratic, and pressure adjustment becomes difficult. So we put a light coat of oil on that spring, which I'll show you when we take it apart, and a light coat of oil on the piston o-ring.

STEW: So you can use petroleum products to lubricate it?

RON: We'd rather the consumer use a urethane-friendly lubricant, a non-penetrating type of lubricant. Over time, the o-ring will become hard or swell and tear if they use distillate-type lubricants. This silicone compound we just started using is an industry standard o-ring lubricant. We find that it works very well. But it's not readily available to all of our consumers. So I recommend a light lubricating oil, friendly for urethane products.

AIR VS. CO$_2$

STEW: So why air and not carbon dioxide?

RON: Carbon dioxide is a compressed liquid gas. It's more unstable than air and very susceptible to temperature changes. Since it's a liquid, we have a problem. Even with an anti-siphon tube, when a player tilts his bottle down, he is going to get some liquid up into the hose that can cause the gun to freeze up. At a minimum, you'll get hot shots in excess of 300 feet per second, which can be potentially hazardous. With the anti-siphon bottles of today, the technology has advanced to the point where it is safer, but there are still problems. There are always temperature fluctuations. Not to say that CO$_2$ is a bad way to do things, you just have to be aware of how it works. The majority of the entry level paintball guns and field owners still use compressed CO$_2$ because it's more affordable at this point. Due to the materials and labor that are involved, our compressed air systems are a lot more expensive than buying mass-manufactured 12-ounce or 20-ounce CO$_2$ bottles, which you can pick up for 40 or 50 bucks, depending on the size of the bottle.

STEW: Does it help with cyclical rates of fire? Remember we were talking about using the Shockers and the Angels. They wouldn't use carbon dioxide, would they?

RON: A low-pressure gun needs more volume. Volume is a big deal. One player in a 10-man competition, two 5-man teams going at it, can go through up to 2500 rounds in one game.

The guns vary. Take an Autococker, for example. There are so many after-market products that change the flow dynamics and the volume characteristics that are available for that gun. The average shot count for an Autococker with a 4500 psi system may be 1600–1800 shots per fill. Variations in barrels and different types of actuating mechanisms will affect performance. Different manufacturers recommend different volumes. So, we say the average is probably about 1800 shots for this system here. But when you get into a Shocker, with its high-rate of fire and particular volumetric efficiency, it's not going to work for a player who wants to shoot 1800–2,000 rounds. That type of gun typically eats more air than others.

STEW: What do they use to get the volume they want?

RON: They use CO$_2$. We can use this same type of bottle with a CO$_2$ valve. The threads are standard. So they can get more with the CO$_2$ in this same sized bottle than you would with compressed air. There's a trade-off, because now you're carrying around 30 ounces of CO$_2$ in a heavy bottle. We looked at that added weight, at the risk level involved with carrying that around, and went with compressed air.

STEW: How does being able to adjust the pressure affect the gun's performance?

RON: Each gun operates at a different pressure which affects performance. By adjusting the pressure, you're modifying it for that type of gun. Automatic style requires 600–900 psi to operate, depending on what type of valve work has been done to the gun. Standard Autocockers require anywhere from 375–500 psi to operate. This allows you to adjust the air system to whatever in-bound pressure your gun requires.

STEW: And then the tournament cap locks that setting?

RON: The tournament cap locks that setting down, so when the air system is de-gassed, there's pressure on the adjustment nut. At that point, when you have to empty your tank, or it is loose in your gear bag, the nut won't float around and change the pressure setting.

Gear

AFFORDABLE
Invaluable
Paintball
Paraphernalia

GET THE BIGGEST BANG FOR YOUR BUCK

Here's a list of simple, low-cost necessities you can purchase that will add to your enjoyment of the recreational paintball experience. Most items can be purchased at general merchandise stores, like Wal-Mart or K-Mart, at sporting goods stores, or at military surplus outlets.

1. **A decent pair of ankle supporting shoes.** High top style cleats are the best.

2. **A pair of gloves.** Can even be gardening type gloves. Less than $1.00 a pair. Cut the fingertips off. Bicycle gloves are great, too.

3. **Knee Pads.** The only way to slide.

4. **Elbow Pads.** Crawl without pain.

5. **A good watch with a timer function or a kitchen timer.** To keep track of time elapsed during games. Glue it to your loader's lid.

6. **Fleece shotgun swab.** A 12 gauge for barrel-cleaning.

7. **M16 Ammo Pouches and belt.**

8. **Wool cap, to protect your head from close range hits.**

9. **Camouflage BDU pants and top.** These come cheap if you buy them used.

10. **MRE's (Meals Ready to Eat).** In case you get hungry during those long games.

11. **Toilet paper.** It's a messy game, after all.

12. **Military helmet storage bag, for your goggles.**

13. **Insect repellent with DEET.** Avoid Lyme disease and keep away the bugs.

—SD

Special Weapons and Tactics

Rob Rubin

Many times when you're playing the bigger games or scenario games in the woods, you'll run into some of the more interesting paintball weapons the game has to offer. This section is going to briefly touch on the basics, and what they're really like to use and have used against you. Remember, we can't possibly cover everything. So always pay attention to the rules of the field and the game to see if they're throwing more special weapons or "exotics" into the game than we mention here.

GRENADES

The most common exotic is the paintball grenade. They come in several types, but all do the same thing: throw liquid paint to eliminate players. How they do it is where you run into two basic types.

First is the "ball bearing" design. This is surgical tubing filled with liquid paint. Then two ball bearings are stuffed into the ends of the tubing, sealing it off. There's also a locking safety device, and usually some safety cap. When thrown, the force of the grenade hitting a solid surface ejects the ball bearings out of the ends of the tube, and it sprays paint in an area.

The second type is a "twist knot" design. This also uses surgical tubing, but the end is wrapped around itself to make a sort of knot. The "safe" device is a rubber band around the end of the tubing. When this rubber band

is removed, and the knot is allowed to unwind, the paint is forced out of the surgical tubing and sprays paint in an area. This is almost like a time-delay fuse on a real grenade.

In either case, the paint grenade is a way to eliminate several opponents at once, providing you use it right. Many players assume it's like a real grenade, and you only need to "get it close." Sorry, but it's not really that easy. These aren't explosives, and they don't throw shrapnel. So if you're going to throw one, you need to know how to do it right.

The paint grenade works best if you can get it to ricochet or bounce around, so throwing it into or onto a hard surface is a must. Honestly, the best luck you're going to have is tossing it into a building or a bunker that has a back wall. It's the best way to get the most splatter for your effort.

Next is understanding physics. When you throw a paint grenade, the stuff in it has momentum going forward. So if you overshoot your target the spray will go right past them. Unlike a real grenade, the fill won't explode backwards. By the same logic, if you undershoot them the paint will never reach them, either. The important thing to learn is how to throw the grenade to either get it to land right where you want it, or to somehow bounce backwards. Here's where that back wall comes in handy.

Finally, you should understand how the rules of paint grenades work. Generally speaking, any splatter from a paintball grenade counts as an elimination. So if you can undershoot your opponents and let the grenade roll into their position, you can eliminate them with the flecks of paint flying forward at them. On the other hand, if they're behind a solid wall, the paint will never splatter on them and you won't get anything more than a spray-painted wall.

So with all this in mind, the best way to eliminate someone with a paint grenade is to either bounce the grenade in front of them and let the fill fly forward, or to ricochet it back at them by bouncing it off a wall and at them. Or find a group of people in a building, toss in the grenade and let the mayhem truly begin.

TRIP-LINE OR TRIP-WIRES

Another use for paint grenades, depending on the design, is for tripwire devices. Before you get all excited, let's talk about safety and tripwires. All trip-line devices must adhere to strict rules. They may not have any kind of explosive charge in them. Most commercially available devices will work using compressed air instead. The player trips the

Players tow tanks to their favorite fields to participate in scenario games...and get attention for Paintball in the process! © T.J. Allcot

The Complete Guide to Paintball

device off, and from there the device uses air power. Normally, a single 12 gram CO_2 powerlet will power a single shot sending the paint flying everywhere.

Furthermore, the "General Scenario Rules of Play" specifically state that all trip-line devices need to use a "breakable" tripwire. This is for everyone's safety! Imagine someone running through the woods and hitting a trip-line that won't break. They'll trip, they'll fall, and they will no longer be having fun playing paintball.

So the best type of trip-line is a cotton sewing thread. It does the job, but it will break if someone runs through it. Trip-lines work well if you have the time to properly set them up. We're not going into those tricks here, as we could spend a lot of time on the sneaky stuff like this. But we'll just say this and move on: if you're resourceful and your options are limited, you'd be amazed at what you can do in a pinch.

Naturally, this leads to actual pre-made "booby traps." You don't see these as commonly as paint grenades, but they are out there. These can work on a trip-line device, or on a pressure plate. Either way, when someone walks over or through it, it throws liquid paint into a small area. Usually, right at the feet of the person who set it off. These are not as commonly found in games as they take a lot of set up time.

My favorite toy is the remote control "mine." These use a radio control device about the size of a key ring. As long as you're within a 300 foot range of the mine, you can set it off remotely. And it doesn't just go off—it sprays paint like a garden hose. They're not cheap, but when you absolutely have to keep a trail clear, this baby does the trick.

PAINT LAUNCHERS

Launching a lot of paint at range can be done too, with the right gear. There are commercially available launchers that you can easily fit 100+ paintballs into and launch mortar style. Normally

The Armored Fist Panther tank at the 2006 Three Rivers Paintball Festival. © T. J. Allcot

Gear

these are used to launch "rockets" to take out tanks. The rockets aren't real, they're small nerf footballs with fins on the back. And before you ask, yes there are rules about launching 100+ paintballs at an opponent. As always, you need to ask the field owner or scenario producer about specific rules of play.

When you're talking about the exotic paintball gear, the sky truly is the limit. If someone can dream it up, it can probably be translated into paintball somehow. The most wild thing I've ever seen in a scenario game was a guy who created a paintball "flame thrower." He had a vintage WW2 flame-thrower, and instead of fuel he filled it with liquid paint. In a way, I felt sorry for some of his victims who were coated head to toe in paint. At least it washed out in the end.

Sights & Scopes

All you have to do is line up opponents in your crosshairs and pull the trigger! It's that easy, right?

not quite...

THE HARD CORE TRUTH ABOUT SIGHTS & SCOPES

Many players use sights or scopes on their paintball guns to help improve "accuracy." I've seen some very impressive 20x-scopes placed on all sorts of paintguns. But do they really help your accuracy? Well, yes and no.

A paintball is not a bullet. Therefore, the accuracy of a paintball cannot be guaranteed. A paintball is filled with liquid, so all sorts of variables affect what happens to it once it's shot out the end of a barrel. The wind can catch it and blow it round. Extreme high velocity can make it unstable. Even the paint can influence your accuracy. Other things that affect the path of a paintball include:

- The gun and barrel brands and how they match-up.

- If your paint is dry or dimpled or wet.

- If your barrel has broken paint in it.
- The phase of the moon. (Just kidding, but you get the point. Many things affect your paintball's path!)

Adco Hot Shot, Adco vision 2000

Smart Parts HI VIZ

Where a paintball is going to go is often an unknown. So, the scope usually out-performs the paint. This isn't to say that a scope or sight is useless. I've had a lot of success using them on my personal paintguns. You just need to understand a few guidelines for the use of these accessories so that you can optimize your experience of them.

HOW TO USE SIGHTS & SCOPES TO IMPROVE YOUR GAME

My opinion is that scopes have limited usefulness. Why? Magnification interferes with your aim. Your magnified perspective will usually be further ahead than the ball will travel. That said, I grant that sights and scopes are useful for looking downfield in the larger "big game" formats of paintball. In other words, use the magnification to look a couple hundred yards ahead to see if your competition is moving around out there, where they're headed, things like this. Of course, opportunities to do this are few and far between for most people. In most cases, you want a sight with no magnification that simply puts a "dot" in space.

Once you've gotten your sight, you want to "Dial it in." What is dialing? In an ideal scenario, realize that a sight can only tell you where the barrel is pointed, not where your paint will eventually go. A little experimentation will tell you where paint is likely to go when you're aiming at something within a certain range. If you can hit a pie-plate at 75 feet, you can calibrate or 'dial' your sight so that it will reflect where the paint usually goes at that dis-

tance. This takes some time and patience. I like to dial in at 75–100 feet, as most of my shooting happens within that range.

In regular "toe-to-toe" play, you usually don't use sights. I find myself just shooting and following where the last ball went, or using the barrel itself as a large point sight. For long angle shots, or for ambush situations, sights work very well. My personal technique may not work for everyone, but it's worth trying.

Place the dot on your opponent's chest area. If a ball drifts in most any direction, it will still probably hit them. I like to keep both eyes open for a stereoscopic view, but some prefer to close one eye to concentrate on the shot. Either way works well. Then, simply pull the trigger in the same way that you would any other time. Don't change that detail, because if you do it won't "feel" right and you probably won't hit the person. Paintguns have no recoil, so slow trigger pulls aren't necessary. In some cases, it may not give you the best shot. Some players put a short "string" of 3 balls on a target, but sometimes that's not necessary.

Using a sight or a scope may or may not improve your game. Your best bet is to invest in an inexpensive sight to try it out. If it helps your game or you just really enjoy using it, you'll find no shortage of variety in terms of available scopes and sights.

—RR

Armson/Pro-Team Products Pro-Dot Sight0

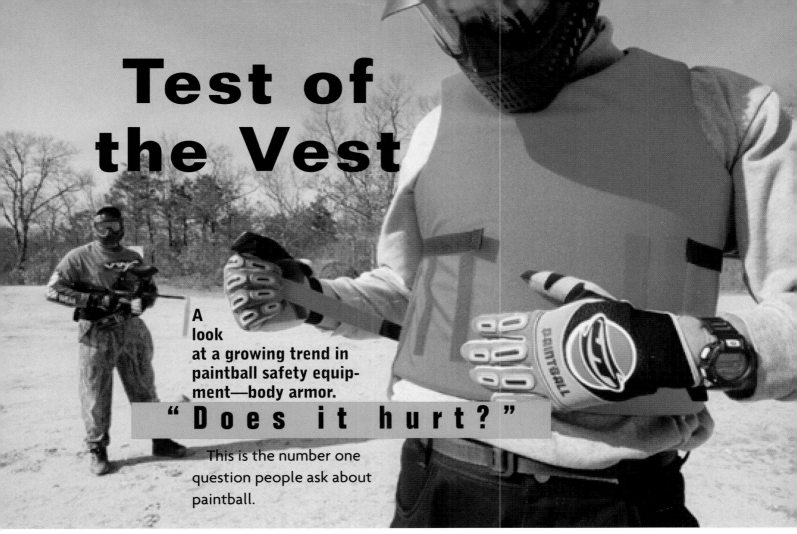

Test of the Vest

A look at a growing trend in paintball safety equipment—body armor.

"Does it hurt?"

This is the number one question people ask about paintball.

With the increase in paintball gun technology pushing the rate of fire ever higher, there is a definite need to provide players with safety equipment that can handle these new conditions. And as more people get into the game, why hurt 'em?

Rose and Dan Drewek have a deep love of paintball that goes beyond playing. Their dream is to have a profound impact on the industry by promoting safety. In 1993, they opened an outdoor paintball field in Canada. In 1996, they opened a retail store to better serve their customers and promote the sport. In 1998, they opened an indoor field.

Rose and Dan have been involved in paintball for 13 years. Dan has always been a tournament player, and has developed a number of local tournament teams. Dan currently plays for the Focus International factory team on the amateur circuit.

"I once had a child cry from the sting of a paintball at his own birthday party," explains Rose Drewek.

"I began to wonder if there were a way to run things so that people didn't have to be afraid of being hit by paintballs."

The Complete Guide to Paintball

With this in mind, Paintball Encounters teamed up with Extreme Adventures, a Canadian manufacturing company, to develop a safety vest. They wanted to maintain authenticity and realism for players. They designed the vest to be the most universal piece of equipment available, next to a goggle system, and called it "The No Flak Jack."

Designed for both players and referees alike—in fact it was selected to be the safety vest worn by the referees at Skyball '99—the No Flak Jack is constructed of heavy Cordura material and is padded with closed cell foam. Two models are available: a recreational vest, which features a removable neck guard and an optional crotch protector (see *The Case for A Cup* and you'll know why this is a good idea), and a field rental version vest, which offers similar protection with a stripped-down design.

We decided to put the utility of a safety vest to the test as part of our field trials for this book. We wanted to see first hand whether the No Flak Jack lived up to the promises of its inventors.

A SIMPLE TEST

Our test was simple: four shots to the back and four to the front from ten feet away. Rob was shooting his Viper. Needless to say, I was reassured by Rob that he'd hit the target every time. This was good news, since I was wearing the vest.

Wham! Wham! Wham! Wham! to my back they came. The third shot landed on top of the second, right in the middle of my right shoulder blade. The impact was felt—in fact, the third shot did sting.

I turned around 180˚ and Rob repeated his

marksmanship skill four more times to my chest. Wham! Wham! The second shot threw paint onto my goggles. Wham! The last shot was a bounce, no break. Pain factor? None.

Removing the vest, there were no obvious welts, just a little redness. Twenty-four hours later when normally bruises would have appeared, there were none.

No marks. No welts. No soreness. Pretty Cool!

Since that day, I have worn the No Flak Jack under my coveralls on the field. I have been wearing the field rental model, because I like the design. Being a big guy, the straps tend to be a bit short, but nonetheless the vest does the trick.

Our conclusion: wearing a vest is an excellent safety precaution, especially as more and more kids are getting into the game. A close shot to the kidneys can indeed cause injury, so why risk it? If I had kids, and they played paintball, I'd make certain they wore a safety vest in addition to their goggle protection. It's a small investment (under $100), and well worth every penny to live to fight another day!

—AF

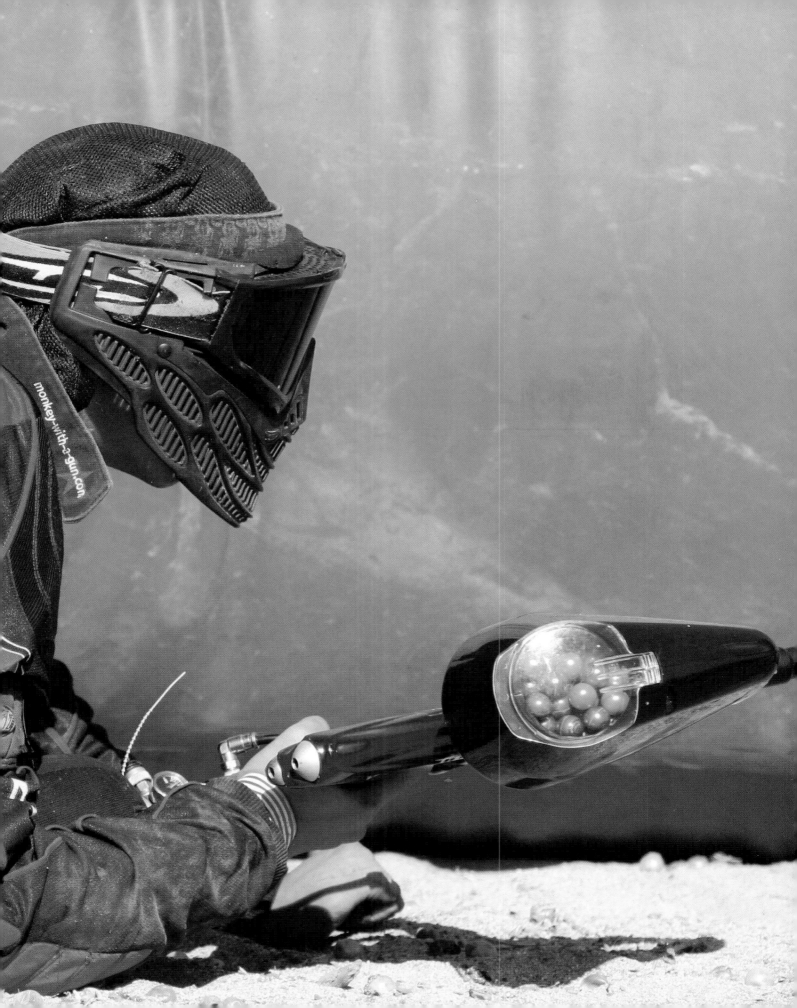

The Well-Dressed Player

Dawn Allcot

DAVE "YOUNGBLOOD" DEHAAN TALKS ABOUT TRENDS IN PAINTBALL WEAR.

The "well-dressed" paintball player used to wear camouflage to stay concealed in the woods. As competitive paintball moved to smaller arena fields the "paintball uniform" changed.

Motocross style jerseys and pants might be "the new camouflage," allowing players to blend in against primary-colored inflatable bunkers. But the tournament look also moved into the recreational market. Many top woodsball teams wear bright yellow or blue jerseys just like the pros.

Styles on rec-ball fields range from pants and jerseys designed for paintball to camouflage BDUs or even loose-fitting pants and sweatshirts. Wearing clothes designed specifically for the sport not only provides protection against the sting of paintball hits, it offers a psychological advantage on the field. It sends a message that you're serious, intimidating opponents before you fire a shot.

Essential paintball wear includes pants, a loose-fitting top, footwear (sneakers, cleats or boots), and goggles. A head wrap is highly recommended, as are gloves. Many players cut the fingers out of their gloves—or purchase them that way—to make it easier to walk the trigger. Padding is built into the knees of paintball pants, but players also purchase separate knee and elbow pads, worn beneath their clothes.

Who better to discuss paintball clothes from head to toe than DYE Paintball owner, Dave "Youngblood" DeHaan?

DAWN ALLCOT: You started out as the best-dressed player on the field, wearing a tuxedo in early games. Now, many pros wear DYE gear. How did the motocross-style jerseys evolve?

DAVE DEHAAN: Some people in the industry have been pioneers, and John Gregory, owner of JT USA, is one of them. He made a conscious effort to leave the camouflage scene and go towards a uniform-style team look. He took a big chance back then. Everybody was wearing camo. John took an existing jersey and pants from his motocross line, changed the colors to black and olive and tan. He started forcing his signed teams to wear these outfits as their playing gear. John Gregory changed the look of paintball to the general public. That was in 1993.

DAWN: When did you launch DYE?

DAVE: I started DYE in 1994. I didn't get into clothing until 1996. I started with barrels. In 1996, we introduced a goggle and a jersey, making our move into soft goods.

DAWN: Today's jerseys and pants are well-padded and ventilated. Is there a limit to how much padding you can offer?

DAVE: There's been a lot of talk about that. There's really not a governing body to determine what is acceptable. For the benefit of the player, with safety in mind, our approach is to give as much padding as we can without offering a performance advantage. As long as balls still break on the player and the fundamental rules of the game are intact, we can offer as much protection as possible. We do an extensive amount of testing to find that limit. You can go overboard, but with rate of fire these days, how small the fields are, and how fragile the paint is, it still wouldn't be an issue.

DAWN: DYE uses unique ventilation technology to keep players cool. Tell us about that.

DAVE: We're really on the cutting edge of using new materials. We introduce new materials into the paintball industry at the same time those materials are introduced, by a company like DuPont, into motocross, into the wet suit business, and other related industries. The sky's the limit with the technology. It all comes down to cost. We've built some pretty interesting stuff, some material that NASA made jackets out of, that keeps your body cool when it's warm and warm when it's cold. But we have to keep costs in mind. If we go crazy with fun stuff, we'll end up producing a jersey that's going to be $300 retail.

DAWN: When did the CORE line of tournament pants and jerseys launch?

DAVE: C4 was the first time we started identifying it by that name. That comes out of the motocross industry. When I worked at JT for a time, I was parallel to the motocross department working in paintball, and they always distinguished their lines by year. They stopped doing that, but we picked up on it. We started with the C4 line and we're almost finished with our C8 line.

DAWN: How has it evolved?

DAVE: Every year, we try and improve on the product from the previous year. We'll get our product to market, we'll watch our pro teams wear it, and we'll watch them beat it up. We'll monitor it, do testing. We'll get back pairs of pants that have been heavily worn and look for wear marks and things we can improve. We get feedback from the pro players to improve the products each year.

DAWN: What about slide shorts and other undergarments? What do you recommend?

DAVE: I believe that players should wear as much undergarment protection as possible. When you're talking about 17-year-old kids, they kind of bounce when they hit the ground, but the older you get, the more you feel that stuff. The guys that we're trying to satisfy around this building are some of the most aggressive, well-known pros in the world. They're pretty serious and they want to be able to dive and hit the ground hard and not even think twice about injury.

We spend a lot of time trying to engineer stuff that will offer as much protection as possible, but will also be lightweight, breathable and not restrictive. We update our body protection every two years. We were the first company to introduce the slide shorts into the industry and now several companies make them. I always recommend that people wear them.

DAWN: Goggles are a player's most important gear. Let's cover head protection and goggles.

DAVE: Goggles and head protection are areas where you shouldn't spare any expense. Don't go cheap. Don't be afraid to spend a little bit more money for something you're going to be comfortable with and enjoy using. In the long term it will be well worth it.

DAWN: What are pro players looking for in goggles?

DAVE: They're all about light weight. They want good vision, clear optics, good peripheral vision, and the ability to hear well. If it was up to them, they wouldn't want it to feel like they're wearing a goggle. We try to find ways to make our goggles lighter and lighter with new materials, new plastics, but still offer all the protection we need to, even beyond ASTM standards.

DAWN: What about softness, flexibility, and a compact size? Is that important, too?

DAVE: Yes. You've got two markets there. You've got a pro player who wants something really compact and lightweight, and you've got the recreational player who really does not want to feel getting shot in the neck. They don't really care about trying to achieve bounce. They don't want to feel any pain in their forehead. We have to design products for different markets.

DAWN: The DYE Invision system is designed for pros. What does DYE offer rec-ballers?

DAVE: We have our PROTO line, which is more competitively priced and certainly broader in its scope of the markets. We have entry-level products for the new player. We have more different families of goggles in the PROTO line than we do in the DYE line. We cover all price points in the PROTO product group.

DAWN: Are fans and timers still important in goggles?

DAVE: Fans are not as big as they once were. The goggles are better equipped for ventilation and anti-fogging capabilities than they have been in the past; they almost don't need fan systems. We make fan systems for both the DYE line and the PROTO Line and they are not big sellers. I think that's good. Timers are still pretty popular. That's a component people like to have.

DAWN: What do players look for in pod packs?

DAVE: It should be lightweight, comfortable, and compact. Certainly, they want the pod to come out of that harness with ease, almost magically. If it takes any degree of fumbling or fighting, they are not going to like it. We're always designing with that in mind. We use some cool materials there, too. We want it to be durable. Harnesses get beat up a lot. At PROTO, we design them to be a little more durable, but not as high-tech. That guy's just not playing in the center X of an X-ball field; he's got more time.

DAWN: For new players, can you explain how much paint each player on the field may want to carry?

DAVE: A lot of times in X-ball, your front guys won't even carry a harness. Maybe they'll carry one pod in their hand. Some of the back guys will carry a lot more. If any of the front guys do carry a harness, it's two pods or three pods. We offer harnesses to carry from four to eleven pods.

DAWN: DYE makes cleats designed specifically for paintball. What makes ATC cleats different from those for other sports?

DAVE: We designed a cleat with a soft sole. When we designed the ATC about four years ago, they didn't make cleats with flexible soles. On baseball or football cleats, the cleat is built onto a hard platform. For paintball, we wanted a lot of flexibility in the shoe but we still wanted a lot of traction. That's when we developed the ATC.

If you look at baseball and football players, they don't spend a lot of time on their knees.

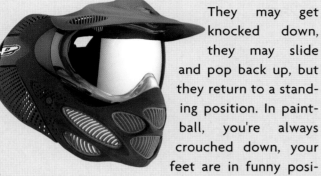

They may get knocked down, they may slide and pop back up, but they return to a standing position. In paintball, you're always crouched down, your feet are in funny positions, and comfort becomes an issue. Today, you can find shoes similar to what we designed in the sporting goods stores. And that's good. It's a better product for paintball players in general.

DAWN: DYE was one of the first companies to get into the market with casual clothing. When did you get into fashion clothes and why?

DAVE: We introduced the fashion clothes in our first catalog, around 2001. Paintball players in general are all trying to have our own identity, as a sport and as players. We thought if we started developing street wear, paintball people would wear it because they take pride in being paintball players. We introduced a line and it did really well. By no means is it a line you find in a mass merchant store, but I think it's something players appreciate. No great marketing plan there, just doing it because we all need clothes in the house.

DAWN: Has that helped build the paintball lifestyle?

DAVE: I think so. There have been a couple of times where we've taken a first step, and it's opened a door that everybody could go through. We started a clothing line in 2001, and today several companies make clothes, which I think is great. All of those companies working in tandem, making similar products, give paintball its own look.

DAWN: There's a trend of camo accents in playing gear. You offer C7s with olive drab. Why do you think everyone is going for this retro look?

DAVE: I think it's because camo made a really big comeback in the casual market on a global basis. We saw that coming. We started doing camo shorts before it really got into the jersey market. If you look at Billabong or Quicksilver, a lot of the prominent surf companies, they all introduced camo. I think it's a trend. It will go for a year or two, and then it will die out and it will be something else.

DAWN: What's the next trend?

DAVE: Plaid is starting to come back. We're introducing a couple of patterned plaid jerseys, a houndstooth pattern. It's going to be just like camo—we expect to see it around for a few years. It's new to paintball, seeing fashion trends recognized the way they are in surfing and other sports markets.

DAWN ALLCOT is Editor-in-Chief of Paintball Sports Magazine. *Her articles have also appeared in* RECON, Paintball News, Paintball 2Xtremes, *and on* Paintball.com.

A diverse freelance writer, Dawn covers topics such as audiovisual technology, wellness, music and the arts for a variety of magazines and websites. Dawn's husband, T.J., introduced her to paintball in 2001. In 2004, he built the Armored Fist Panther tank, and Dawn secured a position as turret gunner. The AF Panther has participated in scenario games from New York to Tennessee, and appeared on a trading card in RECON *Magazine. Dawn is also a Reserve Member of the Tippinators Paintball Team, known for their exemplary sportsmanship and for using Tippmann A-5s in speedball tournaments.*

Dawn, T.J. and their nephews, core members of the Armored Fist Panther crew, play at fields across the U.S., including Cousins Paintball, N.Y., and E.M.R. Paintball, PA.

Lock & Load

Paintball loaders serve one purpose: to feed more paint into a marker more efficiently. The first "Loaders" were tubes that were a permanent part of a paintball gun. To load a paintball you had to rock the gun to roll a paintball into the open breech, and then cock the gun. "Rock-N-Cock" loading systems like this are still evident in Stock Class paintball guns like the PGP, Phantom SC, and P-68SC. Many players added a "speedloader" to these guns to add another tube, and another 10 paintballs.

The widespread desire to carry more paint in a gun led to a simple "Stick Feeder." It was essentially a PVC tube attached to a PVC elbow that was designed to come off the back of an on-gun feed tube. A sock holder prevented the balls from rolling out of the top. It was usually designed to hold another 10–15 paintballs. Anything longer was too much of a target. Later, when direct feed guns were introduced, many players still used a stick feeder for quite some time.

Many people made "Home-brew" loaders from all sorts of objects. The most popular was an old oil can cleaned out, the top made into a lid, and placed onto the neck of a paint-ball gun. "D.A.M. cans" were a mass-produced version of the oil-can loaders. This design eventually lead to the mass-pro-duced "Worr Games Ammo Box." This box held 45 paintballs, and had an opening for tubed paint (as in 10 round tubed paint). The WGP ammo box had the advantage of being smaller and more streamlined than the oil-can style of load-ers. It was an instant hit.

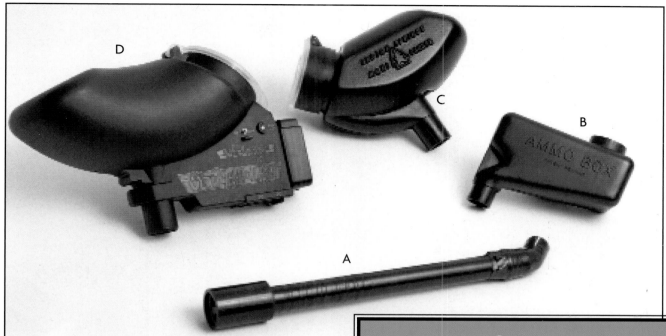

Larger loaders were introduced very quickly. The first was the "Whaler," which resembled a large sausage tube with "Magic Fish Lips" (no, I'm not making this up!) to aid in faster loading. The need for a better loader was answered by Viewloader, a company that introduced a modular 90-round hopper simply called "Viewloader." It had a clear flip lid, which was easy to look into and to load on the fly.

Brief History of the Loader

A. 15 round stick feeder

B. Worr Games Product Ammo Box

C. Indian Springs 120 round loader

D. View Loader Revolution, Brass Eagle, with VL timer

Viewloader also made 45-round hoppers with which one could fill this new loader. Other companies used this same principle to create a plethora of 100–150 capacity loaders. This was the norm, with a few larger loaders becoming available.

The only problem with all this was the paint. Many paintball guns wouldn't create enough of a 'kick' to move the paint around, and jams were common. Imagine having to shoot five times, shake your gun, shoot another five times, shake your gun, and do this all day. Players wanted a solution, and Viewloader delivered one.

The Idema Combat Systems vest, filled with with tube loaders. Introduced 1988 — Discontinued 1991.

Viewloader created the first patented agitating loader, the VL-2000. It works by placing an electronic eye in the feed neck that tells a motherboard to rotate a paddle to move the paintballs around in the loader. They originally designed it on their 200 round loader, but with time and research it's become streamlined and efficient. Many players agree that the 200 round loader is the best for size, weight and capacity.

The latest in high-technology is based on the VL-2000, called the "VL-2001." It's an electronic loader that you plug into the gun itself. The motor rotates and agitates the balls at a predetermined trigger pull. Electropneumatic paintguns like the Angel or the Shocker use this kind of loader, as the guns themselves are electronics-based.

Other loaders are still available. For example Indian Springs makes a 125 paintball hopper that's well suited for pump guns, if you're into vintage old-school play. Many other companies and loaders exist as well. Keep your eyes open for the next best thing—force-feed. But for the time being you have many excellent loaders to choose from.

-RR

THE CASE FOR A CUP

Andrew Flach Recounts a Personal Moment
of Humility & Discomfort

To wear a cup or not wear a cup, that is the question. Of all the answers I've sought in the process of putting together this book, it is the most mercurial of them all. Some people swear by cups, others swear against them, saying they're too uncomfortable and restricting. Many players who never wear them can recall situations where they wished they had.

The first time I ever played paintball was at an indoor field called Dark Armies in Indianapolis, Indiana. As we went through the check-in procedures and briefing, we were informed that protective cups were available for purchase at $7 each. I skipped the additional investment and threw my extra bucks into more paint and a gun upgrade, naturally.

Wouldn't you know, in the early moments of my very first game, as I leaned stealthily out of a doorway. . . Wham! Wham! Wham! Three "precise" shots right in the crotch. Kinda took my breath away. "I'm hit. I'm hit," I cried, hoping to end the flow of balls to my already sore area. The shooter stopped, and I hopped out-of-bounds.

The lesson: paintballs can hurt.
My advice: wear a cup.

Squeegees in a Nutshell

The Fine Art of Squeegee

WHERE TO START

There are two basic styles of squeegees on the market. Picking one is a matter of objective necessity and personal preference. Both clean out your barrel very effectively, but you may like one more than the other.

The first style is a "Stick" squeegee. "Stick" squeegees are long plastic tubes with a rubber disc at one end, and a spring-style action at the other end. To use this effectively, you push down on one end to push the rubber disk out. You need to flatten the disk out, and push it down the barrel. When you release the top spring, the disk comes flat against the plastic tube, filling the barrel. When you pull out the squeegee, it pulls broken paint and shell out with it. Many styles have a cloth on the opposite end, with which you can clean any residual paint out of your barrel.

The other style is a "Pull Through" or "Cable" squeegee. The cable style has several disks on a cord, and sometimes a fluffy "Swab" on the end. To use one, you need to remove the barrel from the paintball gun. You place the end without the disks in one end of the barrel, feeding it to the other side. You then pull on that end to bring the disks through the barrel, cleaning out the paint in your barrel. The "Swab" removes anything that may be left in the barrel, making one clean sweep.

Both styles have advantages and disadvantages.

A. Straight Shot

The Complete Guide to Paintball

B. Jerk

C. Battle Swab®

- Stick squeegees are easy to use and you'll be done in a jiffy, but they may not clean the barrel as effectively as a pull through.

- A pull through can't be used on some styles of paintball guns with "Fixed" (non-removable) barrels.

- Pull through squeegees can be folded, and fit into your pocket.

- Stick squeegees are bulky.

After squeegeeing your gun, you should clean off the disks. Placing a stick squeegee in the back of your knee and wiping it clean is a fast way to do this.

-RR

If you borrow someone else's **squeegee**, it's good form to clean it off before you return it.

D. Power Squeegee

E. Barrel swab

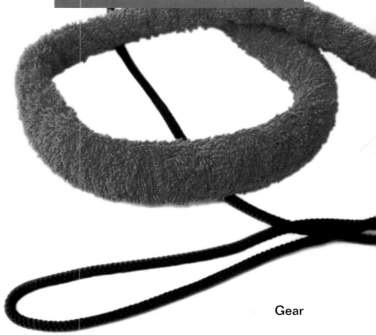

PART 4

DRILLS

Warm Up Play Hot

Prepare Your Body to Optimize Your Game Play

After interviewing some of the top paintball players and field owners in the world, it was apparent that many of the injuries that occur during a paintball game could easily be avoided by a moderate level of fitness and flexibility. In fact, the two biggest injuries are ankle sprains and muscle pulls (hamstrings and lower back). The ankle injuries can be decreased by wearing proper shoes such as high top cleats, and a few basic calf exercises and stretches. The hamstrings and the lower back can also be strengthened by an easy routine of stretching and exercising. This chapter is devoted not only to preventing the most common injuries in paintball, but to assisting adventurous paintball players in becoming more flexible, faster, stronger, and healthier. Follow this step-by-step stretching program during the week and you will be able to splat your opponents with ease during the weekend paintball games.

Stewart Smith graduated from the United States Naval Academy in 1991. He then spent four years on SEAL teams, after which he was put in charge of the physical training and selection of future BUD/S candidates. Stewart currently runs the getfitnow.com family fitness center in Severna Park, Maryland.

WARMING-UP

Warming up prior to stretching, exercise, and playing paintball is absolutely crucial to injury prevention. You will find that your muscles are more flexible and react to stretching far better after a brief 5–10 minute warm-up. Do this by walking, jogging slowly, riding a bike, or doing 50 jumping jacks.

The objective is to get your heart pumping above its normal rate, which will increase the blood flow to the muscles that you are about to stretch and use. Stretching is not only the best way to avoid injuries, but also the best way to prepare yourself to get tight and small behind a bunker, and then explode in a sprint on the attack. Regardless of your age, paintball is a vigorous and challenging sport that will test your stamina. To take your game to the next level, give your body the attention it needs, and follow these simple guidelines.

YO!

We'll be covering only stretches in this book, so we encourage you to check out our workout resources for the active sports enthusiast by visiting the GetFitNow.com web site. As most of our workout books are derived from the finest fitness regimens in the world—those of our United States Armed Forces—we are certain that you will find them extremely helpful in training to become the ultimate paintball warrior!

S T R E T C H E S

UPPER AND LOWER BODY

Arm (Shoulder)

Drop your shoulder and pull your arm across your chest. With the opposite arm, gently pull your arm across your chest and hold for 15 seconds. Repeat with the other arm.

This stretches the back of the shoulder and muscles that attach the shoulder blade to the upper part of the back. This is the very root of most tension headaches. Keeping these muscles flexible will help prevent injuries caused by running and falling to the ground when you are seeking cover from incoming paintballs.

The Most Advanced Piece of Machinery in Paintball? Your Body.

Arm Circles

Rotate your arms slowly in big circles forward and then reverse. This will help prepare your shoulders for pushups, dips, and dumbbell work.

Triceps into Lateral Stretch

Place both arms over and behind your head. Grab your right elbow with your left hand and pull your elbow toward your opposite shoulder. Lean with the pull. Repeat with the other arm.

This stretch prepares you for the dumbbell triceps exercises, pushups, and dips, but also helps stretch the back muscles. This is a very important stretch for upper body exercises!

Chest

Stand with your arms extended and parallel to the floor. Slowly pull your elbows back as far as you can. Hold for 15 seconds. Do not thrust your arms backwards. This is a slow and deliberate stretch designed to prepare your chest for pushups, dips, and other shoulder/chest exercises.

Shoulder Rotations

Rotate your shoulders slowly up and down, keeping your arms relaxed by your side. Your shoulders should rotate in small circles and move up and down in slow distinct movements.

Stomach Stretch

Lie on your stomach. Push yourself up to your elbows. Slowly lift your head and shoulders and look up at the sky or ceiling. Hold for 15 seconds and repeat two times.

Hip Rotations

Place your hands on your hips and slowly rotate your hips in big circles clockwise and counter-clockwise for about 15 seconds in each direction.

**In a game where a miss is as good as a mile,
an extra show of agility,
degree of flexibility, or burst of speed can make the difference
between Triumph and Defeat!**

Thigh Stretch

Lie on your left side. Pull your right foot to your butt by grabbing your ankle with your right hand. Keep your knees close together and hold for 10–15 seconds. Repeat with the other leg.

Calf Stretch / Achilles Tendon Stretch

Stand with one foot 2–3 feet in front of the other. With both feet pointing in the same direction you are facing, put most of your body weight on the leg that is behind you, stretching the calf muscle.

Now, bend the rear knee slightly. You should now feel the stretch in your heel. This stretch helps prevent achilles tendonitis, a severe injury that will sideline most paintball players for at least four to six weeks.

Hamstring Stretch

From the standing or sitting position, bend forward at the waist and touch your toes. Keep your back straight and slightly bend your knees. You should feel this stretching the back of your thighs near the connection of the leg and butt. Now, slowly straighten your legs, feeling the stretch travel down your leg and behind your knees. You have just stretched the entire hamstring. Hold both the straight leg and bent leg stretch for 15 seconds each.

Most people pull their hamstring at the top part of the leg (where it connects to the buttocks). By simply bending your knees while stretching, you will decrease your chances of suffering the most common injury to paintball players.

Groin/Inner Thigh Side Stretch

Stand with your legs spread and lean to the left. Keep the right leg straight while pointing the toes up. Repeat on the other side. This will help prevent groin strains, another common injury to paintball players who play speedball and games with a similar fast-paced tempo.

Hurdler Stretch

Sit on the floor with your legs straight in front of you. Bend your right knee and place the bottom of your foot on the inside of your opposite thigh. With your back straight, lean forward in order to stretch the back of your legs and lower back. Hold the stretch for 15 seconds, switch legs, and repeat.

Ilio Tibial Stretch

Sit on the ground with your legs crossed in front of you. Keeping your legs crossed, bring the top leg to your chest and bend it at the knee so that your foot is placed outside of your thigh. Hold for 15 seconds and repeat with the other leg.

You should perform this stretch before and after running. This will help prevent very common over-use injuries in the hips and knees.

Knees-to-Chest

Lie flat on your back. Pull your knees to your stomach and hold for 20 seconds. You should perform this stretch before and after any abdominal exercise.

As you may know, the lower back is the most commonly injured area of the body. Many lower back problems stem from inactivity, lack of flexibility, and improper lifting of heavy objects. Stretching and exercising your lower back will help prevent injuries to this extremely sensitive area.

Butterfly

Sit on your buttocks with your knees bent and the soles of your feet together. Grab your ankles and place both of your elbows on your inner thighs. Slowly push down on your thighs.

AND NOW YOU'RE READY TO RUMBLE

Underestimating the stress you put on your body when playing this game is a surefire way to get injured or develop chronic aches and pains. If you do these stretches every day, and always perform them before playing paintball, you will be doing yourself a huge favor.

Stewart Smith's Paintball Workout is available on our web site, GetFitNow.com, for those of you interested in the achieving the highest possible performance.

PAUL FOGAL ON FITNESS
Fitness Does Matter

"I think one of the beauties of paintball is that just about anybody can play because you can play to your level of fitness. If you're scared or you're slow or you have a disability or something, you can play a static defense. You can guard the flag. You can be a central source of communication. You have options people who aren't in the best shape don't have in other sports. And if you happen to be in great shape and you're real aggressive, then you can go out on offense and you can run.

It certainly helps to be in some kind of shape, because then you really have your choice of how you want to play. And, of course, small, quick people definitely have an advantage. It's harder to hit a quick and small target. You don't have to be in particularly great shape to enjoy paintball, but the better shape you're in, the more options you have."

Stretch out and you'll feel better before, during, and after you play!

Tactical Drills for the Beginner

TO KICK ASS, YOU MUST DRILL

Our goal in this chapter is to teach paintball playing basics. Of course, you can tailor paintball tactics drills as you see fit. The key is not merely to practice, but to practice the right things.

FIRST THINGS FIRST

Chronograph your paintgun to 285–290 feet per second (fps), the appropriate outdoor playing speed.

Each drill is a scenario. The object of each scenario is similar to what you will face on a normal playing day in both recreational and tournament play. Once you know the moves, you can repeat them with minimal effort. Think of them as "katas" of sorts.

Each drill should be performed from "both ends" if applicable. The idea is to combine all of the aspects of the game into your individual game. Even in a team setting, your individual moving, shooting, and communication skills will make or break a game.

SHOOTING DRILLS

You'll need the following supplies: Paper Plates (pie tins, frisbees, etc.), a stopwatch.

Obstacle course

Object—Run the course as fast as you can, hitting all the targets as you do so. This is a sample course, feel free to adjust it to your conditions and playing field. Just remember that the course should resemble a playing field as accurately as possible.

- On breakout, hit a 100 foot target

- From a bunker position, hit 75' and 50' targets

- Run to new bunker, shoot a 75' offhanded shot (lefty for right-handers, righty for left-handers)

- Run to new position, shooting at a positioned plate as you pass it. (This is called bunkering or a 'takedown').

- From new bunker, take offhand 50', 75' shots, then regular hand 50', 75' shots.

The Complete Guide to Paintball

- Take a 150' long shot from new position, then turn around for a 25' close shot.

- Stop watch at flag station bunker. Repeat the course until you improve your time and accuracy. Then change the course to give yourself a fresh challenge.

A SIMPLE RUN & SHOOT DRILL

Another simple Run & Shoot Drill is to set up a series of targets (in this case soda jugs hanging from a rope) and run past them, shooting as you go. Your motion, as well as the swinging of the jugs, makes this a particularly challenging drill.

Of course, you do have options . . .

Two player option: Follow the same course with a player shooting at you as you run through it.

Team option: On the same course, one player moves while the second gives cover fire. When the target is hit, the second player leapfrogs to the next position.

Pressure option: Same course, teammate runs course behind you. If you do not hit your target before your teammate does, your teammate is allowed to shoot you to get you to move.

BACKFOOT TACTICS DRILL

Timed Offense/Defense

Needed—At least 2 players, position of defense (such as a flag station or a building), flag, stopwatch.

Setup—3 attackers to 2 defenders or 2 attackers to 1 defender

Scenario—For each defender, put 1 minute and 30 seconds on the clock.

Goals
- Defense must prevent a flag pull.
- Offense must grab the flag and get away clean in the time allotted.
- Offense may set up anywhere beyond 150 feet of the defensive flag.
- Defense may set up anywhere within 150 feet of the flag, the closer the better.

Lessons
Offense—Must be aggressive when the numbers are in their favor, and learn to push hard under time pressure.

Defense—Learn how to be patient and kill a clock when outnumbered. Survival is the key, and staying in the game under pressure is hard.

This drill can also be used to simulate defending an opponents' flag station while they are trying to bring your flag in for a win. For this, do 3 on 1. Your solo guy gets a minute to set up. The aggressors have 2 minutes to hang the flag.

WORKING WITH BUNKERS

All bunkers "work" (or are worked) in the same manner. Flat-sided ones are easier to demonstrate on. The drills I'm highlighting here apply for use of trees, brambles, or any similar protection.

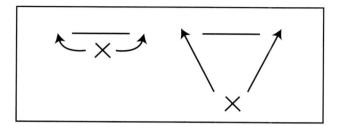

Take A Few Steps Back To Gain Perspective and Expand Your Field of Vision and Kill Zone

Get back if you can. You can cover more space with less effort.

Be Unpredictable

Move around in a position, because "Jack in the Boxes" get hit.

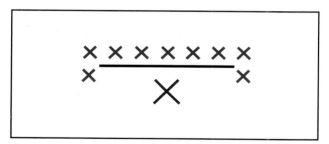

The little red markers represent all of the potential angles from which "X" can pop up and take shots at his opponents. Being unpredictable keeps your opponents waiting for your next move.

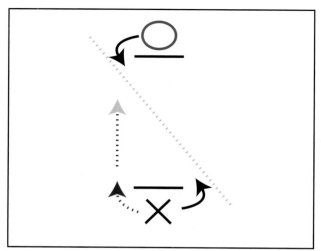

When "X" sees that "O" keeps emerging from the left side, he suspects his opponent is right-handed and relies too much on firing from the same place. They exchange fire along the pink line several times. Then, by shifting to the left side of his bunker and using his left hand, "X" surprises "O", and gets the elimination. "X" is right-handed, but he practices left-handed shooting to gain the advantage in scenarios like this one.

Downfall of the "Right Hand" Conspiracy

Actually, what we're talking about here has absolutely nothing to do with a conspiracy. It just happens to be the case that most people are right-handed and have a natural propensity to favor the right side of their bunker. From your perspective, that means most opponents will be emerging from the left side of their bunker. If you practice shooting with your off hand, you can make better use of your cover to eliminate your opponent.

This is pretty powerful knowledge, but you need to practice taking advantage of it!

Go the other way and take opponents out before they know what hit them.

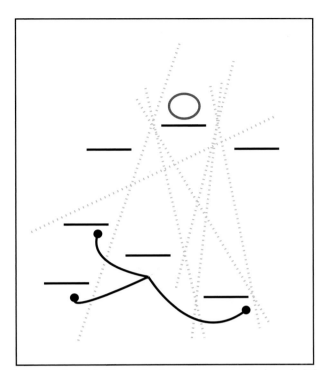

By moving behind different bunkers, even moving backwards, "X" is able to attain new angles of attack against "O." The dotted lines are shooting lanes that "X" can take advantage of if he's willing to take new positions.

Be Dynamic—Move From Bunker to Bunker To Gain New Angles of Attack

Use all the space you have available, even if it means falling back or shifting sideways. One person can take up a lot of space.

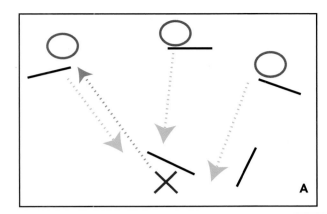

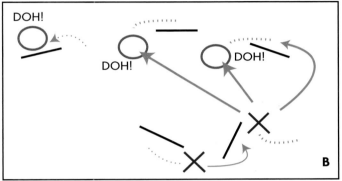

(A) "X" is in a tough spot. One moment, he's occupying two opponents. The next, he finds himself wide open to a flanking "O." While calling for support from teammates, "X" must act fast to maintain his position, using fire to literally "cover" his own position. This can't last for long!

(B) With support from a stealthy teammate who heard his coded plea for assistance, "X" is able to turn the opponents' perception of his weakness against them. As they move in for the kill, they are taken out by "X"'s flanking teammate. Now it's 2-on-1 in favor of our resourceful team "X" who quickly take new positions. Never give up!

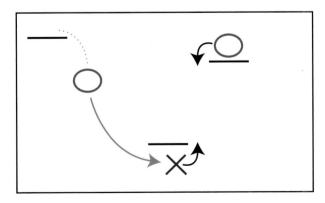

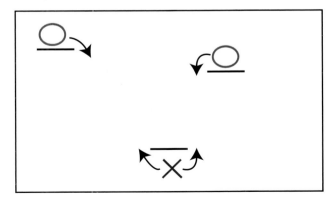

"X" is focused on the "O" right in front of him. This is exactly what Team "O" is counting on. A preoccupied "X" is easy to flank, as we can see from the first diagram. "X" is about to become "American History X."

A more mature "X" is moving in his bunker and looking for enemies on all sides. Here he has a good chance of keeping two opponents at bay, even taking them both out. Observe that if "X" has practiced using both left and right hands, he'll be more effective at keeping his opponents on their heels. Never stop moving behind your bunker. "X" should also communicate that he has two "O"'s in from of him and try to turn the tables on them with help from teammates! "X" may also want to try 'taking a few steps back' to facilitate handling this relatively precarious situation.

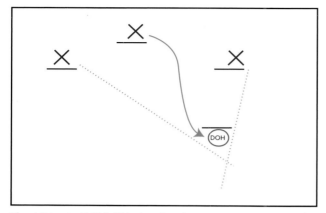

The Ultimate DOH! This is what happens to someone who doesn't communicate and doesn't play as part of a team. Or someone on a team that has been demolished!

If you're the only one left, and you find yourself completely overwhelmed, you still have options. As you can see, if "O" doesn't move, he's a goner. May as well try to take out as many of the opposition as he can!

Avoid tunnel vision!
In a bunker, keep looking and shooting both ways to keep your enemies at bay.

Look for natural holes in cover (like barrels) and shoot through them.

DELUSIONS OF INVINCIBILITY CAN BE USEFUL

Sometimes you need to act in a manner that others will perceive as incredibly daring and maybe even a little crazy. But in reality, a grand (or gutsy) move can blow open a game. Your opponents may fall into the trap of expecting you to be as cautious as they are. Suddenly, you're heading for an extremely aggressive position. They may get distracted by your audacity and pause before responding. If you pull it off, they'll feel demoralized and may be inclined to become preoccupied with your ominous position.

"I can't believe that guy just did that. What's he going to do next?"

This is just one of the questions that you can implant in the minds of your foe with a bold move!

Another benefit of this is that it takes the heat off of your teammates, who should be able to take better positions while the other team is second-guessing itself. Of course, you should scream at your team to do this if they're not responding promptly.

Aggression can be rewarded, as long as you are in control and know what is going on.

DRILLING FOR DOUBLES
Coordinating your game play with one other person makes you a double threat—both defensively and offensively. The following drills will enable you to practice basic coordination techniques that can lead to dramatic results in games. You'll take a couple of steps closer to an elevated understanding of paintball when you practice working in teams. Drilling 2-on-2 is a great way to work on coordinated offense and defense.

Low Man Approach With Cover
High man supplies cover by shooting over crawler. Crawler takes new position and shoots opponent.

Flank'em
One flanks left while other teammate shoots to keep opponent occupied and down. Flanker shoots opponent from new position.

Overbound
One moves, the other takes his place. This is called displacing. Keep moving up like the ends of a centipede.

Bait and Switch

Direct an opponent to one side of a bunker by shooting at one side consistently. It's human nature to move away from incoming fire, so this is likely to work. The opponent is likely to use the other side to "return fire."

Keep paint on the side your flanker is approaching to prevent your opponent from returning fire to that side and discovering your flanker. You are the bait. Your opponent will be flanked and eliminated in no time.

Overwhelming force

Having superior numbers does not guarantee victory. A patient and skilled opponent will pick your teammates off one by one if you're not careful and methodical about eliminating him. The idea is to get angles. The more sides of your opponent you shoot at, the less chance he has to hide behind cover to avoid you.

DO IT AGAIN!

Drills can be fun, but they are not ends in themselves. The point of doing drills is to improve your response to live game situations. **There's nothing as satisfying as bearing witness to your own improvement in paintball. The shortest path to that uplifting experience is a balance of frequent drilling and playing.**

—RR

Drills

Sarah's Drills 2Die4

Here are a few suggestions for drills
from an expert at drilling,
Sarah Stevenson of 2Die4!

Anyone can participate in paintball at any level regardless of size, sex, color, creed, beliefs, habits . . . basically, it's an open party. You don't even have to own your own gun or equipment! However, if you want to be any good at this game, you have to develop certain skills. The old adage about practice making perfect is as true in paintball as it is in any endeavor.

Paintball is a sport in which you cannot look at your opponent and assess them merely on a visual basis. This is primarily a marksmanship and reaction-type sport. So your opponent doesn't have to be the strongest or the fastest adversary to beat you. How do you gain an edge in this game? You must be tuned in to the game, have a full knowledge of your equipment, and play within your own physical abilities.

The whole idea of drills is to help improve your reaction time and target shooting ability. The following drills work very well with a few basic supplies. You will need the following items at your disposal: empty milk jugs or coffee cans, rope, and a stop watch.

Target Shooting

1. Place three targets approximately 15 feet apart and at different heights (place on top of bunkers and hang from trees).

2. Walk approximately 25 feet away and face away from the targets.

3. Count down, 3-2-1, spin, drop to one knee and (shooting only three times at each target) shoot left, center, right.

How many shots did it take to hit the targets? Which one was easier to hit than the others? After you have done this a few times, change the placement of the targets and your distance (either closer or farther away) and repeat it for a while. This drill will help you with your reaction time. When you have two players running at you and they are spaced apart, you won't hesitate to take them on and you'll have success.

Snap Shooting

1. Again, place a jug on top (or on the ground to one side) of the bunker.

2. Place yourself behind another bunker just opposite the target. Crouch on your knees and raise your gun to your shoulder, leaning close to the edge you wish to shoot from. Lean out very quickly, shoot no more than twice, and come back in to your bunker.

3. Repeat until you hit the target.

How many attempts did it take to hit the target? Now, start again, only this time lean out the opposite side from the one you did before. Practice right and left snap shooting. This is a very important drill. This exercise will save you more times than you can count. It applies in either woods play or indoor speedball.

One-on-One

1. Two players take the field at opposite ends, set your clocks for three minutes.

2. Face away from each other completely (gun and all)!

3. 3-2-1, GO! Turn and try and take out your opponent as quickly as you can!

The technique this drill practices helps players try and "rule-the-field." You must take control of the opposition as soon as you come out from your flag station. Start shooting at them, follow where they run to, and do not let them come out from their bunker to shoot at you! As you keep their heads in their bunker, you attempt to move up the field (never taking your eyes off their position), keeping other bunkers between you and your adversaries.

This does not mean that you must shoot at them all the time, but you must be prepared. Your gun should be raised at all times so you can shoot every time you see them move. Soon, you will be close enough to slow down your rate of fire, minimize movements, and watch for them to come out. Then, "WAP!" you got 'em!

After you practice this for a while, try a few two-on-ones, two-on-twos, three-on-ones, etc. This will help build you up to what it is like in a tournament level competition.

RUN & SHOOT

1. Set up a jug on top of a bunker or hang from a string to add motion and increase difficulty.

2. Walk approximately 15 yards away, face away from the target.

3. 3-2-1 countdown, turn and run, holding your gun in an upright position, and shoot at the jug.

At what point did you hit the target? How many shots did it take? Another twist to this is to put the jug in different positions—on the ground either to the right or left side of the bunker, "peeking" through a hole in the bunker, etc. Set up realistic scenarios and run through them until your accuracy and time improve.

Keep practicing and you'll earn the respect of your fellow players!

DRILLING FOR VICTORY

SNAP SHOOTING DRILL

If you have been placed into your bunker and cannot come out, snap shooting allows you to take one or two shots to get your opponent back into his bunker, giving you an opportunity to get out. It is important not to come out from the same spot twice in a row. You change the spots you come out from so opponents won't know where to expect you.

When practicing snap shooting drills, make sure you have someone there to point out areas you are leaving exposed (e.g., your hopper or elbows and knees).

GOOD FORM IS CRITICAL

Left, right, center, it doesn't matter where you come from as long as you never repeat the same pattern twice.

RUNNING MAN DRILL

The purpose of this drill is to learn how to shoot into the empty space that a target is going to enter just in time to hit it. This is called leading.

Use a live moving target—with that person's consent, of course—and stage it so he or she is running perpendicular to your position. Lead the person by putting a stream of paint into the direction they are moving, or over the bunker they are heading toward.

It is good to start at a distance of 100–150 feet. Shoot about 10–15 feet in front of your target, and have that daring soul run his or her fastest. There's no time factor in this exercise, but try to limit the number of rounds to about 20 per drill before starting over.

Drilled Running Man

By increasing the angle of your barrel, you will be able to increase the distance your paintballs will fly. At some point, of course, you shorten the distance the paintball will travel, but increase the slope of its descent.

LONG DISTANCE SHOOTING DRILL

When practicing long distance shooting drills, set up a target 200–210 feet in front of you. Limit the number of rounds in the hopper to time the drill and the number of shots you take. This drill teaches players how to control the arc of their ball so they can get the maximum range out of their shooting skill. Being a long distance shooter with accuracy is a fast track to legendary status in paintball lore.

At 200 feet, paintballs don't break that easily, as Steve points out. The longer the ball is in the air, the less energy it will have on impact.

Hopper Loading Drill

Learn to load your hopper without taking your eyes off the action. At first, perform this drill with an empty hopper and empty guppies. Get the motion down first before using paint (to avoid getting it dirty). With one hand holding your gun, perform your loading routine as follows:

A. Pop your loader's lid open.

B. Reach behind you and open your velcro harness.

C. Firmly grab a full guppy and bring it forward.

D. Pop the guppy's lid with your thumb.

E. Dump paint into your loader.

F. With the bottom of the now empty guppy, flip the loader's lid closed and snap the lid tight.

G. Toss the guppy aside and resume firing.

NOTE: This should be one smooth continuous motion. Practice until you get it right! Practice while you watch your favorite television shows and time yourself.

Blind Shooting Drill

There are times in a game where you are shooting without a clear view of your target. In these cases, you are "shooting blind." Blind shooting can be an effective shooting technique. The key is learning to identify a reference point that you can see from your firing position that relates directly to your opponent's position. This way you can stay safe in your bunker while you rain paint down on your opponent's head. He'll get dumped with paint and you can move on to your next unwitting target.

To practice, you and your buddy face off in opposite bunkers. From a quick peek, see if there is an object directly in line with their position. In these photos, you'll notice a tree directly behind your opponent's position in the background. Now, from the safe haven of your bunker, lay a stream of paint in the direction of the tree without overexposing yourself to return fire. Change the angle of your barrel to increase or decrease the range of your fire. By getting used to the feel of blind shooting in this manner, you'll increase your chances of survival, and become more of an offensive threat.

Out of paint?
Keep shooting anyway. The sound will keep your opponents' heads down while your teammates gain advantageous positions.

Out of air?
Throw paintballs. Heck, it'll keep them guessing and one just might break!

PART 5
TACTICS

A.C.T.

**Rob Rubin's Customized Approach to
Essential Paintball Tactics**

"GETTING" PAINTBALL

When you first start playing paintball, you're literally bombarded with suggestions, advice, and ideas about the game. As is the case with most new players in any sport, it's easy to get overwhelmed just trying to keep up.

There's an easy way around "Information Overload."

You see, I've done a little work to fix this problem. And the good news for you is that paintball can be boiled down to a simple formula that's not only easy to remember, but even easier to carry out.

I call this "The Triad." It will carry you very far in your pursuit of paintball fun. You see, the game is only fun up to the point of elimination. Learning tactics is about learning how to stay in the game.

And the core of paintball tactics is the Triad.

Here it is.

A.C.T.-UNG
Baby!

"Angles" "Communications" "Teamwork"

These are the three basics of paintball, "A.C.T." for short. That's all you need to know. This may sound simplistic, but even professional teams are always working on these three basic principles. Forget the gizmos, forget the gadgets, forget the tech-talk. These are the nuts and bolts of the game. If you want to be somewhere between competent and excellent at paintball, you must master "the Triad."

Why "The Triad"?

Much like a tripod, this particular trio of paintball skills works only as a whole. When you play them all, you get a whole game. It's easier to explain how they interconnect by looking at them in reverse order.

Do It For the Team

Teamwork can be as complex as 10 players moving as one mind, or as simple as finding a buddy and moving together up the tapeline. A second pair of eyes is invaluable, and a second shooter on a target can be the difference between wasting your time and eliminating your opponent.

Teamwork doesn't mean you're on top of one another, but it does mean you're working together for a common goal. One player is shooting at the opponent, the other player is advancing on him. That's great teamwork. One player is yelling positions, the other players are listening and moving accordingly. That's effective teamwork.

You can even have teamwork when you don't know anyone you're playing with!

In open fields or speedball games, I'll be the fool yelling his head off about where I saw players running to, or where they have people positioned. Why? Someone has to, and it may as well be me. Something as simple as "three right, four left, two center" tells your team how they stack up against their foes. Communication accomplishes teamwork.

Communication = Effective Yelling

Sure, anyone can yell their lungs out. But it's effective yelling that makes the difference. Remember that teamwork thing? Here's the second part of it—communication.

Once you've buddied up, or you've decided to be a 'caller,' don't be shy. If you need some help, a simple "Help here!" gets the message across. You can get someone to move up to help you, or flank around to eliminate the opposing player who's shooting at you, and a lot of other things, too.

New players often try to be stealthy, and that works up to a point. One of my rules of thumb: "Once the other team shoots at you, don't bother trying to hide anymore." They've spotted you. It's useless to hide now. What you want to do immediately is get another player to help you out. Give them as much information as you can. For example:

"There are two guys in that bunker! Can you swing around and shoot them?" This brings us to the third leg—angles.

Angles

The term 'angles' covers moving, maneuvering, crawling, leaping, getting skinny behind a tree, and getting into a bunker so the other team can't occupy it.

Paintball is partially a game of real-estate, and getting angles is the way you use real-estate effectively. As an individual player, you want to take advantage of opponents who get 'tunnel vision' (players fixated on what's in front of them) by moving up on their flanks. A tree can only protect from so many directions at a given moment. The key is getting to an angle that renders your opponent's tree useless.

Your most frequent use of angles is to support your teammates. Most shoot-outs take place head on, meaning face to face. The idea behind 'angles' is to get to the side of your opponent while your teammate keeps your opponent's attention. After you make that key elimination, your teammate begins to move up while you support his advance similarly.

Pretty cool, isn't it?

You may already be starting to see the pattern. You can't "do" one part of the Triad well without doing the other two simultaneously.

- If you don't communicate, your teammates won't know you need them to take a better angle on the player shooting at you.

- If your team won't move to better angles, your teamwork breaks down and you get eliminated quickly.

- If you don't work together at all, you'll find the day frustrating, because your team won't communicate and move together in any way.

A.C.T. is a simple formula, and it encompasses the essence of what you need to do to qualify as a great player. It's also adaptable to your later paintball games as well. The concept of "angles" includes 'back doors' and 'key bunkers' and seeing holes in your opponent's line. Simple "communications" later become your team codes. And "teamwork" becomes the backbone of your game.

Putting It All Together

Eventually you combine the elements of the Triad into complex "Swing" moves and "Sweep" maneuvers.

For example, the "Two Man Swing" uses all of "A.C.T." in rapid order. Your buddy starts by telling you the opponent's position (communication), you start shooting to keep your opponent's head down (teamwork) as your buddy moves up (angles), you continue to feed your buddy information about where the opponent is (communications/teamwork) as he slides into his new position (angles). Your buddy begins to shoot (teamwork) and tell you where the opponent is leaning out of (communications) as you move up (angles) to get the elimination.

All of this may occur within ten seconds.

For now, don't worry about achieving that level of play. It takes practice, a good memory, and adventurous spirit to get good at this game. All of that takes time.

For now, have a good time! Enjoy yourself! Try to remember to "A.C.T." Write it on the back of your hand if need be. Talk to your teammates about it, too. It's something that everyone and anyone can do with a little effort.

—RR

Once you have the Triad down, you'll be amazed how fast it can improve your game.

Opening Moves

Military strategy and tactics and paintball, for the most part, do not mix. Military jargon has been adopted by players out of convenience, but the principles of war do not really apply to the game. However, there is at least one aspect of paintball that mirrors almost exactly its military counterpart—the use of surprise.

Napoleon (among many other legendary military commanders) believed that the effect of surprise is the equivalent of having an army ten times its actual size.

Surprise is a critical aspect of tactics and it comes in two flavors—complete surprise and plain vanilla surprise.

Complete and total surprise is an elusive, ideal kind of thing, which doesn't really exist in paintball. At the very least, the other team knows the terrain, your objective, the size of your team, the length of the encounter, and when the contest will start. That's quite a bit of handy information. You can, however, achieve something close to complete 'paintball' surprise, but only at the very beginning of the game.

AT THE BREAK

It is only during the first few crucial seconds that the other team has no idea where you are going to go or what you are going to do. Once the game starts, after no more than about 30 seconds, the other team will at least know where a few of your players are. This is one reason why good teams and players spend more time figuring out their initial move than any other part of the game. The 'Break,' the moment at which a game begins, is your only chance to catch the other team with their pants down around their ankles.

After those first few seconds have passed, you can only hope to achieve vanilla surprises; these would be things like suddenly moving players from one side of the field to the other, a crawler getting into the midst of the other team's positions and spreading havoc, or a sudden push on a section of the field.

THE FIRST STEPS

The start, or opening move of a game, is an all or nothing affair, just like an opening move in chess. How you begin determines the entire outcome of the game: the countermoves your opponent makes and your counters to those countermoves, ad infinitum.

Two very important factors are set at the beginning: what terrain you choose and how you use your players, assuming you are the team captain. You can decide to take positions deep into the field (seizing portions of your opponent's half of the field); you can take terrain at the fifty (the mid-way point); or you can play the terrain

'short'—that is, take much less than your 'half' at the outset.

How you use your players depends partially (but not entirely) on the terrain itself, but more importantly it depends upon the tone of the game you wish to play. Playing an aggressive game generally means that you will commit most or all of your players from the beginning. Committing players means (1) you have given them a job to perform that will occupy all of their effort, and (2) it will be extremely difficult to position them. Playing a defensive game means that you will commit few to none of your players. And, of course, there is the very common tactic of taking those positions that must be taken and then waiting to see what happens, which is essentially a 'middle' strategy.

The three basic methods of playing the terrain and the three basic ways in which you use your players can be mixed and matched for an almost inexhaustible variety of game plans. Some real-world examples may serve to illustrate this.

- During an NPPL tournament game in Chicago, Bob Long sent one of his players to an aggressive location, well over the fifty, on his left tape—an aggressive, deep-field position. He then had that player tuck in, knowing that the other team would be forced to try to take him out. The final outcome was that the Ironmen's opponents lost four players in trying to eliminate the one player Bob had committed.

- At an NPPL in Boston, Renick Miller's Aftershock committed one player to a kamikaze charge down one tape, merely to attract the attention of the other team; this player was covered by two players on that side of the field who moved to about the fifty and then dug in. Meanwhile, the remainder of the team had been sent to the fifty across the middle and other side of the field in a 'waiting' posture. Once they saw the other team commit to attacking the sacrificed

player, the Aftershock players in the middle pushed.

- At an NPPL World Cup in New York, the All Americans received the disadvantaged side of the field and were forced to play in a defensive posture from the beginning of the game; they committed no one to any specific action, but remained loose and mobile, stretched across the field just shy of the fifty, until opportunity came knocking. One bunker move led to another, and they handily won the game.

All of these plays were programmed from the outset of the game, based on the terrain, what the competitors wanted to achieve, and who their opponents were. These opening moves also were based on an honest evaluation of the limitations placed on each team, limitations created by the skill level of their players, by the nature of the terrain, or both.

Let's review the basic advantages and disadvantages of each of these strategies.

PLAYING THE FIELD

Aggressive—Deep Penetration

- Advantages—Surprises the other team, happens very quickly, adding confusion to the mix, and ends a game (one way or the other) quickly.

- Disadvantages—Concentrates a lot of your players in exposed positions; requires you to have 100% aggressive players; must be carried through no matter what, and ends a game (one way or the other) quickly.

Middle Ground—"Taking the Fifty"

- Advantages—As much terrain is taken as possible, without undue risk to players.

- Disadvantages—The other team knows (or should know) all the angles and how to play this area of the field better than just about any other area of the field.

Defensive—Playing the Field Short

- Advantages—Players can get set in position very quickly. Opponents are dealt with on terrain which is less familiar to them; typically opponents will not know shooting angles and will not have any pre-set positions to use.

- Disadvantages—Very little room for maneuver. No place to retreat. Usually restricts players to 'reacting' to opponents' moves.

In general, determining what 'mix' of playing styles to use depends upon what you and your teammates want to accomplish, and how much (or how little) the terrain of a given field will support those opening objectives. It would be foolish to overextend your players past the fifty, if there is nowhere for them to go once they get there.

The objective of an opening move is to prepare your team for the anticipated actions of your opponents and/or (and this is an important distinction) to place your players where they will be able to support your plan for the remainder of the game.

In order to practice these kinds of opening moves, you should constantly look for fields and games that will allow you to test different openings. For example, you can find the fast players on your team (or in your group) and, when playing on a field that has good cover over the fifty yard line, create a plan that pushes some of those players into that cover. Set the remainder of your players in positions that will support the forward players—some shooters who can pick off the opponents who will try to take your forward players out, some defenders on the other side of the field in strong 'hold' positions, a small reserve of players who can follow up on any push that your forward players may make.

On a field that offers good cover on your end of the field, practice setting up an ambush and playing the field short.

If you don't have any idea what a full-bore charge down one tape is like, pick a good field and give it a shot.

If you are playing tournament ball, remember that the number one rule for opening moves is to 'play the field,' not your opponents; it is far easier to analyze terrain before the game than it is to guess what your opponents will do.

-SD

© Cleo Fogal

Smart ideas work, bad ideas don't.

Back to Basics

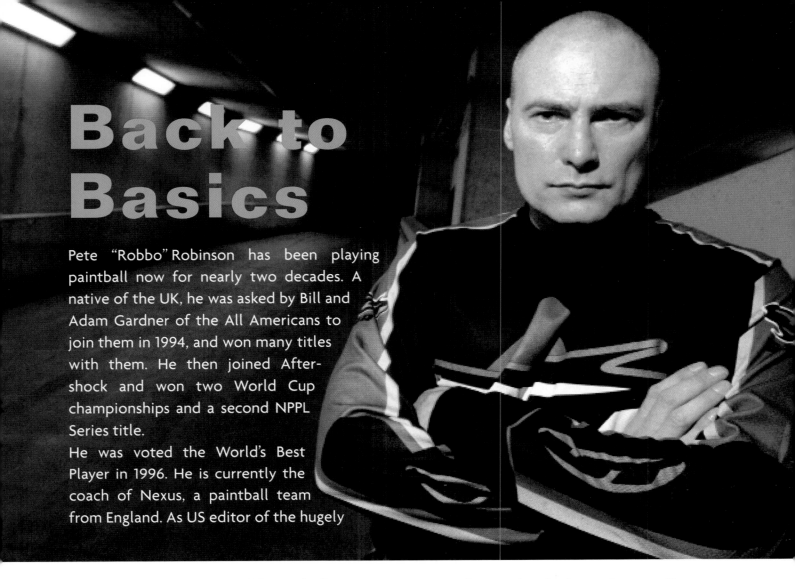

Pete "Robbo" Robinson has been playing paintball now for nearly two decades. A native of the UK, he was asked by Bill and Adam Gardner of the All Americans to join them in 1994, and won many titles with them. He then joined Aftershock and won two World Cup championships and a second NPPL Series title.

He was voted the World's Best Player in 1996. He is currently the coach of Nexus, a paintball team from England. As US editor of the hugely successful *Paintball Games International Magazine,* he has written well over 100 articles spanning ten years of playing professional paintball. It's definitely time to tune in.

THE ONLY WAY TO PLAY PAINTBALL IS TO STAY IN THE GAME

In paintball, there are many people who have opinions about how the game should be played. You will hear and read about numerous theories and approaches, most of which are either unworkable or pretentious.

The game of paintball in its most basic form is the art of eliminating opponents without getting shot. The definitive attribute of a good player, therefore, is his or her ability to stay in the game and eliminate opponents. You will notice that I put staying in the game first. That has to take precedence over all else in the game of paintball. What is the point of being the best shot in the world when you're standing on the sidelines?

It may seem simplistic to say that to become a good player all you have to do is think about staying in the game, but it is neither simple nor easy to keep yourself in the game on a consistent basis.

Let's clarify a few points. The techniques I will be discussing are wholly applicable to all levels of paintball. Whether you are a first time rec-baller, amateur, or pro matters not.

THE TECHNICAL AND THE TACTICAL

The tactical relates to those actions of the team decided upon before the game has started (i.e., whether you push one flank, or five players run down the middle). Anything involving predetermining players' actions on the field is tactical.

That said, however, I must say that the most important part of playing paintball, by far, is the technical component.

Good technical play defeats good tactics!

Techniques are actions a player undertakes to make sure he stays alive while endeavoring to eliminate the opposition. Basically, when you see a player behind a bunker snap shooting, ducking in and out, firing his gun from different spots at different times, you're watching someone employing techniques to enhance the effectiveness of his play.

The Principle of Paintball Technique
You must do all you can so that when you do shoot your gun, you give your opponents the least possible opportunity to eliminate you from the game.

The Complete Guide to Paintball

ESSENTIALS OF TECHNICAL PLAY

Now, let's just run through some hypothetical situations. Imagine a player who sits behind a bunker and never shoots his gun. What is the likelihood he will be eliminated?

The only way this guy would be eliminated is if someone runs over and bunkers him. Stands to reason, right? Nobody else can shoot him because he never breaks cover to fire his gun.

From this we can readily infer that a bunker provides a safe haven. At the same time, it is of no use just to sit there without firing your gun. To win the game, the player has to break cover and endeavor to eliminate opponents or, at the very least, provide suppressive fire.

Herein lies the central problem in paintball. As soon as you come out of cover, you are vulnerable. This fact forms the genesis of the whole philosophy of technical play.

No technique is fail-safe, but good technique can drastically reduce your rate of elimination.

Believe it or not, this is the secret of playing this game on the highest level. The ability to practice this philosophy separates the good players from the great players, great teams from championship teams.

Let me explain why.

If all ten players on a team were to practice the philosophy of play I advocate (i.e., to concentrate 100% on not being shot rather than allowing the secondary need of eliminating opposition to determine actions) then, by definition, the average life of the team as a whole would increase. Furthermore, if players spend more time in the game, that also means that, as a team, they are firing more paint than the opposition. That increases their chances of eliminating the opposition and winning the game.

So you can see that by getting

your team to concentrate on technical aspects of play, everything else seems to fall into place. Even if you're not on a team, it should be clear to you that honing your technique will enable you to survive longer when you're on a losing team, and may make victory possible when you're outnumbered.

A LOOK AT THE ACTUAL TECHNIQUES!

Now that we have established the importance of technical play, we have to look at what those techniques are, in terms of what to do and what not to do.

We can reduce the game of paintball to ten one-on-ones. For the moment, I am using a ten man tournament team as an example, although what is to be discussed is wholly applicable to players at all levels.

If a target player is beading on me (i.e., lining his gun up on me and occasionally firing when I come out to fire at him), then there are a couple of things to remember.

First of all, never come out into an incoming stream of paint. Seems obvious, but you would be surprised just how many mugs do it. You have to wait until your opponent stops firing at you. Alternatively, you can move to the other side of the bunker, but this normally means you will be shooting back-handed, so I will ignore that option for the moment.

If you are right-handed, I take it for granted that you are shooting out of the right hand side of the bunker as you look at it. The reason is obvious; you show a minimum profile to your opponents if you shoot this way. That brings us to snap shooting.

Snap Shooting 101

Accepting that we never break cover into a stream of paint, we now have to create an opportunity to fire at our target. When your opponent stops firing, the best technique is to snap shoot your way into dominance. If your opponent is lined up and just waiting for you to come out, then this is what you should do.

Get in to your mind the approximate location of your opponent. You can do this quite easily by taking a quick look in the direction from which the sound of your opponent's gun is coming. You should already have a good sense of his location because you know he's generally going to be sitting behind a bunker just like yours.

Once you have established his location, then get yourself set to roll out of cover with an upper-body roll movement.

This takes a bit of practice, but generally I would sit with my legs in front of me, usually bent in front of my chest, in a position behind the bunker that just allows me to be safe. In other words, if I were to lean slightly outwards to the right, my opponent could eliminate me, but with a slight roll back in, he would not be able to see me, let alone tag me.

When you're set, roll out, fire two shots, and immediately roll back in. The reason for this rapid-movement, minimal-fire approach is simple. If your opponent has indeed lined up where you're likely to emerge, you have to take a shot at him and get behind cover before you get hit. That's not long at all; if you only shoot twice and roll back in, there is no way that your opponent can react in time to eliminate you. The window of opportunity you gave him is just too small, he will always be one step off the pace you are setting.

If you adhere to this technique, the only way you can get tagged is if your opponent fires randomly and gets lucky.

If you roll out of cover, and a paintball is already winging it's way over to you, you're a goner!

So there remain now two possibilities in this interaction.
1. You eliminate him by snap shooting
2. You have to modify your technique slightly

As you roll in and out of cover and fire your

two-shot bursts, you are relying on a fair amount of luck to get your elimination. Nevertheless, many players are eliminated this way.

The reason you have to roll in and out of cover is because your opponent has the drop on you.

The key here is to turn the tables and get the drop on him!

At present, it looks as though he controls things by making you snap shoot, but what if we could push him back into cover leaving us to line up on him?

To put your opponent on the defensive, you must do two things when you come out to snap shoot. First, watch as you roll back into cover; you are looking for any movement of your opponent that suggests your two shots are so accurate that they forced him to get back behind his bunker. Secondly, listen carefully, because if you hear no shots coming back at you right away, it's likely that you forced him back, but failed to see it.

If you are looking for them, these two clues give you a chance to establish control of the situation. If you take advantage of them, you can line up on the guy who thought he had you right where he wanted you!

Suppress your opponent with protracted fire enabling one of your teammates to bunker him. At the very least, keep him out of the game with continuous shooting.

The big advantage in lining up an opponent is that you get a chance to 'read' all of his movements. After observing him for a while, you'll find that he becomes predictable. This predictability will eventually be his downfall. Be patient and persistent, and you'll know this fine feeling.

In everything having to do with paintball technique, the key is concentration. You must concentrate on staying tight to your cover and on timing your retaliatory fire.

This is the way to optimize your chances of eliminating your opponent and minimize your chances of getting shot.

We have now covered two of the most fundamental aspects of paintball technique. Whether you are an experienced pro or a first timer, staying tight and timing your shots will transform your game overnight.

-PR

© Cleo Fogal

The Complete Guide to Paintball

VISUALIZATION TECHNIQUES

Photo by Rigo Ramirez, © JT USA 2004

Visualization Techniques

Albert Einstein once said that imagination was more important than knowledge. "Knowledge is limited," he said. "Imagination encompasses the whole universe." With that in mind, let's talk about your imagination, and how to harness it for sports performance. Lately it's been termed "sports psychology," but what it really comes down to is the use of visualization techniques.

Visualization techniques require that you use your imagination. Before you write it off as being stupid, put this into your brain: baseball players, football players, downhill skiers, martial artists, and most other serous athletes use visualization as a part of their training. In some cases, it's a matter of being cheaper (sky divers and sky surfers perform what's called a "dirt dive" to practice formations they will do in the air before they jump from the airplane). In others, an athlete can be out of commission due to injury and unable to actually play.

Training Your Mind

To begin, here's a brief introduction to the techniques you'll be using later on. The first is the ability to see things with your mind. Everybody has this ability. For example, if someone told you to picture a pencil in your mind, you would not have a hard time doing it. More than likely, you'll see a long cylindrical object used to mark paper. The trick to using visualization techniques is to be able to visualize the same pencil, but change the eraser's color to yellow, or green, or blue, or any other color for that matter.

What I'm trying to get you to do, is to play with your own imagination a bit, and get used to manipulating things in your minds eye without actually touching them. If you can get to the point where you can mentally tie pencils into knots, you'll have something. The reason this is important is that once you can manipulate things in your mind, you can also start to play in the realm of "what if" and "how can I . . ." Starting with basic items like pencils is a good way to begin.

Seeing the Shot

The true power of visualization is the ability to play games or game segments in your mind. The logical question is "Why?" It's a fair one. Why would you pretend to play paintball when you can really play paintball? The best way to answer that is with an example.

Playing with Palmerized last year at the Knoxville indoor was a real treat. The first day of the 5-man event, I had the chance to walk the field along with everyone else. Up until then, I really had never seen

a purpose to walking a field. I always play cold, I preferred to play cold. The 'Point me to a bunker and I'll get there' kind of thing. But I was there, I figured I may as well walk the fields.

I took some time looking over the corner bunkers, and where my moves would be once I started to move up. From one layer back of the corner bunker I stood to the outside, and visualized the view from the other side of the field into my current position. And in my mind's eye, I could see the view from the other side of the field. I visualized the angle at which you would have to lean out in order to stay mostly protected from the flag area and still shoot into the center dish at the opponent. Even though my view was blocked physically from that angle, I visualized where that spot would be.

Then I looked up field into the barricades, and saw a small gap. It was like kicking a field goal. The left and right poles I had to shoot through were separate bunkers, and I would have to just barely clear the top of both bunkers to land the paint where it needed to go, but there it was. It was a

hole about six inches wide that ended up putting paint on the outside of that key bunker. I could visualize the range of the Stroker, and the arc of paint it would take to hit a kneeling player that I couldn't see. I figured it could work, and I kept it in mind. In the first game I played that morning, I took out an opponent who had stuck his body into my gap, trying to shoot at our guy in the center. I never saw my paint hit him, but I saw a referee get all excited because a player right in front of him took one to the head. All these angles were seen before shooting a single ball on the field.

What I did was play a game segment in my head, visualizing the outcome based on what I knew already. Some would call it good field walking, and in fact, a lot of field walking is visualization. It's the easiest way to take the idea of visualization and put it into your game immediately. Before a single ball is fired, you can try plays and angles. It also has the advantage that you can do all this without showing your opponents what you have planned.

The key to doing this type of visualization is having the ability to see both ends of the field at once, or at least having a sort of overhead view of a field in your mind. Many of the arenas now have a way to physically stand over the field, and look down on it. If you can keep this kind of overhead map in your mind's eye while walking a field, you can see angles on one side of the field while standing on the other.

Doing this kind of visualization also helps you find bunkers that really offer you minimal protection or offer no advantage in field position for your team. While walking the fields, you need to visualize your angles of shooting out at your opponents while sitting or kneeling in a bunker, and who can shoot at you. While in there, try to see it from the other side of the field; are you an easy target? This is a lot of head work, I know, but when you hit your spots perfectly, it's all worth it.

Playing the Scenario

Another type of visualization you can use before you play is running through set plays in your mind. Robbo keeps on talking about "set plays" being the wave of the future, so let's implement it to a degree. To do this, you need to envision your favorite field. You know, the local field that you go to all the time and could probably play blindfolded. Yes, that one. Now we're going to design a set play using visualization techniques.

I may go way over all of your heads here, but stay with me. Right from the break, picture going up to a bunker on the left side of the field that's about half way up the field. How would you get there? Are there any barricades further up the field to block your opponents from shooting at you? Can you run behind any bunkers on your side of the field to mask your movement?

Now for the more interesting concepts and questions: Are there any opportunities to run a path or a route that isn't usually taken? This is what takes a lot of practice on your part. Can you place in your mind's eye positions that are off the beaten trails of that field in order to make it to that central bunker? On concept fields this really is hard to do, but in the woods it's always an option.

Off the break is easy to visualize, but trying to see where you can go while in game is always more difficult. There are a lot of variables, most of which you can't really control. Where did the other team set up? Which way are they looking? Where are your teammates at any given moment? You can't predict every variable, no matter how well you can visualize things. Instead, use visualization to see a more complete view of the field when a game is over. Part of paintball is the BS sessions between games. Even if you don't believe half of what you hear, listen to where people were. What bunkers did they take? What about their teammates? This is important because it will help you visualize more of the overall game. Once you know where everyone was, you can then figure out what you could

have done, and then implement it the next game. Could you have made that move to the next position? Was the snake really cleared? Knowing there was only one person in front of you, would you have made that move on him?

You can also use visualization techniques like this to practice moving up as well. For example, some players like to think of how they can move up to a bunker position using someone else's move. They visualize how fast they can run, the distance between bunkers, and the likelihood they'll get shot at while running. Those players do that to make moves automatic in their minds. They don't have to think about making those moves, they just do it. This is part of building an instinct for the game that will help you overall. Some say you can't train for instinct, but you can by becoming more accustomed to moving in response to things hap-

pening on the field. And the easiest way to train your mind to respond is to visualize scenarios and play them out in your head.

All of this sounds like heady stuff; but when you see some guy looking up field before a game, and you can see his hand moving like a guide, or his head slightly nodding left to right, he's visualizing his opening move. It's really easy to pick up, and it can help your game with a minimal effort. You just need to open your mind to something intangible, and use your imagination.

—Rob "Tyger" Rubin

Mapping Your Game Plan

The Fake and Push

The fake and the push can be used on any field, but must be adjusted according to terrain. A critical component of this and any game plan is that your team should walk onto the field together. Each player must examine his own bunker and firing lanes. Both sides of the field must be walked. It is important to know what positions the opposing team may take. This will help you calculate the firing lanes and angles available from your bunker. This is the time to take note of bunkers that facilitate a pinch play. You and the other player on your team with the pinch shot must work together. Another important thing to keep in mind is that you may want to use the bunkers on the other side of the field as you advance. In this particular game plan the primary objectives are A5, B5, A3, and B3. A5 should be taken by the fastest tape runner. The back player, A1, has found a good shooting lane that cuts off the right side of the field. This lane cuts between bunkers and will be called Zone.

1. The objective for A1 is to eliminate player B3 at the break of the game. The objective for the players on the right side of the field is to eliminate player B5.

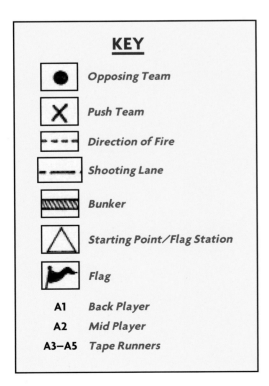

KEY

●	*Opposing Team*
✕	*Push Team*
- - -	*Direction of Fire*
— —	*Shooting Lane*
▨	*Bunker*
△	*Starting Point/Flag Station*
🏴	*Flag*
A1	*Back Player*
A2	*Mid Player*
A3–A5	*Tape Runners*

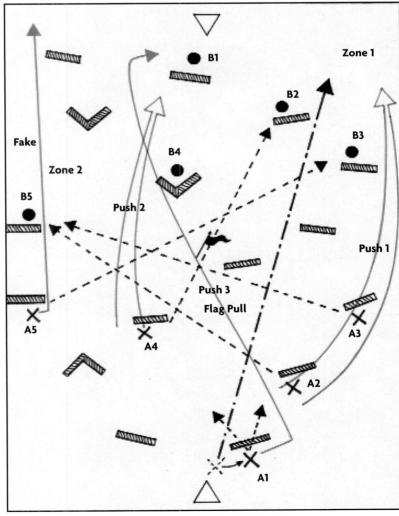

2. Players B1 and B4 are not much of a factor in this game plan. As the back players signal, player A5 runs down the tape line. If player B5 is still in the game, A5 should eliminate him as he passes. A5 continues to run to the back corner of the field. This will cause the opposing team to turn in panic toward A5. It should be noted that if A5 had been eliminated prior to the signal, A4 would fill in. This is called a fake. A5 will most likely be hit performing this move. If he isn't, the opposing team has a huge problem. Timing is essential for this to work. Once A5 has begun his run, A2 and A3 should take advantage of the commotion and push the opposite side of the field. If the game plan has worked they should be able to eliminate some of the opposing team by shooting them in the back. Their primary objective would be to eliminate players B3, B2, and B1 in that order. A2 and A3 have now turned the remaining opposing players toward their side of the field. A4 should leave after A2 and A3. He should be advancing up the same side of the field as A5. His main objective is to eliminate player B4 and anyone else who remains. A1 follows A4 up the field. He should cross centerfield, picking up the flag as he advances. If the other players have done their job, all that is left for A1 to do is to hang the flag. This game plan incorporates four separate pushes. It is designed to keep the opposing team off balance. If it is executed well, the opposing team will be eliminated before they know what hit them. This is a very aggressive game plan. It is not simple to execute. If one player is too early (or late), the game plan may disintegrate, leaving the opposing team with the upper hand.

Shooting Lanes

Shooting lanes should be chosen during field walking. The basic idea is to find a bunker on the opponent's side of the field that is key to their

game plan. Then find a way to eliminate the player who plans on getting into that bunker. The ideal shooting lane is a line of fire devoid of obstacles. The line of fire should drop the paint into the opposing player's running lane. In this example, player A1 shoots for Zone 1, dropping a line of paint into the path of B2 and B3. Mid player A2 stops half way to his bunker and fires into Zone 2, hoping to eliminate B3. This means that player B3 must cross two shooting lanes. This technique is used to increase the chances of eliminating a key player. Once B2 and B3 are in their bunkers (or eliminated), A1 and A2 need to take cover in their bunkers. Example 2 (shown in red) depicts 2 players firing in

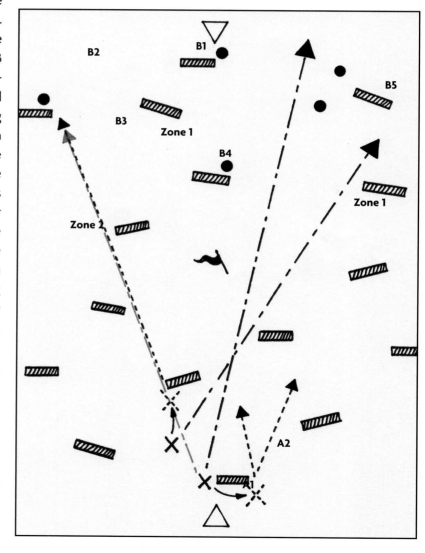

the same lane. This should only be done for an extremely key bunker. Player B5 must cross a firing lane with twice as much paint traversing it. This choice of firing lanes increases the chances of eliminating player B5. Hit or miss, A1 and A2 should get into their bunkers after B5 has passed the firing lane.

Keep in mind that shooting lanes are a great tool. They are not, however, foolproof. There is a certain amount of luck involved. This is a skill-based plan that should be practiced like any other. The back player using the lane needs to get a feel for the appropriate height to aim for. One trick to try is to aim at hip height at the entrance to the bunker. Even if the player comes in low he will usually not be below that point.

—MS

New Players' Guide to Cover

"Work your bunker." "Get angles from your bunker." "Slide out of your cover."

What does it all mean?

Cover is . . . "Anything that protects or shields from harm, loss, or danger."

In paintball, anything between you and an opponent that will stop, disable or render useless a fired paintball is considered "cover."

There are two basic types:

1. "Hard" cover includes medium- to large-sized trees, rocks, and bunkers.
2. "Soft" cover is like grass, small trees, and shrubs.

Both types serve the same function, but you'll learn to use them differently.

Let's tackle hard cover first. Virtually all speedball fields are exclusively hard cover. Meaning there's a very solid object between you and the other guys. Big trees, rocks, and bunkers are solid cover from incoming paintballs. Some fields have berms, hills, and other terrain features that qualify as hard cover.

A berm is a ledge or space between the ditch and parapet in a fortification.

Anything solid you can place your body behind is hard cover. Seeing as most game situations involve bunkers (especially on speedball fields), I'll stick to using that term generically. Do a little mental dance and bunker becomes tree becomes rock becomes fort becomes wall becomes inflatable becomes corrugated piping becomes car becomes anything and everything solid. (Whew!)

I'll avoid the finer points of moving into a bunker. That's dependent on your speed and fitness level. Let's focus on what you do once you're in position. A common mistake is to get as close as you can to your bunker no matter where you are on the field and pop out for eliminations. It's not really a mistake, I guess. It made sense to me when I was new to the game, too. But, after studying videos, watching the experts play, talking to some of the best players I know, and reading stories about other players' approaches, it becomes obvious that this isn't necessarily what you always want to do.

Using Cover in Context

It remains true that the closer to the action you are, the closer to the inside of your bunker you want to be. If you're relatively far away from the action, you can afford to move farther back from your bunker. It's called "sliding back" or "sliding out." This is useful because from farther behind a position, you can control more of the field laterally without overexposing yourself to your opponents. You can watch their movements from a good position and still use bunkers to maximize protection. If your opponents get closer, it's only a matter of moving up a few feet forward into your bunker to counter a move of 20 feet from your opponent. You also can avoid their shots entirely by leaning a few inches, rather than moving a few feet. This allows you to keep your gun in position to shoot back easily, and not have to reset your arm positioning. In the thick of a game, this can be the difference between winning and losing.

By sliding back, you also access more angles. "Angles" is a blanket term for shooting side to side from a position. Very rarely do you shoot at your 12 o-clock from a bunker. You're mostly shooting the 9 to 10:30 angle and 1:30 to 3 o-clock angles. Why? It's easier and faster to lean out the side rather than poke up above a bunker.

On a lean, your head and gun come out simultaneously. On a poke up, your head is seen first, giving opponents a chance to take you out before you shoot.

Speaking of leaning out, most opponents lean out from your left. Why? As I mentioned back in the drills section, it's more natural for right-handed people to lean to their right, which puts them on their opponent's left-hand side. This means that you can anticipate most players' movements by aiming towards the left-hand side of bunkers. How? Tournament players preach playing switch handed. This is just a fancy way of saying, "You should learn how to use both hands." It's tough, but it helps. I lay on my side on the left side of a bunker and wait for their lean to my left and hammer down.

Imagine a line just over the top of your bunker, and just around the sides. This line starts from your

Teaching yourself to shoot effectively both right- and left-handed will help you work both sides of your bunkers and catch opponents off guard while keeping your exposure to incoming paint to a minimum.

opponent's barrel and continues past the sides and top of the bunker. Learning where that line will be when you attain a bunker position is the essence of understanding angles. And learning how you can extend this line will improve your game immensely. Watch your feet, your hands, head, your loaders, your harness—anything beyond that line puts you in jeopardy.

So how do you make these angles work for you?

Good question. The best way to do this is to develop a stable shooting stance that you like. This position should allow you to play in two directions at once, but also give you freedom to slide in when necessary. Some players get on their knees and play from there. Some players crouch down on their toes. And some go on one knee, the other one up. If you wear soft knee/shin guards, go with something like that to shield yourself from incoming

paint. Make sure you're comfortable in your stance. A Team Internet friend of mine has big thigh pains after a full day because of his technique. It works, however, so he still uses it.

With any stance you use, you want to try to layer your cover. For example, if you can line up several trees (or anything else that will protect you from opponents' paint), you can do something called "tree-walking" or simply "walking". Using terrain in this manner will give you a freedom of movement that will make you uncannily effective. Like water, every time you move, your relationship to your terrain shifts. Take advantage of this zen approach, and your game play options will expand dramatically and unpredictably.

THE VIRTUES OF SOFT COVER

This conveniently brings me to soft cover. Soft cover is more about finesse and grace than brute force. Using soft cover requires a little more creative perception and quick-thinking than hard cover does.

Soft cover is anything that may prevent paintballs from reaching you, and is likely to if you are careful, but nonetheless isn't risk-free protection.

We're talking about stuff like twigs, leaves, grass, and small and thin trees.

In many cases, tall grass is just as good as a bunker. Grass will either break paint outright or deflect it in most cases. Unless someone rips a few hundred balls, nothing is going to make it through. Everyone has a story about the guy who hid behind a twig and never got shot. I know a few fields where I can get behind a shrub and nothing gets to me but splatter. This is beautiful cover; it allows you to watch the other guys and communicate what you see to your teammates who may not be able to see it.

Soft cover also includes some things you wouldn't expect. What should you use for camouflage? Get behind some grass or shrubs and lay still. If they don't see you, they can't shoot you.

Going back to our definition of cover, this seems to work. How about moving far enough back so they can't touch you with the longball? If you're fast, you can outrun a shooter between bunkers. Or you can pop your gun up and lay down a wall of paint at the other guy to make him duck. (Ever wonder why it's called "Cover Shooting"?) The three "Out's"—Outrange, Outrun, and Outshoot—are all good forms of cover, if you think of cover more broadly, as doing whatever it takes to avoid elimination.

All of this information takes a long time to master in practice. These are the basics. Take what you learn, build from experience, and enjoy!

-RR

HANDY HAND SIGNALS

Visual signals are used when it's time to be stealthy and quiet. You and your buddy may be crawling to the flag station unnoticed. Why give away your position by talking? Using visual hand signals, you can communicate to each other silently as you plan your attack.

The following hand signals have been adopted from Navy SEAL small unit tactical signals. Of course they've been slightly modified to meet the challenges of the paintball experience.

Stop
Fist held in air.

Hear
Hold your hand up next to your
ear as if you are listening.

Go
Arm up, sweeps from back to front.

Down
Arm forward, sweeps down.

Cover Me
Tap your head with your hand.

See
Point to your eyes.

Go Faster
Fist in air, pumps up and down rapidly.

Out of Air
Fast movement of the hand back
and forth across the throat.

Gun Down
Point "thumbs down" at your gun.

Tactics

Bunker
Open grip. Fingers point downward.

Flag
Palm vertical.

Take Bunker
Thumb up, index finger extended, pointing ahead.
As in, "Full speed ahead—bunker that guy".

Gun Working
Also known as the universal "o.k." symbol. As in,
"Whatever was wrong is now o.k."

Out of Paint
Make zero with your thumb and fingers.

Flag Station
Inverted bunker.

Crawl
Wave index and middle finger in opposing
up/down motion.

Affirmative
Thumbs up! Another universal symbol for "understood."

Put them together and see how they work.

Here's the message: "I see a bunker. Cover me. I'm
going to "bunker" them".

Here's how it looks:

—*Andrew Flach and Stew Smith*

CODES AND COMMUNICATION

WE CANNOT STRESS IT ENOUGH:
COMMUNICATION ON THE PAINTBALL FIELD IS VITAL TO WINNING.

The types of codes you use, and what you use them for, may vary depending on whether you play in the woods or on a field, in a pick-up game or in a tournament. But any way you splat it, you've got to talk it up!

COMMUNICATION BASICS

Lack of communication spells defeat for your team. If the other side has equal skills and is communicating better than you are, you'll be counting far too much on luck to win. Whatever methods you choose, pick a system that is easy to follow and remember. In the heat of the game, you can always rely on plain old English, but codes can be faster if used well, and they can confuse your opponents! Obviously, codes can also add a fun dimension to your game. Why not make up your own code and try it out with your friends!

There are plenty of things to communicate on the field:

- The Status of Your Team—what you are going to do; what's your team's status
- The Status of Your Opponent's Team—what they are doing; what's their status
- The Status of the Overall Game—how much time is left; how many players are left
- Field Locations—where is everyone
- Junk Codes—designed to throw off the opponent, they are meaningless

There are as many different systems of codes and communication as there are paintball teams and styles of play. What follows are some examples to help get you started in developing your own.

VERBAL CODES

Verbal codes are faster to communicate than visual signals. Here are a few examples of verbal codes (and their meanings) that have been developed by actual teams:

Fishing—I've got a gun jam

Sunshine Red—Everyone shoot right

Sunset Blue—Everyone shoot left

Going Shopping—I'm off to "bunker" someone

Mickey Says—Indicates how much time is left in the game. For example, "Mickey Says Three" means there are three minutes remaining in the game.

Exxon—Reloading

Juice—The Flag

Visa—Attack (as in, "Charge!")

Codes can be based on a number of different schemes: car types, breakfast cereals, animals, cartoon characters . . . anything goes so long as it's easy to understand.

Here's another code. This one is based on airline travel:

Passport—The flag

Lost My Luggage—Gun Down

Found My Luggage—Gun Working Again

New York—The Right Tape

LA—The Left Tape

Flight Delayed—Reloading

Cancel the Ticket—Bunker someone

Disneyland—The Opponents Flag Station

The Gate—Your Team's Flag Station

In-Flight Movie—Your team has the advantage

Airline Food—You are in a bad position and could use some cover

Buckle Seatbelts—Everyone attack

Emergency Exit—The flag is in jeopardy

FIELD LOCATIONS

Field Locations can be identified by memorizing a simple grid describing rows and columns, or a clever code system. Draw a grid with an "x" and "y" axis dividing the field into 4 quadrants. Then, draw horizontal lines to delimit 6 "rows." Use colors to divide the field down the middle. "Red3", for instance, might describe a bunker in the 3rd row on the left side of the field. "Blue3" would indicate the same row of bunkers on the right side of the field.

A more complex system, but one which might be easier to remember, can be based on the map of the US, the hands of a clock, or the locations of stores in a shopping mall familiar to your team.

Make certain all players on your team know your code inside-out! You can tape a copy of the day's codes to the inside lid of your loader.

Tournament Talk

By Justin Owens

In the sport of paintball and especially within the ranks of its top tournaments, good teamwork is the key to success. The execution of good teamwork involves the integration of a number of important factors, the single most important of which is communication. Good communication requires commitment and dedication from all members of a team in order to learn how to effectively spread important information during a game. The history of paintball shows us that it is those groups of players who have developed their ability to function as a single unit on the field of play, rather than as five or ten individuals playing individually on the same team, that have been most successful.

An integral part of communication on today's tournament paintball fields involves the widespread use of codes. Today's tournament teams go to extreme measures in order to learn how to communicate effectively among themselves without giving away important information to their opponents. A full set of codes for a single team usually involves code words to account for any relevant circumstance that might be encountered on the field of play.

Here is a list of codes as they might be used by a serious tournament team.

Code Word	Code Meaning	Code Application
Burn 1, 2, 3 . . .	# of opponents eliminated	Calling out "Burn 1" signifies that you have eliminated one of your opponents; "Burn 2" = two eliminations; "Burn 3" = three eliminations; and so forth.
Down 1, 2, 3 . . .	# of own teammates eliminated	Calling out "Down 1" signifies that you have eliminated one of your opponents; "Down 2" = two eliminations; "Down 3" = three eliminations; and so forth.
Reality	amount of time left in game	"Reality four-fifty" = four minutes and fifty seconds left in the game; "Reality ten-ten" = ten minutes and ten seconds left in the game; etc.
Thunder	provide cover fire	This is a code you might call out if you were preparing to shift from one bunker to another and needed cover fire in order to make it happen. Variations of and additions to this code could further specify where the cover fire needed to be directed, for example.
Rabbit	wanting to move	Variations on this code could specify your plan of action, and this code could be used in conjunction with codes such as "Thunder."
Poison	marker down	Use this code to inform the rest of your team that your marker is experiencing problems during the game, or has quit working entirely.
Fast Food	need to reload	Use this code to inform nearby teammates that your marker's loader is running low on paint and that you need to reload.
Choker	bunkering code	In tournament paintball, there are times when it is necessary to run up on an opponent and eliminate him or her at point-blank range. This is commonly known as a "bunker move," and the code to direct teammates to do it or to alert teammates that you are about to do it is one of the most important ones to have.
Wolverine	push upfield	This code is sometimes used near the end of a game when there is danger of time running out. When a team calls it out, the entire team will move upfield at once in an attempt to overrun their opponents and win the game.
Shadow	opponent is across the bunker from you	To warn a teammate that he occupies the opposite side of the same bunker as one of his opponents, call out "Shadow" along with his name.

In addition to learning code words for communicating actions and circumstances effectively across a team, the nature of today's concept fields (especially the inflatable fields) has made it possible for teams and players to give specific names to bunkers with characteristic shapes. By giving specific names to these bunkers, teams are better able to communicate positions and locations on the field.

Can: A cylindrical bunker set on its end, standing approximately seven feet tall with a diameter of roughly four feet. "Cans" are most commonly found in the backfield, nearest each team's respective starting stations.

Steamroller: A "can" that has been laid on its side.

Dorito: This bunker resembles a pyramid, is roughly eight feet in height, and is one of the most popular Sup'air bunkers made.

Baby Dorito: Just as it sounds, a smaller version of the "Dorito."

Wing Nut: Looks like a "can" which has been cut in half, with two fins that stick out from the sides of the bunker.

Snake: There's no mistaking this bunker; it looks exactly like the name implies and is typically found across the midfield running near the out-of-bounds line. "Snakes" are low bunkers and the players who have become most comfortable using them are those who have learned how to crawl and snap-shoot very well.

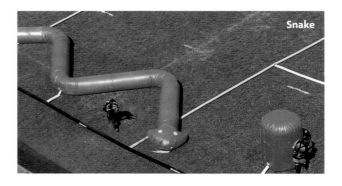

Nessie: This bunker resembles a miniature snake, very short in length and displaying a characteristic "S"-curve.

Car Wash: An arch that forms a long tunnel when set up on the field—hence the name "car wash." It is typically found along the midfield line and can easily provide cover for two or more players from each team, even at the same time!

Cone: Looks like a pointed ice cream cone (a "sugar cone") which has

Carrot

X

T

been turned upside down and sits on its circular surface, pointing towards the sky.

Carrot: A "cone" that has been laid on its side.

Submarine: This is a large bunker that will almost always be found on the midfield line next to one of the tapelines (out-of-bounds borders). It roughly resembles the long-tube appearance of a submarine.

Fish: There is no mistaking this bunker when you see it; it looks like a fish.

Rocket: As is the case above, there is no mistaking the "rocket"; it looks exactly as one would expect a "rocket" to look.

Octopus: This bunker is typically found in the exact center of the field, and resembles a large X laid on the ground with a single cone pointing straight up from the center of the X.

Tombstone: Like the snake, rocket, and fish, the "tombstone" looks exactly as its name implies.

Fish

Cheese: Resembles the shape of a thin, tall, triangular slice of cheese standing on end.

Wedge: Somewhat resembles the "cheese" with its top half cut off.

X: When laid down and viewed from above, this bunker forms an "X" on the ground.

T: Resembles a "T" on the ground when viewed from above.

Taco: This is another no-brainer; it almost perfectly resembles the shape of the typical taco.

Taking & Defending Buildings

I've seen some beautiful buildings in the course of my paintball exploits. And I've seen some ugly ones. I've seen some that were crafted to look like UFOs and castles, others that looked like they were rescued from the garbage dump.

Everyone loves buildings, myself included. I just love attacking them, and you're about to discover why. When it comes to taking a building, I've got it down.

Most people see buildings as fortifications, and this is pretty accurate. In paintball, a building is a good solid piece of cover, which explains its popularity. On the surface, they look like great (read: *safe*) places to hang out. They have small holes to shoot through, combined with little or no exposure to incoming paint. Sounds like a dream come true, right? Newbies tend to see these structures that way, as well. But from outside of the walls, newcomers to this game get discouraged by buildings, and won't move on them. As a result, they get picked off with relative ease as they try to take buildings by force.

© Cleo Fogal

Most paintball buildings are about 2 meters in length and width. (That's about 7 feet for you Americans.) This makes them about 4 square meters of doom that I can exploit as an attacker!

Look at buildings as traps rather than as fortresses, and a world of attack possibilities will open up to you!

LIKE "THE DEATH STAR," BUILDINGS HAVE THEIR WEAKNESSES

When I'm approaching a building filled with paintball players, I know that I have an enormous advantage. First of all, buildings are not mobile. (If they are, they're called tanks.) This fact alone might scare you out of buildings for the rest of your paintball career. (You shouldn't let it, but more on that later.) Once inside a building (especially if there's more than one entrance), this is where you're going to stay. Sure, you can move around inside there, but you're still on the same piece of real estate.

Stuck in a building like a roach in a roach motel.

You can't flank in a building, unless it's an unusually long one. You can't really crawl. You can't do much in there other than defend perhaps three angles that the openings and the doorways will allow. Defenders tend to exploit this to a fault.

They will defend those angles with their last paintball.

You can't win a game based on mobility by taking and defending a building!

As an attacker, exploit the isolation and siege mentality of a building defender. The fact that most of a building is impenetrable also means that its occupants have substantial blind spots. It also means that their ability to hear what you're doing

on the outside is easily compromised, because in many cases the buildings are echo chambers; a few shots against those walls while you're moving will make it hard for them to hear where you're going. Once you know the angles the building allows its inhabitants, you can use different angles they can't cover. If this sounds simple, that's because it is. You just need to be patient, perceptive, and decisive in your attack.

A building can be worked through or over if need be. For example, you can dedicate one shooter to a building and basically stop everyone in that building from poking their heads out. This tactic plays out in the following manner.

If three guys are inside a building structure, they have limited fields of view. They can't all poke out of the same window without missing something and/or becoming a huge target. Here's what you

do. Place one player near the front of the building and have him shoot it up a little to make noise along the building's sides. I call this "knocking," because you're just making them nervous instead of trying to eliminate them.

The next move is a flanking maneuver exploiting the limited visibility of the building's occupants. If you can manage to put paint in the vicinity of or through the openings, you'll make the occupants sloppy and nervous. Before you know it, you'll have cleared the building, because they won't have seen or heard you come right up on top of them. Or, if all of their players are in the building, why bother to take it? If you can ignore the building, grab the flag while they're tied up with a well entrenched front shooter who has a great shot at their escape door.

Tactics for loners who must take a building

What if you're alone? Well, the principles are the same, but in this case I'll tie 'em up infinitely by shooting and maneuvering while they're ducking down from my shots. Either that or I'll just put paint into a hole until some poor dude pokes his head up to see what's happening. Poof—instant elimination!

WHAT BUILDINGS ARE USEFUL FOR

I've said some harsh things about paintball build-

ings. Clearly, buildings are the bane of those who misuse them.

On the other hand, buildings can be helpful to those who use them appropriately. For example, they should be used as cover. Despite everything I've just said, I'd like to remind the reader that buildings are more than just four walls.

When I'm using a building for cover I try to stay on the outside of it as long as I can. In this case, it's used like any bunker with the exception that the holes can line up to form a smaller hole for opponents to shoot through. I can shoot through easily, whereas my opponents can't.

I'll also back away from the building, and use it as a normal bunker that way. Buildings offer the opportunity to become invisible to my opponents. I only use this as a last resort, however. Or I use it as part of my tactical plan. Either way, using a building must serve a concrete purpose for the team.

When you enter a building, you're making a commitment.

Sometimes you'll be making a whole game commitment, because you'll end up in an inescapable hot zone. Of course, if your objective is to make your opponents focus on you, this can work to your team's advantage. If you're not doing anything for your team, you're not doing your job. Too many defenders forget that, and they get eliminated or they simply don't get involved in the game.

After diving into a building, it's important to keep your ears open for teammates' communications and to make your shooting count for something. Like any bunker, you have to work it. Buildings need to be worked harder because you don't have all the openings a bunker provides. Tunnel vision is easier to slip into from inside a building; if the window faces forward, you tend to look forward. Work a building's entryways the same way you work its windows and its cracks. Stay on your toes, or you'll get trampled point blank.

You really need to have a lot of team support for your building players. You need mobile people on the outside of the building to prevent flankers from taking your position. You also can make yourself a 'distraction' so that your teammates shoot the guys fixated on eliminating you. If you lie in a building, they can't touch you. But they'll keep trying because they think they can, and your teammates will just keep getting eliminations.

In January 1998, I played at an outdoor speedball field in Florida that had a few buildings in the center. During one game, I made a very bold move and made the center building. I took a few shots from the outside and realized that my team needed a gun a few feet forward. So I went into the building.

"What's on the right?" I yelled out. Some kid said there was a crawler parallel to me. I turned to look through the door, leveled the barrel, and put 20 shots into the shrubs, just hoping to get something to move, and I got an elimination. Immediately I looked left to see someone moving on the flank. I shot a few balls to stop him. No paint broke, but it stopped him.

The rest of the game flowed this way. A few shots left, a few right, a few more left, working the whole area hard. As the left was shooting at me, I'd work the right side. When the right would start on me, I would swing left.

What amazed me was how they wouldn't move up on me. Instead, they tried to longball my position and get a lucky shot on me. This was crazy; all I had to do to avoid shots in the building was shift a little one way or the other. Had they concentrated on my position and rushed me or worked on my flanks before shooting me, I would have been a goner.

The building provided great protection, but without team support I would have been toasted. Against competition with better tactics, team support would have been absolutely essential to holding that position and turning it to our advantage. I was always trying to keep my flankers informed of our opponents' movements. Since that building was in the center of the field, I was able to act as a team caller, relaying information from side to side with great protection. If you're in a building and are not being useful, leave it before you get abandoned.

My team won the game after the other team wasted a good deal of paint on my position. I figured that the other team shot about 2000 paintballs at me in that game, but they just couldn't take me down because of their lack of coordinated teamwork and intelligent communication.

GETTING BUNKERED IN A BUILDING

The Element of Surprise

Inside a building, getting "bunkered" or "mugged" can be much worse. This is mainly due to the element of surprise. Here's a true story that illustrates what I mean. Once upon a time, there was a big game in Racine, Wisconsin . . .

Both flag stations were two-story castles, which are very impressive to the eye but brutally hard to defend. When the flag was about to come down, the attackers rushed the building, stuck their guns into the windows and opened up point blank. This was FUBAR for anyone in that building. Much bad welting resulted from this.

You see, your main danger, as both an attacker and defender of buildings, is that you're going to find yourself in a point blank scenario and get lit up within a second or two by players whose adrenaline levels are off the charts. Of course, this isn't actually dangerous. You're just going to get hit abruptly at close range and

perhaps a few more times than you'd prefer. Later, you'll laugh about it. But, believe me, when it happens, you're going to rue the day buildings made their way into this game.

In a tournament, this activity can count as "Unsportsmanlike Conduct" or "Overshooting." In a recreational setting, you may be told to sit out a few games for overshooting.

My point? If you're going to rush a building, please be careful. Unlike a rounded bunker, you really won't see anything until the last second, and even then you could get bruised. Personally, I'd prefer to flank a building.

Overall, I try to avoid buildings. I can do more damage outside of them. But, sometimes, they're useful. They definitely make things more interesting for their attackers and defenders, and are part of the exhilarating paintball landscape.

—RR

CHUCK STONER, THE ULTIMATE SNIPER

ANDREW FLACH: What do you do as a sniper?

CHUCK STONER: As a sniper, I'm hunting. When I'm on the field I feel like I'm hunting people and what I try to do is set myself up in situations where people will approach me, enter my effective range, and not know where I am even after I've eliminated them. So whenever I'm on a playing field, I'll make the best possible use of the available vegetation and the terrain and the features on the playing field to make myself invisible.

ANDREW: How long can you possibly sit in one position for a game?

CHUCK: Of course, that depends on the game that's being played. In a scenario game, a 24 hour game, I can be on my own for the whole time.

ANDREW: But in one spot, physically?

CHUCK: It depends on how good the hunting is. If I'm entertained, feel effective, and my position isn't compromised, I can stay for a long time. That's just something that you learn as a hunter. You spend a whole day from sun up to sundown in the woods, usually fairly stationary, especially if you're hunting deer or other big game.

Playing paintball is another hunting experience for me and it's kind of nice because I don't have to drag anything out. I don't have to field-dress anything I shoot.

ANDREW: In terms of picking a spot, what kinds of things would you consider to be important?

CHUCK: I would say that there are half a dozen rules of thumb and one of them is that you're never more dangerous than when your opponent is unaware of your location. As soon as you begin to fire, if your gun is noisy, or if your movements are quick and jerky, you give away your position. Then, your fighting ability is compromised.

This pump gun that I'm playing with is very accurate. It has range that other guns don't and shoots very consistently to the same place, but if I'm competing against semi-automatic guns, once I give my position away I can't function effectively.

People can't fight what they can't see. So, one of my other rules of thumb is that you should always set up fights on your own terms. That means that you're only going to win so many gunfights. I'm not actually on the field to be a gunfighter. I don't want to be a hero. I'm there to be dangerous. That's my function.

ANDREW: To create problems.

CHUCK: Yes. With that in mind, I always set my encounters up so that people fight me on my terms. I choose where to hide, I choose the shooting lane, I choose the terrain. That's how you can be most effective. Human eyes pick up erratic movement very quickly—rapid, jerky movements, swift movements. Our eyes are arranged that way. Consequently, when you move through the forest you should move very little and when you do move, you should move steadily and smoothly.

Even if you're going to be an effective sniper, it's not necessary to move painfully slow because there's just not as much at stake. You want to be able to get around the field and enjoy the game.

Most people are very untalented when it comes to training themselves to be a watcher in the woods. They tend to overlook a lot of things. It's that "you can't see the forest for the trees" thing. When you play the way I like to play you have to see everything. I developed this ability through years of hunting. You always look for bits and pieces of things rather than the whole item. If you go into the woods, and you're looking for a whole paintball player, you might get lucky and see that. Mostly, you're going to see hands and the corner of a goggle, or the tip of somebody's boot. You have to be able to interpret what you see and then incorporate that piece into the whole and identify your target. The same thing happens in the woods when you're hunting deer. You rarely see a whole deer. You see a tail, a leg, a hoof, an ear, an eye, a nose.

I like to play against players who wear colored lenses because I can easily see amber lenses and rainbow lenses. I can pick those out of the woods in a heartbeat.

ANDREW: What is a shooting lane?

CHUCK: A shooting lane is quite simply a path for your projectile to follow to the target. It's very important with paintball, because if you hit a twig at 280 feet per second, your paintball is going to splatter and never make the target. Just like you can effectively hide in a thicket of rhododendrons. You can be mostly in plain sight but people can't get paint onto you. I don't enjoy playing that way because I clean my equipment up after every day of play and if I'm all spray painted with pink paint from head to toe, that kind of detracts from my enjoyment of the game.

As a matter of fact, I play not to be hit. I want to play the entire day and never take a hit, and I do that often, which is kind of unusual.

More than the shooting, I enjoy matching wits with the people that I play with. That's every bit as satisfying as shooting my gun. I try to understand my oppo-

nent right from the get-go. Usually, right after the first or second game, I can get a feel for the mentality of the team that I'm playing against, and I can identify individuals that I regard as dangerous and identify individuals that are a piece of cake.

ANDREW: So you're sort of like the wolf watching the sheep, right?

CHUCK: That's all part of setting up the situation. Remember what I said: "always fight somebody on your terms." It helps to know the fields. I only play here at Skirmish, so I have an advantage. I know the fields very well, so I can use all of the terrain. I can use the creeks. People don't realize it, but one of the most effective stalking techniques is to wear knee-high rubber boots and to move in a creek bed because the noise of the water conceals most of your movements.

ANDREW: Cool.

CHUCK: You're down a foot or two below the line of sight and you usually have creek banks on both sides. People just don't expect to see you wading down a creek that's got a foot or a foot and a half of water in it.

One of the things that's interesting about hiding, and I tell new players this all the time, is that you always find bunkers and trees and log piles and fox holes. Everybody thinks those are the ideal places to hide. I disagree. I want to hide where somebody is not going to look for me, and those places are intrinsically suspicious.

I strive for a shooting lane that provides me an effective, defensible, dangerous position to work from. That's what I try to do.

ANDREW: And a dangerous, defensible position to work from would be . . .

CHUCK: I need shooting lanes, I need to feel confident that I'm

The Complete Guide to Paintball

going to see everything, that I'm going to encounter targets. I need to position myself strategically where I can help my team because I'm not always out there to play for myself. I want to be somewhere useful. I want to encounter other players and I want to effectively engage them and paint them or send them in another direction.

ANDREW: What shooting stance do you prefer as a sniper? Would you use the prone shooting position?

CHUCK: Almost never! I never lay down on my belly. First of all, I've got a pump, and if you lay down in a prone position it makes it harder to work the pump. When you play, you should move very little or not at all. When you do move, move

steadily with smooth movements. When things go south, and you decide that you have to move, be definitive. Move really fast! If you're laying down on your belly, you can't get the heck out of there if you need to. So I always play kneeling or standing.

Some players, especially those coming from military backgrounds, plop down on their belly as soon as they get into a fight. I just eat them up. Shooting from prone position may work in other situations, but when you're playing paintball, it's

not completely effective.

ANDREW: I notice you play with a scope.

CHUCK: Yes I do play with a scope. While I'm picking my targets I keep the yellow lens cover down. If I take a hit in the lens of the scope then I've lost my targeting system. Just before I take my shot I pop up the lens cover and set my sights on the target, giving me a clear field of view.

It's a straight four power (4X) scope. When I originally put it on the gun, I had some problems with it because it made my targets appear so close that I tended to undershoot them. But I've just taught myself to play with it and now it's just part of my equipment and second nature to me.

I can shoot like most people do: looking down the barrel and shooting. My pump gun doesn't have an auto-trigger so my rate of fire doesn't even begin to approach a semi's rate of fire. A Tracer or a Phantom with an auto-trigger can fire faster, but maybe not as accurately.

ANDREW: What shooting gear do you bring to the field with you?

CHUCK: I have my Bud Orr Sniper and I have my backup gun, a Phantom that I played with full-time several years ago. It's a good gun, shoots just as straight and just as far as the Sniper. I play with the Sniper because I like its heft.

I bring a couple of extra barrels and a couple of extra elbows. It's really important to have the right size elbows. A couple of squeegees, some gun oil, a gunsmith screwdriver for making adjustments on the guns. Spare parts, o-rings, various bits and pieces for the guns.

ANDREW: Tell me a little bit about your dress and camouflage. What kinds of things determine your choice of camo?

CHUCK: There are so many patterns out there. You have to have an artist's eye to be able to critically regard the terrain that you're going to play in, and then select the camouflage pattern that

you think will be most effective. I have snow camo, I have camo for the summertime, and I have camo for every season in between.

In the wintertime when there's snow on the ground, I have some white coveralls with some branch lines on them that are actually meant to be tree camouflage. I found that up here in the woods, where there's tons of angular branch features with a white background, such camouflages are very effective. I can almost disappear.

In the Fall, if it rains, the color of the leaves darkens. I have a camouflage pattern that's called Fall Foliage that is a very effective pattern in conditions like that. Like I said, I'm a hunter and an outdoorsman and a paintball player all in one. My investment in all this equipment makes sense.

I wear hand coverings and face coverings. For most people in the woods, those are the most noticeable parts of the body. And again, since human eyes are set up to see movement, concealing your face and hands is rather important.

ANDREW: Do you have any memorable experiences as a sniper you can share?

CHUCK: Here's a classic. I coached a player, Rob,

a couple of years ago. He wanted to become a sniper. At one point in the game, he hid in the top of a blown down tree and four players on the opposing team walked right past him! He and I and some of our other players were working together to set up an ambush. Everybody has to contribute to make those work. Our contribution was to engage the approaching players and have them concentrate on us. Then Rob just raised up out of the blown down tree top (he was fifteen yards behind them) and they were all four lined up with their backs to him and he just went to work on them. It was beautiful. That's how I like to play. It was a most enjoyable success.

ANDREW: That's great. How about yourself? Ever been ambushed?

CHUCK: It happens to the best of us. I like to match wits with people, to out-think them. People are just like deer, very much creatures of habit. It's not usual for someone to surprise me. But it's happened.

I was playing a couple of years ago with a friend and we snuck in on the back side of a flag station and went to work on the defenders and I thought I was doing really well. There was a six-inch puddle of water at my feet and all of a sudden this guy just reared up out of the puddle. He looked like a freaking sea monster, slopping water and wet leaves dripping off of him.

I was astonished and stunned. I stood there with my mouth hanging open and got shot.

MAKE YOUR OWN GHILLIE SUIT

It's easy and fun to make your own ghillie suit. Here is a quick primer on do-it-yourself camouflage.

Items Needed

- A cotton landing net, the kind used for fishing

- Camouflage Webbing: Determined by the season and terrain. Choose several kinds as needed.

- Burlap Strips: Find some raw burlap material and pull it apart to get at the threads.

- Rit Fabric Dye: Choose earthy tones.

At least a day before, dye your burlap strips in various tones by following the directions on the package. Let dry.

Cut the landing net open so you have a rectangular piece as big as possible. Lay this on the ground.

Cut your camo-webbing into thirty-inch strips. (Webbing is preferable because offers a more natural appearance. Most foliage will transmit a diffused light and webbing does that, too. If your ghillie suit is made of fabric, when you're backlit you will present a much darker, more distinctive silhouette. And an easy target!)

Fold the camo strips in half and then girth hitch them to the landing net. Don't just randomly attach them. Think about the patterns in the woods where you'll be using your suit and try to create an interesting, deceptive pattern.

Use the dyed burlap strips to fill in areas and add texture to the suit. Camouflage is an art, not a science. Use your imagination. Make several different kinds of ghillie suits to meet your needs.

Make separate pieces that can be used alone or together. You can make a back cover, a front cover, and a head cover. Attach these to your body with ties made of webbing. For your head cover, sew the landing net to an old cap, then apply camo netting and burlap strips.

Tactics

Paintball Snipers—From Myth to Reality

SOME MYTHS WERE MADE TO BE BROKEN

Occasionally on rec.sport.paintball ("the internet" for the paintball-playing crowd), someone posts the question "How can I be a paintball sniper?" This guy gets a lot of ribbing, partly because of the anti-military movement in paintball, and partly because I don't think most players understand the usefulness of a hidden player in the modern game. There are myths about the paintball version of snipers, let alone the pop-culture version, that simply need to be exposed for what they are. Because of the images we are spoon-fed by hyper-unrealistic movies and television shows, paintball players automatically believe that a sniper wears a bulky black suit, holds a gun longer than he is tall, and sits at the other end of a field putting paint onto a dime in the opponents' flag station. Sorry, no. Not in this game. At least, not any time soon.

Setting the record straight on paintball snipers.

First of all, real "snipers" need not apply. No matter how accurate your gun is (go ahead and spend a fortune on the best barrels, bolts, tanks, triggers, and sites), your projectile is the weak link. Ever seen a paintball decide it wanted to make a hard left? I have. Paintballs have a mind of their own. They're not accurate projectiles. Even in ideal circumstances, you really can't take someone out from as far away as an actual sniper with a special, high-powered rifle is expected to. You may or may not have figured this out yet, but basically, paintball is not, in the end, about the gun. The gun cannot outperform its ammunition. A roughly spherical gel-encased ball of colored vegetable fluids is not high-performance ammunition.

Instead of looking at someone as a "Sniper", look at them as a "Hunter." That's what they have to be in paintball. Sometimes you stalk, sometimes you hide, sometimes you shoot. You never line someone up from 200 yards away. So let's say you want to start playing like a hunter. How do you do it? It's easy, really.

If you move, you're not hiding.

Pick a camo that fits your terrain if you can. If not, make do with what you have. I've used Realtree in a desert setting effectively before and it worked well. You also have to understand what your camouflage does for a living in order to use it.

Tiger Stripe fools the eye into 'sliding' past the camouflage. Realtree, Advantage and Treebark look like the background, and fool the eye into believing they're part of the background. Woodland, Dots, and others of this style appear mottled and try to 'blend in' like a smudged painting. It's much more complex than that, but you get the idea.

In the U.S. region, when in doubt use Woodland. Very universal, very effective. The way I see it, the U.S. government spent a lot of money to make it work well, and they succeeded. Don't use specialty camouflage, French Lizard comes to mind, unless it's broad-based enough to fit in anywhere.

Probably more than you wanted to know, right? Well, if you take being a sniper seriously, this is pretty critical information. Take the time to pick the right camouflage!

The Sniper's Paintgun

I've never been a believer in new barrels, bolts, or anything like that. But you have to realize that I play normally with a fixed-barrel Piranha which is non-modifiable. So I'm biased.

Like many other people, I'm a believer in the target range. I've spent many cases of paint on the target range, and not just shooting for the heck of it. I'll try to hit all the targets on the range in order from front to back, then back to front. Then I'll put paint in the "0" in the number "50" on the sign. Then between the "1" and "2" on the "125 foot" sign. Once I have my effective range down in my mind, I can walk on the field with confidence. I know my range, and I know how accurate I am at that range. That takes years of experience, mind you, and it's not something you can learn from a book. You just have to go out and shoot paint at a target until you have the motion down.

SNIPING

Do Not Try to Be a Sniper...Be a Sniper!

So let's assume that you make it to the field in one piece, and you're ready to give it a go. Try some pre-game mental prep. Do this—hit the target range, plan your route, and review the team strategy.

You have to remember a few key rules here. Once you shoot a ball, the world will know where you are. This can be a good thing, as well as a bad thing. If someone spots you, they'll shoot a lot of paint at you. Either shoot back, dive for cover, or freeze. I'll address this in detail later, but for now, these are your good options. Take your time, relax, listen for opponents or teammates. Aural clues are easier than visual ones, especially when you're stalking.

Shooting is a skill that's a major factor in the game, the be-all-end-all of paintball. But, if you're trying to be sneaky, you generally want to make your first shot count. And the key to this is getting a good stance so your hand is steady.

I like having something I can shoulder up, usually my tank. But I've been using a lighter GTS stock lately, and they work very well with a remote line. It's just easier to hold a barrel steady when it's braced.

Taking aim is key. You want to hit something solid, like the opponent's gun or a harness buckle. Aiming for the chest area is good if you have the time to aim. If the paintball deviates a foot or so, you'll still hit the target.

Some say you should pull the trigger slowly, but I don't. Pull the trigger as you would normally. Don't change anything mechanical that you're used to. It's like changing the engine in your car to drive to a new job. Not really worth it. Just shoot in the same way you always do. If all goes well, you'll have an eliminated and confused player in no time. ("Where'd *that* come from!?!?")

Now, let's say that it all goes wrong.

Your barrel is wet and your ball skids left by a million feet. Your target turns and spots you. Now what?

As I said before, you have options. Three basic choices include the following—(1) shoot back lots of paint, (2) dive for cover, or (3) freeze in place. I've done all three, and they all work depending on terrain, your opponent, and your positioning.

For example, if the terrain is thick and you're fairly far from your opponent, freezing in place will confuse him. He may not see you at all. Presuming you only shot one ball, he won't be able to get a good 'fix' on your position.

If it's more open and there's a lack of hard cover (trees, rocks . . .) let it rip. Keep the initiative in a situation like this. He's off guard, and you can make him react to you. Eventually, he will make a mistake and you'll get an elimination.

You can also dive for cover. But once you go to ground, the initiative is gone, you surrender it to the other team. Once you're on the ground get out of there, move back, move up, move somewhere. Just move! Get back to another position and try all over again. Or, fall back and watch your old position. The other team will probably run up onto it assuming you're still there.

The best way to learn how to do this is actually to do it yourself. Try being a sniper for a game or two; you may be surprised at what happens. It's another trick to put in your bag. Remember, being versatile is a large part of what will make your game more successful and keep it fresh and enjoyable over time.

—RR

DEFENSE

Not enough has been written about defense in paintball, and the reasons are apparent. Very few of us think of playing defense in paintball as either a glamorous or enjoyable experience. Indeed, most players' idea of defense is to hang back and shoot anything not friendly as it comes back to the flag station.

But this isn't defense, it's a siege mentality. Bona fide paintball defense is a multifaceted position that's all about controlled aggression. If you understand the dimensions of paintball defense, you will think twice before leaving it out of your game plan.

The idea of defense that true paintball jedi should employ involves channeling your desire to win into preventing the other team from winning.

Most paintball teams are very concerned with taking ground fast, slamming a tape, and being very aggressive in their actions. But a team has to balance that with some kind of defensive capability, and not in the classical "Old School" sense. Paintball is becoming a game of players with positional strengths. Once you accept that proposition, exploring the possibilities of defense becomes more interesting.

First off, let me define paintball-style defense. Defensive players are those on the team attempting to stop the opposition from scoring points. Eliminations, flag hangs, first pulls—all of these are points that can be prevented with a good defense, and not just in tournaments either. If you play for fun, you can play a solid defense and win with it.

What makes a good defender? The mindset of a defender is a combination of fierce pride and spartan commitment. "You're not getting my flag. You're not shooting my crawler. You're not getting that bunker. Not on my field!" Sounds a lot like an aggressor, yes? The difference is that as a defender, your "aggressive" goal requires actively preventing them from attaining their goals. Hence the phrase, **Controlled Aggression**.

A fat wallet helps. Defense isn't cheap; you can shoot a ton of paint on "D."

So what's the purpose of defense? I've broken it down to four basic categories:

1. **Positional Defense**—Holding a single piece of real-estate with everything you have.

2. **Prevent Defense**—Also known as "Sitting." Play-

ing solely to stop the opposing team from shooting your team or achieving their goals.

3. **Reserve Defense**—Staying in the back with the eventual goal of becoming an attacking player in a later stage of the game.

4. **Team Defense**—Playing the backfield to aid your forward players.

As a defensive player, you have to decide what style is best for your team and its goals and adapt on the fly. In a big game, it means holding the fort. In a tournament, you may prevent the other team from advancing and scoring points. In your rec-ball weekend, it could mean being the last line of defense because the corned beef sandwich you ate for lunch just isn't sitting right and running is more than you can handle. *Remember the team goal is important, and so is not barfing during a game.*

Paintball is, and always will be, a team sport.

Defense falls into two broader styles—"Passive" and "Aggressive." As the names suggest, the two styles reflect two different trains of thought, but one overall goal: denying points and positions to the opposing team. There's a general stereotype here for the two styles. "Rec-Ball" players are 'passive' defenders, whereas tournament players are 'active' defenders. Tournament teams leave no players back, but rec-players always do. Yes, it's a stereotype, but it's almost always true. As in everything else, there's a time to be passive, and other times when being aggressive is necessary. Learning the rhythm of the game is very important. It's key to know when you need to act, to feel the appropriateness of doing something. With this in mind, let's go into a little more detail on the four basic categories of defense.

Positional Defense is mainly a concern of passive defenders, because it requires patience in the beginning and cunning when it hits the fan. Active defenders can use the principles of this to take and hold key bunkers and control zones from one spot on the field. Examples of this can be found mostly in big games where a flag station or a fort must be held. On tournament fields, situations arise wherein a defender holds the last few bunkers and tries to stop the offense.

Most positional defense originates in one location and uses that location to fend off all aggres-

sors. This is a very passive defense, and is very common in rec-play. From a position like this, you want to work around as in a typical bunker. But you have to keep your eyes open because you will more than likely be seeing more than one attacker and they have the maneuverability advantage and often greater numbers.

Aggressive Defense is about players having *zones of influence* that they can claim as their own. This is a very aggressive defense, because you as the defensive player are making the action happen and causing people to react to you. You're grabbing a section of field X by Y in size, staking a claim, and putting up a sign that reads "No trespassers allowed." As a defender, it allows you to move

around more and remain unpredictable. Slide forward to a position to stop them; scuttle to the other side of the bunker and shoot it up. While they're adjusting, move back a position and draw one into your barrel. Take him down and dive to another bunker. Scope out two bunkers you can dive between to make them wonder. If you can keep them guessing so they can't figure out where you are, they will hesitate to move up on you. My girlfriend calls this a "Field Mouse Defense" because it's what a field mouse does and, in her words, "What's more defensive than a field mouse?" Be elusive!

The Surprise Factor

You also want to have the element of surprise. You can accomplish this even if your enemy knows where you are. Consider the following scenario.

At the Ohio Bash, we had a position we had to hold for 5 more minutes so our team captain could touch the station for more points. I had a pump gun, and a few surprises. The team was laying paint heavily into the other team's attacking force. I put my body in front of our captain and began to pump paint to keep their heads down. I kept watching the time, knowing it wouldn't be long. With a minute before the call in, I grabbed a smoke grenade, popped the striker, and tossed it just over the lip of the hill.

It was a good throw, but the smoke wasn't thick enough for my liking. So I popped a red smoker with it and tossed it over the hill as well. "Hammer down!" I yelled. My teammates doubled their rate of fire, stopping our opponents' last minute push. Our captain touched the flag station, and we got our points and vacated the area. The opposing team wasn't expecting a smoke screen, and that stopped them long enough for our team to achieve our goal. This was Controlled Aggression exemplified.

Let it all hang out, but don't take unnecessary risks!

Prevent Defense

Related to positional defense, **prevent defense** uses similar means, but tends to be more useful in tournament settings. Simply put, you're preventing the other team from advancing instead of holding a position. For example, if the opposing team needs to eliminate five of your guys to advance, you fare better by sitting back and making them do the work. They get sloppy or nervous, and they get eliminated. Prevent defense is also easier than position defense because it's not zone oriented. It's more aggressive as well: you hide less and being mobile is emphasized.

I was in Chicago once, and had the opportunity to talk to some guys from Thunderstruck. They were telling me about a tournament field in Vegas some years ago in which they zoned out one bunker at extreme range down a main trail. One guy from the start would take three steps and start laying paint just over that bunker. He made three eliminations in the first two minutes. This is a perfect prevent defense. Other players on his team were making aggressive moves, but this one shooter made the plan work—*controlled aggression is where it's at!*

Most of your defense should be geared towards a "prevent" style. It's very flexible in response to what the other team is doing, but it's not just reactive. If you've done your job before the games start, you should have scoped out the bunkers your opposition is likely to see as advantageous. Dedi-

cate a defense player to preventing them from getting in and/or using that position. Even if someone makes it in, rain paint on their heads so they won't even look up. Now *that's* effective prevention.

Delay Tactic

The other side to a prevent is a **delay tactic** in which you aren't stopping the other team as much as you're stalling the inevitable or forcing them to deal with you. A good friend of mine calls this tactic "The Human Speedbump." We do this in big games all the time. The entire offense is getting routed hard, and we figure that they need a few more seconds to get away. So we stop hard behind a tree and start shooting at the attackers. They always stop to return fire, and we always get eliminated. But we get our teammates a few hundred more feet of running room in the trade, and they can be more effective. You may also have seen a tournament player crash a front bunker and just hug it. The opposing team is forced to deal with that player, because he's a threat in their path. You may not consider this a defensive maneuver until you realize this one player is stopping the entire other team from pushing a side by just sitting there. Again, this is controlled aggression—doing just enough to stop the 'bad guys' and help the 'good guys' without getting hit.

Reserve Player Defense

The **reserve player tactic** is a different defense mostly used in recreational play. The general idea is to hang back and wait to see what the opposing team does. Your time interval for this is up to you. For example, I've been playing a lot of speedball style games lately (no deer ticks, and none of this hiding stuff...). Earlier this summer I played at a field in Wisconsin that was preparing for a tournament, so the speedball field was all nice and dolled up. We were also playing the older speedball style of face the back and turn around on the horn. From the break I spun and saw where people were pivoting to move to. I knew where my guys were going,

The Complete Guide to Paintball

and I didn't have a plan right off the bat. The other team sent most of their players left, while we had a balanced offense. Within three seconds I decided I needed to go on the left to bolster the offense. It worked. Within a minute or two we had held, then cleared the left side. I didn't do it by myself, but my presence was a big help. A few seconds in the "reserve" slot helped the overall offense of the game. I could have slanted right to attack the off side. I could have stayed back and long-balled. I could have sat in the backfield and directed traffic. All of these decisions were opened up to me because I waited to react to the other team.

In an outdoor game, I'll wait a few minutes if need be, listen for the shooting and figure how we're holding. If it seems static, then I'll flank or reinforce. In some cases I'll launch myself up a tapeline and sneak around the shooting. If everyone is too busy to look my way, I can make it all the way behind the flag station.

The idea is to be a 'spare player' with intentions to move up on a flag or objective. Again, controlled aggression is what you're going for. The key to your move can be timed in minutes or seconds. You can also count the eliminated players and move up when half the other team is eliminated. The main thing is you're not going to sit down the whole game and wait for the opponent to come to you. It also makes the other team cocky when they make it to your flag after they think they eliminated everyone already. Free shots.

Team Defense

The last category is a **team defense**. This actually crosses all the previous three categories, but usually sacrifices the defender. The tactic I've already mentioned as "Human Speedbumps" can also be used on a flag return. You run back with the flag runner. If there's any trouble, the runner keeps going but you turn around and return fire. Again, they stop to shoot at you. But your flag runner has a clear path into the station. Any time you make a trade-off like this, think of it as a defensive maneuver. In chess, sacrificing a pawn for a positional advantage that is virtually impossible for your opponent to overcome is a brilliant move.

On the same note, a takedown ("bunkering" or "mugging") can be defensive in nature as well. I can hear you sighing in disbelief from here. But consider: let's say one player is holding your team in one place. That player's goals are to prevent your team from advancing and to keep you preoccupied. To prevent him from achieving his goals, you may want to send in a guy to take him out. Often times you get a trade-off. You and he walk off the field together. But that one move opens up your side and the offense can take control. In this case, bunkering a guy goes from a highly aggressive maneuver to a tactical team-oriented defensive maneuver. This is yet another example of controlled aggression.

Sacrificing yourself isn't the only team defense option. Enter the art of an ambush. Often misunderstood, a good ambush should leave an attacking force saying "What in the world just happened?" A good ambush involves three players, requires good setup time, and demands patience to execute well. In an ambush, it is critical to cover the attackers in paint as fast as you can. Speed is the key; otherwise, they will find cover, regroup, and give you a hard time. Use your cover, stay low, keep your cool, and when they walk into your zone, let them have it all at once. Of course, this can be very nerve-wracking, but it can also rattle your opponents and cause them to stop an attack. I could write a whole article on the ambush alone—it's more versatile than you think.

Team defense also covers people in your backfield—the heavy shooters who should be working in sync with the team. A guy in the way back longballing the other team, while feeding information to his front crawler is very common, and the easiest to see in action. But it can go further. There's been a lot of talk about "set up plays" recently, and your back players are the best judges as to when you should launch one. So they're a lot like quarterbacks, calling the plays and supporting them to make sure they can happen.

The Bottom Line

I've talked a lot about being an aggressive defender, and controlling that aggression in a way that benefits the team. Always consider the team when planning your defense. A solid defense, or at least a planned one, can hold the other team to a points loss or prevent them from organizing that one solid push they need to win the game. Too many teams undermine their best efforts on offense by sacrificing their commitment to defense. If you want your team to be invincible, take a balanced approach to the game. Explore the possibilities of dedicating a few players to defensive postures. One guy suppressing the center could make the difference between winning and losing in rec play or a tournament.

—RR

The Complete Guide to Paintball

Getting Down to Earth

At the outset, you need to know something about me. I am 6'4" and 250 pounds of big, fat, artery clogging American mass. This makes me quite the atypical "crawler." Your stereotypical crawler is a guy 5'5" with sticks for limbs, and a pat of breakfast butter that slipped onto his shoe representing body fat.

But, since I do crawl, I maintain that anyone can. Crawling can be worked into anyone's game; it's just a matter of how and to what degree. A little floor work can enhance your game by making the impossible likely.

Let us start with a situation most likely to pop up in your game. Say you are in a shootout where nothing is happening. Neither you nor your opponent is moving forward. You have a choice: spend all game in a one-on-one "pop-up-and-shoot" scenario, or try the following.

Swing to your left and release a string. Then quickly roll right and crawl ten feet, and then up three to a different tree. Do not run. Crawl. Assuming you did not run, your opponent, who was likely concentrating on your left side, did not see you reach your new spot. When they pop up to shoot your old bunker, tag them on the head. Crawlers hit the turf just at the right times, not all the time. Crawlers try to fool their opponents by stealth, misdirection, or a combination of the two. A ten foot sideways maneuver is a crawl although it does not appear to be.

Successful crawling begins with the right equipment. Contrary to your assumption, "camouflage" is not a top priority for the crawler's kit. Knee and elbow pads are, however. Technically, I can crawl naked, but it would be painful for me and traumatizing for any witnesses. Pads should allow you to feel the ground when you move but still give protection. I use Redz pads and have never regretted it. Next, you need gloves to serve as padding for your hands. Having a good pair of cleats, a stopwatch, and a stick squeegee in your pads is helpful. You'll need to get streamlined and keep all loose equipment off your body. Once you have acquired these priorities, look into camouflages. You can overcome those big, juicy white logos on your chest with a crawl. Your chest is already on the turf, who's going to see it?

Crawling is a combination of patience, skill, and time management. Bob Long once gave me the metaphor that when you commit to a crawl (or anything in paintball), you need to see the door opening, decide when to go for it, and gauge how long you have before it slams in your face.

Although every situation must be treated uniquely, I have found two basic techniques for crawling suitable for different occasions. The first is the "Leopard Crawl," which is useful for low or dense cover. The whole time you are moving, you are on your toes, knees, elbows, and hands, and your belly is literally just over the ground. Most of your forward power comes from digging your spikes into the ground and pushing off of them. While you do this, raise your body over the ground and steady yourself on your elbows and hands. Do this in the manner most comfortable for you. For a long time I used my toe spike, but then I switched to Diggers cleats and changed to a side spike on the ball of my foot. If you are doing it right, it should be like rock climbing on flat terrain (except you don't get jackhammer foot or use carabiners). Using five times the energy to move a quarter of the distance, the disadvantage to the Leopard Crawl is energy expenditure. But in heavy cover and places where the only way to cross to a key position is to dig your nose in the dirt, the Leopard Crawl is the best option. It is quite a rush to crawl up the middle of a field, cross a ravine unseen under rays of paint shooting above you, and attain a key spot.

The second basic technique is the "Three-Point crawl". As the name suggests, you crawl forward with both knees and one hand on the ground while the other hand holds your paint-gun. Keeping an Autococker level as you crawl isn't easy, but do not point it at the ground. If you get surprised, shooting the ground is ineffective and pointless. While you're crawling, do not continuously put all your weight on an open hand; you don't want to hurt your wrists. I crawl on a closed fist parallel with my forearm to minimize injury potential. The Three Point Crawl is a very fast crawl, but it is less stealthy, and, therefore, more perilous. From these two basic techniques you can accomplish a lot of maneuvering. A variation of the Leopard Crawl would be moving more like a snake—making more noise, but crawling faster and lower to the ground. A Three Point can become a

Four Point or even a Two point. Adjust the maneuver to the specific situation. Be mindful of your feet; a beautiful crawl can easily be defeated if your foot becomes a target.

When should you take a chance on crawling? Not all the time. You would gain little from crawling all the way from flag to flag. Getting half way up the field would take the whole game. Instead, crawling should be used to gain an advantage, either with your teammates or on your own. The field—tree roots and shrubs included—looks different when you're a foot off the floor. There are many holes that are only visible at ground level.

The best teacher is experience, so here are some team plays to try.

The "Low-man approach" is a classic. One teammate shoots over your head at an opponent they can not reach due to cover. You start a Three point crawl towards the covered opponent. Speed is the key. Your teammate over you, the High Man, keeps signaling you information: "50 feet, on left! 11-o'clock!" or whatever team codes you use. As the crawler, don't say a word. That would defeat the purpose and destroy the surprise attack. Your back player should shout a code word ("now" will suffice) as a signal for you to pop up and put a string on the opponent. When it works, it's so sweet.

Using the same set up, you can make a "sacrifice" move. The High Man makes a lot of noise, and does a lot of shooting. He will eventually fall back or get eliminated, leaving the crawler, or the Low Man, in the field deep in cover. The crawler waits for the other team to overrun his spot and then fires at them from behind. Either that or run for their flag; they won't expect you to be covering their flag station, will they?

In both cases an aggressive team could argue that you should just make a takedown. This does not work all the time, and circumstances like heavy overgrowth or a bad trail create a difficult situa- tion for "running

up and mugging the bum." Besides, a crawl like this only takes a minute or two. Patience to make a take-down gradually and wisely is rewarding.

Out on a paintball field you have to make quick decisions that can affect the outcome of the game. Crawling may not always be the best thing to do,

but it's worth having in your arsenal as part of an overall plan.

For example, assume that you have a good bunker position, but you spy a better one. There is enough cover to work, so you set up a crawl about thirty feet from the new bunker, going low but fast. You will cover that last thirty feet, the "Three Second" point, by running. Here is the general "Three Second Rule" for sprints: it takes a second to see you, a second to comprehend who you are and what team you are on, and another second to raise a paintgun and shoot. The three seconds of comprehension are three seconds of sprinting you get for free without the risk of getting shot. So crawl to that "Three Second" point and take them by surprise. You can reach the new bunker unseen by slithering right to it. The effect will be the same. Once you get there you have a few free shots, equivalent to those three seconds of sprinting, before the other team adjusts to your new position.

Another field strategy is crawling under a fire-lane, as long your opponent's line of sight does not extend that low. Imagine a line that begins at your opponent and travels straight out along their line of sight. They can not see you as long as their position does not enable them to look over and down. You can crawl literally under their barrel if you possess the nerve.

Stealth is covered extensively in my Woodcraft chapter, but it bears a quick mention. Basically, move quietly, clear your path, and set up for a one-shot "Bingo." Crawling makes stealth easier, as being on the ground makes brushing noisy obstacles out of your path easy. The bragging rights for getting "Bingos" is beautiful (and they save money on paint, too).

Crawling is an important paintball tool among many. Knowing when and where to go to ground can be an asset to your game. Even if you are tall and chunky.

—RR

"ALL-AMERICAN" THINGS YOU CAN DO TO IMPROVE YOUR GAME

"When you attack, you want to attack from the highest heights of heaven. And when you defend, you want to defend from the deepest resources of the earth."
LAO TZU, THE ART OF WAR

BILL GARDNER: First, we'll talk about individual tactics, then we'll talk about squad tactics and team tactics. When I say individual tactics, I mean aspects of the game that improve the individual's play.

And a lot of this comes down to the simple things. For example, there are different ways to load. Obviously, if you stick your elbow out, it becomes a target. You need to learn how to load with your elbow tucked in. These are the little things that make the difference between winning and losing.

You have to develop certain basic skills. First, you have to learn to shoot. You also have to realize that you're not going to be afforded the opportunity to just aim and slowly pull the trigger. You need to work on your snap shooting—the ability to stay within a bunker, then snap out and shoot a target, and then get back behind cover quickly.

Almost every player that achieves any level of skill in this sport gets comfortable with shooting a target at 40 yards or so with a quick snap and a couple of shots. So, from an individual standpoint, you must work on accuracy.

Then, there are bunker tactics—the ways you work a bunker. During a game you often end up behind some structure, either a speedball bunker or a stick bunker in the woods.

Never look from the same place twice in a row. You bring your head up at the same place every time, and the other guy watches your head come up at the same spot, two times before. So he aims at that spot. As you bring your head up again the paint is on its way, and you're wet before you know where it came from. So learn to peek around left, take two shots, then peek around right and take two shots. Keep your opponent off guard.

Paintball is an aural game, too. You can hear your opponent's gun go off. You can hear paint fly through the air; it whizzes. So, you can and should use your ears to determine when to come up and where to shoot.

ADAM GARDNER: People get shot just because they stay up too long. They want to watch their paint fly and then yell about it. Remember, you can call for a paint check just as effectively from behind a bunker. You saw the ball far enough on it's path that you have a pretty good idea of whether you were on line or weren't. If you didn't get him, you can adjust.

You want to come up, take your shots and immediately duck down. Inexperienced players watch their paint fly through the air as if that's the best part of the game. When they get a hit, they freak out and make themselves an easy target.

BILL: Blind shooting is another excellent tactic. If you're playing in a wooded field, look beyond your opponent for reference points you can zero in on from a better, protected position, and put paint in that direction. For example, get a fix on a branch right over the guy's head. You have a good chance of getting a hit and you minimize your risk of being shot. That's the beauty of blind shooting.

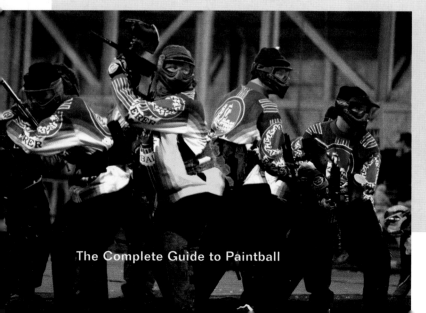

BILL: Different people are interested in different skills. You have your bunker players. You have your back players. People fall into different categories. They may know their orientation towards playing the back positions, and they'll gravitate towards shooting paint a long distance.

So, instead of running down the field, getting as close as they can to the other players, which is an aggressive, front line mentality, their mentality is..."I don't want to get closer,

Some of the best players we've seen will do strange things in the bunker. They'll kick the right side of the bunker as a diversion, then move left. Meanwhile, everyone's thinking that the player is coming out the right side, so that's where they are looking.

We call this working the bunker. Of course, given your athletic ability, there are only so many things you can do. One of our best players is extremely flexible. With his degree of flexibility, he can work a bunker in ways that other people just can't.

It's also good to be skilled at left-handed shooting; this opens up the entire left-hand side of the bunker. So practice shooting with both your left and right hands.

ADAM: A lot of people will take the first shot they can get. You need to practice patience. There are times when you're far better off letting a guy get closer, especially if he doesn't know where you are.

When people don't see you, you want to make sure that the first thing they hear is your paint hitting them. Learn to breathe, relax, and be patient . . . not too patient, though.

I'm going to shoot them at a mile and a half. I'm going to take a ton of paint and just dump it."

If you do this, you're shooting by volume, trying to get one of 50 shots to hit. You have to practice shooting long range targets. I bet a guy here once 10 bucks in one shot I could hit him at 100 yards. I shot one shot and hit him at 100 yards. You can definitely shoot 70–100 yards and eliminate players.

If you wear glasses, get goggles that will hold the glasses. Better still, wear contact lenses. A lot of people say, "I can't wear contact lenses, they're the most uncomfortable things in the world." In paintball, you'd be amazed at how many people finally wear contacts. When you're out on the field, it makes all the difference in the world.

Now there's a thing called being tight in a bunker. Being tight in a bunker means your elbows aren't sticking out. You tuck your harness around the back so it's not exposed. You bring your knees in. You crawl up underneath sections of the bunker, take the harness off completely and lay it on the ground.

ADAM: You can even lay flat on your back and watch the paint fly by. It's a lot easier to see it as you're watching it fly over. Find your best angle and determine where the shooter is.

BILL: The back player is exposed to many different angles of shots, and it is imperative that he survive because he's the eyes and ears and the communication center of the team. If he dies, the team's ability to win is significantly compromised.

ADAM: You have to learn to focus on the most immediate danger. For example: Let's say you have an opponent who's positioned with a couple of trees in between him and you. This makes it hard for him to get a shot. Then, you've got another opponent 30 yards away who can either run at any time and bunker you, or has a clean shot. That's the guy you have to stay focused on. He's the greater threat. If you concentrate on the guy who doesn't have a very good chance of shooting you, the guy who does will blow you away.

People get impatient and forgetful. They look the other way and get caught up in other action. Before they know it, they're out.

If opponents are getting really close or you know that if one of them pops up and you're not looking, he's going to have a good shot at you, you must focus on the immediate danger. Even if it means just pointing your barrel right at that guy and not moving it. Remember that you're on a team. Tell your teammates to keep the other guys off you.

BILL: To summarize individual tactics and techniques: Know how to shoot, know how to live in a bunker, know how to identify the most dangerous target, be patient. Learn to load, squeegee, and do other things when you're not shooting so that you don't expose yourself. Be tricky, be sly, and be unpredictable.

SQUAD TACTICS

The next level is squad tactics. The first thing that comes into play when you have two people is communication. Great communication is the most powerful tool in paintball.

ADAM: A lot of new players start off with five men. So, there are five of them and there are five of you. At the start of the game, say you shoot two of their guys off the left and you lose one of your guys.

You see all of this and call out, "21," which means "two of them are dead, one of ours." It also conveys that they lost their guys on the left side.

If you look downfield and see there are two guys on your right and one guy in the center, you know there's a very good chance that they are weak on the left. You can quickly run behind the other team, take them where they're weakest, and win the game.

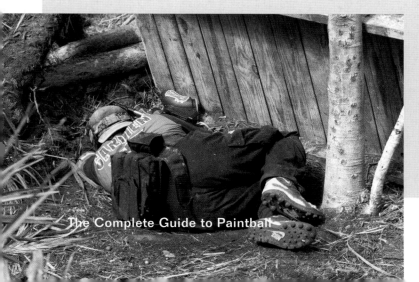
The Complete Guide to Paintball

BILL: People tend to play in squads, just like special forces. The most important element of squad level tactics is coordinated shooting and moving.

Teams come up to me and say, "The time was right, everything was great. We all ran right down to bunker him, and we got killed. What did we do wrong?"

My response is usually, "Well, it's pretty simple. You were all running, no one was shooting."

Only by bringing together the shooting and the moving do you end up with the squad performance that you're looking for.

One of the hardest things to teach players who are moving from the intermediate recreational level to the beginning of tournament play is that you all can't just move at once.

You have to realize that unspoken versus spoken communication comes with experience and effort. I realize, as I run up to this bunker, he's just going to get me if I take one more step. So, I sit down and start shooting, and Adam comes over and does him from another angle. We win because we act to support one another in scenarios that are familiar to us.

A squad that understands shooting and moving works together like clockwork. You get absolute dominance with that combination.

ADAM: Making a good squad or team is about developing that level of trust. I've got to trust the fact that my teammate is going to be there dropping and firing when I'm making my move.

BILL: The squad must combine individual tactics, communication and the aggressive, coordinated movement we've been describing. Now, a good squad of three that has excellent movement will do tremendous damage to an uncoordinated, non-communicating team of five. It's the way teams play together that decides who wins or loses.

TEAM TACTICS

Team tactics bring together all the squad tactics. Now you have to make the squads work. And to be honest with you, we struggle with this to this day. Teams that come together with the trust factor, the right mix of people, that understand it all, have perfect faith in each other, and make it happen; they're unbeatable.

It's a constant struggle to develop that chemistry. You don't just find it. It's almost like managing a business. You start by picking people not only for their playing abilities but for their personalities and their ability to motivate other people.

Young teams often ask me "How can we get to

The Complete Guide to Paintball

be the best team?" My reply is, "Make sure that when you go out and play every weekend, you have fun. Don't pick guys that are jerks." Put people together who will work together, who don't need to be told to be helpful and supportive.

Another team tactic involves learning the fields. You start to walk fields as a team. Identify the vulnerable positions and dominant bunkers. Figure out what positions you need in order to win.

ADAM: We spend a lot of time learning where we want to be and trying to figure out where the opponents are most likely to be. We want to have a game plan. We want to know in advance how the game should go. It takes work, but it pays off tremendously. Once you set that game plan, all your other tactics start to come together—team, squad, and individual.

BILL: We should mention sweet spots. Sweet spots are situations where there's a really nice offensive or defensive advantage. I remember a time where there were thick pines on both sides of a trail that our opposing team had to run about 35 yards through before they could break out their positions. We lined all 10 guns up on the trail. As soon as the whistle blew, our paint was in the air. Ten guns firing 10 balls a second. We took four out before the game even started. We discovered this sweet spot by walking the field in advance of the game.

Another tactic is to break the opponent's line. When you break lines, Adam's done it very successfully, you can come up behind the other team. You come into their line to shoot them all as if you're one of their players. It happens all the time.

ADAM: I snuck behind these guys once and two of them turned around and looked at me. They said, thinking I was one of their team: "Hey Jim!"

I went along with their case of mistaken identity and said, "Yeah, what's up?"

"Jim, we got two of them off the front!" They were pretty worked up.

"All right! Way to go!" I replied.

And as they turned back to me I raised my gun and took them out. "Oh, by the way, I'm not Jim." They were shocked!

Bill: And that was a team of U.S. Marines!

To wrap this up, I want to quote from a book that I love, *The Art of War* by Lao Tzu. I consider it recommended reading for anyone interested in tactics, even emotional tactics. "When you attack, you want to attack from the highest heights of heaven. And when you defend, you want to defend from the deepest resources of the earth," says Lao Tzu.

I interpret it this way: When you attack, your adrenaline is pumped. You attack with such vigor and force that the enemy cannot defend itself. But, when you defend, you don't take stupid chances. You dig in so deep that there's no way that they can shoot you or eliminate you.

PART 6

PLAYING THE GAME

Knowing the Game, Playing to Win

I have always believed that understanding leads to success. Many players play paintball without ever truly understanding the underlying concepts, which is the only way that a person can advance in this sport. As a result of this, many people misinterpret what happens during a game and learn nothing from watching them. Case in point...

After my team, Aftershock, won a game at the World Cup in Orlando, I heard one kid tell his friend, "Oh yeah, you should have seen them. They just mowed the other team down. Aftershock just got up and went at 'em. They smoked 'em, dude." He had completely missed the true nature of what had happened. He seemed to be implying that the win was wholly attributable to Aftershock's attack; it wasn't. He couldn't differentiate between what looked dramatic and what had actually transpired.

Witnessing a team dominate and demolish the opposition, without a doubt one of the most exciting and memorable aspects of paintball, sticks in the mind because it is so dynamic. But it does not tell the whole story. Not by a longshot.

The bottom line is that if you want to progress in this sport, you need to learn how to understand what is going on!

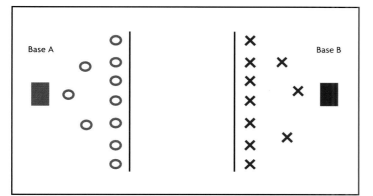

The above illustration is a rough guide to what 99% of tournament paintball teams do when they position themselves at the start of the game. If you look at any tournament game, you will see each team run out to initial positions on the first third of the field, as shown above. The teams will sit in these positions and duke it out until one side gets a few more kills than the other. At that point, the prevailing team will make their move. Only after a significant number of eliminations have been made does the end game unfold. Obviously, the team that gets the most kills in this part of the game normally wins.

Paintball can be broken down, like chess, into three parts: the opening, middle, and the end.

THE OPENING GAME

This is best described as the part of the game where your teammates run out to their primary cover points: the bunkers or trees that you have selected to be your first stopping points.

Now this part of the game, unlike the other two, is completely under your control.

Before the game, your team should have agreed on a selection of bunkers that were not only the

safest to attain, but also provided the best angles for eliminating the opposition.

When the game starts, you should know where you and your teammates are headed, and the path you will use to run to your primary position.

Your team's entry into primary positions should be accomplished without any losses if you have done your prep work correctly.

Having control is important because if you control proceedings then you can predict outcomes Without control, you are a hostage to fortune. Luck will smile on you one day and not the next.

With one hundred percent control, you can do whatever you want with no real interference from the other team. But once you get in this position, the middle part of the game begins, and this is where paintball games are won and lost.

THE MID GAME

Ninety-nine percent of paintball games at tournaments follow similar patterns. Both teams run out to their respective primary positions and start firing their guns. As soon as the mid game progresses, people begin to walk off the field.

The stronger team starts picking off the weaker team one by one. This is where the real damage is done. The determinant of who will actually win the game is generally who gets the most kills off the basic line format. This is one of the fundamentals of tournament play.

All tournament teams try to play this way. They run out to their positions, which roughly extend across the width of a field in a line. In this way, all the bases are covered. Both defensive and attacking capabilities can be optimized across all areas of the field.

The basic layout of a field is the length of it divided into three sections. The first third line is where each team lines up. The middle third line of the field is the killing ground, and the final third line is where (from your perspective as a player) the opposition resides.

The Mid-Game is the Pivotal Phase

As I alluded to earlier, the perspective of the side line observer is limited because the truly decisive and key eliminations are achieved immediately before the *exciting* finale. Indeed, the reality is that by the time you see five or six tournament players get up and run down the last vestiges of the opponents' defense, the most decisive part of the game is already over. A controllable end game results from a successful mid-game.

Since the mid game is so important, what can we do to make sure that it's successful?

Technique is the answer. If you are better than your opposition technically, then the killing ratio will be in your favor. If not, more of your team members will be eliminated and you will lose control of the end game. Lost control means defeat. Period.

Paintball can appear very complex to many people when it is actually very simple. Once you understand the underlying concepts of it, everything makes sense.

There are no secrets in Paintball; everything is common sense.

THE END GAME

After a successful mid game, the end game should be yours. You began the game in control of your primary positioning. You used your technical prowess to acquire a high killing ratio, which left your opponents at a numeric disadvantage. Now you have control. But it isn't over yet; you still have to take advantage of your supremacy.

Almost everyone has heard of heroic last stands from players who have killed five or six incoming

players alone. It happens, but it shouldn't.

Superiority in numbers should mean victory, but there are exceptions when a field bias will sometimes confer an advantage to the team with fewer players. Not everything always goes exactly as planned in the end game. Sometimes the disadvantaged team wins. This sport is inherently unpredictable, but you must give yourself the best possible chance for success.

These are the basic concepts behind the game, but in order to increase your chances of winning, you must have an idea of the other available styles and strategies.

PLAYING STYLES

There are three basic playing styles in paintball: **defensive**, **technical**, and **aggressive**.

The Technical Style

Historically, the All Americans (now the Philadelphia Americans) exemplify the technical approach.

They sit on their line format and eliminate the other team's members with their superior techniques throughout the entire game.

As you watch an American's game, you will notice a procession of their opponents toward the dead box for no reason other than that the Americans shot them first. The trick is to do it consistently. If you want this to be your style, then you need to become an extraordinary sharp-shooter, drill regularly, and practice patience.

The Defensive Style

One of the reasons for playing a defensive game is to counter-attack the other team's offensive attacks. It is not very accepted on the tournament circuit because it is seen as a way of compensating for lack of skill and aggression.

Another reason for playing defensively is when the opposing team is believed to be better than your own. It's safer to move only when you are attacked instead of making an offensive move and opening yourself up to trouble.

The Aggressive Style

This is the most exciting and difficult way to play. It occurs when your team hits the wall of the opposing team, which only happens after significant eliminations have been made. Only two or three teams play this way: Aftershock, multiple World Cup champions, and Bob Long's Ironmen of 1991 to 1994, who were the greatest aggressive team of all time. They attacked with a series of line assaults that could and did break every defense.

KNOWING AND PRACTICING ARE DIFFERENT THINGS

Teams generally acquire their style by default, rather than design, which is a direct consequence of who is on their team. Conservative members play defensively, while eager and slightly crazy members play aggressively. The technical components of each style need to be molded to fit with the technical capabilities of each team. Those who are masterful paintball technicians experience paintball at its most exciting and rewarding. If that's your goal, you are aiming high, and better start practicing now. And now that you know what you have to do, you have no excuses.

—PR

© Cleo Fogal

FIELDS OF DREAMS

Paul Fogal

Achieving the ultimate recreational paintball experience drives Paul Fogal, Founder of Skirmish USA, located in Jim Thorpe, PA. Visit their website at www.skirmish.com.

When it comes to recreational paintball, Skirmish USA is one of the best run facilities out there. It offers plenty of fields to choose from, encompassing a wide variety of playing experiences and environments-from deep woods to wide open spaces. Over 700 acres and 44 fields are devoted to the recreational paintball experience. Every other year, the World Record Game attracts over a thousand players from all over the world.

If you want to know what makes for a great paintball experience, there's one man to ask—Paul Fogal. He has set the standards for recreational play.

ANDREW FLACH: What are your standards for a successful day of paintball?

PAUL: You should have an exciting time running around with your friends in the woods, and no complaints about the service at the field. If you and your friends leave with a smile on your face, we've done our job.

In a way, it's a people movement business. We try and move you efficiently, so you're out there playing as soon as possible and can play the number of games you want. Then we try to change the games and the terrain around so you've got to think a little bit about what you're doing. You shouldn't be running to the same tree all day. You'll play one time and you're on one side of the field and then the other side of the field and sometimes you go to another field

or sometimes you might play three games on a field if you really like it.

We try to give the players the field experience they want. One field might have more open terrain and another might be real thick. One might be dry, another wet. Then we have the Village Fields and the Scenario Fields where there are buildings, structures, and unique bunkers.

ANDREW: A field like The Alamo?

PAUL: Yes, there's a couple like The Alamo. People like to play those fields at the end of the day. They're bigger and they're paint-eaters. Near the end of the day, when players want to run out of paint, we hear them say "The hell with this hunting thing. Let's just shoot it out."

ANDREW: From what I observed from just a brief experience interacting with your staff, it strikes me that there are several keys to your success. And I think these are things all people should expect when they go to a paintball field. Number one is the emphasis on safety. Safety is paramount.

PAUL: The most critical safety issue is that you have to keep your goggles on your face at all times on the field of play. There are some people who don't understand that and you have to keep pushing them and reminding them. Some people just blank out and start to lift their goggles after a game is over. You just can't do that, and we never let people forget it.

Beyond keeping their eyeballs in their heads, we like our players to feel like they're spending most of their time doing what they came to do. Players are there to get their money's worth. They expect to be moved efficiently through the entire process—get their release forms filled out, get their gun and equipment rentals in hand quickly, buy paint, get to the field. Players should be able to start playing very quickly and play as many games as possible during the course of the day. Sufficient logistics are of primary importance.

To accomplish this, we need a professional staff—motivated, helpful people, who know how to treat customers properly and handle situations in an appropriate manner. People who enjoy delivering on customer service.

ANDREW: You're doing something right in terms of the way you're conducting your business. People speak very highly of their experience here. Word of mouth is priceless. People tell other people, "I had a great time at Skirmish. They were really nice people, I felt really comfortable, and their fields are awesome." These are all things that add up to a successful operation.

PAUL: You have to run your field in a professional, businesslike manner. That has been a problem in paintball, but it's improving. For years there were a lot of fields that weren't being run well,

© Cleo Fogal

but as the sport matures, only the fields that have their act together will survive. Most of the poorly run fields are dropping by the wayside. Not long ago, an insurance guy told me he figured that about forty percent of the fields still didn't have any insurance. That's just ridiculous. Wake up, field owners. You could lose everything and hurt paintball's reputation in the process!

ANDREW: It seems that to engineer a fun day

of paintball, a certain plan is required. Are you guys following a program, whereby teams that start on field "A" will move on to field "B", whereas teams that start on field "Y" go on to field "Z"?

PAUL: No, it's not that scientific. There are large, open fields and small, wooded fields, and fields thick with 15-foot-high rhododendron bushes. We have a general manager, Karen, who evaluates the groups and she puts them on the field where she thinks it's appropriate for that group to start. For example, if it's forty people she puts you on a field that would handle forty people size-wise.

During the course of the day, the judges talk to the players, who are usually pretty forthcoming about what they want. They'll request fields, and we try to accommodate them.

There's one person whose job it is to keep track of who's playing where and they radio in about which fields are open. That person will look at the group and see how many people there are, see what fields they've played, which field is open. You just try and vary it a little bit. You're kind of throwing them a curve, keeping things exciting and new.

I really think the secret to our success is that the fields are a little bit bigger and there's a little bit more anticipation before the shooting starts than in most places. Most places really pack you in.

Playing the Game

ON FIELD DESIGN

ANDREW: Who's job is it to design the field?

PAUL: Dewey Green and I are the chief designers. It's a constant tinkering and feedback process. Various judges and players also make suggestions regarding their preferences and desires. Once or twice a year, a group of us will get together over beer and pizza. We brainstorm new field designs and game formats.

THE ROLE OF THE JUDGE

ANDREW: It seems important to have someone on the field who is a representative of the paintball field's operator-the judge. What is a judge?

PAUL: On a recreational level, a judge is a combination of referee and guide. He or she helps the group with their equipment, leads them through the day, and then will make some calls on the field. By the very nature of the fact that you're playing on a number of acres in the woods, the referees cannot make all the calls. There always has to be an honor factor.

The best judges are people with extroverted personalities, who kind of enjoy the woods. A lot of the judges are there because they like to run around in the woods. I often hear them say things like, "I sit behind the computer terminal all week, so it's fun to get out here and get some exercise."

ON CLOTHING

ANDREW: How should I prepare myself for a day of play? What would you recommend as the proper clothing?

PAUL: Just wear old clothes. If you have a set of fatigues, wear them. Dark colors are a good idea—black, brown, green. Clothes that you will not mind getting wet, dirty, muddy, or splattered with paint.

As an option, most fields offer some sort of camouflage overalls, or "cammies," for rent. You just step into them; they fit over your clothes. At the end of the day, you turn them in and let someone else worry about cleaning them.

Shoes are probably the most important consideration. Go for something light with ankle support and avoid heavy boots.

ANDREW: What about food and water?

PAUL: A good field will provide that stuff for you. Of course, you can bring your own. A good field will have adequate food service and drink. You've got to stay hydrated to avoid cramps and overheating.

© Cleo Fogal

Your basic rental gear.

WHAT KIND OF GAMES ARE PLAYED

ANDREW: What are the different games you play at Skirmish?

PAUL: There are an infinite variety of games you can play. Center Hang is when you put one flag in the middle of the field and both teams try to get it and take it through to the other team's side of the field. It's like scoring a touchdown. That's a pretty popular game.

The top one is certainly Capture the Flag. The second most popular game is probably Center Hang. Number three would be Offense/Defense or Attack and Defend. One team defends their position and the other team just attacks it and they usually have to go in and get the flag or pull it down, or take it out beyond a boundary.

Frankly, the twenty-four hour scenario games are my favorite. They are as interesting as the people who come to play them. We're talking serious paintball hobbyists. In a twenty-four hour scenario game, you've got what seems like unlimited time. So you're not worried about it. And the field of play is huge.

You can go out on a mission and it might take you two hours to try

and attain a certain objective. The guy that's directing it, the scenario director, he's just playing with you. He basically sends you out on this mission and then calls up the other coordinators on their radios and he gives them codes that tell them where you're going so that you can be ambushed.

Now, you as a player understand that he's doing this, so you know you have to be careful. Your opponents are going there for the same reason and maybe they've had a half an hour head start on you. Even though you know what's going on, there's still a great deal of suspense.

Sometimes a squad will go out and count how many tents are set up in the enemy's base camp. The players have to try and get that information and bring it back. You earn points if you complete that mission.

Another mission may involve a downed pilot in Sector Five on your map. One of the judges goes out and lays there and makes believe he's the downed pilot. Sometimes they've got to take a stretcher out there, put him on it, and bring him back on it. Very intense stuff.

Whatever the mission, scenario games are highly complex and some people are really into this role

playing. Guys come out here with night vision goggles, radios, set up "booby traps" and ambushes. We even have homemade tanks.

We do run three or four scenario games a year, but we only do two twenty-four hour games. The other ones last about eight hours—we call them "mini-scenarios."

ANDREW: How does outdoor paintball differ from indoor paintball?

PAUL: When you play outdoors, the fields are larger and it takes time before "engaging" your opponents. From your position, you can see them coming and you can watch and you can hide and you don't have to move.

Whenever I've played indoors, there's no ambush factors really. You can hide against this wall, but your opponent is still right there . You cannot set an ambush and watch him moving towards you, waiting for the right moment to open fire. Everything happens at a much further distance in the woods, so it's not quite as scary. Indoors can be pretty scary. People are shooting at close range, surprising you from around corners and obstacles.

ANDREW: That's how I experienced it. Indoors does have a frantic intensity. This one place I went to played the Mission Impossible theme before the game. Everybody gets revved up. Add that to the craziness that you're already experiencing. It was wild.

At the very end of the game, I had run out of paint, but I was still able to get these guys out because I was adrenalized. I just shouted, "You guys are out. Drop your guns right now." They didn't even question it. I love that energy rush. What is it about the game of paintball that you enjoy?

PAUL: I play paintball because I like the game itself. My son and I went out and played the other day. He's starting to play very well, so now I can play with him on an equal basis. It was fun for me-not just because he's my son, but because I'm engaged in

this competitive experience that is so exciting.

Paintball is a great equalizer. Psychological makeup, not social status, really attracts certain people to the game. I played on a team that included a couple of guys that were engineers, a fellow who was working for AT&T, another who was a mason's helper, one was unemployed, another guy drove a forklift in a factory, yet another was a movie stuntman. All different walks of life come to have fun in the woods.

For me, male camaraderie and bonding are a large part of my enjoyment of the sport. I liken it to the way primitive hunters must have felt at the end of the day:

"We just had a successful hunt. We just killed a woolly mammoth." The sense of having survived is unique.

FIELDER'S CHOICE

The appendix in the back of this book provides a list of paintball fields in all areas of the United States and of the world, so you've got plenty of options when it comes to locating a field. If you haven't played for a few years, however, you may be in for the surprise of your life when you get there.

Paintball isn't just that game you play in the woods anymore.

The concept fields used for tournaments are now easily obtainable by field owners willing to set aside space to put them up. There are even parks set up in family fun centers next to go-karts and batting cages! This availability is due to many new companies coming into the arena game market. In addition to the Sup'air system, Ultimate Air has begun to make bunkers that are tubeless, so they can be put up in more remote areas without the pipes Sup'air uses.

Courtesy Challenge Park Xtreme

Courtesy Challenge Park Xtreme

Many fields have gone even further than that. Although theme fields are not new—SC Village has been doing them since the 1980s—they are home to a whole new kind of theatrics. Probably the most graphic example is Challenge Park, just outside of Chicago, IL. They were an established field for years, then moved in order to facilitate something bigger: a theme park for paintball. Their fields include, among others:

- **Bedlam, IL**. This field is a town. Full buildings, cars parked in the streets, mailboxes, phone booth, streetlights, the works.

- **Jungle of Doom** is a wooded field with a full temple built into it.

- **Armageddon** is a bombed-out cityscape with rubble piles and half-destroyed buildings.

Armageddon

Courtesy Challenge Park Xtreme

Meanwhile, in Canada, a field opened up in Toronto using the abandoned set from "Total Recall." Now called "Area 51," the field has a backdrop that is, literally, something out of a sci-fi movie.

The concept isn't new. EMR has had the "Castle" for years, and holds two "Castle Conquests" every year. Skirmish has several theme fields, like "Hood in the Woods." But the level of theatrics has become so high that, again, paintball fields resemble theme parks more and more.

If you just want to play out in the woods, that's still available. But look for theme-park field owners to keep trying to top each other in the years to come. The future of scenario paintball is limited only by what field owners are willing to build—and, for the moment, they show no signs of slowing down.

—*Rob Tyger Rubin*

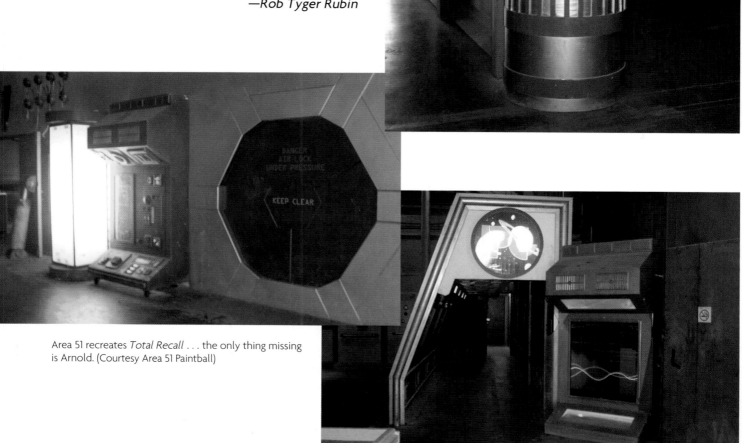

Area 51 recreates *Total Recall* . . . the only thing missing is Arnold. (Courtesy Area 51 Paintball)

Woodcraft

PLAYING THE OLD FASHIONED WAY!

Now you see me ... now you don't!

So many people are getting into arena games that they forget (or sometimes don't even learn) how to play the woods. I'm guilty of it myself. I've definitely been playing indoors too long, and I've been losing my woodland eyes. (It takes a few games to get that vision back, but man, I love it!)

Woodland play is fun for me, when I can get there. I live in Minnesota—land of two seasons: winter is coming and winter is here. (Yes, the movie "Fargo" was a good documentary and "Grumpy Old Men" was filmed on location 20 minutes from my house.)

Personally, the best part of woodland paintball is the stalking. I don't want to sound like some kind of wacked-out, back-country, weird-beard here. I'm just saying that when you're outside, closer to nature than usual, successfully stalking your friends (or whoever your opponents happen to be that day); it's a thrill! I'm a big guy, and somehow I can do it.

What is Woodcraft?

Woodcraft is mainly the art of trickery. The use of camouflage and conceal-ment is a dying art in paintball. Crawlers use a little 'woodcraft' on tournament fields, but it's virtually obsolete because fields are increasingly postage-stamp-sized.

It's a real skill to use terrain to your advantage. It encompasses a number of skills that we either take for granted or don't take seriously as modern players. These days paintball players laugh at people using face paint; back in the eighties, when I started playing, face paint was the norm. The original paintball players used woodcraft because the game was played outside exclusively. The time has come to modernize the use of woodcraft to suit the evolution of our sport.

Know your opponents!

What you need to do is trick your opponent. How? The first thing you have to understand is your opponent. To begin with, he or she is a human being. However noble in reason and spirit they may be, humans are fallible. In paintball, their imperfections are often relatively easy to spot, if you're paying attention.

Paintball tricks work by understanding the general nature of and specific inclinations of your opponents. Generally speaking, most players today are impatient. Instead of waiting for you to walk on top of them, most will shoot as soon as they see you. Most are also deadlocked on the opponent they see in front of them and less likely to check their sides as they advance.

Here's where using your camouflage comes in handy. For example, I was playing at Stalker Paintball Games, a field in Wisconsin that has a dense canopy and not many light patches. I dove into a thicket bush and sat for a few minutes. Basically, I was out in the middle of nowhere, with no solid

cover for 50 feet other than this thicket. But, the other team was making a push up the center. One player in a JT jersey came screaming up the center. I leveled my gun, waited for him, and hammered down as he made a turn into the spool right in front of me.

Sitting still in your cover and using your camouflage to your advantage is the essence of fieldcraft. My opponent was so focused on making his bunker that he got sloppy. I understood that he would do just that, and I acted accordingly. I had control of the situation, he just never realized it.

So with that story in mind, let's start with your camouflage.

The Invisible Advantage

We all wear camouflage, but hardly anyone uses it correctly because of a lack of control or understanding. It's ridiculous that so few people really take advantage of their camos. Many players want to shoot their gun as many times as they can. Fine, go ahead! Don't be surprised that someone saw you from the other side of the field. You're making noise, and now we know where you are.

In order to use camouflage, it's important to understand why it works. There are a few different styles that work in different ways in different terrain. I had a long chat with Tim Schloss of Pursuit Products about camouflage. That's his business, he sells "Tiger Stripe", "Realtree" and "Advantage" styles of camouflage, as well as color blocked styles. Great stuff. He told me there's two basic types of camouflage, and two basic ways they work.

Types of Camouflage

Aggressive camouflage works by fooling the eye into thinking it's a part of the background. Good examples of this type would be US Woodland, Belgian dots, Auscam, and so on. It's made to match a background's overall colors. This stuff works best behind shrubs and shadows. Camouflages like Tiger

Stripe fall into this category, but for a different reason. You see, the human eye is lazy. When we scan for opponents, we scan horizontally. Aggressive camouflage, like Tiger Stripe, encourages the eye to "slide over" it. There are a few other camouflages like this. US Woodland was actually created for a European military theater by the United States government. Tiger Stripe was originally made for the Vietnam conflict, but was modified slightly for paintballers. You don't want to know how much the Australian government spent on developing Auscam, but it's the best stuff for hiding in Australia that I've found.

Passive camouflage works in a different way; it's made to convince the brain it's part of the foreground and totally natural. This would include Advantage, Realtree (and it's derivatives), Mossy Oak, and so on. Each of these types is perfect for specific uses. Advantage looks like the forest floor, while Realtree looks like a tree. These camouflages started as hunting patterns. They are supposed to enable a hunter to stand in front of a tree to get a better shot. That's why they try to be photo-realistic. They're not really meant for other terrain. In their elements, these highly specialized camouflages are excellent.

Then there's a third kind of camouflage, which I call "Weirdo-Flage." These types fit mostly into the "Aggressive" camouflage category. They include, but aren't limited to, JT, Scott, Renegade or Venomwear printed jerseys, Splash clothing. Any of the "Non-Camo" stuff also falls into this category. The

idea behind these patterns is simply to bring paintball into the 'mainstream'. Paintball garb as fashionable accessory...you get the picture. They work toward that end, and, occasionally, as partial camouflage. I love the guys who wear off-the-shelf JT Jerseys. Big, juicy white targets in the center of their chests and on their forearms. Easy target from across the field. Love it.

Some of the non-camo works, but not as well as true camouflage. If you're wearing it to look like a team, cool. If you're wearing it as a true camo... well... umm... yeah...

Whatever you're wearing, the golden rule of camouflage is not to move. The human eye is lazy, but it's also naturally drawn to motion. Motion is perceived as something worth watching.

Paintball players, of course, have to move. Given that fact, note that "Aggressive" patterns allow you more freedom of movement than "Passive" patterns. Aggressive patterns aren't specific to one spot or terrain, and allow you to take a "camouflaged" position anywhere in a broad spectrum of places. If you're wearing Realtree and you're lying down, it doesn't "look" right and you're more apt to be spotted. Tiger Stripe looks more appropriate in any given place you stop.

As a player, you can also use different patterns in different terrain. I have a set of Realtree I've used in the desert. It worked well. This isn't brain surgery, people. The key is simply to match your camouflage as accurately as possible to your surroundings. I've seen pictures of UK players in Tiger Stripe in which the green just blares out against a brown background; we're talking total absence of greenage on the ground level. I've made boo-boos like this before, mostly in my paintball youth. And if it happens by mistake these days, I just change my outlook on the game and adapt. I'll look for colors where I'm close to blending in and go from there.

Camouflage—All or Nothing!

Use a visor on your goggles or at least a hat brim. Goggle flare is a dead giveaway to your position. Don't use chrome or bright, splashy stuff that may glare as well. Matte Black is still your best bet for color. Wear a full mask. Skin tones aren't nature tones and will give you away. Better yet, paint your mask for camo colors or mottle it somehow to break up the "Black Blob" on your face. My favorite trick is hiding your brightly colored armband by burying your arm into a tree or the ground and using your body as a "cloak" over it.

BEHAVING INVISIBLE

There's a time and a place for battle cries and open charges down the middle, but this ain't one of 'em!

Wait your opponent out. They panic when nobody is shooting at them. Take your time and you'll absolutely freak 'em out.

You don't need cool camos or anything like that to hide, however. I could be wearing stark white, and you won't see me if I'm totally behind hard cover (see the Cover chapter). It's that easy. Let's say I'm wearing a really bright jersey and I've got a bright red paintgun. If I'm trying to hide, I'll get behind a rock, a dirt berm, or a hill. Anything I can put my whole body behind relative to an enemy position will hide me.

Nature is one big free camouflage factory!

Use Reference Points and the World Around You

Having a reference point is good as well. I'll often use cover from one angle, knowing that the other team or another player will be coming from that or another angle and crossing my barrel. I can expose myself to one side if I know that side is *safe*. That's why I run the tape as often as I do, I can expose

that whole flank as I wait for you to walk into my dot-sight. Pop, "HIT", Bingo. Thank you.

Terrain is a big part of woodcraft. Your woodcraft skills come from learning how to use what's ahead of you and see what's to the side of you. Lining up trees to conceal your movement toward your opponents is always a good idea. You can't plan on things like shadows, wind, and so on to mask your movement. You just have to do it.

But when it all falls together, you have to recognize it for what it is. If I'm stalking a tape (either by crawl or by crouch), I'm constantly aware of my surroundings. I'm looking ahead for the clearest line in the path that requires minimal effort and noise. Leaves are bad, dirt is good. If I have a choice between twigs or dried leaves, I'll take the twig route. I can push twigs out of my way quieter and faster than I can leaves by just dragging my hand along them and not lifting my knees too far.

I'm always listening to the wind. When it picks up, I move. When it dies down, I slow or stop. I listen for airplanes, cars, trucks, trains, people shooting in the center . . . anything that makes enough noise to mask my movement.

Moves are made quickly and deliberately, and planned two steps ahead when possible. The thought process is: "Big tree to fort. Fort to spool. Spool to shrubs."

I'm always looking ahead. I'm also looking down the field to where opponents should be hiding. I can't predict everything, but if I'm coming up on a big tree or an outcropping of barrels, odds are someone is either in there or wants to be. I'm looking through cover for background shadows. If I don't see any light behind twigs or shrubs, it's either a rock, a tree, or a player.

Sounds play a very important role, too. Especially nature sounds. Most things in nature that produce noisy sounds will stop when something big comes by and scares them. If the birds and crickets stop chirping, someone spooked them and you should get ready. In some cases, an animal may start making a lot of noise if you approach. Listen for any and all audible changes; they're the best early warning system you'll have in the wild.

A bit of woodcraft also goes into using nature to fool people. These are old school tricks, but they're still good. Here are some examples from my experience. I'm lying on the ground while two guys are looking for me. They know I'm out there, but not sure where. With one foot I'll wiggle a small tree or a thick shrub away from me. That will get their attention long enough for me to come up and take 'em out. There's also the "Throw a rock away from you so it makes noise over there" trick, but I stopped doing that out of fear of pelting a ref or well-hidden player. You'd be well advised to throw only relatively light things. I've also been stalking, been spotted, and swayed matching the tree in front of me for movement. The player looked away, and I got moving at the flag. (I was able to get the flag, and not make a single elimination that game.) Then there's the 'ballsy' approach. Someone thinks they see me, and they open a barrage at me. I don't flinch or move. After a few moments, they stop shooting. Why? Nothing shot back, obviously nobody's there. One burst later, they're gone.

CLAIM THIS LOST ART AND PUT IT IN YOUR GAME

To a paintball player who uses woodcraft, tactical possibilities are virtually infinite. I've crawled through a path with no cover in front of me and made it, and I've sat in front of a tree and remained unseen. But if you think this is all there is to know, you're wrong.

I talked to a friend of mine; he plays in ratty old BDU's, uses a pump gun, and wears no mask. He's one of my favorite wire players, because he can just vanish after taking a guy out and pop up thirty paces to the right of where he just was. He's very good. When I started writing this piece, I asked him for help. "Sure!" he said. "Who's gonna read it?" I said new players and tournament competitors. "No way, man!" he said. "I'm not gonna tell 'em all my secrets! I've earned some advantage over them!"

I agree. Some secrets are meant to be discovered rather than shared. Besides, I learned from the best. I can't let out all our trade secrets. Ninja Union Local 151 won't let me.

—RR

Playing the Game

Indoor vs. Outdoor

Paintball was first played outdoors, in the woods. Most games still take place in the great outdoors. But Nature is unpredictable and anything can, and usually does, happen. So players looked for an alternative to being rained, snowed or hailed on, and moved the game inside.

You'd think that the only difference between indoor and outdoor paintball is that one simply has a roof overhead, but you'd be wrong. Bringing paintball indoors creates a whole new game, and many indoor fields can do things that outdoor fields simply cannot. But we're getting ahead of ourselves here.

Indoor paintball is, obviously, played inside. But there's a lot of variety in that loose definition. Some fields have artificial turf set up with airball bunkers. Others have sand floors and cars buried up to the axels. And yet others are designed like a maze, where opponents can be around any corner. There have been indoor paintball fields set up in old movie theaters, old warehouses and even in a storefront of a mall! They can be small or huge, depending on how much space they have available.

Let's start with some of the basic concepts of playing indoors. Indoor paintball is usually played in much tighter spaces than outdoor paintball. Safety first: most indoor fields require paintguns to shoot at a lower velocity than outdoor fields. Generally, 220 to 250 FPS is the legal indoor limit. Compare this to the 290 to 300 FPS limit of outdoor fields and you can begin to see some differences. So be prepared to turn the velocity of your paintgun down to meet the local speed limit. All other normal safety rules apply, with barrel blocking devices mandatory and standard goggles and masks required.

On the topic of safety, let's talk about the play surface. Everything from sand to wood chips to dirt to ground-up recycled shoes to bare concrete has been used for indoor surfaces. Each has its advantages and drawbacks, and most of the time it's the field owner's preference as to what they use. What you want to do as a player is plan ahead. If the surface is dirt, sand, pea gravel or other earthy type material, you want to wear cleats or boots with an aggressive tread. If the surface is carpet or turf, a pair of court shoes may work best.

Footwear is a pretty big deal for indoor play. Paint accumulates on the floor, and there can be dangerous slick spots. Trust me; it's not fun when you go from a full sprint to an unbalanced skid because your shoes just lost traction. So your footing is not going to be 100% solid every time you take a step. Just remember to be careful when you're moving until you learn how your feet and the floor get along. Wearing shoes or boots that brace your ankles, regardless of type, is a good idea.

Wearing knee and elbow pads is also a very good idea. These will help protect you from injury if you should slip on the surface. I would also recommend wearing long pants, a jersey or long sleeve t-shirt and gloves as well. Much like the floors, paint collects on walls and bunkers. Brushing against a wall can make you look like you've just taken a dive into the deepest paint pit on the planet so wearing long

sleeves is important. Because of the close-quarters nature, wearing a neck guard or other "protection" can ease your mind as well.

Before you assume that indoor is worse or somehow "lesser" than outdoor, let's look at some advantages, such as running water—you have real bathrooms. Most indoor fields are closer to large towns, so you're not driving to the middle of nowhere to go play. Indoor fields are also open late at night, so you can play outdoor in the morning, drive to the indoor and play into the evening. Having done it myself, it makes for a very fun day! Indoor paintball also provides fields that you just can't get in the woods. The rush of going from door to door in a dimly-lit environment is something you have to experience for yourself. Some fields have music or sound effects blaring through speakers to add to the whole feel of the game. Sure, you can get the same kind of thing in front of your TV with a video game controller in your hands. But playing a video game has nothing on the real thing. You can't get a real adrenaline rush in front of your TV.

Before your first outing to an indoor field, there are a few things you want to do. First, do a little homework. Almost every field has a website, and you should look at it to learn a little about the field. This gives you a chance to find out all the information about the hours, prices, floor surfaces, and what kind of field they provide. Are there photos of plastic pipes or cars? Do they have buildings up or is it airball bunkers? Take some time to know what the field offers. It also makes it easier to get friends to show up when you can tell them what to expect.

Many people don't know what to wear to an indoor field. Just bring your normal playing clothes. No, really, that's all you need. Wearing gloves helps to take the sting out of hand shots from close range. Some people have specific gear to play indoors, but for your first time indoors you shouldn't need anything special. If you don't have any of your

Playing the Game

own gear, some loose fitting jeans and a long sleeve t-shirt will do just fine.

Here's where doing your homework comes in handy. Many indoor fields will have coveralls you can rent or buy. Don't expect anything special, but it's a lot better than ruining your regular clothing for a day's play. They may also have gloves, hats or other clothing for rent or purchase, too. Finding out this information, and calling ahead to confirm it, can make your life a lot easier. Plus it can give you an idea of what the day will cost you, generally speaking.

If you have it, bring your usual equipment, too: your normal paintgun, hopper, pods, and the rest of the gear you always play with. Because of the lower velocity limits, you might want to bring spare parts to tune your paintgun to a lower speed. Most indoor fields also have a pro shop on site, and they may have the parts you need there. I would also recommend packing a spare bag with a full change of clothing. You'll thank me later.

One comment about goggle lenses before we move on. There's always a question of what color lens to use indoors. Many players will prefer an amber or yellow tinted lens over a clear one. This is to increase the contrast, as it filters out the "blue" light. This is good for low-light conditions. Clear lenses are also fine, and most players have a pair already. Under some conditions, such as an extremely bright indoor facility, you may want to keep a smoke or mirrored lens in your goggles. But, for the most part, you can't go wrong with a clear lens.

As said before, indoor fields vary from location to location, so what you're going to be playing on and around can be just about anything. The intensity of the games you can expect to play is mostly dictated by the style of field, the surface on the floor, the lighting available and how much space you have to play in.

For example, Indoor Field A has a sand floor, and they have mostly airball style bunkers in a very well lit room that is 125'x125'. The style of play will include a lot of shooting. Players won't be sliding into bunkers as the sand surface will stop them in their tracks if they try it. But players will get hit from across the field, and the action will be very fast paced.

By comparison, Indoor Field B has a dirt floor, is minimally lit, and has walls set up to create a building to building maze in a medium sized room. The play will usually slow down as players are not only watching

The Complete Guide to Paintball

Courtesy of Smart Parts

where they're going, but also they're going room to room, which takes more time. Plus the action is going to be very close and personal, so an opponent will be very hesitant to just walk right into a darker room.

When you compare this to other types of outdoor play, you'll see there's nothing quite like an indoor field. So when the weather gets bad, or if you want to play late at night, it's definitely worth a try!

—RR

URBAN PLAY

Paintball is an interesting game. What we play on an airball field can be taken into the woods, or a junkyard, or even into a town setting. It's the latter that we're going to review now: Doing it under urban conditions.

Urban play can take many forms, including everything from an old auto bone yard to glitzy Hollywood sets. But the most basic way to play urban terrain is building to building. One thing that you'll find is that there is no way to take a building with a 100 percent success ratio. It won't happen. No matter how cool your SWAT fatigues look, you will not be able to do it perfectly every time.

The true key to success is being prepared for the urban play environment. If it's paved, it will hurt to play on unless you have knee and elbow pads. We also recommend neck guards, a cap of some kind, and anything else you can think of. Some think it's weak to wear that much padding, but it's really only a sign that you don't want to get unnecessarily injured. Most players have no problems with that.

Now, on to the urban sprawl: let's take a look at any given field that is building to building. Most share a few common items besides buildings. Most are clear cut, meaning the fields are kept to grass and not overgrown. In this case, playing a building field isn't much different than playing any given airball field except you can get into the bunkers as well as hide behind them. Another thing they all share in common is the style of buildings. Most are four walls with windows and roofs. The style may change, but the basics never do.

So right there you can get a few of the techniques down, just by knowing that there are a few constants in how they play.

Defending

We'll start with defense, or playing in or around a building to hold it. Sometimes you can do more good for your team by going into a building, putting out the unwelcome mat, and moving in. A building can offer a sense of security that other structures may not, but that can come back to hurt you.

So let's start by going into a building. When you go in, get an idea of your surroundings before you start to go to town. Check the angles of the doorways and windows and how they relate down the field to your opponents. You want to avoid being "locked in" at all costs. Translation: they keep your head down and you can't come up for air without tasting paint.

As a bunker, look at a building as a place you can work with. One way is to stay outside a building. If you're outside the building, you can line up shooting lanes through windows of a building. It's harder to thread the needle from 70 feet away than it is to shoot from the same "needle" when you're inside it. You also want to work all sides of a building, left and right. Buildings are big structures, usually. So you can go from one side to another without any problems.

Once you're inside a building, don't stop moving around. On more than one occasion, I've held off

numbers I usually would never have a chance with because I move around in a building. Two shots out the left door, two shots from the right side of a window, back to the left door, then the right door, then the window again... Mix it up. For the most part, you have unrestricted movement in a building. Use it all.

You want to come out of windows and doorways at odd heights. The average person, kneeling, is about three feet tall. Standing, it's a little less than six feet. Come out of a door at one foot, poke the barrel out and shoot. They'll never see it coming. For protection, use the corners of windows rather than the sides or bottoms. The advantage is you can conceal more of your paintgun and body from the corner of a window than you can from the bottom or sides.

© Cleo Fogal

If that doesn't work, move to the opposing wall of the building, and kneel down. In this case, it's like playing a loose bunker. You can control more angles of the field without exposing yourself unnecessarily. I like to do this in order to

snapshoot from windows. It gives me more room to breathe, and also offers an opportunity for me to slide to a doorframe or wherever if the window angle is too much.

Speaking of windows, watch your angles. You may be inside a building, and protected from the whole right side, but your left could be exposed to one guy who can thread the needle and hit you. Keep an eye on doorways you're not at currently, and most important, be mindful if the bad guys run up on your building. Point blank exchanges happen, and are not fun.

One more thing: When you're inside a building, have an escape route. Sometimes you go into a building knowing your trip is one-way. You either get eliminated or you own the field. But normally, you want to look at the doorways for a route to exit, if you need to.

Attacking

Now we'll discuss attacking a building. If it's unavoidable, if it's a part of the scenario you're playing, if it's where the opponent's flag is, you're going to have to go in. But before you do, you want to do all you can to soften it up a bit. From long range, pour in the long ball. You may not be a fan of high volume shooting, but in this case it's probably the best thing you can do. When you rain in paint, you make it dangerous for the defenders to poke a head up. By doing that, you make it possible to approach a building from one side without the defenders in the building seeing the move.

Assuming you can do this, and it's easier than you may think, you can pretty much run up to a building. Unless you're Superman, you can't see through walls. Neither can your opponents. Flatten out against the wall, away from the windows and doors. You don't want them to see any part of you from in the building. If they as much put the barrel out the window to shoot, put a ball on it. A barrel hit is just as good as a goggle hit in my book. I've knelt under

a window to shoot up and hit someone's hopper when they stuck it out of a window.

Watch your profile too. If a defender is on the ball, and they're playing the building as hard or harder than you are, they can make a fast move into a corner, see some of your harness, and shoot it. And don't try to pop through the window yourself. The defender is set up, and waiting to do the same thing. At best, you'll trade you for them. At worst, you'll get shot a dozen times point blank because you just scared the blazes out of someone by magically appearing in front of them in a window frame.

Even if you can't get up close to the building, you can play mind games with a defender in a building. Shoot a few balls, then stop. Stay on your position, and when you see movement, put a ball into there. You want to let them feel it's safe to come out the window again, and then put paint on them. You'll get more eliminations by letting the other team run into your paint than any other way.

If you're working a field of buildings, the field boundaries may be a good way to take the field. Depending on the boundary itself, you may be able to work in an alley way, a room to room scenario, or some cover outside the actual town. Keep an eye into the buildings, and move it up. You can also use any natural cover on the boundaries like trees, scrub brush, and so on. Just realize that you may not be able to see inside a darkened building, but they can see out just fine.

Driving

And now, the fun part. Driving. When you're going to enter a hostile enclosure, it's called "driving a building" or "driving through a building." It's a very messy affair, and not a pleasant thing to do from either side of the equation. Even the most highly trained members of a SWAT team drill this over and over, eventually getting it down after hundreds of dry runs.

Ideally, you want at least two people entering a

© Cleo Fogal

At the same time, the second in is pointed straight ahead to clear everything from the back wall to the corner of the room. The second will enter the room as soon as the first steps to the side, but he's over the shoulder of the first before he does this. If you need to, put the barrel literally on his shoulder so the muzzle tip is past him. You don't want to shoot someone in the back of the head point blank if you don't have to, especially your own teammate.

If you have more than that, the next in the room will sweep the room as they enter, and ideally the last in line is watching behind the group. That's the ideal. The reality is that the first guy enters the room, a defender panics and starts shooting. And in the chaos that follows, paint is shot in anger and it can be a mess. If you're going to take a building like that, here's a recommendation: If you've got them, paint grenades are a great tool for clearing a room. You want to throw it in so it hits the opposite wall, and bounces back towards the door. That way you get the maximum coverage of spray with minimum exposure. Just toss it in like a hook shot, hard enough to set it off, and bring your hand back fast while keeping your body completely on the other side of the doorway. It's not the ultimate answer, but it certainly can make taking a room of a building easier if it's already been "softened up." (Of course, it never quite works like that. You're lucky to get an organized move through a doorway, let alone a well choreographed dance of paintballs and players moving like a well oiled machine.)

Urban play is a nice break from the woods style we're all used to. And with many fields building sets, or villages, or even castle structures, odds are you'll be on one sooner or later.

—Rob "Tyger" Rubin

building. Four to five attackers are actually better, but if it's all you have, two will work. Realize that since two people can't usually make it through a door at the same time, the first one in has to be gutsy and trust his partner totally. It's all about knowing a role, trusting your teammate completely, and then doing your job. You want to set up your move by standing against the wall with everyone lined up, ready to push into the building. The lead attacker is the one who decides the moment.

The first one in the building is at the most risk, obviously. But the job of this player is to check the area right inside the doorway, sweeping the barrel toward the inside of the room. So if the door is along the right wall of a room, the lead man steps in, sweeps 90 degrees to his left, makes sure it's clear of bad guys, then sweeps 45 degrees to face the opposing corner.

Durty Games

THERE'S MORE THAN ONE WAY TO . . .

Hi there. Durty Dan here. These games were designed with established fields in mind. That is, the area is all set up, marked out, has flag stations and the like. When writing the rules, I tried not to insult your intelligence by mentioning painfully obvious facts. I figured I didn't have to tell you that the games start and end with a whistle or horn. You will also notice that a lot of rules from the basic Capture the Flag game are repeated in each game, I've done this so you don't have to keep referring back to the original game. Each game stands on its own.

Field owners will find these games an interesting addition to the games they may already run on their field. You may need to adapt the rules to your own particular needs, but remember that safety is always your number one concern.

I purposely did not include games like speedball. (These games and other games requiring structures will already exist where the structures exist on the field.) Not every field will have a speedball course, a village or a fort. The reason for not including these types of games is an attempt on my part to make these games universal. With a little preparation you should be able to play these games on any field in the world.

Speaking of fields, do not confuse "established" fields, with "commercial" fields. Established fields have a playing area already set up to play at least Capture the Flag. Whether it's a "legitimate/commercial" field or a "bootleg/outlaw" field is beside the point.

I have been to some "legitimate/commercial" fields where I was afraid to take off my goggles at any time, unless I was in my car with the windows rolled up. I have also heard of a "bootleg/outlaw" field who sent a guy home for having a hot gun!

Unless otherwise stated, these five rules apply to all the games in this chapter. These are referred to as . . .

GENERAL RULES

1. All players must begin the game at their flag station (or assigned starting point) and cannot leave that area until the game begins.

2. Players who are hit are out of the game.

3. Players who are eliminated may not, by word or gesture, indicate any intentions or locations of the opposing team members.

4. If a player is eliminated while he is carrying the flag, he must drop the flag where he was hit, or hang it on the nearest available object (not another player).

5. When a player is carrying the flag, it must remain visible at all times and be carried in the hand, over the arm, or around the neck.

—DD

Known as the "World's Most Famous Recreational Player," Durty Dan has been playing since 1984. He started his writing career in 1992 when Randy Kamiya (then Editor for *Action Pursuit Games Magazine*) published his first article in the February issue. Since then he has written for *Action Pursuit Games*, *Paintball Sports International* (in his column Rec-Ball), *Paintball Industry Magazine* (no longer in publication), *Paintball News*, *Paintball RAGazine* (no longer in publication), and *Paintball Magazine*. Since 1992, he has had an amazing two hundred and fifty articles published.

CAPTURE THE FLAG

Requirements

Two flag stations.

Two even teams.

Two flags, hung in opponents' flag stations.

Duration

30 minutes

Rules

All players must begin the game at their flag station (or assigned starting point) and cannot leave that area until the game begins.

Players who are hit are out of the game.

If a player is eliminated while he is carrying the flag, he must drop the flag where he was hit, or hang it on the nearest available object. (Never another player).

Players who are eliminated may not indicate any intentions or locations of the opposing team members.

When a player is carrying the flag, it must remain visible at all times and must be carried in the hand, over the arm, or around the neck.

Objective

Capture the opposing team's flag and return it to your base!

CHARGE OF THE LIGHT BRIGADE

Requirements
Two flag stations.
Two even teams.
Two flags hung in opponents' stations.

Duration
20 minutes.

Rules
All General Rules apply.

Objective
Hang your flag in the opposition's flag station.

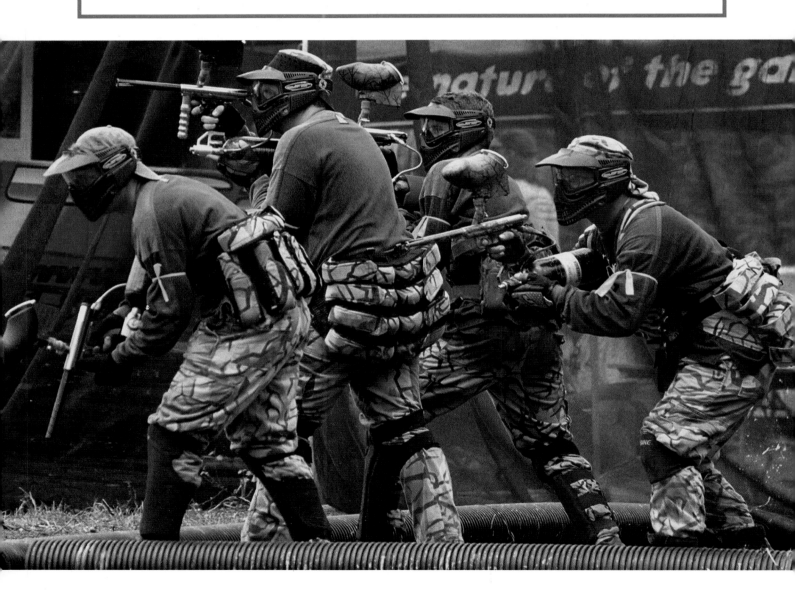

SHOOT THE CAPTAIN

Requirements

Two flag stations.

Two even teams.

The teams are brought to their respective flag stations.

The Captain is tied to one end of a 20 foot rope, the other end of which is tied to an immobile object like a tree or fence post.

To spice up the action, tether the Captain's gun rather than him.

Another variation is to limit all offensive players to 20 paintballs and give the Captains unlimited amounts of paint.

Duration

30 minutes

Rules

The Captain cannot undo his tether.

If playing the tethered paintgun variation, the Captain can abandon his paintgun, but cannot use another paintgun.

If you use the limited paint option, players cannot share paintballs.

General Rules 1,2, and 3 apply.

Objective

Eliminate the opposing team's captain.

DUEL

Requirements
Two players are the duelists with the same type of pistol.
A third person to play the Warder.
A clear area.

Duration
As long as it takes, usually no more than 12 seconds.

Rules
Two players stand back to back.
The Warder is standing about ten feet to the side.
Both players are armed with pistols. The pistols each have one paintball in them ready to fire.
The paintguns can have no other paintballs in them. This is a one shot deal.
The warder then says, "This, Gentlemen, is an affair of honor. You will take ten paces on my command, then turn and fire. If either of you turns before the count of ten, it will be my unfortunate duty to shoot you down." (Or something to this effect.)
The duelists then pace off in time to the Warder's cadence. At the count of ten they turn and fire.
The paintball has to break for the elimination to count.
Players cannot side step or lie down, but they may kneel if they wish.
No other rules apply.

Objective
The person who is not eliminated wins.

ATTACK AND DEFEND

Requirements
Two teams of equal strength:One team, the Attackers; the other, the Defenders.
Choose a defensible area to serve as a flag station.
Defenders should be restricted to the confines of the flag station.
Set boundaries that limit the movement of the defenders out of the flag station.

Duration
10 minutes

Rules
Defenders cannot leave the flag station area, or the areas of the flag station they are charged with defending.
The Attackers can attack from any place on the field.
General Rules 1, 2, 3 apply.

Objective
Attackers: Pull the flag off its support (a string, branch, cone, etc.)
Defenders: Stop the Attackers from pulling the flag.

ANNIHILATOR

Requirements
Set up multiple five man teams.
The maximum limit is four teams for every acre of playing area.
Place teams in the area so that they are not in line of sight of each other.
To make score-keeping easier, the teams may be accompanied by a referee and each team may have their own distinct color of paint.

Duration
30–45 minutes

Rules
Teams will stay in their starting stations until the start of the game signal.
Teams get points for each elimination they inflict on other teams.
There are no points for surviving members of the team.
General Rules 1, 2, 3 apply.

Objective
Survive and be the team with the highest score at the end of the game.

BLACKJACK

Requirements
Two flag stations.
Two even teams.
Two flags, hung in opponents' flag stations.
Each player is only allowed 21 paintballs.

Duration
30 minutes

Rules
Players are not allowed to share paintballs.
Players who shoot all of their paintballs must
   leave the game immediately.
All General Rules apply.

Objective
Capture the opposing team's flag and return it to
   your base!

BUNNY HUNT

Requirements
A "Bunny" (one person) and Hunters (everybody
   else).
One player volunteers to be the Bunny. To give
   the Bunny some kind of advantage, choose
   one of these options.
OPTION 1–Give the Bunny a semiautomatic
   paintgun plus a garbage can lid or other
   device to use as a shield.
OPTION 2–Give the Bunny as much paint as
   he's comfortable with, and restrict the Hunters
   to 20 paintballs each.

Duration
20 minutes

Rules
If the Bunny chooses OPTION 1, hits on the
   shield do not count as an elimination.
The Bunny has a 5 minute head start into the
   playing area.
A signal will be given so that the Bunny knows
   when the game is started.
All hunters must start at the same time and from
   the same place.
When using the limited paint option, if a hunter
   runs out of paint, he is out of the game.
General Rules 1, 2, and 3 apply.

Objective
If you're the Bunny, SURVIVAL IS THE GOAL!
If you're a Hunter, eliminate the BUNNY!

RECON

Requirements

Multiple Five-Man Teams.

Checkpoints (one for every team on the field) are spaced throughout the field. Each is clearly marked with a flag or similar ornament.

Each checkpoint also has a gun hanging from a string. Each checkpoint has a different colored gun.

Each player has a card attached to his wrist (a playing card will do!) by a string, rubber band, or elastic band.

Each team starts near a checkpoint.

Duration

20 minutes

Rules

Players must mark their card with the guns provided at the checkpoint.

Every team member must attempt to mark his card, although this is not mandatory.

Players who are eliminated are not allowed to count the points they collected with their final team score.

General Rules 1, 2, and 3 apply.

Scoring

- 1 point for each different-colored mark on a card.
- 5 bonus points if all team cards are marked by at least two checkpoints.
- 5 bonus points for each additional checkpoint where all team cards are marked.
- 2 bonus points for every team member with card marks from every checkpoint.

Objective

The team with the highest score wins.

GETTYSBURG

Requirements
No bulk loaders, loading tubes or any solid
  apparatus used to hold or feed paintballs.
Two flag stations.
Two evenly numbered teams.
Two flags, hung in their respective flag stations.

Duration
30 minutes

Rules
Players can carry as many paintballs as they
  wish.
Paintballs must be loose or in a plastic bag.
They cannot be in tubes, hoppers, or any kind of
  bulk loading system.
Players can only load paintballs by hand, one at
  a time into their paintguns and cannot load
  another paintball until they shoot the one in
  the paintgun.
General Rules apply.

Objective
Capture the opposing team's flag and return it to
  your base.

DOWN BUT NOT OUT

Basic Requirements
Two flag stations.
Two even teams.
Two flags, hung in their respective flag stations.
One white sock per player to be provided.

Duration
30 minutes

Rules
1. When a player is hit, he calls himself out and lays or sits on the ground (using common sense). The player then places a sock over the barrel of his paintgun to indicate that he has been hit. He cannot move from this location until tagged. This is referred to as Waiting.

2. If a waiting player is tagged by a teammate he is back in the game. (The player, of course, removes the sock.)

3. Players who are waiting cannot shoot or disclose the positions or intentions of opposing players.

4. If a waiting player is tagged by an opposing player, he is out of the game.

5. If a waiting player feels that no one will find him, or he is tired of waiting, he can take himself out of the game. In this case the player cannot be tagged back into the game.

6. There is no limit to how many times a player can be tagged back into the game.

7. Players waiting to be tagged cannot shoot or be shot at.

8. All General Rules 1, 3, 4, and 5 apply.

Objective
Capture the opposing team's flag and return it to your base.

PAINTBURNER

Requirements
Create, depending on group size, as many three man teams as you can.

Odd players out will wait in the Designated Holding Area for enough eliminated players to return and will make up the next in-going team.

Teams start the game in different areas of the field.

Duration
30 Minutes

Rules
1. Once a player is hit, he proceeds to the Designated Holding Area.

2. Once there are three players in the Designated Holding Area, they rejoin the game as a new team.

3. A referee will escort a newly formed team out into the field, away from the action and any other teams, if possible, and signal their entry with a short whistle blast.

4. Players cannot shoot or be shot at while being escorted by the referee.

5. Only General Rules 1, 2, and 3 apply.

Objective
Fun! In which case, everybody wins!

© Michael Wise II, chrono300.com

REINFORCEMENTS

Requirements
Two flag stations.
Two even teams.
Two flags, hung in their respective flag stations.
Flag stations double as Reinforcement Rally points.

Duration
30 minutes

Rules
1. Eliminated players go back to their flag station.

2. One player wears a special armband. This is the only player that can go back to the flag station to get reinforcements.

3. If the player wearing the armband is eliminated, he proceeds back to the flag station. He then collects those players who wish to rejoin the game and he himself rejoins the game. In this case the eliminated players have no choice but to be reinforcements. They cannot stay behind and defend the flag station.

4. Players can elect to stay behind and defend the flag station, with the exception of REINFORCEMENTS Rule 3. When they return to the flag station they are automatically active defenders.

5. Players returning to the flag station must physically tag the flag to become active defenders. If the flag is not at the flag stations the players are considered out of the game as they enter the flag station.

6. Players who are hit are out of the game but the player is only out until he reaches his flag station. Players eliminated at the flag station are out of the game.

7. Only General Rules 1, 3, 4 and 5 apply.

Objective
Capture the opposing team's flag and return it to your base.

KICK THE BUCKET

Requirements
Two flag stations.
Two even teams.
Instead of flags, a bucket is placed on the ground under where the flag usually hangs. This bucket must be made of a light plastic (remember, someone is going to kick this thing).

Duration
15 minutes

Rules
1. The bucket cannot be moved by the team which owns it.

2. If a player is hit before he kicks the bucket, the kick (if completed) does not count as a win; the referee then resets the bucket as quickly as possible.

3. Only General Rules 1, 2, and 3 apply.

Objective
Kick the opposing team's bucket over.

TROPHY HUNTER

Requirements

Players act individually to gather trophies on the field. No teams.

Each player wears three armbands on one arm (these are referred to as trophies).

Players are interspersed in the playing field.

A signal will sound every five minutes (referred to as the five minute signal) and will be different than the start and end of game signal. (The period between these signals will be referred to as the waiting period.)

Duration

30 minutes

Rules

1. Players who are hit must drop to the ground (using common sense) and remain motionless and quiet until the next five minute signal.

2. Another player (not necessarily the one who hit him) has the waiting period to collect one trophy. Once the trophy is taken no more trophies can be taken from the player during that Waiting Period.

3. When the five minute signal sounds the player is immediately in the game.

4. Only general rules 1, 2, and 3 apply.

Objective

The player with the most trophies wins.

HOSTAGE RESCUE

Requirements

Two teams:
1. Rescuers
2. Terrorists

Terrorists pick one Rescuer to act as the Hostage.

Two hostage holding areas are designated. The location of one of the hostage holding areas is disclosed to the Rescuers. Terrorists do not know which location was disclosed.

Establish an area the Rescuers will have to take the Hostage to in order to win the game.

This is known as sanctuary.

Terrorists know where sanctuary is.

Duration

30 minutes

Rules

1. Terrorists are given a five minute head start to take the hostage to one of the hostage holding areas.

2. A start of game signal is given to let terrorists know when the game has begun.

3. Terrorists cannot move the hostage out of the hostage holding area.

4. The Hostage cannot attempt escape.

5. If the Hostage is hit, the team that hit him looses.

6. The Hostage must have at least one Rescuer with him when he reaches sanctuary for the Rescuers to win.

7. If the Hostage finds himself alone for some reason, after being rescued, he must stay where he is and wait for the Rescuers to find him again. He may call out for help if he wishes.

8. Only General Rules 1, 2, and 3 apply.

Objectives

Terrorists: Stop the Rescuers from bringing Hostage to sanctuary.

Rescuers: Bring Hostage to sanctuary.

TAG

Rules

1. No teams—this is a free-for-all!
2. Select a person to be "It."
3. Disperse players in the playing area.
4. The player who is "It" starts the game by sounding the start game signal.
5. The player who is "It" must wear an armband,which must be clearly visible.
6. When a player is hit by "It" he must stand where he is. The player then receives the armband from "It" becomes the new "It."
7. The player who is "It" and the player who is receiving the armband cannot shoot or be shot at.
8. The new "It" puts the armband on and cannot shoot or be shot at until the player calls out "ready."
9. The new "It" cannot shoot at the old "It," and vice versa.
10. When "It" has been eliminated, the game is over.
11. Only General Rules 1, 2, and 3 apply.

Objective

Everybody wins by just having fun.

TRAITOR

Requirements

Two Teams.

Two flag stations required but only as starting points.

A deck of cards is taken, two kings and two jacks are removed, then a number of normal (nonface) cards are taken from the deck.

The number is the total amount of players MINUS 4. (It's minus four because two people will be drawing jack and two will be drawing kings.)

Then two piles are made, a king and a jack goes into each pile and then the remainder of the cards that were drawn will be separated evenly between the two piles.

The two piles are shuffled separately and one team will draw from one pile and the other team will draw from the other.

Duration

30–45 minutes

Rules

1. Only those players who drew the kings are to reveal their cards. The players who drew the kings are the leaders for each team.

2. The players who drew the jacks are the TRAITORS. They do not reveal their identity.

3. Leaders will wear two armbands on EACH arm to designate themselves as leaders.

4. Traitors may turn on their teams at any time they see fit, once the game starts.

5. Only General Rules 1, 2, and 3 apply.

Objective

Eliminate the other team's leader.

(If the TRAITOR eliminates the leader the opposite team wins. e.g. Red team TRAITOR nukes Red team Leader, Blue team wins.)

HITTING HOME ON THE RANGE

I often harp on about marksmanship and accuracy. I advocate shooting hundreds of balls at the range. But, for most people, this is not very entertaining.

Just because I love you guys and gals so much, I've invented seven fun games for you to play on the range. All games can involve any number of players, taking turns, unless otherwise noted. Also, the games are more or less designed to allow a mix of technology; semis can go up against pump and stock classes.

So now, not only will you be having fun, you'll also be learning a valuable skill. (Whether you want to, or not!)

HIDE 'N' SEEK

Requirements
No teams—everyone for themselves.

Rules
1. Select one player to be "It."
2. Establish a "home" area and within it, an object players have to tag to be "home free."
3. Establish two different signals, one as the start/end game signal and one as "home" signal.
4. All players gather at one entrance to the playing field.
5. The player who is "It" begins a slow count to one hundred; during this count the players race into the playing area and hide.
6. At the end of the count the player who is "It" sounds the start game signal and enters the playing field.
7. Players must try to make it back to "home" before getting caught by"It."
8. The player who is "It" does not have to hit the players to eliminated them. He simply calls to them and points them out ("It" has to actually see them at the time) and the player must go back to "home."
9. Players who are hit by other players or the player who is "It" are out of the game and must return to "home."
10. Each player returning home, no matter what the reason, must sound the player "home" signal.
11. The game is ended when the player who is "It" is hit.
12. Only General Rules 1 and 3 apply.

Objective
Long Version—The player, when he or she was "It" who caught the most players. (Players hit by "It" are not included in this number.)
Short Version—(One game) the player who eliminates "It."

How to Settle a Tie
Replay the game from beginning between tied players. Repeat if necessary. With Reach for the Top, replay the last round, players must get 10 for 10. For One Player Duel replay one round for the best time.

RAPID FIRE

Requirements
More than one shooter.
5-10 targets.

Rules
Select a number of targets (between 5 and 10)

Shooters fire at the targets as fast as they can, but are restricted to shooting at a target only once.
An official measures the time with a stop watch.
Penalties: add one second to the time for every miss.
To win: Shortest time.

RANDOM RAPID FIRE

Requirements
Ten targets, each has its own number.

The official calls out the numbers in random order (the order is determined for each player by a random drawing of ten numbered cards, prior to the player's arrival on the range.)

Shooter can only shoot at the target whose number was called.

Official calls the number (after the first target is called) as the player shoots the previous target.

Penalties
Add one second for every miss.

Add two seconds for shooting at the wrong target (hit or miss).

Objective
Shortest time.

SNAP SHOT

Requirements
Players and targets, as many of each as you want.

Rules
1. The paintgun cannot be put to shoulder or brought to eye level.
2. Several targets at several different ranges, number and position are up to the players.
3. Players are restricted to as many paintballs as there are targets, and can only shoot at each target once.

Scoring
Add 1 point for each hit; and

Subtract 1 point for each miss.

Objective
Person with the highest score wins.

LONG SHOT

Requirements
One target—a small can placed on an object at least 3 feet off the ground.

The can must placed so that it will fall over when hit.

Rules
Players shoot at can until they hit it and knock it to the ground.

Official counts the number of shots it took them to knock the can over (including the shot that knocked it over.)

Objective
Knock the can over in the least number of shots.

REACH FOR THE TOP

Requirements
10 targets
—3 at short range (15–20 feet)
—4 at medium range (35–50 feet)
—3 at long range (80–100 feet)

Rules
1. Three rounds of shooting.
2. To pass the round:

First round—minimum 6 out of 10

Second round—minimum 7 out of 10

Third round—10 out of 10 (at this point the player has completed the game).

3. If the minimum is not met, the player cannot proceed to the next round and is eliminated for competition. Players can score higher than the minimum.

4. Players are limited to 10 paintballs per round.

5. Players can only shoot at target once per round.

Scoring
One point per hit.

Objective
Have the highest score.

FOLLOW ME

Requirements
Two shooters.

Rules
The two players flip a coin to see who will be the first shooter.
The first shooter calls a target and shoots at it.
If the first shooter hits the target: the second shooter must hit the target as well;

If the second shooter misses the target, the first shooter gets one point; and the first shooter calls a target and shoots again.
If the first shooter misses the target: the roles are reversed. (e.g., Billy is the first shooter, Joey is the second shooter. Billy misses, Joey takes the first shot until he misses)

Objective
The first shooter to reach 20 points wins.

ONE PLAYER DUEL

Requirements
One player and one target

Rules
1. Player stands with his/her back to the target.
2. On command from official, the player begins to pace off, according to official's count.
3. Player turns and fires when official says "Fire".
4. Player is only allowed one shot.
5. Official starts timer at the start signal and stops if target is hit.
6. If the target is not hit, the round is not counted.
7. Players have three chances (rounds)
8. The players must be at the following distances, order is random, as chosen by the official (one distance for each round). Official draws only three distances out of the five.
   —10 paces;
   —5 paces;
   —3 paces;
   —8 paces; and
   —12 paces.
9. Players take the best time out of the three rounds. If the player missed in all three rounds, the player is disqualified.

Objective
Hit all targets in fewest turns.

The BIG GAME

"When it comes to paintball, I live for the Big Game!"

For some players, the tournament is the highest level of play available. For others, like me, the pinnacle of paintball is **the big game.** An army of players, cheap paint prices, freaky people in hilarious costumes, big-name celebrities, massive confrontations, a sense of comraderie—the big game is where you'll find all of these things and more.

SO WHAT IS THIS BIG GAME THING?

In my neck of the woods when ten people show up to play, we say it's a good sized crowd. If forty people come, we praise the paintball deities for smiling upon us. I've heard some players talk about 200 players just arriving on a single day; if I ever experience anything like that, I'd be temporarily paralyzed with happiness.

But the Big Game blows all of these experiences out of the water.

Technically, the 'Big Game' is one that has a large number of players on the field at any given moment. Regionally, a game with 70 players at an unknown field is certainly awesome, but it pales in comparison to games with well over 500 players. These are the numbers you'll find at the Skirmish World Record Games.

Scenario Game or Big Game?

You may have heard of 'Scenario' games. It's true that those games attract large numbers of players, but they aren't what I mean by big games.

Scenario games either reenact an event of real combat, or invent a plausible chain of events for players to act out in a sort of large-scale, live-action, role-playing game. Role-playing games are not new. The concept has been around in paper formats before 1975 with such staples as Advanced Dungeons & Dragons (TSR). Players are even given a new identity to assume during the course of the game. It's pure fantasy play, and it definitely appeals to many paintball players, but it doesn't have anything to do with the Big Game.

Big Games are still paintball games, only on a larger scale. They have flag objectives and eliminations. Of course, players can assume any identity they wish to, but they are not playing out a 'story' as they would in a scenario game. No matter what or whom they look like, the game they're playing is still "Capture the Flag" or "Total Elimination."

Well-run scenario games have point values for achieving special missions, such as holding a 'bridge,' capturing a specific target, achieving specific operations and so on. This is meant to bring the scenario somewhat close to the actual event that occurred (or, at the very least, to what the organizers want to accomplish). Teams get points for achieving specific objectives, and a winner is tabulated at the end of the game.

The distinctions between scenario games and some big games may blur. Some big games have 'objective flag stations' to be held for points. And some are worth more than others. It helps to be 'in the know'.

Scenario games and Big games do share a bit in common, and, with a little tweaking, you can use the following information in both contexts.

Recon!

The first step is to find a big game. Where should you look? They're advertised in many mainstream publications, and by word of mouth. Ask the guys who run the fields you frequent; they should know (they're probably as eager to go as you are). You may wish to find somewhere close to home, although traveling can be half the fun if you're with friends!

It's very important to know what you're getting yourself into before you play a big game. Once you've discovered one, call for information. You want as much time as possible to plan properly for this kind of event. I recommend at least a month, but three months is better. You want to know the cost of the event and what it covers (e.g., does it include CO_2 and nitrogen refills?), how much paint will cost (or, even better, if you can bring your own?), if food will be provided or available. You get the idea.

If you're not familiar with the area, ask about where you can stay (e.g., local hotels, motels, or campgrounds). Most big game flyers will include this information, but it's still a good idea to verify everything, just in case something has changed.

Another good idea is to ask about the field. Knowing a bit about the terrain can be a good thing. My feet were sore for weeks after playing on the rocks of Pennsylvania. I could have protected them better if I'd learned about the field in advance.

The newest venue for information about big games is on the internet. You may already know about 'rec.sport.paintball' and 'alt.sport.paintball.' Through these two usenet newsgroups you can gain access to what I call the 'paintball hive-mind.' There are also many websites that host their own message forums, such as pbreview.com, warpig.com, and many more. If you have a question about a specific field or a place that you've never played before, you can probably get an answer in a few days from someone who has been there. Some events have web pages about them as well.

The more informed you are, the better time you will have.

GEAR, GARB, AND GOODIES

What Do I Bring to the Big Game?

Bring what you bring to any paintball game! Yourself, goggles, harnesses, gun, gloves, squeegee, and all that stuff you probably play with all the other times you play. If you wear contact lenses, bring your eyedrops. Always bring multiple pairs of underwear and socks and backup sneakers or boots. Just make sure you've packed everything you need. When you're a few states away from home, realizing you forgot your goggles is pretty demoralizing.

Then there are the things you'd never think of bringing, but they don't hurt.

Bring extra money. Whoever thinks you can bring too much money is silly. Some big games have a vendors tent with more goodies to bring home with you. Not to mention how quickly eating out drains your cash no matter how affordable. Bring a tent, or some kind of portable shade; parking lots never have trees in them! Lawn chairs are great (trust me, car bumpers get uncomfortable after a few minutes!), and a cooler filled with ice, water, and Gatorade will make you the envy of many dehydrated participants. Packing a small first aid kit is invaluable as well. You get the idea.

Preparation is the key to playing the big games.

Arrival

As with any major event, showing up early has it's advantages. Better parking is worth it, believe me! If the event starts at 9 AM, you want to try and get there by 7:30 AM. I've had to walk a half a mile to the staging area with all my gear in tow. Avoid this if you can.

Once there you want to sign in right away. The sooner you do, the easier it is to get all your gear together, chronograph in (all guns must fire under 300 fps!), and just get comfortable. It's also pure joy to sit back and watch the people arrive in a panic as they try to prepare for mass orientation in under 10 minutes.

I'm Here, Now What?

First, relax. It's just another game of capture the flag. It's just that this time you've got company. You may have as many as 500 people on your team—way more people than you're accustomed to. But that's still not a problem.

Just like a normal walk-on day, you go through an orientation speech. Pay attention to it! You may have played a billion times before, but it's important that you listen to this orientation!) They will go over the rules of the game, as well as special rule variations specific to the big game. And it's important to be at least acquainted with those rules.

Paintball Sam's in Racine, Wisconsin runs a few big games every year. One of the rule modifications there always involves medics. If you are hit below the knee or below the elbow you are 'wounded.' You can be 'healed' by a designated 'medic' player three times before you are eliminated from that particular game.

For some time, the rule stated that a hit below the knee, elbow, and above the chin line counted as a 'wound.' The year they switched to head shots counting as eliminations was confusing to a lot of the players who weren't paying attention to the orientation speech and frustrating to those of us who lit them up.

Listen to the rules at the beginning of the game!

Motor Easy

One of the things I cherish about the big game format is how laid back players are, in general. Sure, you get your hyper players out there who make down-the-middle rushes. But, for the most part, everyone is in a casual frame of mind. Sometimes players hang up the camouflage for a day. Among the things to expect people will be wearing, I've seen jeans and t-shirts, tuxedos, three-piece business suits, a Fred Flintstone outfit, a Moose hat (I mean antlers and all!), Viking helmets and costumes, even a Waldo sweater (as in "Where's Waldo?"). Me? I wear a deer costume. It's a midwestern thing.

Meanwhile, other players dust off their stock guns to play amongst the other semi-autos. (In the midwest, it's rare to see one on the field at all. Big Games bring them out of hiding.) When there are a few hundred opponents, you know you're going to meet at least a few of them. So some players generally take it easy on firepower for the day.

Before I forget, let me mention that you should leave your temper at home. A big game is not for proving how many people you can eliminate. Angry, overly intense players ruin this kind of experience for everyone else. Your priority at this game is to relax, have fun, meet people, and make friends! This is another major difference between the Big Game and Scenario Games, which tend to be intense because people are making believe that a great deal is at stake (e.g., the future of human civilization, the outcome of WWII).

Tactics aren't as important in the Big Game as they are in normal play. Having a few tricks up your collective sleeves isn't a bad idea, but any more organization than that and you're going to end up in pretty lame arguments with people who have thought way too long and hard about the game to be enjoying it.

As you'd expect, most players will play offense. This is natural. People generally feel safer when they're flanked by hundreds of players. On the offensive side, there's a lot you can do.

As much as I hate to say it, grandiose military tactics can work on big game fields. This is due to the size of the field, and the game's typically longer time frame. Checking with the rules is important here. Do you have enough time for wide flanking maneuvers? Do you have time to make an ambush happen? These are things you need to know to avoid expending tons of energy only to discover that the game is over before you've engaged anyone.

The Big O

Grab as many people as you can for your flanking moves. Sometimes it's a good idea to make a 'sacrifice' maneuver to spring ambushes, or to determine numbers. Also, keep in mind the overall objective. Fifty people chasing five guys for an hour is a waste of time that you could be using to build momentum.

Players have a tendency to group in a circle formation, and you should use this to your advantage. The front-most players should be watching forward, the rear-most players should be watching the back (literally facing backwards and walking backwards!), and players on the sides should be covering your group's flanks. You have to think as a very large pack of wolves on the prowl. You have to trust everyone else in the pack to do their part. **Trust works if everyone is equally committed to it.**

Having a 'team' mentality helps, but knowing how to get your fellow teammates to share it is important as well. You can do this by rallying everyone in earshot to move forward, or go through the bunkers. Or by adding yourself to the push so you can gain some more feet of real estate.

Shouting has its time and place. Once you and another person pushes forward whoopin' and hollerin,' people will be more apt to follow you. This is a 'herding' effect that I touch on in detail a bit later on. By the same token, there's something to be said for people who hang back and observe the whoopin' and hollerin' advance, especially if it's ambushed. Then it's their turn to shout out the position of the other team, direct people to regroup and engage, pursue, or retreat.

Transmitting information from one side of the playing field to the other is vital. Send more than one person as a messenger. The faster you can tell the "center" crowd that the "left" crowd is punching through the left side, the more people you can slam through it, and the more likely it is that you'll win the game. If you hear something about a push, or that the opponents are making a move, pass it along as fast as possible, and make sure you get a few more to pass it as well.

Information is power. Spread the word.

Individual Offense

Big games get chaotic. So, despite their size, what you do as an individual can make a difference. The first thing you should realize is that, outside of your friends, you are surrounded by individuals.

Paintball is a team sport, and remains so even if both teams consist of 300 people a side. Stuff happens, however. Your entire team gets shot, or they all abandon a situation and you find yourself alone. What can you do? Switch gears.

Lone Hunter Mode

Now you are the lone hunter. You are individually outnumbered, but that's not really important. As an individual, you have strengths against big numbers of opponents.

Sink into your camouflage and start to crawl around. It's nerve-wracking to let a team of guys walk past you, but let them go. Sneak up on your opponents and take out a few of them from behind. Then, run for the hills. You may be able to draw them away from your teammates or your flag, weak-

ening their offense. Or, you can go for the other team's flag! You may be able to fake them out, saying you're on their team (if the rules allow it).

As a loner, you'll experience the game at a higher level of alertness. You have to watch your own back. Your movements must be quick, subtle, and quiet. You will only fire your gun if you have a clear shot.

Flaming bones from Animal Paintball (Courtesy Animal Paintball)

Even if you get eliminated, you can still do a lot for your team. If you think in ratios, if you eliminate 5 players, and tie up 20 more in the process, that's 25 guys on you that aren't on your team's flag station. And if you can tie them up for a length of time, you'll really be doing a favor to your team.

Or, perhaps you'll become a spy. As a spy, your challenge is to gather intelligence behind enemy lines about their allocation of resources, sheer numbers of people in certain places and the direction they're moving in, and then to get it back to your forces in time for it to be useful. The cool thing is, you can always switch into 'Lone Hunter' mode if it looks like there isn't enough time to get your information back to your people. Let out a shout that gives away an enemy position (this works better if you have a friends in your main group who will know what you mean when you holler!), take a few of them out, and start running. Of course, doing this kind of thing is dependent on the length of the game.

Which brings me to defense.

"Are we leaving any defenders?"

I actually heard this on a big-game field once.

A Big Game defense is fully dependent on the scenario objective. A game of "Capture the Flag"

will have more defense than, say, capture and hold a point bunker. I'll talk about both types.

First, let's look at Capture the Flag defense. A good defense can hold off an opposing offense. But what is the best defense?

A common 'big game' mistake is to make the offense the defense by not letting anyone through the cracks. This isn't a good idea, because then only a few players can slip through to capture your flag. Leaving a few people behind, or at least near the back of the field is always a good idea.

A good defense is layered. Meaning that you have players 200, 100, and 50 yards out, then the final flag station. (This can be modified, but you get the idea.)

However, the defense should be aware that if they can not stop and rout the offense by 70 yards out, the game is pretty much over (Again, this distance changes from field to field, but if they can longball you en-masse, you're history.) I call this the 'Final Approach' zone. In this zone, the offense gets motivated to win, and your defense has nowhere to go.

Bottom-line
If you run out of real estate,
you're a sitting duck.

Other big games have specific point bunkers. These work differently. Your team gets points by holding such bunkers for allotted periods of time (20 minutes), or on specific time marks (every half hour) Defending this type of bunker is different.

For starters, you probably have to defend against 360 degrees of terrain. So having a lot of defenders is a good idea if you have the power. You are probably going to want to organize the same kind of layered defense as I had mentioned earlier, for many of the same reasons. Your 'final approach' distance will be shorter, but it may be worse. Always try to leave an avenue of escape if you can. That way you can always do an end run and flank behind the other team. If they totally surround you, it's over.

Still, if the other team surrounds you or reaches the "Final Approach," your chances are not totally gone. You can get reinforcements from some angle if the game allows for reinsertions or if your teammates find you. Hold your position as long as you can. If you get eliminated after the points are allotted, you've done your job for your team.

Either way, stopping a rampaging offense is no easy task. You do it through sheer will, determination, and discipline. Shooting a lot of paint doesn't hurt either, but it's not necessary. As a defensive group, you don't want to all concentrate on one 'zone'. You want to take a line of approach, and cover it. Communicate with your teammates, and have overlapping lanes of fire. The idea is to stop their forward movement and rout them.

By halting their approaching push, they have nowhere to drive but backwards. This breaks their attack momentum, and they lose the 'will' to keep driving at you. It's hard to recover from a rout. The hard part is figuring out when to change gears from defense to offense, or even if you need to go at them. That becomes a 'feel' thing, best determined by experience and what's happening on the field.

When the offense gets into the "Final Approach" zone, they tend to get a little blood-thirsty. Meaning that they start to 'smell' the flag, taste the victory. If you get caught as a defender in this situation, you will get pounded unless you can rout them.

If you do get tagged, the best thing to do is scream, "I'm out! I'm hit!" repeatedly and just vacate the hot zone as fast as you can. Keep your paintgun high (Don't worry about your barrel plug, you'll have time to put it in when you're out of the hot zone), Then, put your barrel plug in. It'll save you from getting more welts than you deserve.

The Human Herd

When a few hundred people are milling about, they usually act like a mob. If you have mediocre leadership skills you can guide them. Heck, even if you have none it's really easy. You just may need to shout (or a megaphone will substitute nicely.)

There's always times when you see from your side that another side of the field needs reinforcements. That's when, classically, you start shouting "SHIFT RIGHT! SHIFT RIGHT!" When the shift begins, just guide players to the appropriate area.

Unfortunately, there's usually at least 20 people trying to do this. All you can really do from the rear ranks is become a 'caller'. This is the player who announces to the pack where opponents are. "THREE BEHIND THE SPOOL! TWO BEHIND THAT TREE! TEN ON THE LEFT TAPE!" The caller is the first player to go hoarse, by the way. The caller can also do the same thing from the front line as well.

SOUNDING SCARIER THAN YOU ARE

Once one player starts to scream like a maniac, other players will join in and follow him. I'm not sure why it works, but it does. (I think it's a psychology thing, I'm not sure.) You don't have to scream. But sometimes that really does the trick!

A good example of this happened in Racine Wisconsin's Big Game a long time ago. While sneaking around on the tapeline, I heard someone playing a bugle; it was the classic "Charge" tune. Soon followed by the loudest screaming match I've ever heard, and what sounded like a stampede. Thankfully, the player was on my team. We used that momentum to carry us to the flag and victory.

"Rebel Yells" "Kamikaze Screams" "Whoops & Hollers"

Primal screams do two things. They provide an adrenaline rush to your teammates who will rush into positions without fear. Moreover, it scares the living daylights out of your opponents. This intimidation is infectious on both sides, and can get a lot of results quickly. It burns your team out quickly, however, so use it only when things stagnate or when you need to make the push.

Part two of the process is getting your teammates to go with you. Some people have the charisma to do it, some don't. Sometimes all you need to do is get into a great position and coax your players to join you. Other times you need to make an impression.

Making a bold—read: stupid—charge to take a bunker will do this. People will be impressed you made it and either join you or shake their heads in disbelief. Either way, you'll have their attention. Use the opportunity to yell to them to move up. Keep reassuring your teammates that you're going to win, you've got the opponents on the run, and so on.

The idea here is to get your players to move up as one group rather than piecemeal. See, the more people moving forward, the better your odds are in getting things to go your way. So a lot of people moving together is a good thing. And convincing a bunch of walk-on players to all do this is part diplomacy, part intimidation, part luck.

But when they all go at once, you've got something good happening, and then it's up to you and the two or three other guys who are interested in taking the lead to maintain it!

Radio Communications

The ability to communicate is always important in paintball, especially in the big game format. Knowing what is happening on the other end of your skirmish line becomes more difficult when you can't see the length of it.

Many big games allow the use of radios as long as you do not cross-talk onto the referee channels. Radios put a whole new dimension on the game.

Remember, you're not going to be alone, so some common courtesy is a good thing. Use a 'push to talk' radio system if you can. I've experienced hard breathing sounds and shooting pain in my right ear. That's not fun, by any stretch of the imagination.

Keep your radio chatter as short as possible if you're in a firefight. Too much information can be confusing and useless to your other teammates. Assume that nobody cares what your teammates think of your paintgun or the referees. Save that for after the game.

Be courteous to your fellow players, and let them have some air-time as well. If you need to talk that much, switch stations.

Radios also have a dual-edged purpose as well. Whatever you broadcast can (and usually will) be intercepted by your opponents, and be used against you. I've personally used this phenomenon myself to try to convince opposing players to surrender the flag. (I bribed them with a six-pack of soda! They respectfully declined.) Another use is to run a campaign of false information on the assumption that you'll keep your opponents off-guard if they think you're moving in one direction, but then end up doing the opposite.

Several models of radios are available, I prefer a hands-free model with a remote push-to-talk button. This way, I can control what I broadcast. I place the button in my off hand, and run the wire down the sleeve and under my pullover. This way I don't have to reach over to broadcast anything, and the electronics are protected under my pullover.

For scenario games some players go as far as to use portable CB radios. I've also heard of a few people who used a cellular phone when the situation got desperate. I think that's a bit extreme myself, but go for it if it works for you (and it's allowed by the rules).

Photo courtesy of Jerry Braun

GO GET'EM!

With these small bits of information, you're set to go.

All in all, the 'big game' is tremendously fun, no matter where you go to do it. The key to this kind of event is forethought. To quote a song by Rush "An ounce of perception, a pound of obscure." Being prepared is the best way to enjoy the 'big game' and to avoid unpleasant 'surprises' along the way. And remember: Never say 'follow me' and trip into the creek. You'll have a lot of soggy compatriots.

—RR

A WHOLE NEW BREED OF
SCENARIO GAMES

Scenario games have exploded in popularity over the past few years. Scenario games are somewhat different than the big games mentioned in the first edition of this book. They have storylines, as well as characters, plots, and props—more like miniature movies than paintball games. Each player is assigned a character, usually with cards that have abilities or powers, and they're let loose on the field. Teams complete missions for points, and at the end of the game, the team with the most points wins.

There are a few types of players in every game. Most players will be your basic player. Their characters will usually be ground units of some kind who actually carry out most of the objectives. The minority of players are the "rollers", the role-players. These are the generals, the XO's, the grand pooh-bahs of the game. They achieve mission goals that involve little, if any, actual shooting. Instead, rollers use a lot of talking, diplomacy, and sometimes outright lying in order to carry out their tasks.

Whatever level you're on, your actions can have a major impact on what happens in the game. If you get a mission that

says, "Go get the fuel from the fuel dump and bring it back," your ability (or inability) to do that can affect future missions. You may need the fuel to use a special weapon, or a tank, or any amount of things. The ability to stick to the missions is one of the main factors in determining whether teams win or lose scenario games.

Many people have been playing scenario games in recent years and, win or lose, they've had fun at it. Right now there are several scenario games that make nationwide circuits every year, most notably those produced by MXS, Wayne Dollack Scenario Games, and Viper Scenario Series. It used to be that if you wanted to experience a scenario game, you had to go to a home field of the scenario producer. Now they travel all over the country making scenario games accessible to anyone.

All large scenario games have a few things in common. One is the longer game format. MXS and Dollack both have 24-hour games, meaning they start at noon on Saturday, end at noon Sun-

The Foletta brothers as Sir Bedemere and his squire at The Quest for the Holy Grail

day, and are played all through the night. If you get eliminated, you go to a dead zone and jump back into the game after a specific time interval, usually about 15 minutes. The action can be as non-stop or as casual as you like.

Scenario games are also becoming available locally. Many small fields now offer scenario-style games to play on special weekends. These games are great for casual players who want to try out scenario play without investing in a hotel room and a lot of gas money. Sometimes local venues don't provide the quality of game or staffing that you might get from a larger company, but that's your tradeoff: some quality for a local feel.

If you are in the mood for a road trip, however, there are a lot of field-specific scenario games that are worth the car ride.

With more and more players signing up for scenario games, it's never been easier to find one to suit your needs and interests. Get into the game this season, and try one out for yourself!

—*Rob Tyger Rubin*

Though kneeling, Bea Youngs is ready for action. Note how only one knee is up, and how her back foot is poised on the toes, enabling her to quickly rise and move if necessary.

Competitive Paintball:
What Every Tournament Player Needs to Know

MIKE PAXSON

Paintball falls under the category of "extreme sports" according to the Sporting Goods Manufacturing Association (SGMA) and has been ranked third most popular, behind skateboarding and snowboarding, for several years now. In most extreme sports, youths dominate the scene, but in paintball we're only recently seeing a growing number of youth participation at the competitive level. According to the 2006 SGMA statistics, the largest age group of all paintball players in the country is between the ages of 12 and 17 at 32 percent, with the 18-24 age range at 23 percent. When it comes to the number of players who play more frequently, 79 percent of those players are under the age of 25.

In 2000, the concept of having an all "kids" amateur paintball team was born; that team, Dynasty, would become today's most popular and best professional paintball team. When Dynasty debuted as a national professional paintball team in 2001, they finished in the Top 4 at almost every event they attended and won their first championship title at the 2001 World Cup 10-man event. The average age of Dynasty players was 18.

By the end of 2006, Dynasty had earned the most championship titles on a global scale since the inception of airball field play. With Dynasty's repeated trips to the championship podium, youth participation in paintball grew by leaps and bounds.

NEW FORMATS

As the average age of paintball players got younger, the tournament format also went through some changes. Another national league with a totally new format was launched. The National Professional Paintball League (NPPL) was no longer the only choice for competitive teams on a national level. Paintball Sports Promotions (PSP) swept onto the scene, introducing a new format called "X-Ball."

At the International Amateur Open (IAO) in 2001, the 5-on-5 X-Ball format was presented during an event called "Nations Cup," a kind of all-star game where the best players from each country formed representative teams. Each country's all-star team then competed against the others to determine which country had the best paintball players in the world. In 2002, the PSP was officially formed and the X-Ball format continued on an even larger scale. The concept of franchising teams came to fruition and paintball's most elite professional

© Michael Wise II, chrono300.com

teams competed in a new league called the National X-Ball League (NXL). Game times were extended to run an hour with two halves, penalties, and a time clock, much like a hockey game. The pace of the game increased drastically as teams tried to score as many points as possible before time's end.

With the introduction of the PSP and the NXL, the NPPL also modified its format. Under the leadership of Chuck Hendsch (NPPL President from 2001–2006), the NPPL changed its 10-on-10 format to 7-man and added "Super 7" to its name. With the help of Pure Promotions, the NPPL also introduced a new way to present the games to its spectators. SupAir Paintball, manufacturer of inflatable bunkers, made new bunker designs not only with different shapes, but different sizes, leading to more aggressive field layouts. The bunkers also gave major sponsors of the NPPL more marketing value when the NPPL adorned each field in sponsor logos on bunkers and banners.

The NPPL also brought paintball to large venues, which was conducive to attracting new faces to the sport and helped change the stereotype that paintball is only played in the woods. The 2002 Huntington Beach Super 7 was the start of the new look of paintball's tournament scene—and a new look for the NPPL itself. Because of its location in a tourist hot spot in Huntington Beach, California, the 2002 Super 7 broke spectator attendance records. The tournament attracted thousands of people from all over the world, piquing people's curiosity about paintball and offering great promotional opportunities for the sport as a whole.

The NPPL Super 7 started a trend in tournament presentation, focusing on attracting teams and spectators based on how they created their "show." Having a loudspeaker to make announcements telling teams when to report to their fields helps a tournament run on time. But playing music through those speakers in between games, or using the PA system to introduce the teams to crowds of thou-

sands, increases the excitement at an event and turns it into even more of a spectacle. Commentators and announcers encourage the crowd to cheer on their favorite teams, which inspires the players to put on a good game for the spectators. The Super 7 Series goes as far as having a music stage dedicated to featuring bands, adding yet another form of entertainment to their presentation.

PAINTBALL PLAYER TO PAINTBALL ATHLETE

The birth of the new formats also changed the way players played the game. Paintball "players" now became "athletes," because of the skill and physical fitness level required to play these new, aggressive tournament formats. With smaller bunkers in the backline of the fields, and field layouts designed to encourage run-through moves, competitive players had to learn to become more athletic and versatile. Being short became an advantage, and making the 50 off the break became even more important. This is one reason we're seeing an increasing number of participants who are younger than 25, and also more women, in the sport.

STANCE BEHIND A BUNKER

Because speed became so important on the tournament field, the player's stance behind the bunker also evolved. Movement down the field became a priority; the team to push down the field first most likely wins.

Staying on your toes is better than being in a kneeling position because players must be prepared to move at a moment's notice. Crouching behind bunkers in a squatting position, or with your knees slightly bent, has become the norm. You don't want to get caught down on both knees. If a player has to go to his knees at all, it's better that he's on just one knee where the other leg is on the ball of its foot. Players must also have a clear picture of the "safe zone," that area where you know you are safe to stand behind the bunker from opposing players shots. Players have also learned how to "play off," or stand farther behind, their bunkers without getting shot, especially in a one-on-one situation.

HOLDING YOUR MARKER

When the tournament paintball scene began years ago in the woods, it wasn't necessary for players to be ambidextrous. Today, it's almost a requirement to know how to play both left-handed and right-handed. You don't want to shoot right-handed out the left side of your bunker.

Another mark of an amateur is to "fan" the trigger to increase your rate of fire. The new trend is to "walk" the trigger with two fingers. You also don't want to load your hopper with your gun down. All it takes is a second for the opponent on the other side to move from one bunker to the next. Learning how to keep your gun up with your eyes always forward is the way to play; when you communicate to the player next to you, don't turn to look at him. Keep your eyes forward. Today, not a lot of players hold their gun underneath the tank, either. Instead, they use their upper body strength to hold their markers up. The latest trend is to grip the body of the marker near the area where the barrel and marker meet, creating a tighter profile.

WEARING THE GEAR

Image is everything, but the fact is that baggy is better. Wearing baggier clothes makes it more likely that paintballs will bounce off of you without breaking.

Believe it or not, starting around 2004, it became cool to wear urban camouflage apparel. Whether it was incorporated into the jersey, pants, gloves, or even head gear, the "retro" appeal showed its face. Camouflage headbands and even "do-rags" with built-in headbands featuring sponsor logos across the forehead has become the thing.

Keep your gun up and eyes forward, even when you're loading.

© Michael Wise II, chrono300.com

OFF THE BREAK

Team breakouts have changed in the past few years, as well. In 2003, players would run right off the break, with only a few shooting. Today's breakouts consist of all players shooting right off the break. Front players no longer just run to a 40 position off the break—they shoot and run simultaneously. At the very least, five out of the seven players on the team should be shooting, with the other two running as fast as they can to move up. The more paint that's in the air at the beginning of the game, the more chance you have of eliminating your opponents early on.

ADVANCED COMMUNICATION

Communication between players has changed significantly since the inception of X-Ball. In the PSP league, sideline coaching is encouraged. In the NPPL, where sideline coaching is prohibited, the communication between players has gotten much louder. Hand signals are used, but not as often, because staying forward in a seven minute game is more important than turning around to throw signs up.

FOR THE LOVE OF MEDIA

Players are becoming more savvy about placing logos in the right spots for the sake of getting their pictures in magazines or on websites. The number of photographers on a field has gone from a few to a slew, especially during the Finals games, when it looks like the sidelines of an NFL football game.

The key to getting into magazines is to sport the magazine's logo on your gear somewhere. Photographers are also getting into the game of promotions, passing out stickers featuring their website's logo and encouraging players to make them visible in order to increase their chances of being photographed.

TOURNAMENTS VERSUS SCENARIO GAMES

Competitive Paintball got its start in the woods, but as the years have gone by, modifications have been made to the way it's played. Today, we're seeing the more evolved style of tournament play on what are called "concept fields," also known as "airball fields." Instead of using trees, bushes, and dirt mounds for cover, tournaments have brought in inflatable thick and durable plastic bunkers and placed them on a 100 x 180 feet border to border field (120 x 200 net to net). There are still tournaments played in the woods and scenario games still flourish across the world, but the two styles of play do have their differences.

In the woods, it's better to wear camouflage or some other apparel that blends in with the environment. Paintball companies have even designed jerseys with camouflage patterns and we're seeing that trend appear on tournament fields as well. The photographers love color, however, and teams are starting to realize that their chances of getting in the magazines are higher if they wear bright colors. Camo gear isn't the only thing woodsball players are wearing: many simply wear military clothing and ghillie suits to avoid attracting attention.

Two big differences between tournament and woodsball play is the speed of the game and the equipment. Tournaments are fast-paced and quick, from the movements the players display to the equipment's rate of fire. You'll see the more expensive high end markers like the DM7, Bob Long Rappers, and Planet Eclipse Egos in the hands of tournament players and the less expensive markers like the Tippmanns, Ions, and Spyders in the hands of the traditional recball player. In the woods, it's a more methodical and conservative type of play as compared to what takes place on a tournament field.

To support the speed of the guns in tournaments, players use electronic hoppers like the JT Vlocity hoppers or Halos versus the gravity feed type hoppers used more by the recball players. You don't need to carry a lot of paint in the woods like you do in tournaments, either. In a 7-man 7-minute timed game, some back players have been known to carry up to ten 140-round pods of paint onto the tournament field and shoot every single ball; a woodsball player might take an entire 24-hour scenario game to shoot that much. Because of the difference in paint quantities, tournament players more commonly use compressed air tanks, while recball players more often opt for CO_2.

Woodsball players don't typically start shooting off the break.

Courtesy of Smart Parts

There's less time to get the flag from the middle of the field in a tournament and so you'll see less "backdooring," (players running behind their opponents) on an airball field and more eliminations. Additionally, in an X-Ball format, it's very rare to see a player shoot his opponent from behind because the sideline coach will give away your position before you get close. Contrarily, in a woodsball game, there's more time to capture the flag and a better chance that you'll be able to sneak past your opponents in the woods without detection.

The tension, stress level, and heat of competition are much greater in a tournament situation versus what is experienced in a woodsball environment. Off the break, there's less paint in the air in the woods and rec players typically stay back, whereas a tournament player is shooting paint as soon as the game starts. In the woods, players run off the break and will only shoot when they see the opponent. In tournaments, they shoot the entire time to keep the opposing team from moving down the field. It's more important for tournament players to keep their gun up the entire time, even when they're loading, but for a woodsball player it's more about looking for the right shots, placing

Tournament teams start shooting right off the break
© Gary Baum, paintballphotography.com

them better on the target, and generally making every shot count.

Whatever your style of play, both types are equally fun. Always remember: play it safe, and use good team work to get the win.

MIKE PAXSON is a pro player, coach and clinician. He started the 2007 season with the Los Angeles Ironmen. He has also played for the Bushwhackers, the Men, Chicago Aftershock and Team LTZ. In addition to being a marker tech for DYE's Matrix line, he travels all over the country as an instructor for PaintballSchool.com. Paxson is also a character on the pro level in the video game, Greg Hastings Tournament Paintball MAX'd. Reach him at www.mikepaxson.com.

Courtesy Ricochet Development

Tips for New Tournament Players

Every paintball player who has ever played in a tournament has one thing absolutely in common: They each had a first-time tournament experience. For anyone, playing in a tournament for the first time can be nerve-wracking. It's hard to know what to expect, and easy to feel intimidated and confused. The important thing to realize is that all this is perfectly normal, and comes with the territory more often than you might imagine—in other words, you're not the first to feel this way, nor will you be the last. Bearing this in mind, here are four tips for you to remember when you head out for your first paintball tournament:

1) Relax.

You might think this is easier said than done—and you'd be right—but you can still get there. Most people seem to have a hard time relaxing simply because they're afraid: not necessarily afraid of anything in particular, but afraid of confronting the unknown. Some people are afraid of doing something stupid, or wrong, or dumb, or making mistakes, or any combination of the above. Well, the truth is that on your first tournament outing, all of those things will probably happen.

Yes, you'll likely make the wrong decision.

Yes, you'll make mistakes. Yes, you'll do something that a seasoned tournament player would call "dumb" or "stupid". And yes, that comes with the territory of being a first-timer, so don't worry about it. You can rest assured that every tournament player in history has been guilty of the same exact offenses.

2) Learn.

Once you've come to peace with the realization that what you fear is not only likely to happen, but is also perfectly normal, you can use it to your advantage by learning from your mistakes. All paintball players learn from experience, and personal experience comes in two basic forms: doing something right, and doing something wrong. The key to developing your potential lies in learning from your mistakes, and this should be your focus. Don't let yourself get so caught up in disgust over making a mistake that you forget to realize the value in such a thing. In addition to learning from your own mistakes, you can learn a great deal from others, so when you're not on the field playing, go watch some other teams play and see if you can pick up on certain things that the better players do, and figure out why they do those things. Don't be afraid to talk to those players as well, to ask them questions about their own tournament experience. If there's one thing you can count on, it's that a fisherman's love for storytelling is eclipsed only by the typical paintballer's, and this can be a valuable resource for your own development in understanding the particulars of Tournament paintball.

3) Don't Get Discouraged.

It is inevitable that you will make the same mistake twice, or three times, or four times, or more. It is inevitable that you will feel like you "should have known better." The competitive nature of those who are drawn to Tournament paintball can make it quite difficult for them to take it easy on themselves. After all, the ultimate goal of playing paintball competitively is to win. If you don't win, don't be discouraged. If you make a mistake that seals your defeat, don't be discouraged. Go back to #2 (above) and apply your feelings there. In time, you will be better as a result of everything you've done wrong, so long as you let your mistakes work for your benefit. So rather than

Courtesy Adrenaline Games

Playing the Game

be discouraged, be happy, because you're learning, and that's a great thing.

4) Have One Goal: Enjoy It!

Most importantly, have fun on your first day as a tournament paintballer. This is your first step into the realm of the sport of paintball, a realm that has proven time and time again for many, many players to provide the ultimate in excitement and enjoyment. Playing paintball competitively is a bit like a never-ending journey, because there will always be more to learn, new games to play, and new situations to experience. All journeys have a first step, and this will be yours. Enjoy it for what it is, and welcome aboard!

Tips for Continued Development as a Tournament Player

As you grow more comfortable with tournament play, don't forget that there are always areas for improvement, new things to realize, and rough edges to round out. The players who have made the biggest impact in their games, on their teams, and in this sport are those who have striven continuously to improve themselves. There are four basic ideas that are essential to the continued growth of a dedicated paintball player.

1) Learn to be Ambidextrous.

The ability to hold and shoot a marker equally well with both hands is absolutely invaluable in the sport of paintball. It's difficult for most players to embark upon this task simply because it feels uncomfortable at first to hold the marker's grip in your non-dominant hand. The trick to mastering this technique is commitment and repetition, which, in time, will get you over the hurdle of feeling uncomfortable. Once you are able to shoot your marker well with both hands, your success on the field will improve greatly.

2) Develop Snap-shooting Skills.

On today's concept fields, it is guaranteed that at some point you will find yourself pinned behind your bunker by an opponent who has his or her marker aimed at your position (is "posted" on you) from a relatively close range. If you ease out and exchange fire with this opponent, he or she will likely eliminate you. However, if you have developed a good snap-shot, you can pop out, take a quick shot at your opponent, and pop back behind the bunker before your opponent has the opportunity to hit you with a paintball. If you've taken the time to work on your snap-shot, that single 'ball is all you will need to eliminate him or her. If you haven't taken the time to work on it, it's more likely that you will be the one to leave the field eliminated from play.

3) Learn to Communicate.

In paintball tournaments, the ability of a team to communicate and work together as a single unit on the field of play is essential. Good tournament players need to be able to communicate effectively with their teammates during the game. It can take a while to get the hang of it, so make an effort always to be aware of it when you're playing, and tell your teammates what you're seeing on the field from your vantage point. It's likely that your team will have some codes worked out for various things (such as eliminations, time, etc.), so learn them well and use them whenever appropriate. If one of your teammates yells a code or says something important, get in the habit of repeating it. Good communication takes practice, but once you've got it down you'll never have to think about it again.

4) Be Open to Constructive Criticism.

A closed mind is a terrible thing because it keeps a player from developing his or her full potential. As you develop as a tournament player, it is important that you remain open to receiving constructive criticism from two sources: yourself and others. Constructive criticism from yourself is important because it teaches you to be aware of your own mistakes. Some players make it a point to find something they did wrong after every game, no matter how good the game went or how well they played. The point here is not to be down on oneself, but to find those rough edges that could use some additional improvement. Make no mistake about it: there is always room for improvement. With this in mind, do not make the mistake of taking constructive criticism from other individuals as personal attacks. Their input can be invaluable to personal growth, because other people often observe mistakes in ourselves that we are oblivious to.

—*Justin Owen*

TODAY'S
TOP
TOURNAMENTS

Tournaments abound in paintball. Virtually every game site provides its players with local three- or five-man tournaments, and many participate in regional tournament series held in cooperation with other field operators in the area.

No player wanting to play competition paintball has to travel far to find a tournament. You can also check out any of the major paintball publications and internet sites to discover dates, places and game structures of tournaments organized and managed throughout the world.

Those teams that get hooked on competitive paintball and seek ever greater challenges should start locally, but then look to the major regional tournament series. Several of these series have become major paintball sporting events where 100 or more players compete in several categories for valuable prizes. The XPSL series on the West Coast, the CFOA in the Southeast, the NEPL in the Northeast and the GPL in the Midatlantic and Midwest are the "Big Kahunas" of regional tournament series. College paintballers have not been forgotten—the NCPA (National College Paintball Association) runs a national series of events for college teams. The International Amateur Open, which opened its doors in 1990, catered strictly to the novice and amateur players. Its emphasis on the new player and his introduction to tournament paintball in a festive atmosphere made it a successful enterprise—as of 2007, the IAO is transforming itself into less of a tournament series and more of a paintball conference-cum-gathering called the "Pittsburg Paintball Festival and Industry Conference." There are also paintball tournaments held throughout Europe and Asia.

A LITTLE NATIONAL HISTORY

In 1992, the players and teams wanted more say in the structure and management of tournament paintball. A meeting organized by the heads of eighteen of the top teams took place in Chicago, and the National Professional Paintball League (NPPL) was born. The teams in the NPPL adopted a charter, formed a rules committee, elected officers and selected six venues for new tournaments to be held in 1993. The only existing tournament placed on the NPPL schedule was the World Cup. Although I organized and managed four of the five events in 1993 (San Diego was rained out), my interests centered around the World Cup; I persuaded Aftershock captain Renick Miller to take over the Chicago venue, All-Americans owners Adam and Bill Gardner to manage the Pittsburg tournament, and Dave DeHaan from the Ironmen to handle the West Coast event. The NPPL morphed into Paintball Sports Promotions in 2001. It was the same tournament series with the same promoters and managers, but with a different name. In 2002, the

organization morphed yet again—this time, it split, spawning the Super 7. The Super 7 took the NPPL name with it, but PSP retained most of the top teams. Although the competition and antagonism between the PSP and the Super 7 was pronounced initially, after a few years each group found its own market.

The PSP and NPPL in the United States, and the Millennium series in Europe, are the top paintball tournament series in the world. These are bring-your-own-paint affairs that attract the best players and teams internationally. Each series boasts hundreds of thousands of dollars in prize money, sponsorship from industry leaders, and access to top-notch locations. The games in this level of competitive play are all held at airball concept fields measuring no more than 175–200 feet long and 125–150 feet wide, which makes for some intense and powerful confrontations. There are several divisions of play in each such series from professional—where the top teams in the world vie for tens of thousands of dollars in prize money—to semi-pro, amateur and novice. Those teams planning on attending these major tournaments should secure their airline tickets, hotel rooms and transportation several months ahead of time. Most of the tournaments in each series fill quite quickly, so it is important to get the commitment of attendance from the entire team and pay the entry fee well in advance in order to secure a spot.

PAINTBALL SPORTS PROMOTIONS (PSP) SERIES

The Paintball Sports Promotions tournament series has grown to become the largest of them all. It consists of five tournaments: PSP opens with a game on the West Coast, is anchored by a Chicago event in the summer, and concludes with the World Cup at Disney's Wide World of Sports complex near Orlando, Florida in the fall. The PSP competitions generally attract upwards of 150 teams, with more than 350 teams from about 20 countries vying at the World Cup in both the five-man center flag and X-Ball formats to be crowned the best in the world. X-Ball is structured as a five-man center flag game (it parallels hockey in its scoring and penalty structures), but it is played by teams that have anywhere from 12 to 14 players on the roster. A squad of five goes out to contest for a point, and after that game is concluded, there begins a two minute turnaround time in which another squad of five goes out to play. The contest for points continues until a period ends, and a period can be as short as eight minutes in novice games to 20 to 25 minutes in pro games. PSP tournaments usually begin on Thursday and end on Sunday, with the exception of the seven day World Cup. All PSP events have significant trade shows, but the one at the World Cup spans more than 30 acres and features more than 100 vendors and sponsors. Some vendors build their own "mini-mall" with trailers and gigantic tents equipped with video projections, playing music, and displaying the latest in paintball gear. The World Cup compares in size to about one-third the size of the Summer Olympics. Go to pspevents.com for more information.

The Complete Guide to Paintball

THE NPPL SUPER 7

The Super 7 opens its tournament series each year with a gigantic event at Huntington Beach, California drawing approximately 300 teams from all over the world. It is a five-game series spanning the United States, but it's concentrated in the West and South. Super 7 games are two-flag seven-man format. The tournaments are three day affairs, beginning with preliminaries held on Fridays and Saturdays and concluding with playoffs and finals on Sunday. Information on the Super 7 can be found at nppl.tv.

THE MILLENNIUM SERIES

In the Millennium series, there are five events held throughout Europe. The Millennium can boast of staging its crown jewel tournament at EuroDisney near Paris, usually in the summer. The games played in the Millennium series are two-flag seven-man format and X-Ball. Their website is millennium-series.com.

THRIVING IN CHAOS

Rob Rubin

I want to relate something that happened to me a while ago. I was playing in a local trophies-only tournament on a throw-together team. We finished respectably, but not in the finals. So, the field decided that while the finals were being held on the airball field, the tubes field would be open to anyone who wanted to just play. And, considering that only six teams out of 18 advanced, that was a lot of people to jump in for some extra-curricular play.

What's important here is that only one variable was different. The field was the same five-man hyper-pipes field we'd been playing all day. The tech was the same that we had all been used to all day. The players were the same. The paint was the same. The only variable that changed during the "for fun" games was the numbers on the field. Instead of five on five, we started playing a monstrous 12 on 12. It grew up to a huge 15 on 15 at one point on a field built and designed for five on five play.

The one thing I noticed, over and over, was a total mental lockup of the players. It was as though their brains couldn't handle the numbers. What was a somewhat predictable five on five encounter was now a working example of chaos theory. The well-oiled machine had a liberal number of monkey wrenches thrown in there to kill the machinery.

Now for me this isn't anything new. Every paintball field that has a concept area that I've ever played feels a need to cram the walk-ons into it for a good game of Speedball. The most amazing game I've ever played was 21 on 22 on a five-man hyperball field. And I've played woodland fields that felt more crowded than a Tokyo subway. So how do you deal with these walk-on numbers? Simple, really. Make order of chaos. Simply become one with the universe by listening to TJ Lambini's relaxation tapes before the games begin. You don't have TJ's tapes handy? No problems. We'll just start with making sense of the mess you're getting dumped into.

Pre-Game Planning

A friend of mine, Kennedy How, has a T-shirt that reads "Never underestimate the power of stupid people in large numbers." It's true. Mob mentality rears its ugly head in big games, and to a lesser degree in large walk-on groups. But once you know the nature of people, you recognize the patterns.

First of all, realize that the game does not change drastically with the inclusion of large numbers of people. Walk-on play is the basic game. You shoot your opponent, they get hit, and they walk off. No goofy rules of reincarnation, or reinsertion, or wounds, or anything like that. So the basic terms of engagement apply. If you're used to tournament play, this is important to know.

Second is basic human nature. A poignant joke applies: Two men are hiking in the woods. They round a bend and see a large bear on his hind legs, fangs and claws exposed, looking ready to attack. One hiker throws off his pack, removes the sneakers from the side, and starts pulling at his boots. His

Photo by Rigo Ramirez, © JT USA 2004

Playing the Game

friend says, "What are you doing? You can't outrun a bear!" The first hiker, having already removed the first boot, looks up and says, "I don't need to outrun the bear. I just need to outrun you."

The point is that in walk-on play, it's every person for themselves! Every player there is paying to play for the day, and their main interest is not necessarily in the team, but to shoot paintballs and have a good time doing it. Translated loosely, "Look out for number one." Oh, sure, you can jump in with your five-man team, but the vapor lock I mentioned before happens every time. Which brings me to my third point: the numbers.

If you're used to counting to five or seven, you are in for a shock when you realize there are three people behind that "back 45" you didn't count on. This is probably the number one cause for the vapor lock I keep talking about. You can have a great five-man team in the arena, but it takes only one guy to zone out and get fixated on the count to expose himself to one angle to ruin a good push.

And fourth is the lack of cover. A typical five-man arena has probably six to eight bunkers on one side of the field to use as cover, not counting the stuff in the center. In a five-man game, this is more than adequate. When the numbers start to get to the absurd, 15 people divided by 6 bunkers equals some very strange bedfellows. Not to mention that some of these bunkers are designed to hold one person, barely. So you get a lot of doubling, and sometimes quadrupling up in bunkers.

These fairly simple principles are always lost to people who don't know what to do in what my friends and I call TREs (target rich environments). But once you step back and understand all this, you can prepare yourself for the insanity.

Organization

Off the break, you get your first problem: getting 15 people behind bunkers set for five. Having a pre-game plan is good, so you all know at least where you're going. Nothing fancy, just "Ok, how many are going that way?" is perfectly acceptable. Anything more complex than that and you'll lose your teammates fast.

Once you know who's going right, left, and center, you can work in your small groups to get a more detailed plan. "I'm going to that back can there." "Okay, I'll go to the laydown in front of that." "Sounds good, I'll go with him to the can, and bump up when you move up." Three players now have a loose game plan. They can now work together to make the first five seconds work.

Don't be afraid to plan to have three guys behind a large bunker. In fact, this can be a major plan of your game. One guy gets knocked out and the other team thinks it's a clear bunker. They move up, and run directly into your barrel. I've done that to a few people before, too. Plan this out in advance. Having no surprises in the first few moments is a good thing.

The other reason you want a plan is to avoid stumbles; literally, two players bumping into each other at a full paced sprint trying to dive behind the same small can together. Don't laugh, I've seen it too many times to count them. Even if your plan includes moving up, let the guy you'll be sharing a space with know what you're up to. Avoids a lot of confusion and a lot of headaches when you bump into the guy.

I want to specifically talk about sweet spotting as well, especially in an opening move like this. If only one guy is running across your stream, you might get one. Great. But now if there's four, one may get hit, the rest will make it through. That's the nature of the numbers. I'm not saying you shouldn't sweet spot off the break, I'm just letting you know the odds are against you shutting down a side off the break. But getting the numbers in your favor in the first five seconds, it's worth the risk.

Mid-Game Strategy

Mid-game, a lot of your strategy is normal game strategy. Play as you always would, but throw your count out the window. Unless you know for sure that the teams are 14 on 14, don't bother counting. And, even if you do, don't expect your teammates to pick up on the count, let alone the fact you're keeping track of that kind of thing.

If you're just a solo player, you would be ahead to buddy up with someone. They don't even have to know you're doing it. Ask the guy in the bunker next to you what he's shooting at. If you can see a name on their jersey, use it. "Hey! Hamburger Head! Where are they at?" It's why I wear vanity jerseys! If someone wants to ask me something, my name is right there for them to use. Stick with this system for optimal results. Also, don't always believe a total stranger. Sometimes, their interest is to see if you get lit up from the left or right, so take things with grains of salt.

If you're playing with your team, play as you normally do. Just, like I said, toss the count out the window. Work more with a 'feel' for the field. If nobody is shooting at you from the left, odds are it really might be cleared out. Remember the first principle from before. The game does not radically change, just the number of bodies.

The other thing you can do is teach. Grab a few of the walk-on players and give them a crash course in codes and communications. "We break the field into red, white, blue." Taking a few moments to teach could give you a code that would be very important down the road from the player you take some time with. And if it goes horribly right, then you can find someone new to get into your team later.

I've always been a fan of the idea "the more the merrier." And as long as fields insist on stuffing 20 on 20 in a 5 man field, I'll get to experience that. It's not anything that can not be handled. It's a matter of knowing a few things, relaxing a little bit, and taking the game as it comes to you.

Courtesy of Cleo Fogal

Playing the Game

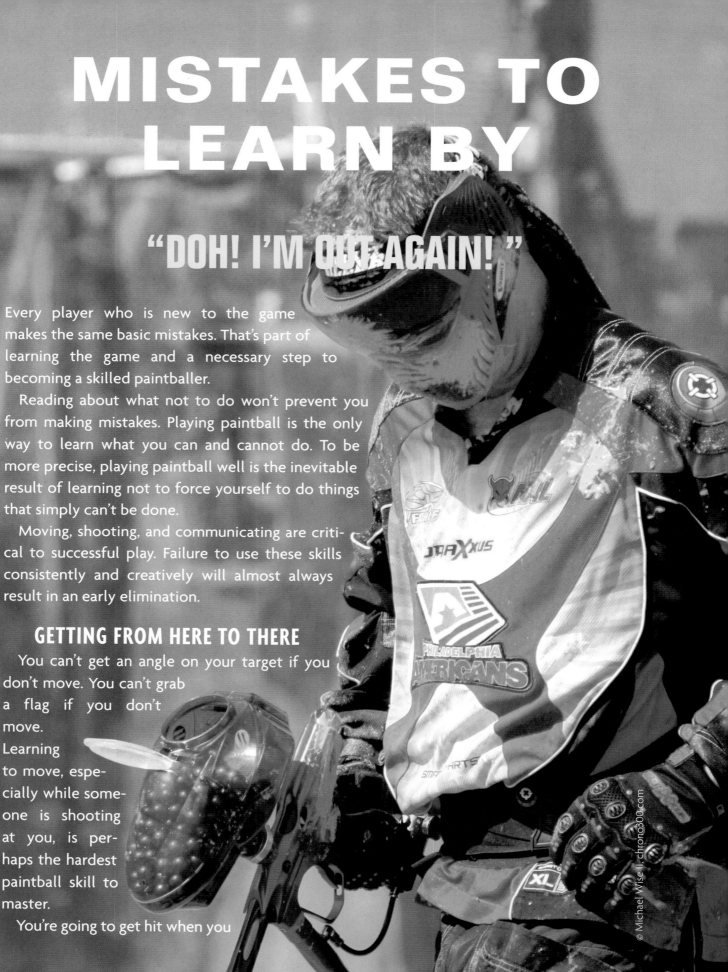

MISTAKES TO LEARN BY

"DOH! I'M OUT AGAIN!"

Every player who is new to the game makes the same basic mistakes. That's part of learning the game and a necessary step to becoming a skilled paintballer.

Reading about what not to do won't prevent you from making mistakes. Playing paintball is the only way to learn what you can and cannot do. To be more precise, playing paintball well is the inevitable result of learning not to force yourself to do things that simply can't be done.

Moving, shooting, and communicating are critical to successful play. Failure to use these skills consistently and creatively will almost always result in an early elimination.

GETTING FROM HERE TO THERE

You can't get an angle on your target if you don't move. You can't grab a flag if you don't move. Learning to move, especially while someone is shooting at you, is perhaps the hardest paintball skill to master.

You're going to get hit when you

play. Even the best tournament player on the face of the planet has been hit thousands of times. Most of those hits occurred while they were moving. That's because they've learned that failing to move will get you eliminated every single time, while moving may offer you some chance of staying in the game.

The purpose of moving is to 'get an angle' on your opponents. If you or one of your teammates can see the side or rear of an opponent, you've gotten the angle, and usually an easy elimination.

SHOOTING

Face it. In order to take someone out of the game, you need to hit them with a paintball. In order to do this, it is necessary to pull the trigger of your gun.

Far too many players get taken out of the game because they fail to realize what a versatile tool

their paintball gun can be. Not only can it be used to shoot an opponent, it can also be used to keep an opponent from shooting at you.

Your paintball gun can be used in a wide variety of offensive and defensive ways—from the 'one shot, one kill' of the sniper to the diversionary shooting of air while reloading. After your brain, your gun is your main tool on the field. Use it.

This doesn't mean that you should start the game pulling the trigger. It does mean that before you play it would be a good idea to step over to the target range and get used to the feel and operation of your gun. Shoot a few targets. See how accurate you are; how fast you can shoot, how far you can shoot. And, once you know what you can do with your paintball gun, remember to use it when on the field.

COMMUNICATING

In order to be able to move, to find targets, or maybe even just to find out how to get back to the flag station, you'll need to communicate with the other players on your team.

During your first few games this may be very difficult, especially if you are playing with a group of relative strangers. Nevertheless, talking can help you stay in the game longer, and may even help you get more eliminations.

The purpose of communicating is to coordinate your moves on the field with your teammates. At first it could be something as simple as asking a fellow player if they can see any opponents ahead of them. Or perhaps even if they know where the other team is!

Courtesy Airgun Designs

Playing the Game

••

The important thing to remember is that your unknown teammate will be very happy to have someone to talk to, and please remember that answering a teammate is just as important as asking your own questions.

As your knowledge of the game increases, communicating will become a very effective tool which you can use to flank opposing players, determine the number of remaining opponents, coordinate

charges or 'pushes' and transmit some very sophisticated information about what is happening on the field.

MORE "LEARNING OPPORTUNITIES"

Once you get past the basics, you'll find yourself running into a whole host of other little lessons and tricks. Learning them will smooth out your game and keep you in the action longer. Although these aren't nearly as important as the three basic skills, learning them will increase your enjoyment of the game.

LOOKING

In order to stay in the game, new players need to avoid tunnel vision, or the tendency to fixate on one object, one opponent or one activity, to the exclusion of all else.

To avoid tunnel vision, practice shifting your attention among all of the activities in the game in a regular order. Look to your left, look ahead of you, look to your right, check your gun's condition, the paint in your loader, check your rear and your front, and then repeat the procedure.

Eventually you will learn to split your attention properly. You will also learn what you need to pay attention to and what you can ignore. Your main goal during your first few games should be to get a pattern down and then remember to use it.

"WHY IS MY GUN SHOOTING SIDEWAYS?"

This is a simple, yet forgettable, skill. Before you go on the field, make sure that your gun is clean, your goggles are clear, "your tank has enough gas," and you're carrying enough paint for the game.

SELF-ELIMINATION

Too many players lose game-time, and valuable experience, by thinking that because they've run out of paint or air, or their gun goes down, the game is over for them.

You can leave the field if you want to, but why would you want to. Stay and concentrate on learning. Find ways to stay in the game longer. Learn to hide. Learn to crawl. Learn to bluff the other team. Get as much playing time as you can, regardless of the condition of your equipment.

FAILURE TO REDUCE THE TARGET

Making yourself small is an important skill. The smaller you are, the harder you are to see and to

NICE & TIGHT

DEAD MEAT

eliminate. In order to 'tuck in' effectively, you have to be aware of exactly where your arms, legs, head, gun, and other equipment are at all times.

This is one of those skills that simply takes time to acquire. However, you can speed up the process by paying attention to where you get hit after the game and by looking at how you take and use cover during the game.

Once in cover, pull your elbows into your body. Tuck your legs in. Get your head down. When you come out of cover to view the field, only expose one eye. While you are shooting, keep your gun barrel as close to the edge of your cover as possible.

Don't use a classic shooter's hold on your gun. Twist the arm of your trigger hand down under the gun. Place the arm of your support hand under the gun as well. When done correctly, both of your elbows should be almost touching on or in front of your chest.

TELEGRAPHING YOUR MOVES

When you break cover, and if you really want to play you're going to have to, you don't want to meet up with a paintball just hanging in the air waiting for you.

Take the precaution of varying where, when, and how you break cover. If your head constantly pops up over the top of a bunker, in the exact same place every time, someone on the field is going to target that spot and keep on shooting at it until you are gone.

To avoid telegraphing, never pop out in the same place two times in a row. Change everything: pop out low on the left, high on the right, from close in on your cover to backed away from your cover.

There are thousands of ways you can break cover, and you should be trying to use every one of them.

FAILURE TO USE ANGLES

If you are using cover properly, the last player on the field who is a threat to you is the one directly in front of you. Once you're down behind that bunker or tucked in behind a tree, you can't shoot at the players to your front, and they can't hit you.

This basic situation means that you must shoot to the sides, or at an angle from your cover. Forget about the players in front of you and look for the ones off to the left and the right. Look deep across the field if you are towards the center, or look out to

the opposite boundary if you are near the tape. You'll be surprised at how many targets you can find.

LACK OF AGGRESSION

Being aggressive does not necessarily mean running straight down the field hollering your head off. And yet, you might be surprised to learn that this actually works once in a while.

Aggression is a finely balanced thing; too much and you end up in an over-exposed position with the inevitable result. Not enough and you end up making your moves too little, too late.

Pushing the envelope will help you learn just how far you can go. Next time you play, try to get

The Ricochet with digital timer/counter

Courtesy Ricochet Development

The Complete Guide to Paintball

to a piece of cover that is just a little closer to your opponents. And then the next, and the next. Try to get behind them. Try running further down the field at the opening of the game. Push it, and then keep on pushing it. If you see an opportunity to win the game, rally your teammates around you, and make it happen.

A MULTI-DIMENSIONAL GAME

Paintball is not just a stand-up game. It's a kneeling game. A crouching game. A lying game. A crawling game. A timing game.

Being in a particular location on the field at the beginning of the game may be very safe. Towards the end of the game, the same spot might be the last place you would want to be.

If you can't move up the field by running, try crawling. If you are lying behind cover and can't make the shot, try it from a sitting position. If you want to move to another position, wait until no one is looking at you.

Use the entire field, all of the time.

—SD

EPILOGUE

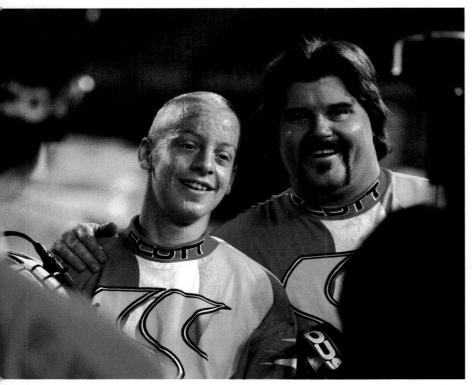

More
Than
Just A
Game

THE REWARDS OF PLAYING PAINTBALL

Jerry Braun Puts Paintball in Perspective

As you have seen, paintball is a game, a sport, a business, an escape, a regimen, an avocation, a corporate training device, a bonding experience, and an all around good time. And still, I would contend, paintball is more than the sum of its parts.

Something about paintball gives a great deal to those who play it. Paintball provides a structure within which players of all ages, backgrounds, physical make-ups, and beliefs can experience the thrill of victory. Its rules are simple and winning is accessible. That's especially important to young people.

Paintball's greatest value comes from what it does for young players. Those who never made the first squad of little league baseball, pee-wee football, or local soccer leagues, who often had to sit on the bench in frustration and embarrassment, can participate and excel in this game. They can score a key elimination, make a sacrifice that helps their team win, and hang the flag to win the game.

In paintball, the recognition, support, and congratulations young people receive from peers build a self-esteem few other activities can foster. To children and their parents, this is where paintball becomes more than just a game.

Travis Jenks takes the flag in front of a cheering crowd at Skyball 1999.

Children who are particularly talented at this game have access to ever increasing levels of difficulty, all the way up to amateur and professional leagues. There are no upper limits for those who seek an extremely challenging competitive experience in this up-and-coming sport.

The game nurtures communication skills, promotes values such as honesty, fair play, teamwork, and goal setting. It also introduces young people to the experience of being decisive, taking risks, and learning from the consequences of their actions. All of this occurs in a safe format and family-friendly atmosphere. In all of these ways, paintball builds character.

Paintball flourishes because it gives so much to its participants in so many different ways. It is an activity that has yet to reach its peak of popularity and its future seems limitless!

Living His Dream

Diagnosed with a rare form of Hodgkins Disease at the age of 16, Travis Jenks is making the most of every moment and taking nothing for granted. Travis seized the opportunity to play with and against the best players in professional paintball in Toronto at Skyball 1999, an international tournament. The Diggers and their owner Jerry Reilly, Operation Paintball, and Mare Island's owner, Matt Crandle, pitched in airfare for the Jenks family, and the Greater Bay Area Make-A-Wish Foundation made hotel arrangements.

Travis was especially grateful to play alongside his personal paintball hero, Bob Long of the Ironmen. This was not their first meeting. The two met initially at the Mare Island fields in California where Travis had his first chance to play with the Ironmen and the Diggers in a scrimmage planned for him by the Greater Bay Area Make-A-Wish Foundation.

"I'd like to get a nice paintball marker and maybe go play with the Ironmen."

The entire paintball industry has rallied around Travis. Bud Orr donated a 98 Autococker and Bob Long gave him a prototype of his new electronic gun, the "Defiant," and a Signature Series Millennium. The Diggers pitched in with a Centerfire AutoMag (complete with Evolution hopper).

Paintball Glossary

ACTION

1. The mechanism by which something is operated, as that of a gun.

2. A military encounter, as a battle or skirmish.

3. Actual combat with enemy forces.

AGITATOR

1. A machine or device for agitating and mixing.

2. In reference to paintball, it is a device that is attached to a paintball hopper or incorporated into the design of the hopper. It has a shaft that enters the inner enclosure of the hopper with some type of impeller attached to the end of it. When activated the agitator rotates the impeller which moves the paintball around inside of the hopper, allowing them to align with the feed port, located at the bottom of the hopper, and fall freely into the hopper feed nipple.

ASA

The abbreviation for Air Source Adapter. See "ASA Adapter".

ASA ADAPTER

Also referred to as CA Adapter. A device that is designed to allow a constant air tank to screw into it and let the CO_2 gas in the tank pass through it. In most cases, the ASA Adapter is designed with a actuating pin. When used with a constant air tank that has a pin valve, the ASA Adapter pin actuator presses in the pin valve's pin and allows the flow of CO_2 gas from the tank into and through the ASA Adapter. The gas then goes to the paintgun's valve mechanism either directly or indirectly via some type of gas line.

AUTO, FULL

Continuous firing and reloading of paintgun as long as the trigger is held down.

AUTO, SEMI

1. Partly automatic.

2. Automatic recocking of paintgun and loading the next paintball but requiring a squeeze of the trigger to fire each shot.

AUTO TRIGGER

A trigger and sear design used with pump action paintguns, that allows the user of the paintgun to have the gun fire each time the pump handle is pulled back, allowing the gun mechanism to be cocked, and then pulled full forward. The gun will fire automatically when pump handle is returned to full forward position—each time the pump handle is cycled from front to rear and back—as long as the trigger is being held down.

BACK BOTTLE SYSTEM

Refers to a constant air system design whereby the gun's ASA adapter is located at the rear of the paintgun and that is where the constant air tank is attached. The constant air tank is used as the gun's shoulder stock and may or may not have a butt plate attached to it. Pump action paintguns usually have the ASA adapter in-line with the barrel and cocking mechanism. Semi Auto paintguns usually have the ASA adapter in-line with cocking mechanism.

BACK BOTTLE ADAPTER

An ASA adapter which is attached to the rear of a paintgun, that is used to connect a gas supply to the gun and is usually in line with either the barrel/cocking mechanism or just the cocking mechanism.

BARREL PLUG

A safety device that is inserted into the front end of a paintgun barrel to prevent a paintball from exiting the barrel.

BARREL, RIFLED, INTERNAL

A barrel that has internal grooves, either straight or in a spiral pattern.

BOLT

The internal part of a paintgun that is common to Stock, Pump Action and Semi Auto paintguns. The bolt usually has O-ring(s) at the front end of it. The O-ring acts as a seal between the bolt and the inner wall of the paintgun barrel when the bolt is in the full forward position. The bolt performs two functions

1. It is the device that moves the paintball from where it is loaded into the chamber of the paintgun, to the bore of the paintgun barrel.

2. It is the device by which CO_2 gas is transferred from the paintgun valve system to the rear of the paintball via the front of the bolt.

BOLT (closed)

One of two design criteria by which semi auto paintguns are manufactured. The closed bolt design means that the bolt is in the full forward position with the bolt O-ring sealing against the inner wall of the paintgun barrel when gun is ready to be fired via the trigger. This is with respect to the paintgun being connected to a CO_2 gas supply (constant air tank or remote air system) and fully pressurized.

BOLT (open)

One of two design criteria by which semi auto paintguns are manufactured. The open bolt design means that the bolt is in the full rear position with the bolt just behind the feed nipple port (the port that allows the paintballs to flow into the paintgun body) when paintgun is ready to be fired via the trigger. This is with respect to the paintgun being connected to a CO_2 gas supply (constant air tank or remote air system) and fully pressurized.

BOLT, VENTURI

A bolt with a concave face. The face of the bolt will have multiple holes in it. These holes are known as thrust ports.

BORE DROP LOADING

Guns using bore systems load into a receiver the same size as the barrel or directly into the barrel itself. This keeps the ball from having to load over any large seams or steep angles.

BOTTLE

1. Slang for tank.

2. A portable container for holding liquids or gases, having a neck and mouth.

3. In paintball it is the container part of a constant air tank.

BLOW BACK

A paintball gun's leakage of CO_2 gases between the bolt and the inner barrel wall and/or leakage of CO_2 gases from the cocking mechanism between the gun's hammer and inner wall of the gun's housing. Blowback may occur for two reasons. First, and easiest to fix, is that the O-rings on the gun's bolt and/or hammer need to be replaced. The second reason for blowback is more complex. It has to do with the positioning of the gun's components at the time that the CO_2 gas is released into the gun's barrel.

BOTTOM LINE

A style of constant air system where the ASA adapter is located at the bottom of the paintball gun's grip frame. This ASA adapter is where the constant air tank is connected to the paintgun. The ASA adapter may be designed into the grip frame so as to be part of the grip frame or it may be a after market ASA adapter that is mounted to the bottom of the grip frame. If it is a after market ASA adapter it will have to have a gas line connecting it to the paintgun in order to allow gas to flow from the tank into and through the ASA adapter to the gas line and then to the paintgun.

BREECH DROP LOADING

Guns using breech loading systems load into an area larger than the inner diameter of the barrel. The ball must then be up into the barrel.

BREECH LOCK SYSTEM

A design that prevents the paintgun from being accidentally pumped twice before it is fired once. Breech locking guns must be fired before the gun can be pumped again.

BUTT PLATE

A device that fits on to the end of a tank allowing it to be used as a shoulder stock.

CALIBER

With respect to a paintball the diameter of a circular section. With reference to a paintgun the diameter of the bore of a gun taken as a unit of measurement.

CALIFORNIA STYLE

A style of constant air system developed in California in the late 1980's that consisted of a paintgun, an 'L' shape shoulder stock with a constant air tank holder located on the bottom side of it, a constant air tank of either 7 or 10 ounce in size with a Thermo on/off valve that would be held in the

shoulder stock's tank holder and a hose with fittings that would connect the tank to the paintgun.

CARBON DIOXIDE

Also known as CO_2. A colorless, odorless, incombustible gas that has many purposes such as dry ice, the carbonation in carbonated beverages, and in fire extinguishers. CO_2 is present in the atmosphere and formed during respiration. CO_2 is a compound gas made of oxygen and carbon. CO_2 stores it's energy when it is in a liquid state and releases it into a usable force through expansion into a gas. Used in paintguns as a pressurized gas (power source) for shooting paintballs out of the paintgun's barrel. With respect to semi auto paintguns, CO_2 is also used for recocking the paintgun.

CGA

Denotes Compressed Gas Association. Usually used to refer to a cylinder valve outlet connection detailed in the CGA pamphlet V-1.

CHECK VALVE

Allows substance (such as gas, liquid or solids) to flow in only one direction. Once passed the check valve the substance cannot flow back through check valve.

CHRONOGRAPH

Electronic device that measures the speed of an object directed across it.

CO_2

The abbreviation for Carbon Dioxide.

CONSTANT AIR

A terminology developed in California in the late 1980's. It refers to the use of a refillable gas tank that is connected to a paintgun and supplies the CO_2 gas necessary to power the operation of the gun. The term "Constant Air" was derived from the fact that the paintgun would have a prolonged supply of gas and would be able to get 300–1000 shots per tank of gas, depending on size of tank and type of gun. This was opposed to paintguns that used 12 gram CO_2 cartridges and only got 15–25 shots per cartridge on the average.

CRITICAL TEMPERATURE

The temperature above which liquid phase cannot exist.

CRITICAL PRESSURE

The saturation vapor pressure at the Critical Temperature.

CYCLE RATE

Indicates the number of cycles a paintgun can perform per second.

DETENT, BALL

Sometimes called Ball stop, anti-doubler, wire nubbin. A device that keeps no more than one paintball from loading into the chamber of a paintgun when the paintgun is executing one cycle. It does this by maintaining the paintball in a stationary position until the paintgun's bolt pushes the paintball into the barrel of the gun.

DEW POINT

The temperature and pressure at which the liquefaction of a vapor begins.

DIRECT FEED

A system by which paintballs are fed directly into the paintgun chamber or barrel via a feed nipple. The feed nipple is usually fastened to side of the paintgun at a 45 degree angle. Feed nipples on pump action guns are usually 1" in diameter and feed nipples on semi auto paintguns are usually 7/8" in diameter.

DISK, RUPTURE

A small copper disk in the valve of a tank that is designed to rupture if the pressure in the tank becomes too great. The rupture disk is usually held in place by a safety plug that has vent holes in it.

DONKEY

Slang for ASA Adapter.

DOT

Abbreviation for Department of Transportation whose Title 49, Code of Federal Regulations regulates the movement of hazardous materials.

DOUBLE ACTION

Requiring only one pull of the trigger to cock and fire.

ELBOW

Slang for hopper adapter.

EXPANSION CHAMBER

A device which conditions CO_2 gas by allowing it to expand before it enters the paintgun's valve system.

FEED NIPPLE

Also known as Feed port. The feed nipple is a short tube that is connected to the paintgun housing at an angle of 45 degrees. It provides the passage by which paintballs move from the paintball hopper, through the hopper adapter, which attaches to the feed nipple, and into the chamber of the paintgun. Commonly, feed nipples for pump action paintguns are one inch in diameter, while semi auto paintguns have seven-eighths inch feed nipples.

FEED PLUG

A plug at the bottom of a power feeder that angles the balls into the feed port. It can also be turned to stop the balls from feeding into your gun.

FEED TUBE

A paintball storage container tubular in form, closed at one end and open at other end with some type of lid covering the opening. When playing paintball the player uses the feed tube to reload his paintgun's hopper.

FEEDER

Slang for hopper.

FILL STATION

An apparatus consisting of at least one valve used for exhausting pressurized fill hose, a fill hose and some type of fill adapter for connecting a constant air tank to one end of the hose. It is used for filling smaller constant air tanks with liquid CO_2 from larger siphon fill tank. The large siphon fill tank is usually 50 to 60 pounds in volume weight.

FITTING, ELBOW, (90 DEGREE)

A fitting that allows the connection of two items at a 90 degree angle to each other, such as a CA hose to make a ASA adapter or paintgun.

FLAG STATION

With reference to the game of paintball, this is a team's base camp and is the location that a team's flag is kept. It is also the location where a team must return the opposing team's flag to in order to win the game.

FLANK

1. The extreme right or left side of an army or fleet.

2. To stand or be placed or posted at the flank or side of.

3. To defend or guard at the flank.

4. To menace or attack the flank of.

FOGGING UP

This refers to those times when a person's breathing and lack of movement will cause the lenses of a persons goggles to fog over, severely reducing visibility.

FORE GRIP

A horizontal grip generally located on the front of a gun. This grip is generally grasped with the player's off hand; i.e. the hand not on the trigger frame; to stabilize the gun for shooting.

F.P.S.

Abbreviation for 'feet per second'. This is the standard method in the U.S. for determining the speed at which a paintgun is shooting.

GAS EFFICIENCY

Refers to the amount of shots a gun gets in relation to the amount of liquid CO_2 it uses. Similar to miles per gallon; i.e. getting 350 shots from a seven ounce constant air tank.

GOGGLES

Eye protection worn by players to prevent eye damage. Paintball goggles are specifically designed for the sport of paintball and should not be substituted with goggles made for any application other than paintball.

GOING LIQUID

Refers to liquid CO_2 entering the paintgun before it has had a chance to expand into a gas or vapor.

GRIPS

Components that fit on the paintgun grip frame and provide surface area by which the shooter may grip the gun. Grips are replaceable on many types of paintguns. Different styles of grips can provide greater comfort and ease of use for the individual paintball player. Different styles of grips include rubber, wood, and wraparound types.

HAMMER

Also known as the lower bolt or the striker. This component, when released from the cocked position, strikes the valve assembly and forces it open. When this striking of the valve assembly by the hammer occurs, CO_2 is allowed to pass through the valve assembly from the gas source to the paintgun barrel.

HAMMER (DOWN)

Refers to pulling the trigger, putting paint on someone in a sudden and intense manner, seizing the moment on offense by showering a target with paint.

HAMMER SEAR

The part of a gun that retains the hammer in a fixed position, usually under main spring pressure. When the trigger is pulled by the shooter's finger, it pushes against the sear, allowing it to release the hammer and thus allowing the hammer to strike the valve assembly.

HARNESS

The combination of straps, pouches and other parts forming the working gear worn by a paintball player to carry paintballs, CO_2 cartridges, tanks, squeegee and anything else he/she requires to play the game of paintball.

HOSE

In paintball a hose is used to transfer gas from one component to another, such as from a constant air tank to an ASA adapter on a paintgun.

HONE

A tool that is mechanically rotated and has abrasive tip(s) for polishing or enlarging holes to precise dimensions.

HOPPER

A container used to hold paintballs, usually with a lid that covers the opening where the paintballs are loaded into it, and a feed nipple at it's bottom.

HOSING

Refers to consistent rapid firing. A tactic typically used when pinning down an opposing player.

HYDROSTATIC TEST

A container test required at definite intervals by DOT to determine the wall thickness via measuring elastic expansion. Purpose of the test is to assure the container is safe for continued use.

I.D.

Abbreviation for inner diameter.

IN-LINE CONFIGURATION

Refers to the manner in which the bolt and hammer of a paintgun are positioned in relation to each other. An in-line configuration indicates that the bolt and hammer are in line with each other—one behind the other.

LENSES, THERMAL

A dual lens system. The outer lens is made of a super hard polycarbonate material. The inner lens is made of a different polycarbonate composition that allows anti-fog gel coat to stick to it. The two lenses are attached to each other by means of a rubber gasket that makes an air-tight seal between the two. The space between the two lenses is called a thermal barrier and helps to reduce fogging on the inner lens.

LOADER

Slang for hopper feed tube.

LIQUID

Slang for CO_2 in liquid form.

MUZZLE

The mouth, or end for discharge, of the barrel of a gun, pistol, etc.

MUZZLE BREAK

1. A pattern of holes or slots machined into the end of a barrel that act as exhaust ports.

2. A machined add-on part with a pattern of holes or slots machined into it that fastens to the end of a barrel either by press fit or set screw fastteners.

MUZZLE VELOCITY

The speed at which a paintball is traveling when it leaves the muzzle of a paintgun barrel.

NELSON BASED

Refers to pump guns (most pump guns) that were designed after the original 007. Nelson based guns have an in-line bolt and hammer system.

NITROGEN (N_2)

Refers to Nitrogen gas. A colorless, odorless, relatively non-reactive gas which is compressed to high pressures. The difference between Nitrogen gas and CO_2 is that Nitrogen is measured by pressure while CO_2 is measured by weight.

N.P.T.

Refers to normal temperature and pressure which is defined as 700° F and 14.696 PSI.

O.D.

Abbreviation for Outer Diameter. Outer diameter refers to distance across an object.

O-RING

A ring of pliable material, such as rubber or neoprene, used as a gasket.

OFF-SET SIGHT RAIL

A sight rail that is mounted at an angle away from top dead center of paintgun body. The off-set sight rail allows a sight to be mounted so that it is unobstructed by other parts of the paintgun.

PAINTBALL

A round capsule filled with brightly colored water based dye that is designed to break upon impact leaving a splat mark on the object it hits. Paintball sizes are .50 Cal., .62 Cal. and .68 Cal., the last being the most current size and readily available. The .68 caliber paintball offers much better range, accuracy, and breakability due to it's size and mass.

PAINTBALL GUN

A mechanical device, usually powered by CO_2 gas, used to propel paintballs.

PAINT CHECK

The time at which a player is checked for splat mark(s). A paint check may be called by referee or player, but may only be invoked by a referee and game may only be restarted by referee. Misuse of the paint check rule by a player is cause for that player to be removed from current game.

POWER FEED

A feed nipple design that incorporates the blowback from the paintball gun to increase the rate at which paintballs are fed into the paintgun. Most power feeds are designed into the paintguns, but there are some after market bolt on power feeds available for guns like the VM-68 series of paintgun and others.

POWERLET

An icon developed by the air gun industry for CO_2 cartridge. In paintball, it refers to 12 gram CO_2 cartridge.

PRESSURE REGULATOR

Regulates the pressure of gas flowing through it. Some regulators are preset to p.s.i., and some are adjustable.

PSI

Abbreviation for pounds per square inch.

PULL PIN

A pin fastener which can be removed quickly to speed disassembly of a player's paintgun.

QUICK CHANGER

A device that is either a part of the paintgun or a separate unit that connects to the gun, usually via the ASA adapter. It allows the rapid loading and unloading of a 12 gram CO_2 cartridge.

QUICK DISCONNECT

Usually made of stainless steel or brass, this unit is composed of two parts, a male fitting and a female coupler that connect together to form an air tight connection. In paintball the quick disconnect is used by the player to quickly disconnect the CO_2 source, such as a remote system, from the paintgun.

RECEIVER

The main body of a paintgun where the bolt and hammer are usually housed. A gun's feed nipple is typically a part of your receiver.

REMOTE SYSTEM

Also known as a "Remote" or "Remote Set-Up". The system usually consists of a constant air tank that is carried on the player's body, usually in a pouch or fanny pack, and a high pressure gas line with quick disconnect and all the fittings required to connect it to the paintgun.

RESTICLE

A network of fine lines, wires, or the like placed in the focus of the eyepiece of an optical instrument.

RIFLING, EXTERNAL

Also know as external porting. With reference to paintball gun barrels, it is a spiral hole pattern which is drilled into the barrel. When a paintball is shot through a ported barrel, the ports allow the air in front of the paintball to escape as the paintball pushes forward. The loss of air restriction in front of the paintball allows the paintball to shoot straighter and further. The barrel porting also breaks up the sound made when the gun is fired, thus the paintgun operates much quieter.

RIFLING, INTERNAL

Grooves or raised points in a barrel that are either straight or spiraled in pattern.

SHERIDAN BASED

Refers to those guns that are based on or are similar to the original Sheridan family of guns. A Sheridan based gun is generally discernible by its stacked design. The hammer and valve system are in the lower section while the bolt is in the upper section.

SIGHT RAIL

Allows the mounting of a sighting system to a paintgun.

SIGHT RAIL, RAISED

A sight rail that is raised up off the body of the gun. The purpose for this is to allow the shooter a better field of view.

SIGHT, RED DOT

An optical sighting device powered by a battery that produces a red dot reticle. Red dot sights do not project a dot on target.

SIGHT RINGS

Adapters to mount your sight to the sight rail. (Note: Different rings are required to mount different sights to different guns.)

SKIRMISH

1. A fight between small bodies of troops.

2. Any brisk conflict or encounter.

SKIRMISH LINE

1. The invisible line between two opposing teams that have confronted each other.

2. A formation taken whereby players are positioned beside each other in a line.

SLIMED BARREL

Slang for when a ball has broken in the barrel of a paintgun and coated it with paint. A slimed barrel will not shoot straight.

SPECIFIC HEAT

Amount of heat required to raise a unit mass of substance one degree of temperature at either constant pressure or constant volume. Usually expressed in BTU per pound per degree F.

SPECIFIC VOLUME

Volume of a unit mass of substance at a given temperature. Expressed as cubic feet per pound at 700° F.

SPLATTER

The residue sprayed on a player by a paintball when it makes impact with an object close to that player.

SPRING, MAIN

The spring that drives the hammer.

SPRING VALVE

The spring that closes the valve after it has been opened by the hammer.

SQUAD

Any small group of persons engaged in a common enterprise; a team or sub-group within a team.

SQUEEGEE

A device used to clean the barrel of a paintgun.

STACKED CONFIGURATION

Refers to the manner in which the bolt and hammer are positioned in relation to each other inside the paintgun receiver. A stacked configuration indicates that the bolt and hammer are stacked one on top of the other.

STICK FEED

A gravity feeder, usually made out of PVC material, which holds the balls stacked in a line one on top of the other.

STOCK 'L'

A shoulder stock that is shaped like an 'L' laying on its side. This stock usually fastens to the bottom of the paintgun's grip frame and may have a constant air tank holder attached to it.

STOCK 'T'

A shoulder stock that is shaped like a 'T' laying on its side. This stock usually fastens to the bottom of the paintgun's grip frame and may have a constant air tank holder attached to it.

SUPPRESSOR

A tubular device that is press-fitted onto the front end of a paintgun barrel, designed to reduce the amount of sound that is made by the gun when it is fired. Also known as Silencer.

TANK, CHILLED

Refers to a tank that has become very cold due to rapid pressure loss. This may be caused by rapid firing or purposefully releasing the remaining air pressure in a tank. (Note, a tank must be chilled before it can be filled with CO_2).

TANK, CONSTANT AIR

A container or structure for holding a liquid or gas. In paintball a tank is made up from two components, a valve and a bottle.

TANK, ANTI-SIPHON

A tank designed to allow only vaporous CO_2 gas to exit the tank through the tank valve.

TANK, SIPHON

A tank specifically designed to draw liquid CO_2 from the bottom of the tank. This is accomplished by a gas line that is attached to rear end of the tank valve and weighting down the other end of the gas line so that it remains located in the bottom area of the tank.

THREAD SAVER

Also know as bottle cap. A protective cap that screws onto a tank valve. This keeps the valve from being damaged while not in use.

TOOL, VELOCITY ADJUSTING

Also called adjusting tool. A tool used specifically for adjusting the velocity of a paintgun.

TOURNAMENT CAP

A cap which covers a gun's velocity adjuster so that the velocity cannot be adjusted during game play, normally required for tournament play.

TRIGGER SHOE

After-market product that fits on the trigger of a gun to provide the trigger finger with more surface area to grip the trigger and a comfortable feel.

TWELVE GRAM

Slang for 12 gram CO_2 cartridge.

TUBE, PAINTBALL

A small cigar-like tube used to carry 10 paintballs.

TUNNEL VISION

Refers to a player who has focused so intently on the player or players directly in front of him that he is not aware of players moving to the side of him.

UN (United Nations) Number

The DOT (Department of Transportation) Number found on the Cylinder (bottle) label. For example UN1066, the "UN" prefix to this number indicates that 1066 is recognized throughout the world as identifying nitrogen. Sometimes "NA" (North America) will appear as a prefix. NA numbers are recognized in the USA and Canada.

VELOCITY ADJUSTER

A component of a paintgun (usually a set screw) that when turned in either clockwise or counter clockwise direction will increase or decrease the paintgun's muzzle velocity.

VALVE

Any device for halting or controlling the flow of something, such as a gas or liquid, through a pipe, out of a bottle neck, or other passage.

VALVE PORTING

The enlarging or drilling of additional holes in a valve body so that more gas will be released when valve system is opened.

VALVE SYSTEM

All the internal parts in the paintgun which control the flow of gas through the paintgun.

WRENCH, ALLEN

A hexagonal tool which comes in various sizes and is used to turn screw fasteners such as hex or button head screws. They are also used to turn anything that has a hexagonal hole. In paintball they are used to adjust the paintball gun's velocity as well as disassemble it.

Field Finder

This resource listing is intended to help you begin playing Paintball, but companies go in and out of business faster than you can tag a target! For the most up-to-date contact information, please visit www.pbreview.com.

ALABAMA

Alabama Paintball Sportz
7300 US Hwy. 431
Alexandria, Alabama 36250
256-473-1440
ken@alabamapaintballsportz.com
http://www.alabamapaintball-sportz.com

Missions Park Paintball
26668 Newby Road
Athens, Alabama 35613
(256) 232-0220
missionspark@aol.com
http://www.missionspaintball.com

Phoenix Paintball Division
24970 Hwy 72
Athens, Alabama 35611
256-232-9599
phoenixpaintball@bellsouth.net
http://www.phoenixpaintballdivision.com

Alabama Paintball Park
1501 Hwy 150
Bessemer, Alabama 35020
(205) 481-1591
pat@alabamapaintball.com
http://www.alabamapaintball.com

Sand Mountain Shooters Club
626 Bloodworth Rd.
Boaz, Alabama 35956
256-593-8027
smsc@cybrtyme.com
http://www.sandmtnshootersclub.com/paintball.htm

Splatzone Paintball
1550 Avalon Drive
Cottondale, Alabama 35453
205.462.0550
webmaster@splatzonepaintball.net
http://www.splatzonepaintball.net

N2 Paintball
80 County Road 1507
Cullman, Alabama 35058
(256) 338-8270
rkfloyd@hiwaay.net
http://www.n2p8ntball.com/

Liberty Paintball, LLC
935 Liberty Road
Danville, Alabama 35619
256-773-8922
info@libertypaintball1.com
http://www.libertypaintball1.com

Allsport
2608 Beltline Rd. SW
Decatur, Alabama 35601
(256) 355-9706

Wiley's Outdoor Sports
1620 6th Avenue S.E. Unit U
Decatur, Alabama 35601
http://www.wileypaintball.com

Dothan Survival Games
141 Cowarts Rd.
Dothan, Alabama 36301
(334) 793-8202
http://www.dsgpaintball.com

Hotshots
3775 Napier Field Rd
Dothan, Alabama 36303
334-618-8051
info@alabamaindoorpaintball.com
http://www.hotshotsfun.com

Paintball Planet
Gaylesville, Alabama 35973
256-779-6454
tim@paintballplanet.net
http://paintballplanet.net/

Mt. Doom Paintball
3071 Co. Rd. 515
Hanceville, Alabama 35077
mtdoom@hiwaay.net
http://www.mtdoom.de.vu/

FPS Paintball
1228 Putman Dr NW
Huntsville, Alabama 35816
256-864-2670
fpspaintball@fps-paintball.com
http://www.fps-paintball.com

BIG Fish Paintball
200 County Road 123
Jemison, Alabama 35085
205-688-5500
shawn_bright@hotmail.com
http://www.bigfishpaintball.com

Storm Fortress Paintball
565 Country Road 499
Lexington, Alabama 35648
256-229-5668
stormfortresspb@bellsouth.net
http://www.stormfortresspb.2ya.com

Paintball Quest
8651 Serene Drive
McCalla, Alabama 35111
rhatch@hiwaay.net
http://www.paintballquest.com

Bob's Paintball
3428 Dawes Road
Mobile, Alabama 36695
(251) 639-8245
http://www.bobspaintball.biz

Xtreme Paintball
900-A Schillinger Rd S
Mobile, Alabama 36695
(251) 639-0399
http://www.xpb.us/

High Speed Paintball
313 Wesley Childers Rd.
New Hope, Alabama 35760
256-723-3084
larry@hspaintball.com
http://www.hspaintball.com/

Elite 1 Paintball
1030 Bright Star Road
Snead, Alabama 35952
(205) 466-3972
elitepaintball@hopper.net
http://elite-1-paintball.com/

Tradin Paint
6510 Spanish Fort Blvd
Spanish Fort, Alabama 36527
(251) 621-6630

Advanced Alabama Adventures
7880 Bear Creek Road
Sterrett, Alabama 35147
(205) 672-2860
jamesroberts@paintball-aaa.com
http://www.paintball-aaa.com

Southern Paintball
4941 Montee Rd
Theodore, Alabama 36582
(251) 490-6049
Southernalpaintball@yahoo.com
http://www.angelfire.com/al4/sou
thernpaintball/Sthrnpaint.html

Venture Sports and Outdoors
618 15th Street East
Tuscaloosa, Alabama 35401
205.758.3900
http://www.venturesportsandout-
doors.com

North Alabama Paintball
655 Baker Lane
Tuscumbia, Alabama 35674
256-381-9918
northala@northalabamapaintball.com
http://www.northalabamapaint-
ball.com

Splatter Sports
Waverly, Alabama 36879

Xtreme Sports - Wetumpka
Paintball
787 Cedar Lane
Wetumpka, Alabama 36093
(334) 567-0149
sales@wetumpka-paintball.com
http://www.wetumpka-paintball.com

ALASKA

907 Paintball / Element Paintball
Klatt Road and Tower Road
Anchorage, Alaska 99508
(907) 351-4606
http://www.907paintball.com

ALBERTA

Fortress Paintball
Bowden, Alberta T0M 0K0
(403) 506-8248
nclark@fortresspaintball.com
http://www.fortresspaintball.com

Xcalibre Paintball
Boyle, Alberta T0A 0M0
1-780-576-2211
mitzymitz@xcalibrepaintball.com
http://www.xcalibrepaintball.com

Capture The Flag Indoor
7th Ave - 28th Street N.E.
Calgary, Alberta T2A 4L6
info@capturetheflag.com
http://www.capturetheflag.com

M.R. Paintball/Bragg Creek
510 77 AVE SE
Calgary, Alberta T2H 1C3
info@braggcreekpaintball.com
http://www.braggcreekpaintball.com

M.R. Paintball/Paintball Zone
510 77 Ave SE
Calgary, Alberta T2H 1C3
sales@mrpaintball.ca
http://www.mrpaintball.ca

Rampage City Indoor
4839-47 St. S.E.
Calgary, Alberta T2W 3G7
403-251-5166
eatpaint@telusplanet.net
http://www.eatpaint.com

Rampage Paintball Outdoor
Calgary, Alberta T1X 1E1
brian@eatpaint.com
http://www.eatpaint.com/

Ballbreakers Xtreme Paintball
Box 21
Clyde, Alberta T0G 0P0
1-877-348-2626
john@ballbreakersxtreme.com
http://www.ballbreakersxtreme.com

Capture The Flag Outdoor
7th AVE-28th street N.E.
Cochrane, Alberta T2A 4L6
(403) 247-8887
info@capturetheflag.com
http://www.capturetheflag.com/

Jazz Paintball
7004—Meridian Street
Edmonton, Alberta
(780) 668-6275

Paintball Action Games (Indoor)
4804-90 Ave
Edmonton, AlbertaT6B 3J7
info@paintballaction.net
http://www.paintballaction.net

Paintball Action Games (Outdoor)
Edmonton, Alberta T6B 3J7
http://www.paintballaction.net/

Players Sports Park
13150 Meridian Street
Edmonton, Alberta
780 491 0222
info@playerssportspark.ca
http://www.playerssportspark.ca

Urban Paintball Indoor Range
17412 105 Avenue
Edmonton, Alberta T5S 1G4
dallas@urbanpaintball.ca
http://www.urbanpaintball.ca

Urban Paintball Outdoor
Stonyplain Rd. & Anthony Henday
Drive
Edmonton, Alberta T6L 2N4
(780) 708-3048
dallas@urbanpaintball.ca
http://www.urbanpaintball.ca/

Valley Paintball Adventures
Elk Point, Alberta T0A 2J0
780-724-2337

Pure Paintball
Abasand
Fort McMurray, Alberta T9J 1J5
purepaintball@hotmail.com

Quest For Adventure
Gibbons, Alberta T6C 4A9
info@paintballqfa.com
http://www.paintballqfa.com

Northen Lights
Grande Prairie, Alberta T8W 2G7
(780) 532-8088
http://www.splatterpaintball.ca

Paintwars
High Prairie, Alberta T0G 1E0
(780) 536-7041

Lethbridge Velocity Paintball
Lethbridge, Alberta T1H 0A1
(403) 320-0757
lavelocitypaintball@hotmail.com
http://www.lavelocitypaintball.com

Paintball Outfitters
4015 Mayor Magrath Drive South
Lethbridge, Alberta T1K 6Y7
403 331 3134

Col. Pepper's Paintball
5 mins. SW on Hwy #3
Medicine Hat, Alberta T1A 7G7
403-504-4505
colpeppers@canopycanada.net
http://www.colpeppers.com

War Party Paintball
Morinville/Alexander, Alberta
T8R 1B7

Silver Creek Paintball
RR2
New Norway, Alberta T0B 3L0
(780) 855-2247

Weekend Warriors Paintball
Twp. Rd. 3202 and Range Rd. 23
Olds, Alberta
mike@weekendwarriors.ab.ca
http://www.weekendwarriors.ab.ca/

Ponoka Paintball
Ponoka, Alberta
403-704-1047
ponokapaintball@hotmail.com
‹ponokapaintball@hotmail.com›
http://www.connect.ab.ca/~woodt
ikrus/

Red Deer Paintball
4816 50 Ave
Red Deer, Alberta T4N 0A1
403-309-8885

TAG Paintball Games
Ryley, Alberta T0B 4A0
tagpaintballgames@hotmail.com
http://www.tagpaintballgames.com/

ESG Paintball
Sherwood, Alberta T8G 1G1
(780) 449-2518
Darren@esgpaintball.ab.ca
http://www.esgpaintball.ab.ca

Young Guns Paintball
RR 13 Highway 16A
Stony Plain, Alberta T7Z 1X2
(780) 945-3958
sales@younggunspaintball.com
http://www.younggunspaintball.com

Hell Dorado Paintball
Sylvan Lake, Alberta T4S 1P1
(403) 358-2468

Sylvan Lake Paintball
RR 39-2
Sylvan Lake, Alberta T4S 1P7
403-887-4487
sylvanlakepaintball@hotmail.com
http://www.sylvanlakepaintball.mo
onfruit.com

ARIZONA

Wild Planet Paintball
4517 N Curry Rd.
Casa Grande, Arizona 85222
480-227-8486
wildplanet@earthlink.net
http://wildplanetpaintball.com

FT. Huachuca Sportsman Center
Ft. Huachuca, Arizona 85613
(520)-459-3782

Cowtown Paintball
Peoria, Arizona 85345
602-301-2679
http://www.cowtownpaintball.com

23 BPS
2209 N. 99th Ave.
Phoenix, Arizona 85037
623-293-8162
http://www.23bps.com

Westworld Paintball Adventures
4240 W. Camelback RD. STE C-3
Phoenix, Arizona 85019
602-447-8200
http://www.westworldpaintball.com/

Xtreme Pursuit
4240 W Camelback C-3
Phoenix, Arizona 85019
602-447-8200
fun@westworldpaintball.com
http://www.westworldpaintball.com

Splatter Ranch
Jomax Rd. and Scottsdale Rd.
Scottsdale, Arizona 85255
602-447-8200
fun@westworldpaintball.com
http://www.westworldpaintball.com

Southwest Paintball
Bell Rd. And Crozier Rd.
Surprise, Arizona 85374
info@southwestpaintball.com
http://www.southwestpaintball.com

Desert Fox Paintball
9651 S. Houghton Rd
Tucson, Arizona 85747
520-574-9232
RRYager@earthlink.com
http://www.desertfoxpaintball.com

Sudden Impact Paintball
Tucson, Arizona 85712
http://www.paintballhq.com

Combatalley Paintball (C.A.P. Field)
51212 US. Highway 60/89
Wickenburg, Arizona 85390
928-684-5950
john@combatalley.org
http://www.combatalley.org/

Wild West Paintball
2654 E. 16th Street
Yuma, Arizona 85365
(928) 343-1802
bannersplusroy@yahoo.com
http://www.bannersyuma.com/Wild%20West%202.htm

ARKANSAS

Arkadelphia Paintball Supply/
Hardcore Paintball
425 Snyder Rd
Arkadelphia, Arkansas 71923
870-246-7933
kimvrba@yahoo.com

JC Paintball Field
103 Racetrack Road
Bismarck, Arkansas 71929
jcpaintballfield@yahoo.com
http://www.jcpaintballfield.com

All American Paintball
26811 Highway 22
Charleston, Arkansas 72933
pb@allamericanfield.com
http://www.allamericanfield.com

SWAT Indoor Paintball
2125 Harkrider St
Conway, Arkansas 72032
501-336-4096

Extreme Paintball
90 Tucker Mountain Rd
Dover, Arkansas 72837
479-967-7528
http://www.doverxtremepaint-ball.com

Point Blank Paintball Park
803 Rheas Mill Rd
Farmington, Arkansas 72730
479-442-4166
http://www.pbpbp.com

Northeast Arkansas Paintball
329 CC 392
Jonesboro, Arkansas 72401
870-932-5399
register@neapb.com
http://www.neapb.com

Gator Park
11411 W. Baseline Road
Little Rock, Arkansas 72209
501-455-3750
ally@gatorparkfun.com
http://www.gatorparkfun.com

X-treme Paintball of South Arkansas
81 Columbia Road 261 East
Magnolia, Arkansas 71753
870-696-3178
brian@southarkpaintball.com
http://southarkpaintball.com

Paintball Arkansas
558 Sturgis Road
Mayflower, Arkansas 72106
501-470-4400
paintballarkansas@sbcglobal.net
http://www.paintballarkansas.com/

Hillbilly Paintball
642 Ceder Hill Rd.
Midway, Arkansas 72651
870-431-5430

Wild World Paintball
Tontitown, Arkansas 72770
http://www.wildworldpaintball.com

Boon-Doc's Paintball Park
3325 Catcher Rd
Van Buren, Arkansas 72956

BRITISH COLUMBIA

J&J Paintball
Campbell River, British Columbia

Adrenaline
53480 Bridal Falls Road
Chilliwack, British Columbia
V0X 1X0
604-794-7409
info@paintballrush.com
http://www.paintballrush.com

Sniper'z Paintball
46201 Chilliwack Lake Rd.
Chilliwack, British Columbia V2R
4M8

Gemini Paintball
1245 Lake Trail Rd
Courtenay, British Columbia V9M
1A2
250-890-2049
http://www.geminipaintball.com

Final Rule Paint Tag
RR#2
Dawson Creek, British Columbia
V1G 4E8
(250) 782-3010

Midway Paintball
5500 Indian Rd
Duncan, British Columbia V9L 6T5
250-748-6588
action@midwaypb.com
http://www.midwaypb.com

A & J Paintball Field
Barnheartvale Rd.
Kamloops, British Columbia V2C
5H8
twistedchaos_andrew@hotmail.com

Armageddon Paintball
Sugarloaf Rd.
Kamloops, British Columbia V2B 1P4
miles@paintyourfriends.com
http://www.paintyourfriends.com

Kamloops Paintball Games
Harper Mountain Road
Kamloops, British Columbia V2H
1N9
aaron@kamloopspaintball.com
http://www.kamloopspaintball.com

Panther Paintball
19022 16th Ave
Langley, British Columbia V3A 4N4
info@pantherpaintball.com
http://www.pantherpaintball.com

Maple Ridge Paintball
14448 224 St.
Maple Ridge, British Columbia
V4R 2P8
604-466-2744
paintballgod@budweiser.com
http://www.mapleridgepaintball.com

Northwest Paintball Adventures
14448 224th Street
Maple Ridge, British Columbia
V4R 2P8

Paintball Xtreme
Maple Ridge, British Columbia
(604) 462-1466
paintballxtreme@shaw.ca
http://www.paintballxtremes-
ports.com/

Stormin Norman's
Paintball Adventures
Metchosin, British Columbia
250-642-2525
paintballvictoria@shaw.ca
http://www.storminnormanpaint-
ball.com/

Bastion Paintball
Nanaimo, British Columbia V9S 1G8
info@bastionpaintball.com
http://www.bastionpaintball.co

Kootenay Kombat
1946 Cox Rd.
Nelson, British Columbia V1L 6J9
1-877-825-4074
play@kootenaykombat.com
http://www.kootenaykombat.com

North Shore Paintball
100 Lower Capilano Rd.
North Vancouver, British Columbia
V7P 3P6
(778) 896-7529
http://nspaintball.ca

Action & Adventure Paintball
Penticton, British Columbia V2A 8L7
playtime@aapaintball.net
http://www.aapaintball.net

Predator Paintball Park
Prince George, British Columbia
250-564-5632
predatorpaintball@shaw.ca
http://www.predatorpaintball.ca

Thunder Grounds Paintball
2361-60th Ave N.E
Salmon Arm, British Columbia
V1E 2A9
1-250-833-9088
thunder_grounds@yahoo.ca
http://www.thundergrounds.com

Ambush Paintball
7550 160th Street
Surrey, British Columbia V3S 3T2
(604) 812-2379
info@ambushpaintball.com
http://www.ambushpaintball.com

Northcoast Paintball Association
Terrace, British Columbia

Big Shots Paintball
Tsawwassen, British Columbia
V3M 6H1
604-813-4386
http://www.bigshotspaintball.com/

Tsawwassen Paintball Games
Highway 17 & Tsawwassen Drive
Tsawwassen, British Columbia
http://www.bcpaintball.com/

BadBob's Paintball
Hwy 16 East, 698 Rose Road
Vanderhoof, British Columbia
(250) 567-5858
crazystamps@uniserve.com

Bushwacker Paintball
3104 32 Street
Vernon, British Columbia V1T 5M5
(250) 542-1170
info@bushwackerpaintball.com
http://www.bushwackerpaintball.com

TNT Paintball
Victoria, British Columbia
250-658-1177
tntpaintball@tntpaintball.com
http://www.tntpaintball.com

Victoria Paintball Adventures
Victoria, British Columbia
info@victoriapaintball.com
http://www.victoriapaintball.com

Whistler Paintball Adventures
Whistler, British Columbia
(604) 932-3524
tim@whistlerpaintball.com
http://www.whistlerpaintball.com

Tiger-Land Paintball
Williams Lake, British Columbia
V2G 4R1
1-250-392-9131
http://www.tiger-land.com

CALIFORNIA

Paintball Fury
3840 Crown Valley Road
Acton, California 93510
661-947-1135
info@paintballfury.net
http://www.paintballfury.net/

American Canyon Paintball Jungle
2 Eucalyptus Drive
American Canyon, California 94591
707-552-2426
karen@paintballjungle.com
http://www.paintballjungle.com

OC Asylum Paintball Park
1440 S. Anaheim Blvd.
Anaheim, California 92802
(866) 818-5221
info@ocasylum.com
http://www.ocasylum.com

Antioch Paintball Park
1201 West 10th Street
Antioch, California 94509
925-757-2468
Jeff@golfngames.com
http://antiochpaintballpark.com/

Mile High Battle Zone
182 Fawnskin Rd
Apple Valley, California 92308
760-265-5263
oakspringsranch@msn.com
http://www.oakspringsranchriding-stables.com

Gorilla Paintball Indoor
5421 Aldrin Court
Bakersfield, California 93304
(661) 323-1066
info@gorillapaintball.com
http://www.gorillapaintball.com/

On Target Paintball & Airsoft
1000 E. Hosking Ave.
Bakersfield, California 93304
(661) 398-9445
ldhayek@sbcglobal.net
http://www.ontargetpaintballca.com

Poso Creek
Bakersfield, California 93312
661-399-4999
jacksonizzy@sbcglobal.net
http://www.posocreekpaintball.com

Hollywood Sports Park
9030 Somerset Blvd
Bellflower, California 90706
gio@hollywoodsports.com
http://www.hollywoodsports.com

Bear Creek Pursuit Paintball (Outdoor)
Boulder Creek, California 95006
(408) 946-7676
http://www.bearcreekpaintball.com/

Splat Factory
428 N. Berry Way
Brea, California 92821
(714) 990-9900
bookings@splatfactory.com
http://www.splatfactory.com

Splat Hill
6851 Marysville road
Browns Valley, California 95918
916-971-2772
info2@splathill.com
http://www.splathill.com

Bay Area Paintball
1864 Rollins Road
Burlingame, California 94010
(650) 552-9939
info@bapaintball.com
http://bapaintball.com

Crossfire Paintball Arena
487 Calle San Pablo
Camarillo, California 93012
805-383-5585
CrossfirePaintball@cox.net
http://www.crossfirepaintballarena.com

California Paintball Park
Charley Canyon Rd.
Castaic, California 91384
(310)261-2439
hybrid240z@verizon.net
http://www.paintballpark.net

Warped Paintball Park
Castaic, California 91384
310-966-1100
warpedsportz@earthlink.net
http://www.warpedpaintballpark.com

Venture Games Paintball
2340 Morgan Territory Rd
Clayton, California 94517
925-757-5150
venturegames@sbcglobal.net
http://www.venturegamespaintball.com

SC Village
Hellman Road and River Road
Corona, California 92880
949-489-9000
info@hollywoodsports.com
http://www.scvillage.com

Davis Paintball Center
24998 County Rd. 102
Davis, California 95616
530-757-7700
info@davispaintball.com
http://www.davispaintball.com

Mr. Paintball USA Field
25320 Lake Wohlford Road
Escondido, California 92027
proshop@mrpaintballusa.com
http://www.mrpaintballusa.com

Canyon View Church Field
23221 Foresthill Rd
Foresthill, California 95631
(530) 367-2272

Pine Ridge Paintball
1783 Pineridge Dr
Fortuna, California 95540
707-725-1558

Agape Playing Fields
8106 S. Fruit Ave
Fresno, California 93245
(559) 213-3786
http://www.agapeplayingfields.com/

Blackbeards
4055 North Chestnut Diagonal
Fresno, California 93726
(559) 292-4554
chrisj@blackbeardsfresno.com
http://www.Blackbeardsfresno.com

Splats Paintball Field
3860 N. Cedar Avenue
Fresno, California 93726
(559) 229-0054

Woodstalk Paintball (Formerly
Breakout Paintball)
Ft. Ord, California 93944
(831) 763-3959 (fax only)
index@woodstalk.com
http://www.woodstalk.com

Conquest Paintball Park Osborne
Glendale, California 91205
(818) 503-7627
mockingbyrd@earthlink.net
http://www.conquestpaintball.com
Mountain Valley Paintball
Grenada, California 96038
(530) 905-1137
cunningham63@juno.com
http://www.mtvalleypaintball.com

Operation Paintball
1932 West Winton Avenue Bldg. 3
Hayward, California 94545
(510) 783-2011
http://www.operationpaintball.net

The Adventure Game (TAG Paintball)
Hollister, California 95023
http://www.800tag5150.com/

United States Paintball Nation
(USPN)
1533 Shore Rd.
Hollister, California 95023
831-636-8877
http://www.uspn.biz

Paintball Playground
5145 West Lake Blvd.
Homewood, California 96141
smile@skihomewood.com
http://www.paintballplayground.com

Jungle Island
14881 Temescal Canyon Road
Lake Elsinore, California 92530
951-775-9316
gunnymt@jungle-island.com
http://www.jungle-island.com

Paranoid Paintball
11900 17th Ave
Lemoore, California 93245
(559) 924-5520
info@paranoidpaintball.com
http://www.paranoidpaintball.com

Enemy Territory Paintball Park
413 East Lockeford St.
Lodi, California 95240
209-368-1888
pbpark@enemypaintball.com
http://www.enemypaintball.com

The Shack
625 E Hwy 246
Lompoc, California 93436
805-737-9600
http://theshack-surf-dirt.com/

Bear Creek Paintball (Indoor)
1001 Yosemite Drive
Milpitas, California 95035
(408) 934-9408
http://www.bearcreekmilpitas.com

Extreme Paintball Field
7336 Dusty Lane
Modesto, California 95356
info@extremepaintballfield.com
http://www.extremepaintball-
field.com

Combat Zone Paintball Park
4444 Pacific Heights Road
Oroville, California 95965
http://www.combatzonepaintball.com

Urban Quest Paintball
Gonzales Rd.
Oxnard, California 93036
dave@urbanquestpaintball.com
http://www.urbanquestpaintball.com

Franklin Hotsprings
3085 Creston Road
Paso Robles, California 93446
805-712-5373
info@franklinhotsprings.com
http://www.franklinhotsprings.com
/paintball.html

Norcal Paintball Park
175 Fairgrounds Dr.
Petaluma, California 94952
(707)939-8550
info@norcalpaintballpark.com
http://www.norcalpaintballpark.com/

Lenix Paintball
9339 Vinton Rd
Phelan, California 92371
760-403-3074
info@lenixpaintball.com
http://www.lenixpaintball.com/

Sierra Paintball Park / ROA Paintball
2751 La Paz Pd
Placerville, California 95667
530-626-1011
info@sierrapaintball.com
http://www.sierrapaintball.com

NFinite Edge Paintball Park
101 Jackson Road
Plymouth, California 95669
916-638-2775
chadp@nfiniteedge.com
http://www.nfiniteedge.com

California Xtreme Paintball
Highway 190 & Road 284
Porterville, California 93257
(559) 805-5130
jess@cxpaintball.com
http://www.cxpaintball.com
Velocity Paintball
Warnock Dr and San Vicente Rd
Ramona, California 92065
field@velocitypaintball.com
http://velocitypaintballpark.com/

Diamonds Edge
Diamond's Edge Paintball
Redding, California 96001
(530) 347-5279
http://www.diamondsedgepaint-
ball.com/

Paintball Hill
Spring Gulch Rd.
Redding, California 96002

Redding Indoor Paintball
6771 Eastside Rd
Redding, California 96001
(530) 243-4204
short2grnd@aol.com
http://www.reddingindoorpaint-
ball.com

Action Paintball Games
Ione Road
Sacramento, California 95821
http://www.actionpaintballsac.com

Sinister Paintball
Sacramento, California 95834
916-802-6022
Sinistersports@yahoo.com
http://www.sinistersports.com

Camp Pendleton Paintball Park
San Diego, California 92055
800.899.9957
http://www.cppaintball.com

Wild West Paintball
255 E. Soboba Road
San Jacinto, California 92583
http://www.jtpaintball.com

Santa Clara Paintball / Fairgrounds
Paintball Park
344 Tully Rd
San Jose, California 95111
http://www.santaclarapaintball.com

Real Action Paintball Indoor Arena
5151 Lafayette Street
Santa Clara, California 95054
408-727-3144
info@rap4.com
http://game.rap4.com

Field of Fire Paintball Adventures
Santa Clarita, California 91380
tgmann@mediaone.net
http://www.fieldoffire.com/

Paintball USA Close Encounters
(Simi)
1250 W. Tierra Rejada Rd
Simi Valley, California 93065
(800) 919-9237
http://www.paintballusasimi.com

Sunol Paintball
7900 Vallecitos Road
Sunol, California 94586
(510) 489 9499
info@sunolpaintball.com
http://www.sunolpaintball.com/

Rankin Field
20000 Rd. 140
Tulare, California 93274
559-685-8986
rankin_field@earthlink.net
http://rankinfield.com/

Midway Paintball Xtreme
4901 Midway Road
Vacaville, California 95688
(707) 399-9400
info@midwaypaintball.com
http://www.midwaypaintball.com

Sherwood Forest Paintball
2 Eucalyptus Dr.
Vallejo, California 94589
Mike@paintballforest.com
http://www.paintballforest.com/

Desert Kombat Zone
10220 Solano rd.
Victorville, California 92392
760-956-2523
kenny@dkzn.com
http://www.dkzn.com

The Paintball Zone
22742 Yosemite Blvd
Waterford, California 95386
http://www.thepaintballzone.com

Wild Adventure Paintball
Zamora, California 95698
splat@wildadventurepaintball.com
http://www.wildadventurepaint-
ball.com/

COLORADO

Tunka
Boulder, Colorado 80301
admin@tunka.com
http://www.tunka.com

Breckenridge Paintball
6061 Tiger Road
Breckenridge, Colorado 80424
(970) 453-7468
Info@BreckenridgePaintball.com
http://breckenridgepaintball.com/
home/index.php
Dragon Man Paintball
1225 Dragonman Dr.
Colorado Springs, Colorado 80929
(719) 683-2200
http://www.dragonmans.com/

Splat Master's Paintball Park
6855 Constitution Ave.
Colorado Springs, Colorado 80915
(719) 574-7004
richardj@splatmasters.com
http://www.splatmasters.com

Peak One Paintball
Copper Athletic Club
Copper Mountain, Colorado 80434
(970)668-5709
peakonepaintball@hotmail.com

Blitz Paintball
4558 Weld County Rd 12
Dacono, Colorado 80514
720-338-7607
the1mib@hotmail.com
http://www.blitzpaintball.net

American Paintball Coliseum (APC)
4100 Grape Street
Denver, Colorado 80216
303.298.8573
customerservice@apcpaintball.com
http://www.apcpaintball.com/

The Paintball, Airsoft & Reball
Center (The PARC)
6100 E 39th Ave
Denver, Colorado 80207
303-336-7272
postmaster@denverparc.com
http://www.denverparc.com

Shutdown Xtreme Paintball
15300 East Arapahoe Rd
Englewood, Colorado 80122
720-641-7670
http://www.sxpaintball.com

Adrenalized Paintball
4103 B South Mason Street
Fort Collins, Colorado 80525
970-225-1117

Take Cover Paintball
31220 Rd. 4.25
Fowler, Colorado 81039
719-263-5374
http://www.takecoverpaintball.com

Alpine Adrenaline Paintball
Glennwood Springs Rodeo Grounds
Glennwood Springs, Colorado 81601
970-404-7911
manager@alpineadrenaline.com
http://www.alpineadrenalinepaint-
ball.com

Shot in the Dark Paintball
404 Noland Avenue
Grand Junction, Colorado 81501
970-248-9331
shotinthedarkpaintball@yahoo.com
http://www.shotinthedarkpaint-
ball.com

Action Pursuit / Colorado
Indoor Paintball
22495 Hwy 34
Greeley, Colorado 80631
actionpursuit1@yahoo.com
http://www.actionpursuitpaint-
ball.com

Guru Sports (Longmont)
41 S. Main
Longmont, Colorado 80501
(303) 651-6882
gurusportsllc@msn.com
http://www.gurusports.net

Victory Paintball
729 N. Madison
Loveland, Colorado 80537
970-613-8846
info@victory-paintball.com
http://www.victory-paintball.com

Xplod Paintball
146 Main Street
Montrose, Colorado 81401
(970) 249-4975
http://www.xplodpaintball.com/

ColorSplash Paintball
139 30 1/2 Lane
Pueblo, Colorado 81006
719-544-1560
jc@colorsplashpaintball.com
http://www.colorsplashpaintball.com

Guru Sports (Rollinsville)
Rollinsville, Colorado 80474
303-258-0900
blue@gurusports.net
http://www.gurusports.net

Signal 20 Paintball
16105 Hwy 50
Salida, Colorado 81201
719-539-2795
info@signal20paintball.com
http://www.signal20paintball.com

Paintball Adventures
Sedalia, Colorado 80135
pbaadv@aol.com
http://www.paintballadv.com

Area 51 Paintball
321 S. Front St.
Sterling, Colorado 80751
970-522-2939
http://www.area51pball.com

CONNECTICUT

Matt's Outback Paintball
677 Riley Mtn Rd.
Coventry, Connecticut 06238
860-742-0201
mattsoutback@hotmail.com
http://www.mattsoutback.com/

Strategy Plus Paintball
Bear Swamp Rd
East Hampton, Connecticut 06424
800-952-9007
info@strategyplus.com
http://www.strategyplus.com

Xtreme Paintball
149 North Road
East Windsor, Connecticut 06088
860-627-6666
info@xtreme-paintball.com
http://www.xtreme-
paintball.com/

Lebanon Sports Center
74 Norwich Ave.
Lebanon, Connecticut 06249
860-886-2477
lebanonsportcentre@sbcglobal.net
http://www.lebanonsportscentre.com

Hogan's Alley Paintball
998 North Colony Rd.
Meriden, Connecticut 06450
hogansalleypaintball@aol.com
http://www.hogansalleypaintball.com

Splatter Zone LLC
Milford, Connecticut 06460
203-878-0693
SplatterZoneLLC@yahoo.com
http://www.splatterzonellc.com

Eastern Paintball Supplies
150 Foxon Road
North Branford, Connecticut 06471
203-488-5721
http://www.connecticutpaintball.com

Paintball Madness
55 Market Street
Stamford, Connecticut 06902
info@stamfordpaintball.com
http://www.stamfordpaintball.com

Final Shot Paintball
96 Ekonk Hill Rd.
Voluntown, Connecticut 06384
860-376-5114
finalshot@finalshotpaintball.com
http://www.fspaintball.net

Extreme Paintball
476 Boyden Street
Waterbury, Connecticut 06702
proshop@extremepaintball.com
http://www.extremepaintball.com

DELAWARE

Graveyard Paintball
4367 Kirkwood St Georges Rd
Bear, Delaware 19701
302-836-4373
http://www.graveyardpaintball.com

Mansion House Farm
Porter Rd and Mansion House Rd
Bear, Delaware 19701
302-834-6723
http://www.co.new-
castle.de.us/neighbor/home/web-
page8.asp

Splat Zone
Milford, Delaware 19963
302-422-7052
splatzone2@yahoo.com
http://www.splatzoneinc.com

A 2 Z Paintball and Skateboarding
(Red Mill)
Red Mill Rd.
Newark, Delaware 19702
302-366-8280
Bear@a2zpaintballandskateboard-
ing.com
http://www.a2zpaintballandskate-
boarding.com/

Paintball Action Games
3124 Old County Road
Newark, Delaware 19702
pbreview@paintballactiongames.com
http://www.paintballactiongames.com

ECX Action Sports
21 W. Market St.
Newport, Delaware 19804
ecx@comcast.net
http://www.ecxactionsports.com

FLORIDA

Al's Army
1440 E Altamonte Dr
Altamonte Springs, Florida 32701
(407)-834-2000
http://www.alsarmynavy.com

F.A.U. Renegade Paintball
Yamato Rd and U.S. Hwy 441
Boca Raton, Florida 33498
754-235-9885

Hi-Tec Paintball
State Road 64
Bradenton, Florida 34206
(941) 746-5866
play@hi-tecpaintball.com
http://www.hi-tecpaintball.com

MVP Sports
3326 Cortez Rd.
Bradenton, Florida 34207
941-751-2204
info@mvpextremesports.com
http://www.MVPExtremesports.com

War Basics
4728 30th Ave E
Bradenton, Florida 34208
941-962-5007
warbasics@aol.com
http://www.warbasics.com

Triad P8ntball
543378 US Highway #1
Callahan, Florida 32011
912-227-0476
http://www.triadp8ntball.com

Wild Bill's Paintball
543378 US Highway #1
Callahan, Florida 32011
904-879-6978
wildbillspball@aol.com
http://www.wildbillspball.com

Mike Greenwells Family Fun Park
35 Pine Island Road
Cape Coral, Florida 33909
239-574-4386
http://www.greenwellsfamilyfun-
park.com

Shoots and Splatters Paintball
16060 NE 58th Ave
Citra, Florida 32113
352-595-4712
sandsp8ntball@earthlink.net
http://shootsandsplatterspaint-
ball.net/index.html

Hosers and Snipers Paintball
37644 Trilby Road
Dade City, Florida 33523
Kim@hosersandsniper.com
http://www.hosersandsniper.com/

Paintball Pro Shop & Field
Dania, Florida 33004
954-929-1466
http://www.paintballproshop.net/

Reball Madness
1701 Green Rd. Suite E
Deerfield Beach, Florida 33064
954-725-0009
reballmadness@hotmail.com
http://www.reballmadness.com

Hit Spot Paintball
Deland, Florida 32720

Calvary Chapel Fort Lauderdale
Area 32:8
2401 West Cypress Creek Road
Fort Lauderdale, Florida 33309
954-315-7531
justiny@calvaryftl.org
http://www.calvaryftl.org

Crossfire Indoor Paintball
2558 4th St.
Fort Myers, Florida 33901
239-337-7678
http://www.crossfireindoorpaint-
ball.com/

Big Red's Paintball
2721 S.US # 1
Fort Pierce, Florida 34982
772-461-0580

Invincibles Paintball
2525 Center Rd.
Fort Pierce, Florida 34946
772-812-0000
http://www.invinciblespaintball.com

Rocky Creek Paintball
10614 SW Archer Rd
Gainesville, Florida 32608
352-371-2092
info@rockycreekpaintball.com
http://www.rockycreekpaintball.com

Extreme Rage Park
6401 Sheridan Street
Hollywood, Florida 33024
954-986-9089
http://www.miamirage.com

Cobra Club Paintball /
Tropical Fun Center
27201 South Dixie Highway
Homestead, Florida 33032
305-246-3731
info@tropicalfuncenter.com
http://www.cobraclubpaintball.com

Gator Paintball
11122 Houston Ave.
Hudson, Florida 34667
(727) 862-2222
http://www.gatorpaintball.com

Ledgen's Field
11820 Hudson Ave
Hudson, Florida 34669
727-560-6866
ledgensfield@hotmail.com
http://www.ledgensfieldpaintball.com

Paintball Adventures
13264 Grover Road
Jacksonville, Florida 32226
904-645-7127
info@paintballadventures.com
http://www.paintballadventures.com

Righteous Paintball
Jupiter, Florida 33478
http://www.righteouspaintball.com

Rush Paintball of Jupiter
17047 Beeline Highway
Jupiter, Florida 33478
305-389-9273
sharon@rushpaintball.net
http://rushpaintball.net

Osceola Extreme Sports
1300 Poinciana Blvd
Kissimmee, Florida 34741
407-933-7785
Ron@osceolaextremesports.com
http://www.oes.cc/

Paintball Nutz
908 SE Country Club Rd
Lake City, Florida 32025
386-623-5155
paintballer88@yahoo.com
http://www.paintballnutz.com

Full Throttle Paintball
845 Pineda Road
Lake Helen, Florida 32744
fullthrottlepaintball@yahoo.com
http://www.fullthrottlepaintball.com

Central Florida Paintball
9365 US Hwy 98
Lakeland, Florida 33809
863-858-3154
cpaintball@tampabay.rr.com
http://www.centralfloridapaint-
ball.com

Off the Wall Adventures
2055 Sheperd Rd.
Lakeland, Florida 33811
863-709-9255
http://www.offthewalladventures.
com

Paintball Experience
2070 E. Edgewood Drive
Lakeland, Florida 33803
(863) 640-0433 / 640-2617
paintballexperience@msn.com
http://www.paintball-
experience.com

PSI Xtreme Sports
8228 Ulmerton Rd.
Largo, Florida 33771
727-538-9946
http://www.psixtremesports.com/

Paint Ballistics
18000 Boyette Road
Lithia Springs, Florida 34689
(727) 937-2640
http://www.paintballistics.com

Hotshots Paintball
16169 Southern Blvd.
Loxahatchee, Florida 33470
(561) 798-4717
http://www.hotshotspaintball.net
Jungle Games Paintball
Lutz, Florida 33559
727-937-1755
http://www.paintballtampabay.com/

First Coast Paintball
520 S Lowder Street
MacClenny, Florida 32063
904 259-2439
http://www.firstcoastpb.com/

Hurlburt Field Paintball
Highway 98
Mary Esther, Florida 32569

Combat Zone
785 N Courtenay Pkwy
Merritt Island, Florida 32953
(321) 454-2374
http://www.combatzoneindoor-
paintball.com/

Master Zone
6990 NW 25st
Miami, Florida 33122
(305) 500-9906

Ruff n Tuff Paintball
13200 NW 43 Ave.
Miami, Florida 33054
305.953.7776
info@ruffntuffpaintball.com
http://www.ruffntuffpaintball.com

Spray Paint Paintball
12781 SW 280 Street
Miami, Florida 33032
305-258-9244
sppaintball@aol.com
http://www.sppaintball.com/

Paintball Brothers
3887 Darlene Rd.
Middleburg, Florida 32068
904-608-8299
paintballbrothers@paintballbroth-
ers.com
http://www.paintballbrothers.com

Renegade Paintball
Collier County Fair Grounds
Naples, Florida 34134
1.239.825.7380
Bob@RenegadePaintballPark.com
http://www.renegadepaintball-
park.net

First Strike Paintball, Inc.
5619 SE CR 337
Newberry, Florida 32669
info@firststrikepaintball.com
http://www.firststrikepaintball.com

Niceville Rec Paintball
Palm Dr and N Partin Dr
Niceville, Florida 32578
(850) 729-0758
paintball@niceville.org
http://cityofniceville.org/youth-
center.html

Ozzie's Kamikaze
15760 S.W. 20 Ave. Road
Ocala, Florida 34473
352-347-0938
webmaster@ozziespb.com
http://www.ozziespb.com

Wayne's World of Paintball
4841 S. Pine Street
Ocala, Florida 34480
352-401-1801
wd24hour@atlantic.net
http://www.waynes-
world.com/wwopen.html

Old River Paintball
9911 SE 170 Ave Rd
Ocklawaha, Florida 32179
oldriverpb@aol.com
http://www.oldriverpaintball.com/

Weekend Warriors Paintball
12650 NE 56th Avenue
Okeechobee, Florida 34972
863-357-9972
sharon@tnni.net
http://www.weekendwarriorspaint-
ball.com

Epik Paintball
14200 East Colonial Drive
Orlando, Florida 32826
407-273-6899
epikpaintballer@aol.com
http://epikpaintball.com

Hypersports Park
5080 Hoffner Ave
Orlando, Florida 32812
407.855.5566
Adminhypersportz@cfl.rr.com
http://www.hypersportspark.com/

Orange County Paintball
1251 S CR 13
Orlando, Florida 32765
407-383-4769
ocpzone@aol.com
http://www.ocpzone.com

Orlando Paintball
7215 Rose Ave.
Orlando, Florida 32810
http://www.orlandopaintball.com/

Stingers Paintball
8615 Florida Rock Rd.
Orlando, Florida 32824
407-582-0024
stingerspb@yahoo.com
http://www.stingerspb.com

Fury Paintball Park
770 Hurricane St SE
Palm Bay, Florida 32908
321.255.1114
Fury@SplatActionSports.com
http://www.SplatActionSports.com

Hurricane Paintball Park
770 Hurricane St NW
Palm Bay, Florida 32908
321-255-4044
hurricane@splatactionsports.com
http://www.palmbayflorida.org/D
epartments/Parks&Rec/City%20Par
ks/paintball_park.htm

Panhandle Paintball
2305 Sherman Avenue
Panama City, Florida 32405
850-785-2030
Tyndall AFB
Panama City, Florida 32403
(850) 283-3199
http://www.tyndallpaintball.org/

EastCoast Paintball
1820 Byrd Rd
Pierson, Florida 32180
386-566-0355
ecpaintballemail@aol.com
http://www.eastcoastpaintball.net

BattleZone Paintball
4416 N. Cooper Road
Plant City, Florida 33565
(813) 986-8812
field@battlezonepaintball.com
http://www.battlezonepaintball.com

East Coast Extreme Sports
7710 Wiles Road
Pompano Beach, Florida v33067
954 757 0222
info@ecepaintball.com
http://www.ecepaintball.com

Kohn Sports
Balm Road and Balm Boyette Road
Ruskin, Florida 33570
813-814-2774
http://www.kohnsports.com

Murder Inc. Paintball
2780 State Road 16
Saint Augustine, Florida 32092
904-819-6933
http://www.murderincpaintball.com/

Adrenaline Dunes Paintball
Behind the Lakeshore Mall
Sebring, Florida 33872
(863)382-4000
web@adrenalinedunes.com
http://www.adrenalinedunespaint-
ball.com/

Elite Paintball
4644 Keysville Ave.
Spring Hill, Florida 34608
352-584-6438
springhillpaintball@hotmail.com
http://www.springhillelite.com/

Xplex Sports / Daytona Beach
Paintball
3838 SR44
Spruce Creek, Florida 32168
386-214-1939
info@daytonabeachpaintball.com
http://www.daytonabeachpaint-
ball.com

St Cloud Paintball
223 Kissimmee Park Rd.
St. Cloud, Florida 34769
http://www.stcloudpaintball.com

Tallahassee Paintball Park
427 Crossway Road
Tallahassee, Florida 32305
904.509.9506
http://www.tpppaintball.com/

Orbital Paintball
7mi N of I4 on Hwy 301
Tampa, Florida 33592
(813) 789-8159
Jeff@OrbitalPB.com
http://www.orbitalpb.com

Break 50 Paintball
Tarpon Springs, Florida 34689
727-934-8900
http://www.break50paintball.com

Indian River Paintball
4710 S. Washington Ave.
Titusville, Florida 32780
321-385-0747
http://www.indianriverpaintball.com

B & D Army Navy and Paintball
1231 Us Highway 41 Byp S
Venice, Florida 34292
941-484-7045
http://www.venicepaintball.com

DRW's Rapid Fire Total Scenario
Paintball
River Rd. and Center Rd.
Venice, Florida 34292
941-497-1886
drwsrapidfire@comcast.net
http://www.drwsrapidfire.com/

Firestorm Paintball
180 Lee Rd.
Venice, Florida 34292
941-921-1818
http://www.firestormpaintball.us

Cypress Gardens Adventure Sports
5630 Cypress Gardens Blvd
Winter Haven, Florida 33884
(863) 324-0559
info@cypressgardensadventures-
ports.com
http://www.cypressgardensadven-
turesports.com

Shooters Den
7608 Aloma Ave, Ste 128
Winter Park, Florida 32792
407-671-2081
mshaffer@theshootersden.com
http://www.theshootersden.com

GTF Paintball
960 Goodbread Rd
Yulee, Florida 32097
904-548-7256
robert@gtfpaintball.com
http://www.gtfpaintball.com

GEORGIA

Paintball Atlanta
Shiloh Rd
Alpheretta, Georgia 30076
pbaatl@aol.com
http://www.paintball-atlanta.com

Rush Paintball
3644 Wrightsboro RD.
Augusta, Georgia 30909
(706) 228-5540
info@rushpaitnballinc.com
http://www.rushpaintballinc.com

A-1 Paintball Field and Supplies
276 W Pine Chapel Rd NE
Calhoun, Georgia 30701
706-602-0330

Nitro Paintball
204A Lower Bethany Rd.
Canton, Georgia 30114
770-720-8466
mario1948@hotmail.com
http://www.nitropaintballga.com

Ultimate Paintball
2788 E. Cherokee Dr
Canton, Georgia 30115
support@ultimatepaintballgeorgia.com
http://www.ultimatepaintballgeorgia.com

Chicken Hawk Paintball
4001 Hwy 320
Carnesville, Georgia 30521
706-384-3047
admin@chickenhawkpaintball.com
http:///www.chickenhawkpaintball.com/

Knights Crossing Paintball
(Commerce)
260 Cowart Rd
Commerce, Georgia 30501
770-530-3984
paul@knightscrossingpaintball.com
http://www.knightscrossingpaintball.com/

Wildfire Paintball Games (Conyers)
2051-B Hwy 138 NE
Conyers, Georgia 30013
wild@akorn.net
http://wildfirepaintball.com/Conyers/Conyers.htm

Vision Paintball
8050 Villa Rica Highway
Dallas, Georgia 30157
Visionpaintball1@aol.com

VRK Paintball
8050 Villa Rica Hwy (Hwy 61)
Dallas, Georgia v30157
770-456-4044
http://www.vrkpaintball.com

24 Hour Games
3751 S. Lower Dug Gap Road
Dalton, Georgia 30720
770-656-9221
info@24hourgames.com
http://www.24hourgames.com

Paintballs and More
3751 Dug Gap Rd SW
Dalton, Georgia 30720
706 428 9675
http://www.paintballsandmore.com

Paintball-Outfitter
1180 Lagrange Hwy
Greenville, Georgia 30222
706-882-8721
wendell@paintball-outfitter.com
http://www.paintball-outfitter.com

GA Xtreme Paintball
105 Cherokee Dr.
Guyton, Georgia 31312
(912) 667-2678
http://www.gaxtremepaintball.com/

Paintball City
Hinesville, Georgia 31313

Dans Land Paintball
Jackson, Georgia 30233
770-851-2000
http://www.dansland.com

Arkenstone Paintball
3292 Cedarcrest Rd
Kennesaw, Georgia 30101
770-974-2535
http://www.apbfields.com

South Eastern Adrenaline Sports
Kingsland, Georgia 31548
912-674-5248
http://www.seaspaintball.com/

Knights Crossing Paintball (Lagrange)
1591 Vernon Rd
LaGrang, Georgia 30240
706-407-4117
bill@knightscrossingpaintball.com
http://www.knightscrossingpaintball.com

Wild Bills Paintball
280 Arnold Road, Suite B
Lawrenceville, Georgia 30044
info@wildbillspaintball.com
http://www.wildbillspaintball.com

Classic Paintball
1320 Blairs Bridge Road
Lithia Springs, Georgia 30122
770-732-1110
generalinfo@classic-paintball.com
http://www.classic-paintball.com

Low Country Paintball
Ludowici, Georgia 31316
912-545-2369
locopaintball@yahoo.com
http://www.locopaintball.com/

Divers Supply
5208 Mercer University Dr
Macon, Georgia 31210
478-474-6790
diving@divers-supply.com
http://www.diverssupplyusa.com/

On Target Paintball Georgia
7450 Hawkinsville Road
Macon, Georgia 31216
478-714-2003
jwpfeil1@earthlink.net
http://www.ontargetpaintballga.com

Splatters Outdoor Adventure
862 Sparta HWY NE
MilledgevillevGeorgia 31061
478-451-0705
admin@splattersoa.com
http://www.splattersoa.com

Average Joe's Paintball
327 Meriweather Rd.
Millegeville, Georgia 31061
478-968-5774
information@averagejoespb.com
http://www.averagejoespb.com

Newnan Paintball
Newnan, Georgia 30263
http://www.newnanpaintball.com

Maximum Paintball
4315 McEver Road
Oakwood, Georgia 30566
http://www.maximum-
paintball.com

Ringworm Paintball
423 Pine Grove Rd
Ringgold, Georgia 30736
706-891-8001
ringwormpaintball@catt.com
http://www.ringwormpaintball.com

Big Daddy's Paintball
2567 Cedartown Hwy.
Rome, Georgia 30161
706-235-1413
Bigdaddypaintball@comcast.net
http://www.bigdaddyspaintball.net

Scenario Paintball Games
709 Livingston Rd
Rome, Georgia 30161
770-364-8444
scenariopaint@aol.com
http://www.scenariopaintball-
gamesga.com/

Gorilla War Paintball
Rydal, Georgia 30171
770-757-9152
MasterSergeant@gorillawarpaint-
ball.com
http://www.gorillawarpaintball.com/

Savannah Paintball
74 W. Montgomery Cross Roads
Savannah, Georgia 31406

Fat City Paintball
2917 Highway 85
Senoia, Georgia 30276
(770) 487-3993
skot44@yahoo.com
http://www.fatcityonline.com

Wildfire Paintball Games (Snellville)
3725-C Stone Mountain Hwy
SnellvillevGeorgia 30039
wild@akorn.net
http://www.wildfirepaintball.com/

Boroball
Statesboro, Georgia 30458
912-488-2320
info@boroball.com
http://www.boroball.com

A.W.O.L. Paintball
Thomasville, Georgia 31792
http://www.awolpaintball.com

Major Paintball
Toccoa, Georgia 30577
866-625-6772
http://www.majorpaintball.net

Splatter Swamp
Moody AFB
Valdosta, Georgia 31699
229-257-1375
http://www.moodyservices.com

Valdosta Paintball
2953 Touchton Rd
Valdosta, Georgia 31601
(229) 630-5628
tony@valdostapaintball.com
http://www.valdostapaintball.com

GotBallz Paintball
Warner Robins, Georgia 31088
http://www.gotballz.net

American Paintball Club
662 Highway 211 NW
Winder, Georgia 30680
770-725-1000
http://www.americanpaintball-
club.com

Dynamic Games Paintball Supply
(DGS)
223 Pickle Simon Rd
Winder, Georgia 30680
dynamicgames@alltel.net
http://www.dgspaintball.com

Athens Paintball
305 Lakeview Dr.
Winterville, Georgia 30683
(706) 583-8600
info@apball.com
http://www.athenspaintball.com

Carnage Paintball
283 Hames Road
Woodstock, Georgia 30188
(404)314-5338
toric@carnagepaintball.com
http://www.carnagepaintball.com

HAWAII

Hawaii All-Star Paintball Games
Honolulu, Hawaii 96813
808-842-STAR
hawaiiallstar@hawaii.rr.com
http://www.hawaiiallstarpb.com/

Paintball Hawaii
Marine Corps Base Hawaii
Kailua (MCBH), Hawaii 96734
paintball-hawaii@hawaii.rr.com
http://www.paintballhawaii.com

Big Island Paintball Supply
Kaloko Dr.
Kailua-Kona, Hawaii 96740
BIpaintball@aol.com

Xtreme Paintball Complex
91-201 Malakole St
Kapolei, Hawaii 96707
(808)864-1610
xpc@808paintballhawaii.com
http://www.808paintballhawaii.com

Run-A-Muck
Paridise Park Right on 28
Keaau, Hawaii 96760
808-937-9298
http://www.PbHeaven.com

D & D Paintball
Kula, Hawaii 96790
(808)-572-1424

Bellows Recreational Field
Waimanalo, Hawaii 96795
(808) 422-8058
info@island-paintball.com
http://www.island-paintball.com

IDAHO

Splat Paintball
3131 Harvard St.
Boise, Idaho 83705
208.363.7230
evilmaster@splatpaintball.net
http://www.splatpaintballonline.com

Pirate Paintball
Off Tyhee Road
Chubbuck / Pocatello, Idaho 83201
PiratePaintball@cableone.net
http://myweb.cableone.net/wtid-
well/piratepaintball.htm

Adventure City Paintball
Hayden, Idaho 83814
ACPidaho@aol.com
http://www.ACPball.com

G&H Paintball
Idaho Falls, Idaho 83402
(208) 681-1961

BK Paintball
22739 Access Rd.
Lewiston, Idaho 83501
info@bkpaintball.com
http://www.bkpaintball.com

Aktion Zone
37 East Broadway
Meridian, Idaho 83642
info@aktionzonepaintball.com
http://www.aktionzonepaintball.com/

The P.A.S.S.
8450 W. 5th
Pocatello, Idaho 83204
208-232-6900
thepass@gotadrenalin.com
http://www.gotadrenalin.com

QC Paintball
Rexburg, Idaho 83440
656-0591
woodyim8@hotmail.com
http://www.qcpaintball.com

Schweitzer Splat! Mountain
10000 Schweitzer Mountain Road
Sandpoint, Idaho 83864
1-800-831-8810
http://www.schweitzer.com/sum-
mer/content_main.php?paren-
tid=2&secid=97

ILLINOIS

Funtime Square
11901 S. Cicero Ave
Alsip, Illinois 60803
(708)388-3500
http://www.funtimesquare.com

Over the Edge
Forrest Baptist Church Rd
Benton, Illinois 62812
618-923-1316
sippl7@yahoo.com
http://www.otepaintball.com

Paintball Pit
15649 N. Legion Ln.
Bluford, Illinois 62814
618-732-0719
thepit44@mvn.net
http://paintballpit.20m.com

Friendly Fire Paintball
200 Olive St.
Bridgeport, Illinois 62417
(618) 945-7380
speedy@friendlyfirepaintball.net
http://friendlyfirepaintball.net

Da Nuke Paintball Games
3485 N. German Church Road
Byron, Illinois 61010
(815) 978-6081
bradandtina@danukepaintball-
games.com
http://www.danukepaintball-
games.com/

Outback Xtreme Paintball
Carbondale, Illinois 62903
http://paintballJim.com

Norman Paintball
19085 State Hwy 16
Charleston, Illinois 61920
217-549-4577
joshnorman@normanpaintball.com
http://www.normanpaintball.com

Chilli Paintball Pits
21324 N. Benedict
Chillicothe, Illinois 61523
joeandron@chillipaintball.com
http://www.chillipaintball.com/

The Badlandz
Elm's Court Lane and Route 394
Crete, Illinois 60417
708.862.2222
http://www.thebadlandz.com/

Realms Of Ruin Paintball Park
19733 Bauer Rd
Custer Park, Illinois 60481
gazelle@realmsofruin.com
http://www.realmsofruin.com

Take Aim Paintball
8251 S. Lemont Road
Darien, Illinois 60561
630-985-7529
http://takeaimpaintball.com

Firemark Paintball
2453 Country Road, 600E
Dewey, Illinois 61840
(217) 643-2620
drdew2@pdnt.com
http://www.firemarkpaintball.com

Area 51 Extreme Sports
140 House Rd.
Elkville, Illinois 62932
618-568-1311
webmaster@area51xsports.com
http://www.area51xsports.com/

Chicago Reball Center
655 W Grand Ave Suite 360
Elmhurst, Illinois 60126
630-833-4513
keith@reball.us
http://www.reball.us/

Warzone Paintball
1322 Watercress Lane
Flora, Illinois 62839
618-662-3637
warzone_paintball@hotmail.com
http://www.geocities.com/war-zone_paintball

Chicagoland Paintball
537 W 195th Street
Glenwood, Illinois 60425
708 756-1166
chicagolandpb@hotmail.com
http://www.chicagoland-paint-ball.com

Paintball Blitz
Sterns School Rd. and Route 41
Gurnee, Illinois 60031
847-437-4227
info@paintblitz.com
http://www.paintballblitz.com

Operation Paintball
15N850 Brier Hill Rd.
Hampshire, Illinois 60140
paul@operationpaintball.com
http://www.operationpaintball.com

CPX Sports
Schweitzer Rd.
Joliet, Illinois 60436
815-726-2800
play@cpxsports.com
http://www.cpxsports.com

Paint Pursuit Games
Joliet, Illinois 60431
(815) 577- 0044
http://www.paintpursuitgames.com/

Area 52 Paintball
702 Smith St
Mackinaw, Illinois 61755
309.359.5252
info@area52paintball.com
http://www.area52paintball.com/

Paradise Paintball
9200 U S Hwy 136
Macomb, Illinois 61455
http://www.paradisepaintball.info/

Adventure Sports Paintball
12800 Prosperity Rd
Marion, Illinois 62959
ASPaintball@excite.com
http://www.aspaintball.com

Sudden Impact
7290E 550N Rd
McLean, Illinois 61754
309-874-3338
http://www.sipaintball.net/

Fox River Games Paintball
10389 Fox River Dr
Millington, Illinois 60537
contact@foxpaintball.com
http://www.foxpaintball.com/

Wacky Warriors Paintball (Illinois)
Mine Haul Road
Millstadt, Illinois 62260
paintbal@wackywarriors.com
http://www.wackywarriors.com/

Xtreme Paintball Park
3545 Douglas Road
Millstadt, Illinois 62260
618-476-9273
xtremepaintballpark@hotmail.com
http://www.xtremepaintballpark.com

Factory Paintball Arena
2400 Commonwealth Ave.
North Chicago, Illinois 60064
james@factorypb.com
http://factorypb.com

Action Games, Inc.
Ottawa, Illinois 61350
630-554-2555
http://www.action-paintball.com

Ballistic Paintball
1775 Chessie Lane
Ottawa, Illinois 61350
815-434-3385

Out Numbered Paintball
407 Milton St.
Paris, Illinois 61944
217-463-1220
rebel91@webtv.net
http://www.geocities.com/onppaintball

Pekin Paintball
1214 Koch Street
Pekin, Illinois 61554
(309)353-2121
info@pekinpaintball.com
http://www.pekinpaintball.com

Mississippi Valley Paintball (MVP)
3701 207th St. North
Port Byron, Illinois 61275
brian@mvpaintball.com
http://www.mvpaintball.com

Tri-State Paintball Club
4329 N 12th street
Quincy, Illinois 62305
217-222-3200
http://www.tristatepaintballclub.com

Croegaerts Paintball
3900 11th St.
Rock Island, Illinois 61201
(309) 283-0420

Wyld Side Paintball
230 Arnold Street
Rockford, Illinois 61108
815-636-9970
mail@wyldpaintball.com
http://www.wyldpaintball.com/

PaintballToGo
RR3 Box 135
Roodhouse, Illinois 62082
info@paintballtogo.com
http://www.paintballtogo.com

SaltFork Paintball
2053 County Road 1100 N.
Sidney, Illinois 61877
217-778-7793
saltfork_paintball@mchsi.com
http://home.mchsi.com/~salt-fork_paintball

RM Paintball
Texico, Illinois 62889
(618) 755-4865

Odyssey Fun World
19111 S. Oak Park Avenue
Tinley Park, Illinois 60477
708.429.3800
bjones@odysseyfunworld.net
http://www.odysseyfunworld.com

Level X Paintball Park
1110 N County Road 2050 E
Villa Grove, Illinois 61956
(217) 832-5225
levelxpaintball@hotmail.com
http://www.levelxpaintball.com

Wildcat Paintball Park
Third Street
Williamson, Illinois 62088
1-800-965-4206
Staff@wildcatpaintball.com
http://www.wildcatpaintball.com/

The Coloseum
1901 E. Edwardsville, Rd
Wood River, Illinois 62095
618-251-4966
paintball@stlindoor.com
http://www.stlindoor.com

Reball Training Center
205 Beaver Street, Unit 2
Yorkville, Illinois 60560
630-553-7125
stacy@centerflagproducts.com
http://www.reballtrainingcenter.co
m./rtchome.html

INDIANA

White River Paintball
925 Anderson-Frankton Rd.
Anderson, Indiana 46011
765-642-7139
info@whiteriverpaintball.com
http://www.whiteriverpaintball.com

Apocalypse Games
302 W. Gilmore
Angola, Indiana 46703
(260) 668-1022
http://www.apocalypsefun.com/

Paintball Barn
5800 N. 820 E.
Attica, Indiana 47918
daver@paintballbarn.com
http://www.paintballbarn.com

Kobra Paintball Fields
405 South Federal Avenue
Butler, Indiana 46721
260-705-1231
kobrapaintball@comcast.net
http://home.comcast.net/~kobra-
paintball/wsb/index.html

Paintball at The Fun Farm
2690 Breckenridge Rd
Corydon, Indiana 47112
800-952-3580
info@paintballfun.com
http://www.paintballfun.com

Decatur Golfworks & Paintball
1740 W. US Hwy. 224
Decatur, Indiana 46733
260-728-4633

Crossfire Paintless Paintball
14914 101st Ave.
Dyer, Indiana 46311
708-341-3255
taylmade@yahoo.com
http://www.crossfirereball.com

Elkhart Indoor Paintball
1919 Cassopolis St.
Elkhart, Indiana 46514
(574) 262-8027
store_field@elkhartindoorpaint-
ball.com
http://www.elkhartindoorpaint-
ball.com

Chase Paintball Field
800 Glasgow Ave.
Fort Wayne, Indiana 46803
1-866-50-SPLAT
info@chasepb.com
http://www.chasepaintball.com

Adrenaline Rush Paintball Field
600 N College Ave
Greencastle, Indiana 46135
adrenalinerush_ccr@yahoo.com
http://www.geocities.com/adrena-
linerush_ccr/home.html

Blast Camp Paintball
600 N.
Hobart, Indiana 46342
(219) 947-7733
blastcamp@verizon.net
http://www.blastcamp.com/

Ben Davis Paintball Club
Indianapolis, Indiana 46214
(317) 726-9888
webmaster@bdpaintballclub.com
http://www.bdpaintballclub.com

Dark Armies Paintball
2525 N. Shadeland Ave.
Indianapolis, Indiana 46219
email@darkarmies.com
http://www.darkarmies.com/

Indy F.O.G.
7532 Indian Lake Rd.
Indianapolis, Indiana 46236
http://www.indyfog.net

Blast Factory Paintball
100 E North St
Kokomo, Indiana 46901
(765) 457-3227

Sycamore Sports & Recreation Park
3437 W. Syacamore St.
Kokomo, Indiana 46901
765-457-3227
blastfactory@insightbb.com
http://home.insightbb.com/~blast-
factory/

Sherwood Forest Paintball
3497 North US HWY 35
La Porte, Indiana 46350
loxley@netnitco.net
http://www.sherwoodpaintball.com

Arrows III Adventures
2888 State Road 25 N
Lafayette, Indiana 47905
(765) 429-4747

Catfish Lake
1700 West Wabash Ave.
Logansport, Indiana 46947
(574) 753-6551
info@catfishlake.net
http://www.indianapaintball.com/

Paintball Splat Attack
5435 North Huntington Road
(St Rd. 9)
Marion, Indiana 46952
765-651-0750
atkinson@comteck.com
http://pbsplatattack.com/

Action Park
11951 Harrison Road
Mishawaka, Indiana 46544
574-674-4263
webmaster@actionparkpaintball.com
http://www.actionparkpaintball.com

Gator Pit Paintball
S.R. 67
Mooresville, Indiana 46158
gatorrod@iquest.net
http://www.gatorjoes.com

Paintball Valley
2620 Valley Branch Rd.
Nashville, Indiana 47448
valleybranchretreat@yahoo.com
http://www.valleybranchretreat.com

Paintball Paradise
5199 Prospect
Newburgh, Indiana 47630
853-5616
http://www.paintballparadisein.com

Paintball Heat
8320 Union Road
Plymouth, Indiana 46513
574-935-3073
info@paintballheat.com
http://www.paintballheat.com

Xtreme to Chaos
415 Water Street
Portland, Indiana 47371
(260) 726-3888
http://www.xplexpark.com

Silver Spur Splat Paintball
Route 3 Box 253
Princeton, Indiana 47670
SettlePops1@aol.com
http://www.silverspursplat.com

The Predator Zone
Richmond, Indiana 47374
(765) 966-7562
thepredatorzone@netzero.com
http://www.thepredatorzone.com

Wicked Trigger
2322 Whiskey Hollow Rd.
Salem, Indiana 47167
wickedtriggerpaintball@yahoo.com

Paintball Heaven
7499 North US. Hwy. 31
Seymour, Indiana 47274
(812) 522- 5333

The Proving Grounds
4440 St. Rd. 47
Sheridan, Indiana 46069
(317) 758-6622
info@pgpaintball.net
http://www.PgPaintball.net

Cliff Edge Paintball
1306 Hyden Rd
Spencer, Indiana 47460
812-829-4622
Paintballtran@hotmail.com
http://www.cliffedgepaintball.xaper.com

Tree Huggers Paintball
133 E County Road 450 N
Sullivan, Indiana 47882
812-382-4419
pb@treehuggerspaintball.com
http://www.treehuggerspaintball.com

Pines Ski & Family Rec. Area
674 N. Meridian Rd.
Valparaiso, Indiana 46385
(219) 477-5993
pinesskiarea@verizon.net
http://www.pinesskiarea.com/paintball.html

Rat City Outdoor Paintball
5585 S Country Club Rd.
Warsaw, Indiana 46580

Fort Knox USA
7485 N US Highway 35
Winamac, Indiana 46996
574-946-4988
fortknoxusa@yahoo.com
http://www.fortknoxpaintball.com

River Valley Paintball
Yorktown, Indiana 47304
rivervalleypaintball@aol.com

IOWA

Paintballs Afire
1147 710th Place
Albia, Iowa 52531
(641) 660-2876
info@paintballsafire.com
http://www.paintballsafire.com

TDR Paintball
4487 Kingbird Avenue
Alton, Iowa 51003
1-712-756-4433
altonplastics@midlands.net
http://www.tdrpaintball.com

Archery Field
3725 NE 56th St.
Altoona, Iowa 50009
(515) 265-6500
http://www.archeryfield.com

ACP Warfield
Bevington, Iowa 50033
http://www.acpwarfield.com

Seven Oaks Recreation
1086 222nd Drive
Boone, Iowa 50036
515-432-9457
sevenoaks@opencominc.com
http://www.SevenOaksrec.com

Jokers Wild Paintball Field
12457 Y-Camp Road
Burlington, Iowa 52601
TMyers8974@aol.com
http://www.jokerswildpaintball.com

Wise Guyz Paintball
124 6th Avenue South
Clinton, Iowa 52732
563-357-8016
sales@wiseguyzpaintball.com
http://www.wiseguyzpaintball.com

Prairie Fire Paintball
Conrad, Iowa 50609
dielhj@prairieinet.net
http://www.geocities.com/prairie_
fire_paintball/index.html

Metro Paintball Games
20595 McPherson Avenue
Council Bluffs, Iowa 51503
712-325-GAME
http://www.metropaintballgames.com

ICU Paintball
Des Moines, Iowa 50323
icupaintball@email.msn.com
http://www.icupaintball.com

Best Shot Paintball
Bankston Park
Dubuque, Iowa 52004
bestshot@mcleodusa.net
http://www.bestshotpaintball.com/

Sure Shooting Paintball Park
Greene, Iowa 50616
DennisDelp@SSpaintball.com
http://www.sspaintball.com/

Edge Paintball
131 Marion Boulevard
Marion, Iowa 52302
319-373-1274
http://www.edgepaintball.net/

Action Jack's Paintball Games
521 N. 2nd Ave. E.
Newton, Iowa 50208
ActionJacks2000@hotmail.com
http://www.actionjackspaintball.com

Adventure Park
3176 61st Street Lane
Shellsburg, Iowa 52332
bill@thinkpaintball.com
http://www.thinkpaintball.com

Plains Paintball
Stone Avenue
Sioux City, Iowa 51106
712-251-4526
contact@plainspaintball.net
http://www.plainspaintball.net

Okoboji Paintball
3310 Hwy 71
Spirit Lake, Iowa 51360
712-336-6970
bobyarger@okobojipaintballs.com
http://www.okobojipaintballs.com/

DOA Paintball
St. Charles, Iowa 50240
515-462-3596
http://www.doapaintball.com

Northwest Iowa Paintball
1712 East Milwaukee Ave.
Storm Lake, Iowa 50588
dave@nwiapaintball.com
http://www.nwiapaintball.com

Iowa Paintball Park
2575 59th Street Dr.
Vinton, Iowa 52349
mdulin@uswest.net
http://www.iowapaintballpark.com

Center Mass Paintball
2450 Hwy 76 SE
Waukon, Iowa 52172
1-563-568-4352
centermasspaintball@yahoo.com
http://www.centermasspaintball.com/

Velocity Paintball Field
West Liberty, Iowa 52776
store@velocityiowa.com
http://www.velocityiowa.com

KANSAS

Bone Creek Paintball
787 N. 210th Street
Arcadia, Kansas 66711
info@bonecreekpaintball.com
http://www.bonecreekpaintball.com

Kansas Paintball Ranch
Arkansas City, Kansas 67005

Lakeside Paintball
1288 E. Lapsley
Assaria, Kansas 67416
info@lakesiderec.org
info@lakesiderec.org
http://www.lakesiderec.org/paint-
ball.html

Graffiti Paintball
1127 N. Seneca
Belle Plaine, Kansas 67013
graffiti_paintball@hotmail.com
http://www.graffitiks.com

Frog Holler Paintball
9430 So. Bluff
Derby, Kansas 67037
316-789-9991
http://www.froghollerpaintball.com

Tornado Alley Paintball
6431 NW 50th
El Dorado, Kansas 67042
tornadoalley@cox.net
http://www.TornadoAlleyPaint-
ball.com

Extreme Crossfire Paintball Park
5 N Mowhawk Rd
Hutchinson, Kansas 67501
620-960-1839
http://www.extremecrossfire.com

BattleSplat
1534 1400th street
Iola, Kansas 66749

JC Paintball
1805 Monroe Street
Junction City, Kansas 66441
785-238-8354

Drop Zone Paintball
Lawrence, Kansas 66061
http://www.dropzonepaintball.com

Homeland Paintball
6341 E. 268 Hwy
Quenemo, Kansas 66528
785-418-7700
punisher@homelandpaintball.net
http://www.homelandpaintball.net

The Edge Paintball
K-96 & Ridge
Wichita, Kansas 67205
316-773-0537
matte@nps.kscoxmail.com
http://www.edgepaintball.com

KENTUCKY

Wizard Land
Aurora, Kentucky 42048
(270) 474-8712

N-tense Sports
2101 Morgantown Rd
Bowling Green, Kentucky 42101
270-792-6246
sanpat@ntensesports.com
http://www.ntensesports.com/

Paintball Hill
438 Windflower Way
Bryantsville, Kentucky 40410
859-433-3801
paintballhill@juno.com
http://www.paintballhill.com

Jebb's Club
Butler, Kentucky 41006

S&S Paintball
1693 Miller Rd
Campbellsville, Kentucky 42718
270-932-9519
REASER007@AOL.COM

Open Range
6401 Cross Keys Blvd
Crestwood, Kentucky 40014
502.243.8282
http://www.openrangesports.com

War Wizard
958 Elderberry lane
Dexter, Kentucky 42036
warwizardpaintball@yahoo.com

Conder's Paintball
813 Hawkins Drive
Elizabethtown, Kentucky 42701
dconder@kvnet.org
http://www.conderspaintball.com

Unlimited Paintball
8171 Dixie Highway
Florence, Kentucky 41042
(859) 647-7255
http://www.unlimited-paintball.com

Ft. Campbell Paintball
Fort Campbell, Kentucky 42223
http://www.fortcampbellpb.tk

Bullseye Paintball
Frankfort, Kentucky 40601
502-229-2952
jdeere160@hotmail.com
http://www.bullseyeky.com

Greensburg Paintball
4385 Ebenezer Rd.
Greensburg, Kentucky 42743
(270)932-5708

Hometown Paintball Supply
Hwy. 69 North
Hartford, Kentucky 42347
hps@kypaintball.com
http://www.kypaintball.com

West Kentucky Paintball
La Center, Kentucky 42056
1 270 665 5696
http://www.westkentuckypaintball.com

Paintball Asylum
3101 Pond Station Rd
Louisville, Kentucky 40272
502-937-9370
Yakuza1ken@aol.com
http://www.pbasylum.com

Third Eye Paintball—
Reball Training Center
102 Outer Loop
Louisville, Kentucky 40214
502-367-6522
info@thirdeyepaintball.com
http://www.thirdeyepaintball.com

Shooter Supply Paintball Field
3919 Cairo Road
Paducah, Kentucky 42001
270-443-3758
padshoot@comcast.net
http://www.pssguns.com/

High Velocity Paintball
Richmond, Kentucky 40475
8596249449

Lake Cumberland Paintball
630 Miller Short Rd.
Russell Springs, Kentucky 42642
(270)866-2942
lcp@duo-county.com
http://www.lakecumberland.com

Rapid Engagement
1667 Stilesville Rd
Science Hill, Kentucky 42553
606-423-5001
cdaniels@rapidengagement.com
http://www.rapidengagement.com

Diehard Paintball
526 River Road
Silver Grove, Kentucky 41085
tim@diehardpaintball.com
http://www.diehardpaintball.com

Kryptonite Caynon
Somerset, Kentucky 42503
http://www.kryptonitepaintball.com

Crossfire Paintball Park
Verona, Kentucky 41092
859-342-9386
gmiller@crossfirepaintballllc.com
http://www.crossfirepaintballllc.com

Thunderstruck Paintball
99 Graefenburg Rd.
Waddy, Kentucky 40342
502-829-0122
http://www.thunderstruckpaint-
ball.com

Game On Paintball
1220 Enterprise Dr.
Winchester, Kentucky 40391
800-779-5544
pb@customcyl.com
http://customcyl.com/fields/

LOUISIANA

Campbellot
10775 Highway 961
Clinton, Louisiana 70722
225-683-5515

Wildwood Paintball
8488 Wildwood Dr.
Denham Springs, Louisiana 70706
(225) 270-2879
wwpb@cox.net
http://www.wildwoodpaintballon-
line.com/

Wilderness Paintball
1780 Williams Colony Road
Downsville, Louisiana 71234
318-396-5901
wilderness_paintball@yahoo.com
http://www.wildernesspaintball.com

Off Limits Paintball
608 Robinson Road
Elm Grove, Louisiana 71051
318-987-2696
offlimitspball@aol.com
http://www.offlimitspaintball.com

LAdrenaline Paintball
22192 Greenwell Springs Rd
Greenwell Springs, Louisiana 70739
225-262-0315
ladrenaline@bellsouth.net
http://www.ladrenalinepaintball.com

Bull Run Paintball
15587 Club Deluxe Rd
Hammond, Louisiana 70403
985-419-8478
http://www.bullrunpaintball.com

Shell Shocked Paintball
Coteau Rd.
Houma, Louisiana 70363
(985) 223-1700
http://www.shellshockedpaint-
ball.com

Paintball Command
21268 Emile Strain Rd
Mandeville, Louisiana 70471
p8nt@bellsouth.net
http://www.paintball-
command.com/

Bayou Dragon Paintball
7625 Barataria Blvd.
Marrero, Louisiana 70072
http://www.bayoudragon.com/

Bayou Paintball
1 Garr Road
Monroe, Louisiana 71203
http://www.bayoupaintball.com/

Paintball Planet
New Orleans, Louisiana 70112
(504) 832-9991
http://www.neworleanspaintball.com

Atomic Blast
608 Bayou Road
Saint Bernard, Louisiana 70085
(504) 682-0988
atomicblast@cox.net
http://www.atomicblastpaintball.com

Splatz Paintball
2750 West Willow St.
Scott, Louisiana 70583
337-289-9828
splatzpaintball@hotmail.com
http://www.splatz.com/

Paintball Warehouse
400 3rd Street
Shreveport, Louisiana 71101

LA Xtreme Paintball
37000 Receiving Rd
Slidell, Louisiana 70460
985-863-8895
mike@laxtremepaintball.com
http://www.laxtremepaintball.com

Battle Hill Paintball
Hwy 546 South
West Monroe, Louisiana 71201
bhillpaintball@jam.rr.com

Paint Check
Zachary, Louisiana 70791
http://www.paintcheckonline.com

MAINE

Lost Valley Paintball
200 Lost Valley Road
Auburn, Maine 04210
207-784-1561
Paintball@LostValleySki.com
http://lostvalleyski.com/paint-
ball/index.html

Splatz Paintball
1640 Hammond St
Bangor, Maine 04401
207.947.7997
bhanson1@maine.rr.com
http://www.splatz.net

Johnson Sporting Goods
206 Bath Road
Brunswick, Maine 04011
207-725-7531

Adventure Sports
1937 Rt. 7
Dover-Foxcroft, Maine 04426
207-564-8156
http://www.adventuresportsof-
maine.com

Easy Street Paintball
9 Easy Street
Farmingdale, Maine 04344
207-622-4813
kevie_kev@easystreetpaintball.com
http://www.easystreetpaintball.com

Triple T Paintball
521 Dorsey Road
Fort Fairfield, Maine 04742
(207) 473-9370
donna@tttpaintball.net
http://www.tttpaintball.net

P&R Paintball
285 Main Street
Fryeburg, Maine 04037
207-935-1900

Bennett AllWeather Paintball
463 Fort Hill Rd.
Gorham, Maine 04038
proshop@bennettallweatherpaint-
ball.com
http://www.bennettallweather-
paintball.com

Flying Dutchman
Sebec Shores Rd
Guilford, Maine 04443
207-564-3369
dutchman@kynd.net
http://www.flyingdutchmanpaint-
ball.com/

Firestorm Paintball
127 North Road
Limington, Maine 04049
info@firestormpaintball.com
http://www.firestormpaintball.com

Westside Paintball
72 Emery Street
Sanford, Maine 04073
(866) 570-3023
westsidepb72@yahoo.com
http://www.westsidepb.com

Rogue Paintball
190 Northeast Road
Standish, Maine 04084
Kirt@RoguePaintball.com
http://www.roguepaintball.com

Seacost Fun Park
US Route 3
Trenton, Maine 04605
207-667-3573
http://www.seacoastfunparks.com

Birch Hill Paintball
76 Birch Hill Rd.
York, Maine 03909
207-363-6416
kjpl@aol.com
http://www.birchhillpaintball.com/

MANITOBA

Ambush Tactical
545 Assiniboine Ave.
Brandon, Manitoba R7A 0G3

Renegade Paintball
Dauphin, Manitoba R7N 0R7
(204) 638-8427
pshumka@mts.net
http://www.mts.net/~pshumka/in
dex.html

Splatters Paintball
22-6-5e
Kleefeld, Manitoba R0A 0V0
204.377.4038
schroederman@Hotmail.com
http://www.splatterspaintball.com

XROSSFIRE Paintball Park
Kleefeld, Manitoba R0A 0V0
sheldondyck@yahoo.ca
http://www.xrossfirepaintball.com

CanadianPaintball.com
Richer, Manitoba
204-453-1077
sales@canadianpaintball.com
http://www.canadianpaintball.com

Paintball Paradise (Outdoor)
Junction 415
St. Laurent, Manitoba R0C 2S0
(204) 338-1535
info@paintballparadise.com
http://www.paintballparadise.com

Heartland Paintball
10-K Keenlyside St
Winnipeg, Manitoba R2L 2B9
204.661.5670
info@heartlandpaintball.ca
http://www.heartlandpaintball.ca

Paintball Paradise (Indoor)
568 Prest Ave
Winnipeg, Manitoba R2V 4R9
info@paintballparadise.com
http://www.paintballparadise.com

MARYLAND

Outdoor Adventures Paintball
16680 Governor Bridge Road
Bowie, Maryland 20716
karen@oapaintball.com
http://www.oapaintball.com/

Be The Hunted Paintball
11312 Ore St N.E.
Cumberland, Maryland 21502
301-724-3216
mike@bthpaintball.com
http://www.bthpaintball.com

Absolute Paintball
229 S. Bridge Street
Elkton, Maryland 21921
410-398-0052
http://www.absolutepaintballfun.com/

Fort Detrick Paintball
Frederick, Maryland 21701
301-619-0247
http://www.detrick.army.mil/well-
being/mwr/paintball.cfm

Paintball Sportsland
10418 Old Liberty Rd.
Frederick, Maryland 21701
paintballsportsland44@hotmail.com
http://www.paintball-
sportsland.com/

Robin Hood Paintball
2130 Pulaski Hwy
Harve de Grace, Maryland 21078
(410) 273-1555
robinhoodpaintball@msn.com
http://www.robinhoodpaintball.net

Paintball Shooters
Laurel, Maryland 20708
410-987-8019

Wisp Resort Paintball
296 Marsh Hill Rd.
McHenry, Maryland 21541
301-387-4911
info@skiwisp.com
http://www.wispresort.com

Adventure Park USA
New Market, Maryland 21774
301-865-6800
info@adventureparkusa.com
http://www.adventureparkusa.com

Delmarva Paintball
1922 North Salisbury Blvd.
Salisbury, Maryland 21804
443-260-0959
http://www.delmarvapaintball.net
/index.html

Paintball Adventure Park
3939 Old Taneytown Rd.
Taneytown, Maryland 21787
http://www.paintballwholesalers.com

Route 40 Paintball
11011 Pulaski Highway
White Marsh, Maryland 21162
(410) 335-7622
http://www.route40paintball.com

MASSACHUSETTS

Xtreme Paintball
369 Main St
Agawam, Massachusetts 01001
413 626 8212
xtremepbma@yahoo.com
http://www.xtremepbma.com

University of Massachusetts Paintball Field
North East Street
Amherst, Massachusetts 01002
grapalermo@yahoo.com
http://www.umass.edu/rso/paint-
ball/

Executive Paintball
239 Otis Road
Blandford, Massachusetts 01008
Gregg@executivepaintball.com
http://www.executivepaintball.com

Cape Cod Paintball
1 Mcarther Blvd
Bourne, Massachusetts 02532
508-759-5130
info@capecodpaintball.com
http://www.capecodpaintball.com

PnL Paintball Bridgewater
1221 Bedford Street
Bridgewater, Massachusetts 02324
http://www.pnlbridgewater.com

Camelot Paintball
610 New Lombard Rd
Chicopee, Massachusetts 01020
(413) 348-5878
chad@camelotpaintball.com
http://www.camelotpaintball.com

Hoops Archery and Paintball
104 Sterling Street
Clinton, Massachusetts 01510
1-866-365-7601
frank@hoopsarchery.com
http://www.hoopsarchery.com

Showtime Paintball
909 Dwelly St. 2nd. Fl.
Fall River, Massachusetts 02724
(508) 673-5040
http://www.showtimepaintball.net

Mill Street Speedball
Feeding Hills, Massachusetts 01030
http://www.freewebs.com/camelo
tslayers

Camp Paintball
Pottle Street
Kingston, Massachusetts 02364
cp.pb@verizon.net
http://www.camppaintball.com/

Planet Paintball
360 Merrimac St.
Lawrence, Massachusetts 01843
(978) 327-5969
info@planetpaintball.com
http://www.planetpaintball.com

West End Paintball
1759 Main St
Leicester, Massachusetts 01524
(508) 721-0003
xfirepaintball@xfirepaintball.com
http://www.westendpaintball.com/

Mill City Paintball
92 Bolt Street
Lowell, Massachusetts 01852
978-452-3332
jrobles@millcitypaintball.net
http://millcitypaintball.net

Airsports Paintball
1102 Center St
Ludlow, Massachusetts 01056
413-583-8200
airsports@charter.net
http://www.airsportspb.com

Maynard Paintball Club
45 Old Mill Rd.
Maynard, Massachusetts 01754
617-605-6056
gameinfo@maynardpaintballclub.com
http://www.maynardpaintball-
club.com

Randolph Paintball
410 South St.
Randolph, Massachusetts 02368
paintball@tiac.net
http://www.randolphpaintball.com

Boston Paintball
43 Foley Road
Somerville, Massachusetts 02145
Matt@bostonpaintball.com
http://www.bostonpaintball.com

P&L Paintball (Indoor)
391 W Water St
Taunton, Massachusetts 02780
508-822-7788
pnlpaintbal@aol.com
http://www.pnlpaintball.com

Action Games Paintball
1078 South St
Tewksbury, Massachusetts 01876
781-942-9222
actiongames@attbi.com
http://www.actiongamespaintball.com

Fox 4 Paintball
159 Milford Street
Upton, Massachusetts 01568
fox4paintball@yahoo.com
http://www.fox4paintball.com

Friendly Fire Paintball
108 Grove Street
Upton, Massachusetts 01568
info@friendlyfire-paintball.com
http://www.friendlyfire-paintball.com

PlayBoyz Paintball / The Habitat
(The Hab)
374 West Street
Uxbridge, Massachusetts 01569
508-278-9888
info@thehab.com
http://www.playboyzpaintball.com

Ultimate Paintball
356 South Ave. (Rte. 27)
Whitman, Massachusetts 02382
1-(781)-447-2260
info@ultimatepaintball.com
http://www.ultimatepaintball.com

MICHIGAN

Hole In the Wall
24262 66th Street
Bangor, Michigan 49013
269-427-1511
hitwp@hotmail.com
http://www.holeinthewallpb.com

Hole In the Wall
24262 66th Street
Bangor, Michigan 49013
269-427-1511
hitwp@hotmail.com
http://www.holeinthewallpb.com

Woodland Paintball
6688 Ingalls Road
Belding, Michigan 48809
Ross@woodlandpaintball.com
http://www.woodlandpaintball.com

Victory Paintball
401 N. 8th Street
Benton Harbor, Michigan 49022
269-926-2876
brian@vicpaintball.com
http://www.vicpaintball.com

TC Paintball G.R.
500 One Hundredth SW Suite B
Byron, Michigan 49315
616 877 0341
infogr@tcpaintball.com
http://www.tcpaintball.com

Chaos Paintball
3262 McConnell Road
Charlotte, Michigan 48813
chaospaintballfield@hotmail.com
http://www.chaospaintballfields.com

Action Sports Paintball
229 North Main
Cheboygan, Michigan 49721
admin@actionsports-paintball.com
http://www.actionsports-paintball.com

Broken Cookie Paintball
4833 E. Dover
Clare, Michigan 48617
1-989-429-5359
Brokencookiepb@hotmail.com
http://www.BrokenCookiePaintball.com

Adventure Zone
125 W Chicago Rd
Coldwater, Michigan 49036
517-278-9663
matt@278zone.com
http://www.278zone.com

RJ Performance
1444 North Irish Rd
Davison, Michigan 48423
(810) 658-5274
http://www.rjperformancepaintball.com

Mad Frog Paintball
Eastpointe, Michigan 48021
586-482-7228
wc_inc@ameritech.net
http://www.madfrogpaintball.com

Barrell 2 Barrell Paintball
11555 80th Ave.
Evart, Michigan 49631
231-734-3885
barrell2barrell@hotmail.com
http://www.dezign-net.com/b2b

Pirates Park Paintball
4175 Miller Rd.
Flint, Michigan 48507
810-230-7800

The Bunker
4510 South Dort Highway
Flint, Michigan 48507
810-744-1008
todd@reball.tv
http://www.reball.tv

Panek Attack Paintball
305 List Street
Frankenmuth, Michigan 48734
989-652-6777
ace@panekattackpaintball.com
http://www.panekattackpaintball.com

Colors Paintball
7412 S. 200th
Fremont, Michigan 49412
(231) 854-4487
randy@colorspaintball.com
http://www.colorspaintball.com

Splat-U-Later
8547 O Lane
Gladstone, Michigan 49837
(906) 428-9599
splatulater@myvine.com
http://splat-u-later.com

River Front Paintball
300 Front Street
Grand Rapids, Michigan 49503
(888)246-5985
blitz@gunlakepaintball.com
http://www.riverfrontpaintball.com

Dementia Paintball
5590 136th Ave
Hamilton, Michigan 49419
s.gerke@sbcglobal.net

Ultimate Paintball Challenge
41300 Production Dr.
Harrison Twp., Michigan 48045
info@upcindoor.com
http://www.upcindoor.com

Crossfire Paintball Arena
A-4054 146th Ave
Holland, Michigan 49423
616-928-1293
crossfirepb@gmail.com
http://www.xfirepb.com

M-40 Paintball
Lincoln Road
Holland, Michigan 49423
info@m-40paintball.com
http://www.m-40paintball.com/

MTU Paintball Club Field
Pilgrim Road
Houghton, Michigan 49931
paintball@mtu.edu
http://www.cockertech.com/mtu

Famous Guy Paintball
10445 Beech Ave.
Howard City, Michigan 49329
231-937-4853
info@famousguy.com
http://www.famousguy.com

Fantasy Paintball Park
13600 Day Road
Hudson, Michigan 49247
(517)448-8586
hudsonyc@yahoo.com
http://www.angelfire.com/mi4/fpp

Combat Zone
1951 E Sterling Rd.
Jonesville, Michigan 49250
517-617-0884
Combatzonepb@Yahoo.com
http://www.czpaintball.com

.68 Caliber Paintball
1809 Reed Ave
Kalamazoo, Michigan 49001
(269) 226-8586

R&S Paintball
6071 West D Avenue
Kalamazoo, Michigan 49009
269-553-6896
http://www.rspaintball.net

TC Paintball Indoor Field
829 Us Highway 131 N
Kalkaska, Michigan 49646
info@tcpainball.com
http://www.tcpaintball.com/

Predator Paintball
103 E State St
Laingsburg, Michigan 48848
(989) 224-8189

Futureball Paintball (Indoor)
Seven Mile Rd. and Middlebelt Rd.
Livonia, Michigan 48150
(248) 446-0772
jim@futureball.com
http://www.futureball.com

Killer Paintball Indoor Park
Livonia, Michigan 48152
248-476-1300
killerpaintballpark@gmail.com
http://www.killerpaintball.com

R&R Paintball
3869 Clyde Rd
Lyons, Michigan 48851
616-527-5514
randrpaintball@yahoo.com
http://www.geocities.com/randr-
paintball

Area 51 Paintball
3005 Westwood Rd
Mancelona, Michigan 49659
231-313-3111
labrat@area51paintball.com
http://www.area51paintball.com

Paintball Extreme Arena
77 Hancock St.
Manistee, Michigan 49660
231-723-2811
http://www.paintballextreme.biz

Precision Paintball
1126. N. Third Street
Marquette, Michigan 49855
906 228 9991
precisionpaintball@chartermi.net
http://www.precisionpb.com/

Lone Wolf West Paintball
4000 S. Lapeer
Metamora, Michigan 48455
1-800-875-WOLF
lonewolfpaintball@wowway.com
http://www.lonewolfpaintball.com

Lone Wolf East Paintball
237 N. River Road
Mount Clemens, Michigan 48038
1-800-875-WOLF
lonewolfpaintball@wowway.com
http://www.lonewolfpaintball.com

Total Control Paintball
3023 S. 11th Street
Niles, Michigan 49120
(574)277-4493
totalcontrolpaintball_niles_mi@
yahoo.com
http://www.totalcontrolpaintball.net

RIP Radical Impact Paintball
Carland Road
Owosso, Michigan 48867
(989) 666-3644
oviattms@chartermi.net
http://www.rippaintball.net

Hell Survivors
619 D-19/Pearl St
Pinckney, Michigan 48169
(734) 878-5656
HellSurvivors@ExoticSportz.com
http://www.HellSurvivors.com/

Bunkers and Banners
3446 West Emery Road
Prudenville, Michigan 48651
989-240-7773
http://home.earthlink.net/~swamp
y68/

Empty Hopper Paintball
Reed City, Michigan 49677
231-832-4034
http://www.emptyhopper.com

Paintball Revolution
6690 N. Leaton Rd.
Rosebush, Michigan 48878
989 - 400 - 3722
Ryan@pbrevolution.com
http://www.pbrevolution.com

Bandit Paintball
Saginaw, Michigan 48603
989-249-4346
http://www.banditpaintball.com

Tri City Paintball
1020 N. Outer Drive
Saginaw, Michigan 48601
989-753-1302

Operation Ambush
218 N. 20th Street
Springfield, Michigan 49015
http://www.operationambush.us

Crossfire Creek Paintball
6760 Frith Rd.
St. Clair, Michigan 48079
crossfirecreek@sbcglobal.net
http://www.crossfirecreek.com

Pine River Paintball
3701 W Pine River Rd
St. Louis, Michigan 48880
989-681-4857
pineriverpaintball@rural-net.com
http://www.pineriverpaintball.com

No Limits Extreme Action Park
Lange Rd
Taylor, Michigan 48180
734-425-2545
nolimitspark@hotmail.com
http://www.nolimitspark.com

Splatmandu Paintball
Three Rivers, Michigan 49093
http://www.splatmandu.com

TC Paintball Outdoor Field
1350 South Airport Road
Traverse City, Michigan 49686
231-933-0717
info@tcpaintball.com
http://www.TCPaintball.com

R.A.M.B.O
5350 Stambaugh Rd
Uble, Michigan 48475
jerry@rambopaintball.com
http://www.rambopaintball.com

Thunderball Paintball
1781 E Wadsworth Road
Ubly, Michigan 48475
989-658-2905
thunderballpaintball@yahoo.com
http://mi.local.yahoo.biz/thunder-
ballpaintball

Mayhem Sportz
2547 3 Mile Rd NW, Suite C
Walker, Michigan 49544
(616) 453-0987
Info@mayhemsportz.net
http://www.mayhemsportz.net

Gun Lake Paintball
891 129th Ave
Wayland, Michigan 49348
blitz@gunlakepaintball.com
http://www.gunlakepaintball.com

Futureball Paintball (Outdoor)
9269 E Mi State Road 36 (M36)
Whitmore Lake, Michigan 48189
(248) 446-0772
jim@futureball.com
http://www.futureball.com/out-
door.php

MINNESOTA

Viking Paintball
6533 County Rd 87 SE
Alexandria, Minnesota 56308
(320) 491-4438
thor@vikingpaintball.net
http://www.vikingpaintball.net

Annandale Paintball
Annandale, Minnesota 55302
320-274-8242
jtsales@annandalepaintball.com
http://www.annandalepaintball.com

Devotion Paintball
1706 Paul Bunyan Drive SE
Bemidji, Minnesota 56601
(218)-333-3630
info@devotionpaintball.com
http://www.devotionpaintball.com

Special Forces Paintball
Buffalo, Minnesota 55313
beyerjeff@msn.com
http://www.specialforcespaint-
ball.com

Pure Paintball
Cambridge, Minnesota 55008
justpaintballmn1@aol.com

Spirit Mountain Extreme Paintball
Duluth, Minnesota 55807
paintball@spiritmt.com

X-treme Paintball Of Duluth
W. Grand Ave
Duluth, Minnesota 55810
1-218-624-4226
http://www.x-tremepod.com

Xphere Paintball
24242 Appleton Ave.
Faribault, Minnesota 55021
(507)-333-9500
xpherepaintball@hotmail.com
http://www.xpherepaintball.com

Combat Zone
Hinckley, Minnesota 55037
combatzoneinc@msn.com
http://www.combatzoneinc.com

Just Paintball
Hinckley, Minnesota 55037
justpaintballmn1@aol.com
http://www.northsidesports.com/
justpaintball/

Mission Creek Paintball
912 Weber Ave.
Hinckley, Minnesota 55037
320-384-6015
missioncreekpaintball@gmail.com
http://www.missioncreekpaint-
ball.com

Northwoods Paintball
4156 Town Rd 219
International Falls, Minnesota 56649
218-324-0755
http://www.northwoodspaintball.com

Action Packed Paintball
8200 Old Highway 169 Blvd
Jordan, Minnesota 55352
952-492-6776
info@actionpackedpaintball.com
http://www.actionpackedpaint-
ball.com

MN Pro Paintball
22554 Texas Ave
Lakeville, Minnesota 55044
952-484-1126
info@mnpropaintball.com
http://www.mnpropaintball.com

Aimless Enterprises
Luverne, Minnesota 56156
507.227.7889
chad@aimless.biz
http://www.aimless.biz

Air Assault Paintball
5130 Industrial Street
Maple Plains, Minnesota 55359
763-479-3113
info@airassaultpaintball.com
http://www.airassaultpaintball.com

Run-N-Gun Paintball Sports
RR 1 Box 248AB
Mazeppa, Minnesota 55956
507-990-0913
http://www.run-n-gun.net

All-Terrain Paintball. Inc.
48341 St. Hwy. 87
Menahga, Minnesota 56464
1-866-346-6701
atp@all-terrainpaintball.com
http://www.all-
terrainpaintball.com

Zumbro Valley Paintball
Wabasha CO 11
Millville, Minnesota 55957
507-798-2290
http://www.paintball-
games.com/zumbro_valley/index.htm

Splatball Inc.
2412 University Ave. SE
Minneapolis, Minnesota 55414
612 378 0385
jim@splatball.com
http://www.splatball.com

It's a Blast Paintball
Mountain Iron, Minnesota 55768

Tommy Guns Paint Wars
48306 235th Street
New Ulm, Minnesota 56073
tommy@tommygunspaintwars.com
http://www.tommygunspaintwars.com

Thunder Alley
1100 Northland Drive
Princeton, Minnesota 55371
(763) 566-7733
info@indoorspeed.com
http://www.indoorspeed.com

Diehard Paintball
14622 Ferret St NW
Ramsey, Minnesota 55303
steve@diehardpaint.com
http://www.diehardpaint.com/

Northside Sports Park
14662 Ferret Street NW
Ramsey, Minnesota 55303
763-427-3892
info@northsidesports.com
http://www.northsidesports.com

Paintball Plus
4680 Hwy 63 N
Rochester, Minnesota 55906
507-261-8033
http://www.paintballplusmn.com

Adventure Zone
13410 Court House Blvd
Rosemount, Minnesota 55068
952-890-7981
http://www.theadventurezone.net

Back 80 Paintball Sports
RR1 box 1046
Rushford, Minnesota 55971
stolpa2@charter.net
http://www.back80.com

Paintball Gods Outdoor
County Roady 75
Sabin, Minnesota 56580
hq@paintballgods.com
http://www.paintballgods.com/

Crossfire Paintball Inc.
3820 Roosevelt Rd &
Clearwater Road
St. Cloud, Minnesota 56301
320-253-5630
info@crossfire-paintball.com
http://www.crossfire-paintball.com

Red Seal Paintball
Willow River, Minnesota 55795
7637531212
MikeJesmer@redsealpaintball.com
http://Redsealpaintball.com

CEW Paintball
337 Oxford Street
Worthington, Minnesota 56187
(507) 376-9149
league@cewgtn.com
http://www.cewgtn.com/paint-
ball/league

Alamo Paintball
Young America, Minnesota 55397
http://www.alamopaintball.net

MISSISSIPPI

Paintball War Zone (PWZ)
2050 Birdsong Rd
Bovina, Mississippi 39183

Action Pursuit Games of Brandon
Clark Creek Road (near the end)
Brandon, Mississippi 39047
601-825-1052
http://www.apgob.com

Delta Paintball Park
1550 Archer Range Rd.
Greenville, Mississippi 38701
662-820-0067
http://www.deltapaintballpark.com

Hattiesburg Paintball
5009 Old Hwy 11
Hattiesburg, Mississippi 39402
601-579-9722
aaron@hattiesburgpaintball.com
http://www.hattiesburgpaintball.com/

The Paintball Project
17 Pioneer Rd.
Hattiesburg, Mississippi 39402
601-261-2664
paintballproject@earthlink.com
http://www.paintballproject.com

Cedar Hill Farms
008 Love Road
Hernando, Mississippi 38632
(662) 429-2540
Cedarhfarm@aol.com
http://www.cedarhfarm.com

Mississippi Splatter Games
3301 Maben-Bell Schoolhouse Rd
Maben, Mississippi 39750
662-263-4445
monster@vcmails.com
http://www.geocities.com/automa
gtoo/mississippisplattergames.html

Abbey's Paintball
1079 Dunaway Rd.
McComb, Mississippi 39648
abbeys@cableone.net
http://www.cableone.net/abbeys

Game-On! Family Paintball Park
205 Lower Rockport Rd.
New Hebron, Mississippi 39140
601-847-7337
gameon205@bellsouth.net

Swat Paintball
6314 Washington Ave
Ocean Springs, Mississippi 39564
http://www.swatpaintball.com

Legends Paintball
13706 Highway 25 S
Sturgis, Mississippi 39769
662-779-4049
legendspaintball@yahoo.com
http://www.legendspaintball.com

Whitetail Ridge
Tupelo, Mississippi 38828
662-869-2925
compshoot@netbci.com
http://www.whitetailridgeout-
doors.com/

MISSOURI

Blodgett Paintball Planet
Blodgett, Missouri 63801
http://www.blodgettpaintball.com

Crowley Ridge Paintball
20366 Co Rd 510
Bloomfield, Missouri 63825
573-568-3942
crowleyridgepb@yahoo.com
http://www.geocities.com/crow-
leyridgepb/

Bulldog Front Paintball
Bloomsdale, Missouri 63627
573-483-2873
Bulldog@Bulldogfrontpaintball.com
http://www.bulldogfrontpaint-
ball.com

Bonne Terre Paintball
8614 Berry Road
Bonne Terre, Missouri 63628
(573) 358-2872
bonneterrepaintball@yahoo.com

Gateway Paintball Park
Missouri Bottom Road
Bridgeton, Missouri 63044
field@gatewaypaintball.com
http://www.gatewaypaintball.com

Bunker Ridge
18 Largo Lane
Buffalo, Missouri 65622
417-345-5332
bunkerridge@hotmail.com
http://www.bunkerridge.com

Big Sky Paintball
5364 SE Elm Court
Cameron, Missouri 64429
bigskypaintball@starband.net

Fat Cat Paintball
5400 West Vanhorn Tavern Rd.
Columbia, Missouri 65203
(573) 874-8179
http://www.fatcatpaintballetc.com/

Inferno Extreme Park
Exselsior Spring, Missouri 64024
816-637-9666
Sales@demonguns.com
http://www.demonguns.com/field/

Atomic Paintball
151 Apple Grove Rd Foley, MO
63347-2513
Foley, Missouri 63347
636-734-1403
admin@atomicpaintballpark.com
http://www.Atomicpaintballpark.com

SlaughterHouse Paintball
4287 Highway 63
Freeburg, Missouri 65035
573-744-5777
SlaughterHousePaintball@hotmail.com
http://SlaughterHousePaintball.com

Battle Blasters
612 Highway D
Hawk Point, Missouri 63349
(636)338-4493
http://www.battleblasters
paintball.com

The Pines
5645 Old Hwy 21
House Springs, Missouri 63051
mypaintballstore@aol.com
http://www.thepaintballstoreinc.com

Splat Paintball
Jefferson City, Missouri 65109
573-893-4144
sales@splatpaintballsupply.com
http://www.splatpaintballsupply.com

Paintball Ridge
3483 Coyote Dr.
Joplin, Missouri 64836
417-781-7703
webmaster@paintballridge.com
http://www.paintballridge.com

Underground Paintball
2710 N. Rangeline
Joplin, Missouri 64801
14172069300
info@joplinunderground.com
http://www.underground-paintball.com

Jaegers Subsurface Paintball
9300 NE Underground Drive
Kansas City, Missouri 64161
jaegersp@earthlink.net
http://www.jaegers.com

Battle Creek Paintball
3643 County Road 221
Kingdom City, Missouri 65262
play@battlecreekpaintball.com
http://www.battlecreekpaintball.com

Maverick Paintball
Kirksville, Missouri 63501
660-665-2692
maverickpb@hotmail.com
http://www.maverickpaintball.net

Baileys Battlefield
Niangua, Missouri 65713
417 839 9299
willimoalso@aol.com
http://www.woodlandwarriors.com

Ozark Paintball
671 Jackson Spring Rd.
Ozark, Missouri 65721
(417) 443-6633

Pork Chop Hill Paintball
1981 West Grapevine
Ozark, Missouri 65721
417-230-5087
http://www.pchpaintball.com

Bushwackers Paintball
5893 Lost Hill Lane
Pacific, Missouri 63069
(314) 579-9933
http://www.bushwackerspaintball.net

Fearless Fighters Paintball
Pacific, Missouri 63069
636-271-7771
bobward@fearelssfighters.com
http://www.fearlessfighters.com/

Smak Zone Paintball
Rte 1 Box Z-12
Patterson, Missouri 63956
mwm@smakzone.com
http://www.smakzone.com

66 Paintball
16219 Route 66
Philipsburg, Missouri 65722
417 589 2677
http://www.66paintball.com

Shockzone Paintball
State Highway 160
Poplar Bluff, Missouri 63901
573-989-3515
shockzonepaintball@ruralroute.net
http://www.shockzonepaintball.com

The Front
Richmond, Missouri 64085
http://paintballthefront.com

The Bing Shop
1010 South Dr
Saint Charles, Missouri 63301
636-724-6666

Paint Games Plus
1411 W. Kearney St.
Springfield, Missouri 65803
417-866-8862
paintgames@sbcglobal.net
http://www.paintgamesplus.com

Springfield Paintball
2160 E. Blaine
Springfield, Missouri 65802
(417) 869-4263
http://www.springfieldpaintball.com

MO-JO Paintball
4807 Saint Joseph Avenue
St Joseph, Missouri 64505
816-387-7111
doc@mojopb.com
http://www.mojopb.com

No Hard Feelings
155 Blunt Rd.
Steelville, Missouri 65565
(573) 786-7422
nhfpaint@msn.com
http://www.nohardfeelingspaint-
ball.lbu.com

Sullivan Paintball
Sullivan, Missouri 63080
573-468-3807
info@sullivanpb.com
http://www.sullivanpb.com

Wacky Warriors Paintball
(Wentzville)
Wentzeville, Missouri 63385
paintbal@wackywarriors.com
http://www.wackywarriors.com/

Top Dog Paintball
215 N. Lindsey Rd.
Winfield, Missouri 63389
314-420-4798
topdogpaintball@lycos.com
http://www.topdogpaintball.net

MONTANA

Mark'em Village
799 Big Hole St
Belgrade, Montana 59718
406.539.3823
info@markempaintball.com
http://www.markempaintball.com

Diamond Paintball
Billings, Montana 59105
questions@diamondpaintball.com
http://www.diamondpaintball.com

Glacier Paintball
1 mile south of the hwy 40 & 2
Columbia Falls, Montana 59901
406-250-7301
http://www.glacierpaintball.com

Darkside Paintball
1518 Tower Street
Missoula, Montana 59803
406-880-2628
admin@darksidepaintball.org
http://www.darksidepaintball.org

Speedball Freak
2098-2099 Twin Creeks Way
Ronan, Montana 59864
406-212-2320
info@speedballfreak.com
http://speedballfreak.com

Awesome Paintball
Highway 21
Simms, Montana 59477
406-899-5800
http://www.awesomepaintball.com

NEBRASKA

High Altitude Paintball
2312 LaPlatte Road
Bellevue, Nebraska 68123
402-250-1508
travis@highaltitudepaintball.com
http://www.highaltitudepaintball.
com

Slaughter Zone
12243 S 190th St
Bennet, Nebraska 68317
432-1442
slaughter_ Zone@yahoo.com
http://www.geocities.com/
slaughter_zone

A L L Paint
Riverlane Ranch
Grand Island, Nebraska 68980
(308) 379-3582
allpaint@gmail.com

Splatterbox
Hershey, Nebraska 69143
308.534.8153
info@splatterbox.org
http://splatterbox.org

Warped Sportz Paintball Park
1206 Ave M
Kearney, Nebraska 68847
308-234-9277
warpedsportz@warpedsportz.com

Mad Cow Paintball
11212 Cedar Creek Road
Louisville, Nebraska 68037
(402) 234-2024
teri@madcowpaintball.com
http://www.madcowpaintball.com

Ker'Splat Paintball
9006 Maple St
Omaha, Nebraska 68134
402-573-6858
fred@kersplatpaintball.com
http://www.kersplatpaintball.com

Twin Creek Paintball
Orleans, Nebraska 68966
ksrobert@csb.swnebr.net

Husker Paintball Adventures
Split Drive
Plattsmouth, Nebraska 68048
402-291-5041
val@huskerpaintball.com
http://www.huskerpaintball.com

CJ's Paintball
Hwy 33 and S.W. 14th
Sprague, Nebraska 68438
cjslincoln@alltel.net
http://www.cjslincoln.com

NEVADA

Herbies Paintball
P.O. Box 2434
Fernley, Nevada 89408
neil@herbiespaintball.com
http://www.herbiespaintball.com

Desert Storm Paintball
Las Vegas, Nevada 89128
(702)595-2555

Paintball Fields at Event Center LV
121 E. Sunset Road
Las Vegas, Nevada 89119
702-457-6900
http://www.sportcenteroflasve-
gas.com

Westside Paintball
2550 S. Rainbow Blvd. E-2
Las Vegas, Nevada 89146
702-227-6621
Westsidepaintball@earthlink.net
http://www.westsidepaintballlv.com

Pahrump Paintball Complex
6095 H & S Lane
Pahrump, Nevada 89048
775-727-1453
pahrumppaintball@aol.com
http://www.pahrumppaintball.com

HPA Sports
2450 Valley Rd
Reno, Nevada 89512
(775) 324-7486
http://www.hpasports.com

Tonopah Paintball
#1 Ray Tennant Rd.
Tonopah, Nevada 89049
775-482-6336
tonopahpaintball@lnett.com
http://www.tonopahnevada.com

NEW BRUNSWICK

Renegade Paintball
Bathurst, New Brunswick
renegadepaintball@hotmail.com

Apocalypse Paintball
Edmundston, New Brunswick
Apocalypse_Paul@hotmail.com

Alantic Archery Center/ Capital
City Paintball, Fredericton
New Brunswick
http://www.atlanticarcheryand-
paintball.ca/

Lameque Paintball Equipment Enr.
64 Rue De L'Ecole
Lameque, New Brunswick
E8T 1B6
(506) 344-8163
patn@nb.sympatico.ca
http://www.lamequepaintball.com

Inferno Painball Feild
Sutton Rd.
Miramichi, New Brunswick
E1N 4E1

Combat Zone
Dieppe, Moncton
New Brunswick
382-6045
colsen@nb.sympatico.ca
http://www.combatzone.ca

Domus Silvae
Elmwood Drive
Moncton, New Brunswick
E1A 7G1
(866) 857-0707
don@domussilvae.ca
http://www.domussilvae.ca

Mystique Paintball
59 Till Rd.
Perth-Andover, New Brunswick
E7H 4Z4
506-273-1809
mystiquepaintball@hotmail.com
http://www.mystiquepaintball.picz
o.com

Megiddo
19520 Route 2 Highway
River de Chute, New Brunswick
506-391-5457
info@megiddo.ca
http://www.megiddo.ca

Hurricane Paintball
Grandbay Westfield
Saint John, New Brunswick
(506)650-3092
http://hurricanepaintball.piczo.com

Tornado Paintball
29 GreenHead Rd.
Saint John, New Brunswick
E2M 5N7
(506)696-6966

NEW HAMPSHIRE

OSG Paintball
1053 North Barnstead Road
Center Barnstead, New Hampshire
03225
1-800-707-PLAY
osgpaintball@yahoo.com
http://www.osgpaintball.com

Party Time Paintball
3849 Claremont Rd (RT 12)
Charlestown, New Hampshire
03603
603-542-9351
PartyTimeFFZ@aol.com
http://www.PartyTimeFFZ.com

E & R Paintball
502 Route 4
Enfield, New Hampshire 03748
1-866-GOT-BALS
http://www.erpaintball.com

Owen's Farm Paintball
Route 175
Holderness, New Hampshire 03245
http://www.owensfarmpaintball.com

Vindico Sports
PO Box 756
Lincoln, New Hampshire 03251
603-745-8525
http://www.vindicosports.com

Granite State paintball
273 Derry Road
Litchfield, New Hampshire 03052
(603) 491-2839
granitestatepaintball@yahoo.com
http://www.granitestatepaintball.
com

Madison Paintball Club
Madison, New Hampshire 03849
mpbclub@madison-paintball-
club.com
http://www.madison-paintball-
club.com

Martel Ventures Paintball
317 Brushwood Road
North Haverhill, New Hampshire
03774
(603) 787-9052
martelventures@earthlink.net
http://www.martelventures.com/
index.htm

Adventure Games Paintball
Weare, New Hampshire 03281
http://www.agpaintball.com

Frontline Paintball
20 Snow Rd.
Winchester, New Hampshire 03470
603-239-4840
info@gofrontlinepaintball.com
http://www.gofrontlinepaintball.com

Canobie Paintball
47 Roulston Rd
Windham, New Hampshire 03087
(603) 893 1863
contact@canobiepaintball.com
http://www.canobiepaintball.com

NEW JERSEY

B. Bonds Grand Slam
910 Oak Tree Ave
South Plainfield, New Jersey 07080
908-756-4446
info@BBondsgrandslam.com
http://www.bbondsgrandslam.com

Blackbeard's Cave
136 Route 9
Bayville, New Jersey 08721
(732) 286-4414
http://www.blackbeardscave.com/
bbc/act_pb.html

PaintBall Thunder
1345 Hurffville Rd, Rt.41
Deptford, New Jersey 08096
856-227-7500
information@paintballthunderon-
line.com
http://www.paintballthunderon-
line.com

EHT PAL Paintball
2590 Ridge Ave. EHT
Egg Harbor Township, New Jersey
08234
609-645-8413
wklearning@comcast.net
http://www.ehtpal.com/paint-
ball.htm

New Jersey Reball Center
204 Passaic Avenue
Fairfield, New Jersey 07004
973.575.0002
http://www.njreballcenter.com

ABC Paintball
1745 Greenwood Lake Trpk
Hewitt, New Jersey 07421
http://www.abcpaintball.com

Top Gun Paintball Games
567 Monmouth Rd
Jackson, New Jersey 08527
732-928-2810
topgun@csionline.net
http://www.topgunpaintball.com

Cousins Paintball
Manchester, New Jersey 08753
1 800 FLAG 007
http://www.playpaintball.com/

Gino's Mini Golf and Paintball
671 Bridgeton Pike
Mantua, New Jersey 08051
(856) 468-1643
manager@ginosgolfandpaintball.com
http://www.ginosgolfandpaint-
ball.com/

CountyPaintball Club
5378 Route 49
Millville, New Jersey 08332
mike@countypaintball.com
http://www.countysports.com/pai
ntball/club/club.htm

E.T. Paintball Park
Netcong, New Jersey 07857
(973) 347-FUNN
etsales@etpaintball.com
http://www.etpaintball.com/Park/
index.htm

Paintball Authority
104 Texas Road
Old Bridge, New Jersey 08857
(732) 656-3320
http://www.oldbridgepaintball-
club.com/

Fireball Mountain Paintball Games
(Old Bridge)
1959 Englishtown Rd (Rt 527)
Oldbridge, New Jersey 08831
(732)-656-9566
fireballmountain2@hotmail.com
http://www.fireballmountain.com

Del Hobbies Paintball
322 Artillery Ave
Pedricktown, New Jersey 08067
http://www.delhobbies.com

On Target Paintball
35 Sheep Pen Hill Rd
Pemberton, New Jersey 08068
(609) 894-4330
on-target@erols.com
http://www.ontargetpaintball.com

Pyro Paintball
SandBridge rd
Pittsgrove, New Jersey 08318
856-933-2884
chuck@pyropaintball.org
http://www.pyropaintball.org/

Campbell's Paintball
1000 State Highway 47
Rio Grande, New Jersey 08242
609-889-0004

E-Jam Paintball (Indoor)
208 Huyler St
South Hackensack, New Jersey
07606
201-487-6542
info@ejampb.com
http://www.ejampb.com

Atlas Paintball Park
339 Route 31 South
Washington, New Jersey 07882
908-689-8050
atlaspaintballpark@verizon.net
http://www.atlaspaintballpark.com

E-Jam Paintball (Outdoor)
625 Macopin Road
West Milford, New Jersey 07480
973-208-7825
info@ejampb.com
http://www.ejampb.com

NJ Paintball Club
Weaver Road
West Milford, New Jersey 07480
973-838-7493
contact@njpaintball.com
http://www.njpaintball.com

Paintball Depot
1204 Union Valley Road
West Milford, New Jersey 07480
(973) 584-2220
http://www.paintballdepot.com

Shooters 365
492 US HWY. 22 West
Whitehouse Station, New Jersey
08889
rooster@shooters365.com
http://www.shooters365.com

Accurate Paintball
1535 N. Tuckahoe Road
Williamstown, New Jersey 08094
856-629-7509
fsantos1@comcast.net
http://Accuratepaintball.com

Paintball Invasion
192 S. Route 73
Winslow, New Jersey 08037
609-704-7787
http://www.paintballInvasion.com

Picasso Lake Paintball
Winslow Township, New Jersey
08095
1-800-21-FIELD
Picpaintbl@aol.com
http://www.picassolake-
paintball.com

Fireball Mountain Paintball Games
(North Hanover)
281 Meany Rd.
Wrightstown, New Jersey 08562
(609)758-0855
fireballmountain2@hotmail.com
http://www.fireballmountain.com

NEW MEXICO

Hinkle Super Challenge Paintball
12931 Indian School Road NE
Albuquerque, New Mexico 87112
(505) 299-3100
colleenjwyatt@aol.com
http://www.hinklefamilyfuncen-
ter.com/index.htm

Paint-Ball Action (PBA)
9808 Central SE
Albuquerque, New Mexico 87123
505-332-3310
http://www.paint-ballaction.com

Valley Diesel Paintball
2101 North Roselawn
Artesia, New Mexico 88210
505-746-9530

All American Paintball
2029 S Prince
Clovis, New Mexico 88101

Casel-Land Fun Center
Clovis, New Mexico 88101
505 742-1356

Splatter Zone Paintball
2029 S. Prince
Clovis, New Mexico 88101

Urban Survivors
Los Alamos, New Mexico 87505
sprueitt@losalamos.com
http://www.urbansurvivors.com/

Rio Rancho Paintball
4051 Sara Road SE
Rio Rancho, New Mexico 87124
(505) 891-1823

CJ's Paintball Park
Located off Exit 152 on I-25
Socorro, New Mexico 87801
(505)507-2008
armijocj@hotmail.com
http://www.cjspaintballpark.50meg
s.com

NEW YORK

First Prize Paintball
245 Morris Road
Albany, New York 12206
(518) 449-BALL (2255)
info@firstprizepaintball.com
http://www.firstprizepaintball.com/

High Energy Paintball
4755 RT-30
Amsterdam, New York 12010
nexus@highenergypaintball.com
http://www.highenergypaintball.com/

Hornetsnest Paintball
746 Roche Lane
Ancramdale, New York 12503
518-329-2255
bobm@hornetsnestpaintball.net
http://www.hornetsnest
paintball.net

Combat Zone Paintball Park
3060 Gates Road
Auburn, New York 13021
315-277-1120
http://thecombatzonepaintball.com/

Extreme Action Sports
7249 Van Buren Road
Baldwinsville, New York 13027
315-635-1158
info@easpaintball.com
http://www.easpaintball.com

High Velocity Paintball Indoor Field
235 South Fehr Way
Bay Shore, New York 11706
info@hivipaintball.com
http://www.hivipaintball.com

GRC Paintball
5907 Vanallen Road
Belfast, New York 14711
585-466-3050
Rob@GRCPaintball.net
http://www.GRCpaintball.net

Elementz Paintball
245 old rte 11
Canton, New York 13617
315-386-2141
field@elementzpaintball.com
http://www.elementzpaintball.com

Hyper-Son Paintball Inc.
7572 State Route 5
Clinton, New York 13323
315-853-7529
Hyperp8nt@hotmail.com
http://www.hypersonpaintball.com

AAA Paintball Park (Constantia)
303 County Rte 23
Constantia, New York 13212
http://www.aaapaintballpark.com/

Grand Slam Paintball
Route 28
Cooperstown, New York 13326
607-437-1637
http://www.grandslampaintball.info

Cousins Paintball
of Coram Long Island
Coram, New York 11727
http://www.playpaintball.com/

High Velocity II
Outdoor Paintball Field
426 Mill Road
Coram, New York 11727
(631) 242-2096
info@highvelocitypaintball.com
http://www.hivipaintball.com

Agape Farms Paintball
4839 Rt 9N
Corinth, New York 12822
518-654-7777
http://www.geocities.com/
agapefarm

ABV (Accuracy by Volume) Paintball
Corning, New York 14870
607-962-1140
abvpaintball@yahoo.com
http://www.abvpaintball.com

TNT Extreme Paintball
780 Campbell Road
Earlville, New York 13332
315-837-4200
tntextreme@tntextremepaintball.com
http://www.tntextremepaintball.com

Fury Paintball
1404 State Rout 5
Elbridge, New York 13060
315-689-9339
info@furypaintball.net
http://www.Furypaintball.net

Route 4 Paintball
Fort Ann, New York 12827
http://www.route4paintball.com

Cousins Indoor Paintball
114 Parkway Drive South
Hauppauge, New York 11788
info@cousinspaintball.com
http://www.playpaintball.com

Operation Paint
3400 County Line Road
Holley, New York 14430
http://www.operationpaint.com

Ithaca Paintball
619 West State Street
Ithaca, New York 14850
jspada@twcny.rr.com
http://www.ithacapaintball.com

Jello Factory Paintball
57 North Street
Le Roy, New York 14482
(585) 768-9380
info@jellofactorypaintball.com
http://jellofactorypaintball.com/

Summerhill Paintball
5903 Howell Rd.
Locke, New York 13092
(607) 898-4256
http://www.summerhillpaintball.com

Head Hunters
3652 Ewings Rd.
Lockport, New York 14094
716-778-0742
headhunters1@zoomshare.com
http://www.headhunters1.zoomsha
re.com/

New York City Paintball
47-11 Van Dam Street
Long Island City, New York 11101
1-888-PBALLNY
info@newyorkcitypaintball.com
http://www.newyorkcitypaintball.
com/

Pine Hill Paintball
3411 Pine Hill Rd.
Marathon, New York 13803
(607) 849 4115
info@pinehillpaintball.com
http://www.pinehillpaintball.com/

Montgomery Sporting Goods
380 Bartbull Dr.
Middletown, New York 10941
845-457-4678
MSGPaintball@aol.com

Ring Homestead Camp
257 Lybolt Road
Middletown, New York 10941
Info@ringhomesteadcamp.com
http://www.ringhomesteadcamp.
com

Crazy Paint
1949 East Main Street
Mohegan Lake, New York 10547
914-526-0806
http://www.crazypaint.net

Paintball Madness North
Monticello, New York 10941
http://www.paintballny.com/

Albany Paintball Emporium
3167 Columbia Turnpike
Nassau, New York 12123
(518) 452-4373
alex@albanypaintball.com
http://www.albanypaintball.com

Club PB of WNY
665 River Rd
North Tonawanda, New York 14120
716-725-8966
clubpbwny@hotmail.com
http://www.freewebs.com/club
pbwny/

Extreme Paintball Park
Route 12
Norwich, New York 13815
(607)-334-2001
mail@norwichpaintball.com
http://www.norwichpaintball.com/

Adrenaline Zone Paintball
134 Forest Way
Otego, New York 13825
607-432-7465
patrick22j@usadatanet.net
http://cooperstownusa.com/adren
alinezonepaintball/

El Ranch De Paz
2857 Montrose Turnpike
Owego, New York 13827
(607) 687-2238
elranchodepaz@aol.com
http://www.elranchodepaz.org

R&M Paintball
445 Miller Beach Road
Owego, New York 13827
607-754-5018
Brett@randmpaintball.com
http://www.randmpaintball.com

Liberty Paintball
Rt. 22 South
Patterson, New York 12563
(845)878-6300
http://www.libertypaintball-
ny.com/

Red's Paintball
31 Clair St.
Pine Valley, New York 14872
607-795-0411
redpb@stny.rr.com
http://www.redspaintball.com

Cousins Paintball of Newburg /
Formerly Survival New York
Camp Sunset Road
Plattekill, New York 12568
info@cousinspaintball.com
http://www.playpaintball.com

Champion Paintball
39 Degarmo Road
Poughkeepsie, New York 12603
845-462-1304
service@championpaintball.com
http://www.championpaintball.com/

3 Guys Games & Paintball
Queensbury, New York 12804
(518) 792-8845
http://www.3guysgames.com

POW Paintball
3435 New Rd
Ransomville, New York 14131
pow_paintball@yahoo.com
http://www.powpaintball.com

Joshua's Paintball Jungle
1039 N. Greece Road
Rochester, New York 14626
JPJ@fbbc.info
http://www.joshuaspaintball
jungle.com

NVP-Paintball
1046 University Ave.
Rochester, New York 14607
585-473-7529
info@NVP-Paintball.com
http://www.nvp-paintball.com

The War Club
7624 Watson Hollow Rd
Rome, New York 13440
(315) 337-6259
http://www.thewarclub.com

Spazz Paintball
160 Malden Tpk Bld 3
Saugerties, New York 12477
845-24P-AINT
http://www.spazzpaintball.com

Rickz Gamez
619 W. SPEARS RD
Silver Creek, New York 14136
716-934-4316
info@rickzgamez.com
http://www.rickzgamez.com/

Paintball Quest NY
5610 South Geneva Road
Sodus, New York 14551
315-483-4951
http://www.PBQNY.com

Tater Wilderness Paintball
6188 Vermont Hill Rd.
South Wales, New York 14139
716-655-7580
taterspaintball@cs.com
http://www.taterspaintball.com

My Uncle's Paintball Field
109 Main Street
Sparrowbush, New York 12780
845-856-3387
sales@myunclespaintball.com
http://www.myunclespaintball.com

Staten Island Paintball
2727 Arthur Kill Road
Staten Island, New York 10309
info@sipaintball.com
http://www.sipaintball.com/

AAA Paintball Park (Syracuse)
1020 Hiawatha Blvd West
Syracuse, New York 13204
315-472-9988
deona21@hotmail.com
http://www.aaapaintballpark.com

HeadRush Syracuse
3417 Walters Rd
Syracuse, New York 13209
315-453-RUSH
mike@headrush.com
http://www.headrush.com

Play To Win Paintball Indoor
222 Chapel Dr.
Syracuse, New York 13219
315-487-7887
MikeG@playtowinpaintball.com
http://www.playtowinpaintball.com

HeadRush Rochester
160 School St.
Victor, New York 14564
585-398-1220
info@headrush.com
http://www.headrush.com

Discoveries USA
4498 State Route 9
Warrensburgh, New York 12885
518-623-4567
discover@discoveriesusa.com
http://www.discoveriesusa.com

Northside Paintball Sports
120 Breen Ave., Watertown NY
Watertown, New York 13601
315 782-3050
info@nspbs.com
http://www.nspbs.com

Island Paintball Arena
400 Patton Ave.
West Babylon, New York 11704
(631) 694-2707
anthony@islandpaintball.net
http://www.islandpaintball.net

Paintball Arena
400 Patton Avenue
West Babylon, New York 11704
anthonyjr@islandpaintball.net
http://www.islandpaintball.net

Mountain Invasion Paintball
Windham, New York 12496
http://windhammountain.com/summer/html/pnt_home.php

NEWFOUNDLAND AND LABRADOR

Paintball Adventures
Corner Brook
Newfoundland and Labrador
don.anstey@nf.sympatico.ca
http://www.paintballadventures.cjb.net

Paintball TAG Rentals
Nicholsville
Deer Lake, Newfoundland and
Labrador A8A 1V4
paintballtag@hotmail.com
http://www.freewebs.com/paintballtag

Front Line Paintball
Mount Pearl, Newfoundland and
Labrador

Hellhounds Paintball Club
St. John's, Newfoundland and
Labrador A1L 2B2
Hellhoundspaintball@hotmail.com
http://www.hellhoundspaintball.cjb.net

Frontline Paintball
1152 Topsail road
St.John's, Newfoundland and
Labrador A1N 3L6
747-4653
http://www.newfoundlandpaintball.com

NORTH CAROLINA

Carolina Paint Slingers
1500 Richey Rd.
Taylorsville, North Carolina 28681
828-495-4100

Madd Paintball
Cranberry Road
Boonville, North Carolina 27011
336-468-2441
maddpaintball04@yahoo.com
http://www.maddpaintball.com

BlackHawk Paintball
240 Water Springs Hollow Road
Burnsville, North Carolina 28714
828-765-3799
blackhawkball@bellsouth.net
http://www.uswoodsball.com

Carolina Paintball Park
480 Beaver Loop
China Grove, North Carolina 28023
http://www.carolinapbsite.com/

Wicked Sports Paintball Complex
340 Beaver Loop
China Grove, North Carolina 28023
support@wicked-sports.com
http://www.wicked-sports.com

Hematoma Paintball
607 Haw Branch Rd
Chocowinity, North Carolina 27817
(252) 975 2289
http://www.hematomapaintball.com/
NC Tactical Paintball
372 Davis Ave.
Clemmons, North Carolina 27012
336.782.9556
williamboyterpr@yahoo.com
http://www.nctacticalpaintball.com

Black River Paintball
526 Carson Gregory Road
Coats, North Carolina 27521
allen@brpaintball.com
http://www.brpaintball.com/

Triangle Paintball
7312 Hwy 98th
Durham, North Carolina 27703
(919) 598-5000

Pirate Paintball
644 Old Hertford Highway
Elizabeth City, North Carolina 27909
757-287-2537
piratepaintball@cox.com
http://www.piratepaintballfield.com

Danny's Paintball
436 Flack Road
Forest City, North Carolina 28043
828-247-1070
http://www.DannysPaintball.com

Toms Paintball Supplies
200 Coffey Road
Forest City, North Carolina 28043
828-289-2557
store@tomspaintball.com
http://www.tomspaintball.com

Freedom Paintball
Fort Bragg, North Carolina 28307
910-860-4469
http://www.freedompaintballusa.com/

Nature of the Game
13200 Hwy 17
Hampstead, North Carolina 28443
910-270-4898
notg@charterinternet.com
http://www.notgpaintball.com

Camp Splat Paintball
3600 Weldons Mill Rd
Henderson, North Carolina 27537
orion@gloryroad.net
http://www.campsplat.com

Wolverine Paintball
500 Brookside Camp Rd.
Hendersonville, North Carolina
28792
828-697-4263
http://www.wolvpb.com

Lockes Paintball Field
17 Blue Valley Rd.
Highlands, North Carolina 28741
828 787 2427
ncpaintballman@aol.com

Predator Paintball(NC)
1113 Kenion Road
Hillsborough, North Carolina 27278
(919)-732-6327
Ronin14@msn.com
http://predatorpaintball.org

Line of Fire Paintfields
923 Gilreath Loop Rd
Horse Shoe, North Carolina 28742
loftjg316@aol.com
http://www.lofpb.com

Coastal Paintball
2586 Wilmington Highway
Jacksonville, North Carolina 28540
http://www.coastalpaintball.com

Milty's
6192 Richlands Hwy
Jacksonville, North Carolina 28574
910-324-5401
miltys@miltys.com
http://www.miltys.com

The Sportsmans Lodge
Jacksonville, North Carolina 28546
910-937-6334

Carolina Paintball
King, North Carolina 27021
336-983-8067
http://www.carolinapaintball.com/

Gold Diggers
Meadow Creek Church Rd.
Locust, North Carolina 28211
info@bossproshops.com
http://www.bossproshops.com

Blue Ridge Paintball Park
1007 Fairview Road
Marion, North Carolina 28752
828-652-2590
shoot@blueridgepaintball.com
http://www.blueridgepaintball.com

Paintball Kingdom
2407 Ansonville Road
Marshville, North Carolina 28103
smoke@paintballkingdom.com
http://www.paintballkingdom.com

CJ's Paintball
13720 HWY 601 South
Midland, North Carolina 28107
ken@cjspaintball.com
http://www.cjspaintball.com

Scrap that Paintball (Indoor)
525 Purser Street
Monroe, North Carolina 28110
704-361-5874
customersupport@scrapthatpaint-
ball.com
http://www.scrapthatpaintball.com

Scrap That Paintball (Outdoor)
1411 Tom Boyd Rd
Monroe, North Carolina 28110
704-361-5874
customersupport@scrapthatpaint-
ball.com
http://www.Scrapthatpaintball.com

Swing Zone Family Fun Park
4605 East US Highway 70
New Bern, North Carolina 28560
252-634-GAME
info@swingzone.net
http://www.swingzone.net

Veteran's Field
North Wilkesboro, North Carolina
28659
336-838-3606
PMuellerfamily@earthlink.net
http://www.wilkespaintball.com

Real McCoy Paintball
9395 Hwy 70 East
Princeton, North Carolina 27569
mccoypaintball@aol.com
http://www.mccoypaintball.com

Rocky Mount Paintball Complex
7500 Highway 4
Rocky Mount, North Carolina 27809
252-446-2854
josh@rockymountpaintball.com
http://www.rockymountpaintball.
com

Gotcha Paintball
176 Darius Pearce Rd.
Rolesville, North Carolina 27571
god@gotchapaintball.com
http://www.gotchapaintball.com

PBC Sports Park
6106 Burlington Rd.
Sedalia, North Carolina 27249
(336) 228-3800
field@pballcentral.com
http://www.pballcentral.com/

Wolf Creek
1311 Spies Rd.
Star, North Carolina 27356
910-220-7184
http://www.wolfcreekpaintball.com

The Meadow Paintball
Mountain Park Road
State Road, North Carolina 28676
336-874-7525
http://www.TheMeadowPaintball.com

Adventure Beach Paintball
85 Lays Lake Dr.
Tabor City, North Carolina 28463
Ellis@adventurebeach.com
http://www.adventurebeach.com

Command Decisions Paintball
84 Reganswood Drive
Taylorsville, North Carolina 28681
(828) 495-4155
ferg@cdpaintball.com
http://www.cdpaintball.com

North Carolina Paintball Park
Thomasville, North Carolina 27360
336-292-1102
info@ncpbonline.com
http://www.ncpbonline.com

Long Branch Paintball
2790 Ten Mile Fork Rd.
Trenton, North Carolina 28585
252-448-1614
longbranchpb@hotmail.com

Gotcha Covered Paintball
1995 Juniper Lake Rd
West End, North Carolina 27376
910-295-9703

A Great Escape
8 Funtime Blvd.
Winston-Salem, North Carolina
27103
336-725-1150
jim@agreatescape.net
http://www.agreatescape.net

Xtremist Paintball
735 McGregor Rd.
Winston-Salem, North Carolina
27127
336-830-2959
xtremist_paintball@hotmail.com
http://www.xtremistpaintball.com

Dickens Farm Paintball Field
3605 Horseshoe Rd.
Yadkinville, North Carolina 27055
336-463-4344
http://www.dickensfarmpaintball.
com/

NORTH DAKOTA

Prairie Paintball
1131 59th Ave SW
Beulah, North Dakota 58523
701-873-2305
prairiepaintball@hotmail.com
http://freewebs.com/prairie
paintball

Valley Paintball
Sabin MN
Fargo, North Dakota 58103
701-367-1931
webmaster@valleypaintball.com
http://www.valleypaintball.com

Goose River Paintball
Hillsboro, North Dakota 58045
701-610-6197
erstad@gooseriverpaintball.com
http://www.gooseriverpaintball.com

Combat Ranch
216 1st West
Jamestown, North Dakota 58401
701-320-7660
webmaster@combatranch.com
http://www.combatranch.com

NOVA SCOTIA

Black Watch Paintball
Barrington, Nova Scotia
902-637-3426
info@blackwatchpaintball.com
http://www.blackwatchpaintball.com/
Splatter Zone Paintball
Beaver Bank, Nova Scotia B4C 1C7
902-497-9821

Never Blink Twice Paintball
Guysburo, Nova Scotia
1-877-628-8988
http://www.nbtpaintball.com

Mersey Road Paintball
292 Mersey Road, East River
Hubbards, Nova Scotia
902-857-9745
merseyroad@merseyroad.com
http://www.merseyroad.com/

Storm Warning Paintball Games
Lakewood Rd and Saxon St.
Kentville, Nova Scotia B4N 2P2
sales@brucesonline.com
http://www.brucesonline.com

Overkill Sportz (Indoor & Outdoor)
41 Etter Rd (exit #3 on HWY 101)
Mount Uniacke, Nova Scotia
B3G 1H4
(902) 830-2376
overkillsportz@ns.sympatico.ca
http://www.overkillsportz.com

Splatz Insane Paintball
52 Tanner Hill Rd.
Salt Springs, Nova Scotia B0K 1P0
902-754-9805
Ryan@Splatz.ca
http://www.splatz.ca

Ambush Gardens Paintball
1498 Gays River Road
Shubenacadie, Nova Scotia B0N
2H0
(902) 956-1358
ambushgardens@hotmail.com
http://ambushgardens.tripod.com

Ballistic Paintball
Tatamagouche, Nova Scotia B0K 1V0
1-902-657-2034
jasonlangille@canada.com
http://www.geocities.com/
ballistic_paintball_tata

Armymans Paintball
1082 Salmon River Road
Truro, Nova Scotia
(902) 899-8183
armymans@armymanspaintball.com
http://www.armymanspaintball.com

SNL Paintball
2782 No. 311 Hwy North River
Truro, Nova Scotia B2N 5B4

Hawkeye Ridge Paintball
RR#1 Tusket
Yarmouth, Nova Scotia B0W 3M0
http://www.hawkeyeridge
paintball.piczo.com

OHIO

3D Sports
13500 Union Ave.
Alliance, Ohio 44601
330-821-5666
threedsports@aol.com
http://fairwind.net/3DSports/

Paintball Madness
1601 Homeworth Avenue
Alliance, Ohio 44601

TPA (Total Paintball Addicts)
1601 Homeworth Ave
Alliance, Ohio 44601
330-823-9692
tpapaintball@yahoo.com
http://www.totalpaintballaddicts.
com

Blister Park
3142 Pymatuning Lake Road
Andover, Ohio 44003
(440) 813-3252
info@blisterpaintball.com
http://www.blisterpark.com

GoodTimes Sharp Shooter Paintball
33777 Chester Rd.
Avon, Ohio 44011
440-937-6210
http://www.goodtimesfun.com

Xtreme Combatzone Paintball
3299 St. Rt. 540
Bellefontaine, Ohio 43311
937-539-8660
xtreme_combatzone_paintball@hot
mail.com
http://www.kindweb.com/xtreme-
combatzone

Great Lakes Paintball
11903 Dining Rd
Bellevue, Ohio 44811
(419)483-7800
Jim@GreatLakesPaintball.com
http://www.greatlakespaintball.com

Paintball Xcape
7320 Myers Rd NE
Bloomingburg, Ohio 43106
614.390.9789
warpedsportz27@yahoo.net
http://www.deliriouspb.com/Paint
ballXcape/Home%20page.htm

Rocky Fork Recreational
Cabridge, Ohio 43725

Splat Paintball
333a Lafayette
Canal Fulton, Ohio 44614
330-323-7706
Gable19@yahoo.com
http://www.splatpaintball.org

Intense Paintball
3000 Atlantic Blvd NE
Canton, Ohio 44705
330-456-3456
Intense@intensepaintball.net
http://www.intensepaintball.net

Lost City Paintball /
Victory Hill Church
4000 Coonpath Rd
Carrol, Ohio 43112
740-756-7563
vhyouth@victoryhill.org
http://www.victoryhill.org

Pinnacle Woods Paintball
10241 Old State Rd.
Chardon, Ohio 44024
pinnwoods@aol.com
http://www.pinnaclewoods
paintball.com

Steve's Paintball
12810 Heath Rd
Chesterland, Ohio 44026
stevespaintball@aol.com

Paintball Junkeez - First Baptist
Church of Mt. Healthy
1210 Compton Rd.
Cincinnati, Ohio 45231
tpnewman23@hotmail.com
http://paintballjunkeez.com/

Paintball Proshop and Customizing
(PPC)
5490 Mclean Mill Rd.
Circleville, Ohio 43113
(740) 477-6237
contactppc@aol.com
http://www.PPCPaintballProshop.
com

Hueston Woods Paintball Club
College Corner, Ohio 45003
513-664-3551
tarvan@xanterra.com
http://www.hwpaintball.com/

The Land Paintball
4999 Old Rathmell Court
Columbus, Ohio 43207
614-732-1623
thelandpaintball@yahoo.com
http://thelandpaintball.
servegame.com

Stonegate Paintball
Coolville, Ohio 45723
(740) 350-2252
http://stonegatepaintball.tripod.com

Farmer Jims
Cortland, Ohio 44446
eminem610187@aol.com

Walsh Farms Paintball
18723 Grill Rd.
Doylestown, Ohio 44230
330-658-6125
pwalsh@bright.net
http://walshfarms.net/

Paintball City
20001 Euclid Ave.
Euclid, Ohio 44117
216-404-0400
roger@pbcity.com
http://www.pbcity.com

Prime Time Paintball
3319 State Route 141
Gallipolis, Ohio 45631
(740) 446-8463
milt@theultimatemadness.com

Warpaint Paintball Field
12006 Fenstermaker Rd.
Garretsville, Ohio 44231
(440)-548-2442
http://www.targething.com

Gonzo Paintball
6568 North Ridge West
Geneva, Ohio 44041
house@gonzopaintball.com
http://www.gonzopaintball.com

Cedar Ridge Paintball
13680 Friend Road
Germantown, Ohio 45327
wayne@crpaintball.com
http://www.crpaintball.com

The Silent Sniper
Glenford, Ohio 43739
(740) 344-6920
grigsbyj@thesilentsniper.com
http://www.thesilentsniper.com

Red Dragon Paintball
2726 Lucas Rd.
Hamersville, Ohio 45130
dragonslayer1145@aol.com
http://www.reddragonpaintball.com/

Cabin Creek Paintball
4117 Eaton Road
Hamilton, Ohio 45013
http://www.cabincreekpaintball.com

Paintball Country
5110 Lesourdsville West Chester Rd.
Hamilton, Ohio 45011
billmiller@woh.rr.com
http://www.paintballcountryohio.
com

Pev's of Ohio 8721 Airport Highway
Holland, Ohio 43528
419-868-8417
admin@pevsohio.com
http://www.pevsohio.com

Battlefront Paintball
Rt 304
Hubbard, Ohio 44425
330-766-1253
contactus@battlefrontpaintball.com
http://www.battlefrontpaintball.com

I-70 Paintball
7750 Wildcat Road
Huber Heights, Ohio 45424
937-237-7070
service@i70paintball.com
http://www.I70Paintball.com

Midwest Paintball
5120 Waynesville Jamestown Rd
Jamestown, Ohio 45335
937-675-3755

Mohawk Paintball
453 County Road 2000
Jeromesville, Ohio 44840
(419) 368-4089
http://www.mohawkpaintball.com

The Dude Ranch
Lebanon, Ohio 45036
http://www.theduderanch.com/pa
intball.htm

Paintball Zone
8252 Norwalk Rd
Litchfield, Ohio 44253
330-722-1867
paintballzone@msn.com
http://paintballzoneinc.com

Battle Zone Paintball Park
809 Poth Rd
Mansfield, Ohio 44906
(419) 747-6400
BZpaintballpark@aol.com
http://www.battlezonepaintball-
park.com/

J&J Sporting Goods
220 Casto Rd.
Marietta, Ohio 45750
info@jjpaintball.com
http://www.jjpaintball.com

Marysville Paintball
22840 Johnson Road
Marysville, Ohio 43040
(937) 642-3345
mvpaintbal@midohio.net
http://marysvillepaintball.com

Rapid Fire Paintball
2262 Kenyon Ave. S.W.
Massillon, Ohio 44647
(330) 837-9277
http://www.rapidfirepaintball.8m.c
om

RUSH Paintball
1530 E. Central Ave.
Miamisburg, Ohio 45342
(937) 545-1721
burkhart@rush-paintball.com
http://www.rushpaintball.com

Survivor Paintball
628 Cochran Rd
Midland, Ohio 45148
937-783-0159
http://www.survivorpb.com

Splatter Park
5560 C.R. 109
Mt. Gilead, Ohio 43338
1-888-8-SPLATT
mail@copaintball.com
http://www.splatterpark.com

Valley's Edge Paintball
8295 State Rt. 121
New Paris, Ohio 45347
765.598.4544
info@valleysedgepaintball.com
http://www.valleysedgepaintball.com

Paintball Valley
1909 Dayton Road
Newark, Ohio 43055
740-349-0939
info@paintballvalley.net
http://www.paintballvalley.net

Splatterball Paintball
5027 Stoney Ridge Rd.
North Ridgeville, Ohio 44039
(440) 864-4640
general@splatterballpball.net
http://www.splatterballpball.net/

Paintball Village
8501 Stearns Rd
Olmsted, Ohio 44138
440 235-9900
http://www.paintbvillage.com/

Operation Elimination
11496 Burro Ln
Orient, Ohio 43146
operationelimination2003@yahoo.
com
http://www.operationelimination.
com

Splat Shack Paintball
14849 Fosnight Rd.
Orrville, Ohio 44667
330-264-5117
splatshack@netzero.net
http://www.splatshack.com

Fran Bar Park
13861 E. Broad St.
Pataskala, Ohio 43062
http://www.franbarpark.com/mega
paintball.htm

Wild Willy's 2
4700 W State Route 36
Piqua, Ohio 45356
937-773-1902
wildwillysfarmandpet@yahoo.com
http://www.wildwillys2.com

Bull Creek Paintball
9703 Greensburg PK
Portage, Ohio 43451
419-266-4799
rbgames@aol.com
http://www.bullcreekpaintball.org/

Wolfpack Paintball
11990 Old Rainer Rd
Roseville, Ohio 43777
740-697-0833
wolfpackpb@hotmail.com
http://www.freewebs.com/wolf
packpaintball

Cutter's Paintball Valley
1881 Miami-Conservancy Rd
Sidney, Ohio 45365
937-492-6548

Professor Lumpy's
Paintball Academy
County Road 18
Smithfield, Ohio 43948
740-435-0230
spiro@blackcatpaintball.com
http://www.academypaintball.com

Metro Paintball
7968 E. National Road
South Charleston, Ohio 45368
937-605-6267
metropaintball@woh.rr.com
http://www.metro-paintball.com

Greenridge (Free and
Noncommercial)
1939 Green Road
South Euclid, Ohio 44121
bryon4@cox.net
http://www.clevelandpaintball.com

U-Do Paint Games
844 S. Crissy Rd
Toledo, Ohio 43601
419-478-5815
udopaintgames@aol.com
http://www.u-dopaintgames.com

Gaul City Paintball
10135 State Route 160
Vinton, Ohio 45686
740-388-0282
gaulcity@excite.com
http://www.gaulcitypaintball.com

Paintball World Indoor
601 South Main Street
Wellington, Ohio 44090
440-647-9373
http://www.paintballworldohio.com

Bruno's Paintball
204 Electric Park Road
Wellston, Ohio 45692
740-384-6466
bruno@magicohio.com
http://www.brunospaintball.com/

TnT Recreation Paintball
West Layfayette, Ohio 43812
(740)-545-7054

Five Alarm Paintball
28979 Bassett Road
Westlake, Ohio 44145
fivealarmpaintball@hotmail.com
http://www.fivealarmpaintball.com

Poplar Ridge Paintball
2685 Armstrong Rd
Wooster, Ohio 44691
330 345 7949
info@poplaridge.org
http://www.poplaridge.org

Outback Paintball
1280 Spring Valley Alpha Rd
Xenia, Ohio 45385
937-673-1982
Outback@Outbackpaintballfield.com
http://www.outbackpaintballfield.c
om

Seek-N-Destroy Paintball
125 Fairground Rd.
Xenia, Ohio 45385
937-554-1871
shaneanderson@seekanddestroy-
paintball.com
http://www.seekanddestroypaint-
ball.com/

OKLAHOMA

Splatters Paintball
I -35 Exit 40
Ardmore, Oklahoma 73401
580-223-5646
splatters_paintball@yahoo.com
http://www.splatters-
paintball.com

AMS Paintball
Blair, Oklahoma 73521
allen@amspaintball.com
http://amspaintball.com

The Paintball Club of Choctaw
14850 East Reno
Choctaw, Oklahoma 73020
405-613-4611
http://www.paintballfieldclubof-
chowtaw.com

Paintball Land
Collinsville, Oklahoma 74021
(918) 371-4044
PBL@paintballland.com
http://www.paintballland.com

Paintball Ranch
Copan, Oklahoma 74022
918-532-1832
http://www.xanga.com/Paintball-
Ranch

Nightbreed Paintball
109 S. 2nd Maint Street
Durant, Oklahoma 74701
580-924-3115

Adventure Zone
2651 East Seward Rd.
Guthrie, Oklahoma 73044
405-936-0606
http://www.shaggybrotherspaint-
ball.com

Arena Paintball Park
2607 SE 75th Street
Lawton, Oklahoma 73501
paintballpro@lcisp.com
http://www.arenapaintballpro.com

Safari Country Woodsball
8220 SE Flowermound Road
Lawton, Oklahoma 73501
580-353-0748

Thunder Moon Paintball
33440 W 51st Street South
Mannford, Oklahoma 74044
kihsm@thundermoonpaintball.com
http://www.thundermoonpaint-
ball.com

The Paintball Field
500 N Portland Ave
Newcastle, Oklahoma 73065
405-366-7694
http://www.thepaintballfield.com

Adventure World Indoor Paintball
3020 NW 16th St.
Oklahoma City, Oklahoma 73107
405-942-1914
marvin@adventureworldpaintball.
com
http://adventureworldpaintball.com

Green Country Paintball
Oolagah, Oklahoma 74053
(918) 371-7077
http://www.greencountrypaint-
ball.com

Dodge City
Peidmont, Oklahoma 73078
(405)-373-3745
http://www.dodgecitypaintball.com/

Wild West Paintball & Supply Inc.
21251 180th Street
Purcell, Oklahoma 73080
(405) 527-2525
wildwestpb@aol.com
http://www.wildwestpb.com

Paintball Adventure Games
10242 S 49th W. Ave
Sapulpa, Oklahoma 74066
http://www.pbadventuregames.com/

I-40 Paintball Field
I-40 & Indian Meridian Rd
Shawnee, Oklahoma 73145
405-733-9066
http://www.gamedaypaint.net/ind
ex.html

Ball Busters
600 Victor St.
Tahlequah, Oklahoma 74464
1-918-431-2065
ron@tahlequahpaintball.com
http://www.tahlequahpaintball.com

Incredible Paintball
8314 East 71st Street Suite A
Tulsa, Oklahoma 74133
918-392-2820
robert@incrediblepizza.com
http://www.incrediblepaintball.com

Paintball Sports Inc.
3887 W. 43rd Street North
Tulsa, Oklahoma 74127
918-428-7742
mick@psipaintball.com
http://www.psipaintball.com

Paintball Fury
NS204 and EW44
Woodward, Oklahoma 73801
580-254-1854
http://www.paintball-fury.com

The Bunker
68950 E. Hwy 60
Wyandotte, Oklahoma 74370
http://www.oklahomadday.com

ONTARIO

Niagara Paintball Games
2136 Allanport Road
Allanburg, Ontario L0S 1A0
(905) 227-4787
http://www.niagarapaintball-
games.com/

FlagSwipe Outdoor Paintball
Alymer, Ontario N5V 1A1
519-671-9636
info@flagswipepaintball.com
http://www.flagswipepaintball.com

DZ or Dead
Arnprior, Ontario

Tour of Duty
RR#3
Ayton, Ontario N0G 1C0
519-665-7604
tourduty@wightman.ca
http://www.tourduty.com

Georgina Paintball
Baldwin, Ontario L0E 1A0
(905)-722-9066
http://www.georginapaintball.com/

Barrie Paintball Adventure Club
8200 10th Line Essa Twp.
Barrie, Ontario 705-733-3393
barriepaintball@hotmail.com
http://www.barriepaintball.com/

Paintball Wilderness
Belle River, Ontario 519-776-4702
play@paintballwilderness.net
http://www.paintballwilderness.net/index.php

Pro Advantage Paintball
130 Adams Street
Belleville, Ontario K8N 2X9
(613) 967-6557
http://www.proadvantagepaintball.com
Rapidfire Paintball
Gilead Road
Bloomfield, Ontario K0K 1G0
613.399.2280
info@rapidfirepaintball.ca
http://www.rapidfirepaintball.ca

Action Adventure Games
Bowmanville, Ontario L1C 3K4
905-728-3985
actionadventuregames@sympatico.ca
http://www.actionadventuregames.com

Emalkabe's
Bracebridge, Ontario P1L 1S1
705-645-7763
emalkabes@bellnet.ca
http://www.emalkabespaintball.com

Dragonfire Paintball
2500 Williams Parkway
Brampton, Ontario L6S 5M9
905-799-9444
http://www.dragonfirepb.com

Angry Hunters Paintball
80 Rush Road
Brighton, Ontario K0K 1H0
613-475-5617
Angry_Hunters-Paintball
@sympatico.ca
http://www.angryhunterspaintball.50megs.com/

Camp X Paintball
Brooklin, Ontario 1-800-542-8089
Tyson0707@rogers.com
http://www.campxpaintball.tk

RLD Games Limited
350 Brawley Road West
Brooklin, Ontario L1M 1M1
info@rldgames.com
http://www.rldgames.com

Flag Raiders (Outdoor)
1500 Kossuth Road
Cambridge, Ontario 519.653.3322
info@flagraiders.com
http://www.flagraiders.com/

Base Borden Paintball Club
CFB Borden, Ontario L0M 1C0
705-424-1200 x3884
bordenpaintball@f5production.com
http://www.f5production.com/bbpbc/pages/Splash.asp

Ottawa Paintball (Outdoor)
1536 Lacasse St
Clarence-Rockland, Ontario
(613) 745-2515
http://www.ottawapaintball.ca

A&D Paintball
70 Baseline Road,RR#1
Coboconk, Ontario K0M 1K0
705-454-3762
dennis.weedman@sympatico.ca
http://www.a-dpaintball.com

Camp A and D Paintball
Coboconk, Ontario
http://www.a-dpaintball.com

Panic City Paintball
7003 Country Road 45
Cobourg, Ontario K0K 2X0
(905) 349-2800

Xtreme Powerball
24 9th Street East,
Cornwall, Ontario K6H 2T8
613-932-2255

Diehard Paintball
County Road 8
Cottam, Ontario N0R 1B0
Dennis@diehardpaintball.on.ca
http://www.diehardpaintball.on.ca

Shoot to Splatter
1470 Cedar Spring Road
Elmira, Ontario N3B 2Z1
519-669-3916
shoot2splatter@hotmail.com
http://www.shoot2splatter.ca/

Paintball City
35 Stoffel Drive
Etobicoke, Ontario M9W 6A8
info@paintball-city.com
http://www.paintball-city.com/

Ground Zero Paintball
384 Marblerock Rd
Gananoque, Ontario K7G 2V4
marc@groundzeropaintball.ca
http://www.gzpaintball.ca/

Renegade Paintball
490 York Rd.
Guelph, Ontario N1E 6V1
(519) 824 1351
travis@renegadepb.net
http://www.renegadepaintball.ca

Screaming Eagle Paintball
Haliburton, Ontario
705-754-1840
screamingeag@screamingeagle-paintball.com
http://www.screamingeaglepaint-ball.com/default.htm

Cameron Speedway & Paintball
2633 Upper James (Hwy#6 South)
Hamilton, Ontario L0R 1W0
905-679-2122 (ext 30)
shayne@cameronmotorsports.com
http://www.cameronspeedway.com

Paintball Adventures
247 Centennial Parkway North
Hamilton, Ontario
905-560-9281
sales@paintballadventures.ca
http://www.paintballadventures.ca

Quest Paintball Games
Ivanhoe, Ontario K0K 2K0
613-391-7219
info@questpaintballgames.com
http://www.questpaintballgames.com

SMT Paintball (Outdoor)
1560 Abbey Dawn Road
Kingston, Ontario K7L 4V1
smt@smtpaintball.com
http://www.smtpaintball.com/

Flag Raiders (Indoor)
259 Gage Ave
Kitchener, Ontario
(519) 570-2769
info@flagraiders.com
http://flagraiders.com

The Paintball Arena
69 Agnes Street
Kitchener, Ontario N2G 2E9
519-579-7585
thepaintballarena@yahoo.ca
http://www.novicepaintball.com/

General Splatters
HWY 2
Lancaster, Ontario K0C 1N0
613-347-2452

SMT Paintball (Outdoor)
80 Otter Lake Rd
Lombardy, Ontario
smt@smtpaintball.com
http://www.smtpaintball.com/

FlagSwipe Indoor Paintball
529 Philip St.
London, Ontario 519-642-0908
info@flagswipepaintball.com
http://www.flagswipepaintball.com/

SunyJim's Paintball Club
London Area, Ontario N5Y 4W2
sunyjim_paintball@hotmail.com
http://sunyjimspaintballclub.2ya.com

Carnage Paintball
4382 Gregoire Road
Marionville, Ontario K4R 1E5
(613) 229-3207

Bunker's Hideaway Paintball
239 Station Road
Marmora, Ontario K0K 2M0
info@bunkershideawaypaintball.ca
http://www.bunkershideawaypaint-ball.ca

Adrenaline Paintball
6457 Riverside Drive
Melbourne, Ontario 519 453 0434
adrenaline@londonpaintball.com
http://londonpaintball.com

Camp Combat
437 6th Concession Road East.
Millgrove, Ontario L0R 1V0
905-690-4585
info@campcombat.com
http://www.campcombat.com

Ultimate Paintball Adventure
Sideroad #25
Milton, Ontario (905) 893-1815
http://www.ultimatepaintball.ca/

Paintball Nation (Indoor)
6200 Ordan Drive
Mississauga, Ontario L5T 2B3
905-795-8866
info@paintballnation.ca
http://www.paintballnation.ca

Pepiniere Paintball
Moonbeam, Ontario
marslee@hotmail.com

Soldiers of Fortune Paintball
6320 English Church Road
Mount Hope, Ontario L0R 1W0
trevor@sofpaintball.com
http://www.sofpaintball.com

Newcastle Outback Paintball
134 Cowanville
Newcastle, Ontario L1B 1L9
905-987-5391

Ballistic Paintball
294 Roy Drive
North Bay, Ontario P1B 8G3
705-476-1581
info@ballisticpaintball.ca
http://www.ballisticpaintball.ca

M&B Paintball
170 Littledown Lane
North Bay, Ontario P1B 8G2
(705) 472 9055
mbpaintball@sympatico.ca
http://www.mbpaintball.ca

North End Paintball
Oshawa, Ontario

Commando Paintball
Dunning Road South
Ottawa, Ontario
http://www.commandopaintball.ca

Ottawa Paintball (Indoor)
2339 Ogilvie Road
Ottawa, Ontario K1J 8M6
(613) 745-2515
bccincorporated@hotmail.com
http://www.ottawapaintball.ca/

Ottawa X-treme Paintball
Ottawa, Ontario
ottawa_x-treme@rogers.com
http://www.ottawapaintball.com

Paint Storm Paintball Games
1966 Featherston Dr
Ottawa, Ontario K1H 6P8
info@paintstorm.ca
http://www.paintstorm.ca

PSI Paintstorm Indoor
1000 Belfast unit 170
Ottawa, Ontario K1G 4A2
613.244.0188
info@paintstorm.ca
http://www.paintstorm.ca

Sitting Duck Paintball
614 Craig Road, R.R.1
Oxford Mills, Ontario K0G 1S0
613-258-0646
sittingduck@electricbriefcase.com
http://www.sittingduckpaintball.com

Valley Paintball
Biggs Rd.
Pembroke, Ontario K8A 6W6
(613) 732-8326
valleypaintball@hotmail.com
http://www.valleypaintball.ca

Next Paintball
645 Kingston Road
Pickering, Ontario L1V 3N7
(416) 284-0746
info@nextpaintball.com
http://www.nextpaintball.com

Paintball Revolution
Princeton, Ontario N0J 1B0
paintballfrontier@hotmail.com
http://www.paintballrevolution.ca

Bunkers Paintball
664 Queen Street East
Sault Ste. Marie, Ontario P6A 2A4
bunkers@sympatico.ca
http://www.bunkerspaintball.com

Gladiators Paintball Arenas
3475 Danforth Ave.
Scarborough, Ontario M1L 1C9
416-691-1919
http://www.gladiatorspaintballare-
nas.ca/

Splatzone Paintball
23 Colborne St
Simcoe, Ontario N3Y 3T1
1-519-428-2828
splat@kwic.com
http://www.splatzonepaintball.com

SMT Paintball (Indoor)
Smith Falls, Ontario
smt@smtpaintball.com
http://www.smtpaintball.com

Niagara Tactical Adventure Games
St. Catharines, Ontario L2P 1H7
800-823-8694
ntag@sprint.ca
http://www.niagaratactical.com

Paintball Park
Falconbridge Hwy
Sudbury, Ontario P3A 4K4
(705)566-9757
info@paintballpark.ca
http://paintballpark.ca

Camp Splatoon
County Road #6
Teeswater, Ontario
1-519-357-5069
Contact@CampSplatoon.com
http://www.campsplatoon.com

TFS Paintball
RR#2
Thamesville, Ontario N0P 2K0
(519)692-4437
info@tfspaintball.com
http://www.tfspaintball.com

Blue Mountain Paintball
201 Scenic Caves Road
The Blue Mountains, Ontario
L9Y 4S3
705-333-3384
watric@yahoo.com
http://www.georgiantriangle.org/
members/showBusiness.php?mem-
berId=683

DMZ Pursuit Games
Thorold Townline Rd.
Thorold, Ontario
905 988 9000
dmzpaintball@hotmail.com
http://www.dmzpaintball.ca

Paintball Encounters (Outdoor)
Pike Lake Road
Thunder Bay, Ontario P7B 5E3
807-683-7071
tbaypaintball@msn.com
http://www.paintballencounters.com

Area 51 Paintball Sportsfield
Tillsonburg, Ontario N4G 3C4
519-688-0431
info@area-51.on.ca
http://www.area-51.on.ca

Rapid Fire Paintball
Mahoney Road
Timmins, Ontario P4N 4M6
705-268-1825
http://www.rapidfirepaintball.dynu
.ca/

Area 51 Paintball Park (indoor @
Downsview Park)
75 B Carl Hall Road-Downsview Park
Toronto, Ontario M3K 2B9
416-636-0657
info@area51paintballpark.com
http://www.area51paintballpark.com

Eastie Boyz Paintball
20 Lockport Avenue
Toronto, Ontario M8Z 2R7
(416) 233 5888
info@eastieboyz.com
http://www.eastieboyz.com/

Sgt. Splatters
54 Wingold Avenue
Toronto, Ontario M6B 1P5
416-781-0991
dstevens@idirect.com
http://www.sgtsplatters.com

Outer Limits Paintball
Vanastra, Ontario
vanastraolp@outer-limitspaintball.com
http://www.outer-limitspaintball.com

Vaughan Extreme Paintball
3481 Rutherford Rd.
Vaughan, Ontario L4H 3G8
416-678-5806
http://www.vaughanextremepaintball.com

Wasaga Beach Paintball Adventure
3600 Vigo Rd.
Wasaga Beach, Ontario
1-866-322-6321
info@wasagapaintball.on.ca
http://www.wasagapaintball.on.ca

Ballistik
11943 Graham Road
West Lorne, Ontario N0L 2P0
519-318-0425
info@ballistik.ca
http://www.ballistik.ca

CA Paintball
Lennon Road
Westport, Ontario K0G 1X0
(613) 273-4263
http://www.capaintball.on.ca/
http://www.capaintball.on.ca

Guerilla Paintball
111 Industrial Dr Unit 15
Whitby, Ontario L1N 5Z9
905-556-9601
info@guerilla-paintball.com
http://www.guerilla-paintball.com

Master Blaster
62 Mill
Woodstock, Ontario N4S 8P1
519-533-0301

Maverick Paintball
36 Main St
Zurich, Ontario N0M 2T0
519 236 7990
info@maverickpaintball.com
http://www.maverickpaintball.com

OREGON

Albany Outdoor Paintball
150 41st Ave S.E.
Albany, Oregon 97321
lee@albanyoutdoorpaintball.com
http://www.albanyoutdoorpaintball.com

Front Line Sports
33520 NW Pebble Creek Road
Buxton, Oregon 97109
503-310-9983
jnaylor1938@peoplepc.com
http://www.myspace.com/frontlinesports

Action Acres
10381 S. Mulino Rd
Canby, Oregon 97013
(503) 266-5733
info@actionacrespb.com
http://www.actionacrespb.com

Paintball Island
6255 Arndt Road
Canby, Oregon 97068
paintballisland@mail.com
http://www.paintballisland.com

DMZ Paintball / SilverBack Sports
Gephart Rd
Central Point, Oregon 97501
541-770-2620
dmzpaintball@yahoo.com
http://www.dmzpb.com

Southern Oregon Extreme Paintball
Central Point, Oregon 97502
carter@rottenpaintball.com
http://www.rottenpaintball.com/field.htm

Corvallis Sports Park Reball
Corvallis, Oregon 97333
541-757-0776
http://www.corvallissportspark.com

Paintball Palace
1820 W 7th Avenue
Eugene, Oregon 97402
541-465-4766
paintball@paintballpalace-or.com
http://www.paintballpalace-or.com

Over the Top Paintball
2950 Highway 101
Gearhart, Oregon 97138
503-738-5900
glenn@overthetoppaintball.com
http://www.overthetoppaintball.com

Woody's Paintball
1680 A Williams Hwy
Grants Pass, Oregon 97527
woody@woodysproshop.com
http://www.woodysproshop.com

Oregon Paintball
40 N.W. 2nd St. Gresham
Gresham, Oregon 97030
info@oregonpaintball.com
http://www.oregonpaintball.com/

JLT Paintball
80224 Rayton Lane
Hermiston, Oregon 97838
541-567-3498
contact@jltpaintball.com
http://www.jltpaintball.com

Hosking Supply Paintball
36205 Middle Ridge Drive.
Lebanon, Oregon 97355
541-258-3232
http://www.hoskingsupply.com

Weekend Warriors NW
38200 S. Nowlens Br. Rd
Marquam, Oregon 97362
WarriorNW1@aol.com
http://www.weekendwarriorsnw.com/

Ambush Indoor Paintball Inc.
449 Pech Rd
Medford, Oregon 97504
541-664-3642
info@ambushindoorpaintball.com
http://www.ambushindoorpaintball.com

Southern Oregon Paintball
Association (SOPA)
6121 HWY. 62 Central Point Oregon
Medford, Oregon 97501
dadomo@charter.net
http://www.splattpaintball.com

Splat Action Paintball
32155 S. Grimm Rd.
Molalla, Oregon 97038
nwpl2000@yahoo.com
http://www.splataction.com

Ontario Paintball Challenge
Ontario, Oregon 97914
208-741-0509
opcfieldman@hotmail.com
http://www.ontariopaintball.com/

Portland Paintball
631 NE Grand Ave
Portland, Oregon 97232
portlandpaintball@msn.com
http://www.portlandpaintball.us/p
dxpaintball/

Warpaint International
3046 Portland Rd. N.E.
Salem, Oregon 97303
503-585-9477
staff@warpaintpb.com
http://www.warpaintpb.com/

Pioneer Paintball
19712 SE Canyon Valley Rd
Sandy, Oregon 97055
(503) 668-0250

Camp Dakota
1843 Crooked Finger Road
Scotts Mills, Oregon 97375
503-873-7432
John@campdakota.com
http://www.campdakota.com

Sniperz Den Paintball Park
20794 French Prarie Rd
St. Paul, Oregon 97137
1-971-235-0000
http://sniperzden.com

SPLATT Paintball
White City, Oregon 97503
541-890-7865
dadomo@charter.net
http://www.splattpaintball.com

PENNSYLVANIA

Jaw Paintball (Outdoor)
11400 Carter Road
Albion, Pennsylvania 16401
814-756-3942
http://www.jawpaintball.com

Alpha Paintball Field
James Ln & State St
Alburtis, Pennsylvania 18011
610-324-6984
alphapaintballfield@comcast.net
http://www.alphapaintballfield.com

Capt'n Carl's Paintball Games
1-A Dutton Mill Road
Aston, Pennsylvania 19014
http://www.CaptnCarls.com

Stonemak Indoor Paintball
355 Bowers Rd
Berwick, Pennsylvania 18603
(570) 752-6330
http://www.stonemakpaintball.com

Operation Paintball
336 Station St
Bridgeville, Pennsylvania 15017
OP_Paintball0334@hotmail.com
http://www.op-paintball.com/

Urban Assault
Bridgeville, Pennsylvania 15017
info@urbanassaultpb.com
http://www.urbanassaultpb.com

Alumni PB
435 Route 36
Brookville, Pennsylvania 15825
(814) 220-0008
http://www.alumnipb.com

Destination Earth Paintball
Fernwood Resort, Route 209
Bushkill, Pennsylvania 18324
1-888-FERNWOOD
fernrs1@ptd.net
http://www.resortsusa.com/am_p
bal.php

1 Shot Paintball
345 Social Island Road
Chambersburg, Pennsylvania 17201
717-816-7481
matt@1shotpaintball.net
http://www.1shotpaintball.net

Back Creek Paintball
2674 Weber Road
Chambersburg, Pennsylvania 17201
717-977-1993
http://www.backcreekpaintball.net

Wise Guy Paintball
2820 Newcomer Rd.
Chambersburg, Pennsylvania 17201
717-263-2975
wiseguypaintball@pa.net
http://www.wiseguypaintball.net/

Ambush Paintball
Hill Top Drive
Conestoga, Pennsylvania 17516
717-871-8632
info@ambush-paintball.com
http://www.ambush-
paintball.com/

Command Post Paintball
Lower Demunds Rd.
Dallas, Pennsylvania 18612
570-829-3818
joezam@commandpaintball.com
http://www.commandpaintball.com

Rogue Element Paintball
Delano, Pennsylvania 18220
shawnbarrett@repaintball.com
http://www.repaintball.com

Wanna Play Paintball
Dillsburgh, Pennsylvania 17019
717-432-7997
http://www.wannaplaypaintball.com

Lehigh Valley Paintball
405 South 5th Street
Emmaus, Pennsylvania 18049
610-965-0377
Info@lehighvalleypaintball.com
http://www.lehighvalleypaintball.
com

Velocity Paintball
14 N Church st
Ephrata, Pennsylvania 17522
717-738-p8nt(7868)
vpi14@aol.com
http://www.VcityPaintball.com

Jaw Paintball (Indoor)
2121 State Street
Erie, Pennsylvania 16503
814-756-3942
nick@jawpaintball.com
http://www.jawpaintball.com

Team Combat Paintball
225 Lincoln Highway
Fairless Hills, Pennsylvania 19030
215-949-4600
info@triagepaintball.com
http://www.triagepaintball.com

Pentagon Paintball Discount Pro
Shop and Fields
6901 Avonia Rd.(Rt 98)
Fairview, Pennsylvania 16415
814-474-5580
Parker@pentagonpaintball.com
http://www.pentagonpaintball.com

Impact Zone
RD# 1 Box 19
Falls Creek, Pennsylvania 15840
814-371-9701
impactzone@adelphia.net
http://www.impactzoneinc.com

Three Rivers Paintball
284 Rochester Road
Freedom, Pennsylvania 15042
724-775-6232
trpaintball@attbi.com
http://www.trpaintball.com

Blood & Fire Paintball
5333 Meadville Road
Gap, Pennsylvania 17527
bloodfire@amgministries.com
http://www.bloodfirepaintball.com

Paintball World
3458 Harts Run Rd.
Glenshaw, Pennsylvania 15116
412-767-5177
Joel@IceCreamWorld.net
http://www.icecreamworld.net/Pai
ntball_World.html

All American Paintball Park
123 Paintball Park Lane
Greensburg, Pennsylvania 15601
724-805-0188
info@allamericanpaintballpark.com
http://www.allamericanpaintball-
park.com

Statlers
R.D. #7 Box 261-B
Greensburg, Pennsylvania 15601
(724) 539-7655
http://www.statlers.com/

Cobra Command
307 Swartley Road
Hatfield, Pennsylvania 19440
(215) 996-0620
info@cobracommand.com
http://www.cobracommand.com

Hot Shots Paintball
20 W. Indiana St
Homer City, Pennsylvania 15748
http://www.paintballhs.com

Skirmish USA
1519 State Route 903
Jim Thorpe, Pennsylvania 18229
1.800.SKIRMISH (754.7647)
info@skirmish.com
http://www.skirmish.com/

WB Sportsman's Club
2657 Schoonover Road
Kylertown, Pennsylvania 16847
(814) 345-5542

Paintball Adventures
124 Starr Road
Landenburg, Pennsylvania 19350

Revolution Paintball
925 Roundtop Rd.
Lewisberry, Pennsylvania 17339
skiroundtop@skiroundtop.com
http://www.revolutionpaintball.com

Linglestown Paintball
5974 Linglestown Road
Linglestown, Pennsylvania 17112
717-541-8323
info@linglestownpaintball.com
http://www.linglestownpaintball.
com/

Outlaw Paintball
283 South Oak Street
Manheim, Pennsylvania 17545
outlaw_paintball@hotmail.com
http://www.outlawpaintball.net

Encounter Sports USA
7271 W. Market St.
Mercer, Pennsylvania 16137
(724)-981-0902
info@encountersportsfield.com
http://www.encountersportsfield.
com/

Grip N Rip Paintball
600 Schoolhouse Rd
Middletown, Pennsylvania 17057
(717) 773-9518
http://www.gripnrippaintball.com

AEL Paintball Field at Fort Boone
Route 405
Milton, Pennsylvania 17847
(570) 490-1939
staff@aelpaintball.com
http://www.aelpaintball.com

Paintball Thunder
Mt Carmel, Pennsylvania 17851
http://www.paintballthunder.com

Point Break Paintball
Muncy, Pennsylvania 17756
570-546-3405
erin@pointbreakpaintball.com
http://www.pointbreakpaintball.net

Pocono Mt. Paintball
PO Box 65
Nesquehoning, Pennsylvania 18240
1-800-876-0285
mailto:playpaintballhere@playpaint-
ballhere.com
http://www.playpaintballhere.com/

Ultimate Pursuit Paintball
426 N Croton Ave
New Castle, Pennsylvania 16101
(724) 657-3355

E.M.R. Paintball Park
RT. 706 and 601
New Milford, Pennsylvania 18834
(570) 465-9622
EMRPB@epix.net
http://www.emrpaintball.com

Next Level Paintball
50 Pine Grove Rd.
Nottingham, Pennsylvania 19362
717-291-1060
info@kellyspaintball.us
http://www.kellyspaintball.us

Sandy Ridge Paintball
1144 Dale Road
Phillipsburg, Pennsylvania 16866
info@sandyridgepaintball.com
http://www.sandyridgepaintball.com

Paintball On the Fly
586 Sckuylkill Road
Phoenixville, Pennsylvania 19460
610-489-2472
staff_mail@paintballonthefly.com
http://www.paintballonthefly.com/

Riverside Renegades
Pittsburgh, Pennsylvania 15217
412-462-4661
riverside@riversiderenegades.com
http://www.riversiderenegade.com

Poco Loco Paintball
Pottstown, Pennsylvania 19408
1-87PLAYHERE
http://www.pocolocopaintball.com/

SureShot Paintball
340 Blackburn Rd.
Quarryville, Pennsylvania 17566
(717) 786-5511
info@sureshotpb.com
http://sureshotpb.com

Paintball Row
Miller St.
Shoemakersville, Pennsylvania 19555
610-926-5312
pballrow@juno.com
http://www.geocities.com/pball-
row/

Mountain Valley Paintball
Smithfield, Pennsylvania 15478
(304) 554-3877
info@mvppark.com
http://www.mvppark.com

Splatterzone Paintball Park
822 Route 981
Smithton, Pennsylvania 15479
724-838-8292
Paintballzombie@Direcway.com
http://www.Splatterzonepaintball-
park.com

Thornton Paintball
170 Dilworthtown Rd
Thornton, Pennsylvania 19373
questions@thorntonpaintball.com
http://www.thorntonpaintball.com/

Rockys Paintball
Rt 414
Towanda, Pennsylvania 18848
570-265-9208

Crazy Daves Paintball
Volant, Pennsylvania 16155
crazydave@crazydavespaintball.net
http://www.crazydavespaintball.net

Greene County Paintball
439 Haines Hollow Rd
Waynesburg, Pennsylvania 15370
724-627-7932

Paintball Extreme
4075 Homestead Duquesne Rd.
West Mifflin, Pennsylvania 15122
Pbxpaintball@aol.com
http://www.pbxpaintballonline.com

Iron Triangle Paintball Club
Zionsville, Pennsylvania 18092
http://www.iron-triangle.com

PRINCE EDWARD ISLAND

Blitz Paintball
Hunter River RR#2
Cavendish, Prince Edward Island
C0A 1N0

Mackay's Paintball
1504 Barbarweight Road
Summerside, Prince Edward Island
C1N 4J8
902-888-2307
mackayspaintball@hotmail.com

Spikes Paintball
York, Prince Edward Island
(902)393-1820
http://www.spikespaintball.net

QUEBEC

Elite Paintball Quebec
660 Cote Bidard
Charlesbourg, Quebec G1G 3T2
418-809-0255
info@elitepaintball.ca
http://www.elitepaintball.ca

Centre Recreatif Les Patriotes
955 Montee St-Roch
Contrecoeur, Quebec J0L 1C0
1-877-743-4977
info@centrepatriotes.com
http://www.centrepatriotes.com

Oxide Paintball
4517, Boul. St-Joseph
Drummondville, Quebec J2B 3G1
(819) 474-8569
oxide@oxidepaintball.com
http://www.oxidepaintball.com

TACTIK Paintball
1870 Boulevard Maloney
Gatineau Ottawa, Quebec J8R 3Z4
(819) 360-5376
http://www.tactikpaintball.com

Arnold Paintball (Outdoor)
474 Chemin Covey Hill
Havelock, Quebec J0S 2C0
arnold@arnoldpaintball.com
http://www.arnoldpaintball.com

XTreme Paintball
1896 Kahnawake
Kahnawake, Quebec J0L 1B0
450-638-2416

Skorpion Paintball
4885 Highway 440
Laval, Quebec H7P 5P9
info@skorpionpaintball.com
http://www.skorpionpaintball.com

Mirabel Paintball
17706 Rang Ste-Marguerite
Mirabel, Quebec J7J 2E7
paintball.mirabel@sympatico.ca
http://www.paintballmirabel.com/

Action Commando Paintball
5592 Rue Hochelaga
Montrial, Quebec H1N 3L7
actioncommandopaintball@yahoo.ca
http://www.actioncommando.com

Combat Enr.
50, Chemin Gosselin
North Hatley, Quebec J0B 2C0
(819) 822-2692
http://paintball-combat.hyper-mart.net/

Le Jeu Du Guerrier
Parisville-St-Ferdinand, Quebec
1-800-475-1395
ph-guerrier@hotmail.com
http://www.bxpaintball.com

Paint Storm Paintball Games
Perkins, Quebec
info@paintstorm.ca
http://www.paintstorm.ca

Giniration X Paintball
Quebec City, Quebec
info@genxpb.com
http://www.genxpb.com

Paintball Le Fou de l'Ile
Repentigny, Quebec
1-866-333-4777
http://www.lefoudelile.com

WarZone Paintball
388 Chemin St-Georges
Rigaud, Quebec J0P 1P0
514-328-2793
info@warzonepaintball.ca
http://www.warzonepaintball.ca

Club de Paintball Rimouski
Rimouski, Quebec G5L 2M8
418-722-4553
goomba756@hotmail.com
http://www.paintballrimouski.tk/

Bigfoot Paintball
1380 Route 343
Saint-Alphonse Rodriguez, Quebec
J0K 1W0
bigfoot-paintball@sympatico.ca
http://www.bigfoot-paintball.com/

Paintball New-Glasgow
1100 Achigan est
Sainte-Sophie, Quebec J5J 2P9
1-800-561-1238
http://www.paintball-new-glas-gow.com

Paintball L'aventurier
2301 Rang St-Malo
Ste-Marthe du Cap, Quebec G8V1X6
1-877-693-8020
contact@aventurierpaintball.com
http://www.aventurierpaintball.com

SXC Games (T2 indoor)
7155 Transcanadienne
St-Laurent, Quebec H4T 1A2
http://www.sxcgames.com

Max Paintball
Val Bilair, Quebec
info@maxpaintball.org
http://www.maxpaintball.org

Arnold Paintball (Indoor)
8136, Jean-Brillion
Ville Lasalle, Quebec
arnold@arnoldpaintball.com
http://www.arnoldpaintball.com

Paintball City
187, Route 112
Waterloo, Quebec J0E 2N0
asapaintballcity@hotmail.com
http://www.asapaintballcity.com

RHODE ISLAND

Warzone RI Paintball
North Kingstown, Rhode Island
02879
Rendo11@aol.com
http://www.warzoneri.com

RipTide Paintball
553 Old West Main
Portsmouth, Rhode Island 02871
401-293-0669
http://www.riptidepb.com

Providence Indoor Paintball
199 Thurston Street
Providence, Rhode Island 02907
(401) 467-2815
info@providencepaintball.com
http://www.providencepaintball.com/

Gorton Field
Warwick, Rhode Island 02888

Rhode Island Paintball
1268 Post Rd
Warwick, Rhode Island 02888
401-369-7575
scorpionpaintball@cox.net
http://www.ripaintball.net

Painted Warriors Paintball
New London Turnpike
West Greenwich, Rhode Island
02817
info@paintedwarriors.com
http://www.paintedwarriors.com/

SASKATCHEWAN

Paintball Action Games Asquith
Asquith, Saskatchewan S0K 0J0
(306)329-4404
paintballasquith@yahoo.ca
http://www.sasktelwebsite.net/pai
ntac

PN Paintball
MacDowall, Saskatchewan S6V 5R3
info@pnpaintball.com
http://www.pnpaintball.com

Paintball Paradise (Prince Albert)
Prince Albert, Saskatchewan S6V 5S6
888-764-9444
info@paintballpa.com
http://www.paintballpa.com/

Maxwell's Amusements Paintball
Hwy 1 East - Eastgate Drive
Regina, Saskatchewan

Paintball Paradise (Regina)
Regina, Saskatchewan
(306) 775-2022
http://www.paintballparadise.ca

Battlefield Paintball
Saskatoon, Saskatchewan S7M 4Y1
(306)227-2570
bpaintball@shaw.ca
http://www.battlefieldsask.com

Merrill Dunes
1039 Merrill School road
Saskatoon, Saskatchewan
http://www.dunesadventure.com

MR Paintball Indoor
355 Valley Road
Saskatoon, Saskatchewan S7L 6C3
1-306-477-2468
sales@mrpaintball.com

http://www.mrpaintball.ca
Paintball Paradise (Saskatoon)
Saskatoon, Saskatchewan

Saskatoon Paintball Games
Saskatoon, Saskatchewan
(306) 975-0133
roger@saskatoonpaintball.ca
http://www.saskatoonpaintball.ca

SOUTH CAROLINA

Proving Grounds Paintball
Beaufort, South Carolina 29904
roy@provinggroundspaintball
http://www.provinggroundspaint-
ball.com

What A Rush Paintball /
Beaufort Fun Park
591 Robert Smalls Pkwy
Beaufort, South Carolina 29906
843-524-2267
party@beaufortfunpark.com
http://www.beaufortfunpark.com

Firelake Paintball
1897 Chedder Rd.
Belton, South Carolina 29627
864-847-4200
sales@firelakepaintball.com
http://www.firelakepaintball.com

Gold Dragon
586 Robinson Bridge Road
Central, South Carolina 29630

Triggertyme Paintball
429 Koon Store Road
Columbia, South Carolina 29203
brian@triggertyme.com
http://www.triggertyme.com

Patriot Paintball
Conway, South Carolina 29527
843.369.4386
patriotpaintball@sc.rr.com
http://www.patriot-paintball.com

Palmetto Paintball
3760 Peach Orchard Rd.
Dalzell, South Carolina 29040
803-316-5399
info@palmettopaintball.com
http://www.palmettopaintball.com

Paintball Central Greenville
120 Rogers Rd.
Duncan, South Carolina 29334
864-486-9287
ken@pballcentral.com
http://www.pballcentral.com

New Generation
108 Semper Fidelis Rd
Easley, South Carolina 29640
(864)859-5561
http://www.newgenonline.com

Duck N Dive Paintball
425 John Paul Jones Road
Effingham, South Carolina 29541
843-317-9302
info@duckndive.net
http://www.duckndive.net

Liberty Paintball LLC
905 Camp Wiggins Rd
Florence, South Carolina 29506
843-319-5710
liberty.paintball@gmail.com
http://www.libertypb.com

Weekend Warrior Sportz Park
161 Verdin Rd
Greenville, South Carolina 29607
864-297-1775
info@weekendwarriorsportzpark.com
http://www.weekendwarrior-
sportzpark.com

VHA Badlands
14211 B West Wade Hampton Blvd
Greer, South Carolina 29651

Saluda Paintball
180 Youth Camp Rd
Honea Path, South Carolina 29654
864-617-9184
info@saludapaintball.com
http://www.saludapaintball.com

Ground Zero Paintball
2078 Bermuda Road
Lake View, South Carolina 29505
http://www.gzpaintball.com

Adrenalin Rush Paintball
3888 Columbia Hwy (Hwy 378)
Leesville, South Carolina 29070
XtremeActionSports@msn.com
http://www.adrenalinrushpb.50me
gs.com

Ballbusters Paintball
4952 Sunset Blvd.
Lexington, South Carolina 29072
803-957-5822
jburke@ballbusters-paintball.com
http://www.ballbusters-
paintball.com

Planet Paintball
380 Blackwood Store Road
Moore, South Carolina 29369
864-525-3200
info@planetpaintballsc.com
http://www.planetpaintballsc.com

Paintball USA
6925 Hwy 707
Myrtle Beach, South Carolina 29588
mike@paintballusa.biz
http://www.paintballusa.biz

COLORS Paintball
North Augusta, South Carolina
29841
colorspaintball@hotmail.com
http://colorspb.50megs.com

Paintball Charleston
7100 Cross County Road
North Charleston, South Carolina
29418
http://www.paintballcharleston.net

Strike-Zone
Highway 170
Okatie, South Carolina 29909
843-524-1800
http://www.strikezonepaintball.com/

Paintball Central Charlotte
1680 E. Main St.
Rock Hill, South Carolina 29730
704-752-9774
http://www.pballcentral.com/

Palmetto Hills Paintball
1481 S Anderson Rd.
Rock Hill, South Carolina 29730
803-366-3801
jcrpg@radcad.net
http://www.rockhillpaintball.com

Extreme Outdoors
231 Griggs Rd
Six MIle, South Carolina 29682
864-868-4288
http://www.extremeoutdoor-
spaintball.com

Psycho Paintball
10573 Hwy 78 East
Summerville, South Carolina 29483
843-821-2337
psychopaintball@bellsouth.net
http://psychopaintball.net

Pee Dee Paintball
Weaver Street
Timmonsville, South Carolina 29161
843-346-2622
peedeepaintball@aol.com
http://www.peedeepaintball.com

Hwy 11 Paintball
530 N Hwy11
West Union, South Carolina 29696
864-638-6368
coll8407@bellsouth.net
http://www.hwy11paintball.com/

Red Fox Games
1 Red Fox Run
Woodruff, South Carolina 29388
redfoxgames@cs.com
http://www.redfoxgames.com

SOUTH DAKOTA

Splat Attack Paintball
43719 258th St.
Bridgewater, South Dakota 57319
bruce@paintthefarm.com
http://www.paintthefarm.com

Darkside Paintball Arena
Brookings Mall 720 22 Ave. S.
Brookings, South Dakota 57006
605-696-0701
darksidepaintball@mchsi.com
http://www.darksidearena.com

Urban Warfare
Dell Rapids, South Dakota 57028
chad@siouxfallspaintball.com
http://www.urbanwarfare1.com/

James River Valley Paintball
39280 148th St.
Mellette, South Dakota 57461
605-228-0531
info@jrvp.com
http://www.jrvp.com

Reckless Assault
5570 Airport Road
Pierre, South Dakota 57501
(605) 773-6586
recklessassault@hotmail.com
http://recklessassault.tripod.com

Ballisticks Paintball
Radar Hill Rd.
Rapid City, South Dakota 57701
605-343-4010
ballisticks@hotmail.com
http://www.ballisticks.com

Flags and Wheels
405 12th St.
Rapid City, South Dakota 57702
605-341-2186
http://www.flagsandwheels.com/
paintball.htm

Splat Zone
6400 S Highway 16
Rapid City, South Dakota 57701
(605) 388-1177

Dacotah Blue Sky Paintball
321 4th Ave E
Sisseton, South Dakota 57262
605-698-9086

The Feud Ranch
St. Onge, South Dakota 57779

TENNESSEE

The Alternative Sport
409 Overhill Dr.
Blountville, Tennessee 37617
thealternativesport01@yahoo.com
http://www.thealternativesport.com

ZXS Paintball Arena
155 Essex Dr.
Bluff City, Tennessee 37618
http://www.zxspaintball.com

Insane Paintball
1200 Wisdom Street
Chattanooga, Tennessee 37406
(423) 624-2121
jared@insanepaint.com
http://www.insanepaint.com

Play Paintball
4350 Jearoldstown Rd.
Chucky, Tennessee 37641
423-348-6161
mbrantner@playpaintballnow.com
http://www.playpaintballnow.com

Red River Paintball
900 Vaughn Rd
Clarksville, Tennessee 37043
931-358-3692
motoplex@midsouthmotoplex.com
http://www.redriverpaintball-
games.com

Ultimate Paintball Plus
78 Mouse Creek Road
Cleveland, Tennessee 37312
(423) 559-0678
service@ultimatepaintballplus.com
http://www.ultimatepaintballplus.c
om/

Paintball On The Plateau
225 Keyes Rd
Crossville, Tennessee 38571
billybob_85_2000@hotmail.com

Hollow Buzzard Paintball
8464 Covington Rd.
Eagleville
Tennessee 37060
info@hollowbuzzard.com
http://www.hollowbuzzard.com/

Splattag-N
1446 E Broad St
Elizabethton, Tennessee 37643
info@splattag-n.com
http://www.splattag-n.com

Paintball Park Memphis
9640 E Davies Plantation Rd
Ellendale, Tennessee 38029
(901) 372-3383
memphispaintball@aol.com
http://www.memphispaintball.com

Bear Claw Paintball
41 Brown Teal Rd.
Fayetteville, Tennessee 37334
info@bearclawpaintball.com
http://www.bearclawpaintball.com
Grace Xtreme
3279 Southhall Road
Franklin, Tennessee 37064
615-591-5091
holli@gracechapel.net
http://www.gracextreme.net

Goode Shot Paintball
Greeneville, Tennessee 37745
(423)639-6639

East Tennessee Paintball
144 Dickey Valley Rd
Harriman, Tennessee 37748
865-882-8181
easttnpaintball@aol.com
http://www.EastTennesseePaint-
ball.com

Carter's Shooting Supply
6210 Highway 58
Harrison, Tennessee 37341
423-344-1099
cartershooting@comcast.net
http://www.cartershooting.com

Yellow Jacket Paintball
Hartsville, Tennessee 37074
615-374-1663
actionpaintballstore@comcast.net
http://yellowjacketpaintball.com

Nashville Paintball Inc., Hermitage
3020 Brandau Rd.
Hermitage, Tennessee 37087
nashvillepaint@aol.com
http://www.nashvillepaintball.com

Music City Paintball Club
Jackman Road
Joelton, Tennessee 37080

Olde Town Paintball
2018 Highway 11-E
Jonesborough, Tennessee 37659
423-753-3800

Down Range Paintball
2000 Stonebrook Place
Kingsport, Tennessee 37660
(423) 384-1542
http://www.downrangepaintball.com

Knoxville Paintball Sports
Brushy Valley Rd.
Knoxville, Tennessee 37918
http://www.knoxvillepaintball-
sports.com

Players Club Paintball
125 Dante Rd.
Knoxville, Tennessee 37918
865 687-1909
Lisa@playersclubpaintball.com
http://www.playersclubpaintball.com

Riptide Paintball
4432 Middlebrook Pike
Knoxville, Tennessee 37921
(865)-584-9878
sales@riptide.us
http://www.riptide.us

Sir Goony's Paintball
10925 Kingston Pike
Knoxville, Tennessee 37922
865-675-3262
ohsuzanna@knology.net
http://www.sirgoonys.net

Nashville Paintball Sports
6455 Old Murfreesbro Rd E
Lebanon, Tennessee 37090
(615) 444-8988
http://www.nashvillepaintball-sports.com

Cross-Eyed Paintball
4721 McDonald Rd.
McDonald, Tennessee 37353
423-396-4364
http://www.crosseyedpaintball.com

Adam King Memorial Paintball
Playground
Nunnelly, Tennessee 37137
justinp228@yahoo.com

Horse Creek Paintball Arena
11470 Hwy 69 South
Savannah, Tennessee 38372
zregister@charter.net
http://www.horsecreekpaintball.com

Dream Tactics Paintball
1171 Robinson Gap Road
Sevierville, Tennessee 37876
1-865-774-7221
http://www.dreamtactics.net

Smoky Mountain Paintball
103 Pleasant Hill Rd.
Sevierville, Tennessee 37862
865-428-7072
John@smokymountainpaintball.com
http://smokymountainpaintball.com

Big Sky Paintball
1054 Frank Martin Rd
Shelbyville, Tennessee 37160
931-680-1557
bigskypaintball@earthlink.net
http://www.bigskypaintball.biz

Middle Tennessee Paintball
4215 Kedron Road
Spring Hill, Tennessee 37174
http://www.middletennesseepaintball.com

Moose Man Paintball
5274 Concord Rd
Springfield, Tennessee 37172
Mooseboy1686@aol.com
http://www.pageofjeremy.20megsfree.com

Valley Paintball
146 Hwy. 283
Whitwell, Tennessee 37397
csjets14@hotmail.com
http://myweb.ecomplanet.com/vapa5819

Caddy's Family Funland
Winchester, Tennessee 37398
931-649-2343
www.caddysfamilyfunland.com
http://www.caddysfamilyfunland.com

TEXAS

Spinner'z
1873 Maple Street
Abilene, Texas 79602
(325) 677-3866

Paintball Knights
13289 La Vernia Rd
Adkins, Texas 78101
(210) 649-3147
http://www.paintballknights.com

Fort Paintball
Dillahey Rd
Allen, Texas 75002
972-442-9777
fortpaintball@hotmail.com
http://www.fortpaintball.com/

DFW Pro Paintball Park
2940 FM 2738
Alvarado, Texas 76009
817-790-3831
questions@dfwpro.com
http://www.dfwpro.com

Ultimate Paintball of Texas
Alvin, Texas 77511
Ultimatepaintballoftexas@
hotmail.com
http://www.ultimatepaintball
oftexas.com

Aggression Paintball
4911 Dumas Dr.
Amarillo, Texas 79108
(806)-383-5688

Field of Dreams
1300 E Amarillo Blvd
Amarillo, Texas 79107
(806) 371-0120

Power Sports Paintball Park
9351 S. Georgia
Amarillo, Texas 79118

Texas Paintball
18300 Medina Vista Lane
Austin, Texas 78645
512-257-8728
sales@txpb.com
http://www.txpb.com

WiseGuy's Paintball
10311 S. FM 730
Boyd, Texas 76023
http://www.gorillaspaintball.net/
WiseguysPaintballPark.html

Circle A Paintball
808 N Horton St
Brenham, Texas 77833
(979) 421-9922

Adrenaline Rush
Brownsville, Texas 78520
(956) 544-2772
http://www.AdrenalineRushPaintball.com

Texas Justice
300 N Broadway
Brownwood, Texas 76801
325-642-7613
darby@txjpaintball.com
http://www.txjpaintball.com

Winkeydoodles Paintball Adventure
401 Anthony Rd.
Canutillo, Texas 79835
winkeydoodles@mail.com
http://www.winkeydoodles.com

Collin County Paintball Park
3222 County Rd. 210
Celina/Anna, Texas 75009
972.369.9955
info@terryspaintballtown.com
http://terryspaintballtown.com

Battlegrounds Paintball
16564 Old Houston RD.
Conroe, Texas 77302
281-572-1479
Battlegroundspaintball@earthlink.net
http://www.Battlegroundspaint-
ball.net

Paintball Mania
924 Butler Rd.
Conroe, Texas 77301
936-588-3128
mfaust@lcc.net
http://www.paintball-mania.com

Twisted Texas Paintball Games
14590 FM 1314
Conroe, Texas 77302
832 372-7953
TwistedGamesTX@consolidated.net
http://www.twistedgames.net

The Bunkers
3699 FM 2657
Copperas Cove, Texas 76522
(254) 518-3279
bunkers.paintball@yahoo.com
http://www.thebunkerspaintball.com

Splatter Action (Corpus Christi)
2110 Highway 286
Corpus Christi, Texas 78415
(361) 814-3830
sonny@playxtremesports.com
http://www.PlayExtremeSports.com/

Bunker Hill Paintball
Crockett, Texas 75835
(936)-544-9494
http://www.bunkerhillpaintball.com

#1 Paintball - Grant Rd Park
15550 Grant Rd.
Cypress, Texas 77429
713-768-0283
Eli@1pb.com
http://www.1pb.com

Valley Paintball
3207 East Vaughn
Donna, Texas 78537
956-464-5559
http://warwhoop.com/RogelioH-
ernandez/page10.html

Dyess A.F.B. Outdoor Rec.
Dyess A.F.B., Texas 79607
325-696-2402

Paintball at Ricky's
1773 Pali
El Paso, Texas 79936
915-855-7474
http://www.rickyspb.com

Suncity Paintball
5352 Doniphan Dr
El Paso, Texas 79932
(915) 833-7633
http://www.suncitypaintball.com

Webe Playing Paintball
Field & Pro Shop
12655 Star Duster
El Paso, Texas 79928
915-820-8884
http://www.webepaintball.com

Snake Pit Paintball
136 Spence Ln
Elgin, Texas 78621
(512) 281-2502

Hurricane Paintball
250 C.R. 255
Fairfield, Texas 75840
field@hurricanepb.com
http://www.hurricanepb.com

Farmers Branch Paintball
3404 Beltline Rd
Farmers Branch, Texas 75234
http://fbpaintball.com

Official Paintball Games of Texas
(Forest Hill)
6629 Anglin Dr
Forest Hill, Texas 76140
866-432-3487
info@officialpaintball.com
http://www.officialpaintball.com

Official Paintball Games of Texas
(Forney)
17437 Adams Trail
Forney, Texas 75126
info@officialpaintball.com
http://www.officialpaintball.com/

Fun on the Run Paintball Park
2621 Roberts Cut Off
Fort Worth, Texas 76135
splat@flash.net
http://www.paintballplayerssup-
ply.com/

Mad Ivans Paintball
1813 W Bowie St
Fort Worth, Texas 76110
817-308-3930
http://www.madivan.com

Sudden Impact Paintball
Giddings, Texas 78942
979-366-9386
scott@suddenimpactpaintball.com
http://www.suddenimpactpaint-
ball.com

Goodfellow AFB Outdoor
Recreation
310 E Kearny Blvd
Goodfellow AFB, Texas 76908
(325)-654-3247
http://www.goodfellowservices.com

Unplugged Sports
1711 E. Hwy. 377
Granbury, Texas 76049
817-579-0131
UnpluggedSports@yahoo.com
http://www.unpluggedsports.com

Xdrenalin Zone Paintball
2500 Fairway Dr
Grapevine, Texas 76051
972-471-3200
information@xdrenalinzone.com
http://www.xdrenalinzone.com

Paintball Max
2223 Private County Road 3342
Greenville, Texas 75402
903-456-8143
robert6621@sbcglobal.net
http://www.paintballmaxpark.com

Blue Panther Xtreme Paintball
28981 Rangerville Rd
Harlingen, Texas 78552
(956) 412-8877

Tactical Paintball Texas
12590 FM 794
Harwood, Texas 78632
830-540-4200
http://www.tacticalpaintball.com/

Choo Choos Family Fun Center
14300 Wallisville Road
Houston, Texas 77049
713-451-3010
http://www.choochoos.net

Paintball Bonanza
Houston, Texas 77024
713-935-0552
bkers@paintballbonanza.com
http://www.paintballbonanza.com

Paintball Zone
2811 Dixie Farm Road
Houston, Texas 77089
paintballzone@excite.com
http://www.paintballzone.net

Survival Games of Texas 2309 Aldine
Meadows Rd
Houston, Texas 77032
(281) 442-2284
survivalgameoftexas@ev1.net
http://www.paintballstoreinc.com

Urban War Zone
2215 Telephone Rd
Houston, Texas 77023
713-480-4716
info@urban-warzone.com
http://www.urban-warzone.com

Outdoor Adventures Paintball Park
2920 CR 904
Joshua, Texas 76058
817-447-3483
doug@burlesonscuba.com
http://www.burlesonscuba.com/ou
tdooradventures.html

Tank's Katy Paintball
899 Westgreen Blvd
Katy, Texas 77450
713-862-5555
http://www.tankspaintball.com

Kerrville Paintball Adventure
316 Camino Real St
Kerrville, Texas 78028
830-895-2747

Mandatory Fun
1001 East Veterans Memorial Blvd.
#401
Killeen, Texas 76541
254 554 7268
http://www.mandatoryfun.net

GatSplat
582 N TX-121-BR (N)
Lewisville, Texas 75057
972-956-5500
gatsplat@gatsplat.com
http://www.gatsplat.com

Panther Creek Paintball
10658 CR 175
Lola, Texas 77861
936-394-4000
panthercreekpaintball@yahoo.com
http://www.panthercreek
paintball.com

Longview Paintball
Pine Tree Rd.
Longview, Texas 75604
903-297-8978
jamie@longviewpaintball.com
http://www.longviewpaintball.com

Paintball Extreme
Los Fresnos, Texas 78566

Apache Acres Paintball
7511 14th ST
Lubbock, Texas 79416
806-787-5528
apacheacres@hotmail.com
http://www.apacheacrespaintball.com

Challenge Park
Corner of Loop 289 & E 50th St Lbk
Lubbock, Texas 79423
806-792-4551

Putt-Putt SplatZone (Lubbock)
5110 29th Dr.
Lubbock, Texas 79414
806-795-2312
info@puttputt-lubbock.com
http://www.puttputt.com

Chupacabra's Paintball Resort
41318 Wood Way
Magnolia, Texas 77354

Xtreme Paintball
7415 Burleson Manor Rd
Manor, Texas 78653
(512) 796-9760
http://www.xtremepb.net

Hit & Run Paintball
12245 County Road 528
Mansfield, Texas 76063
http://www.hitandrunpaintball.com/

Markham Paintball
Markham, Texas 77456
979-241-1256
speedball@ykc.cc
http://www.markhamspeedball.com

Marshall Paintball
201 Marshall Str.
Marshall, Texas 75762
903-926-0714
draggingslab@yahoo.com
http://www.marshallpaintball.com

Celebration Station
4040 Towne Crossing Blvd
Mesquite, Texas 75150
972-279-7888
tmarek@celebrationstation.com
http://www.celebrationstation.com

Double D Ranch
12809 Eastgate Dr
Mesquite, Texas 75181
http://www.ddranchdallas.com/paintball.htm

Adventure Park Paintball
5001 Princeton
Midland, Texas 79703
432-686-7333

Midland Paintball
4501 E. CR 55
Midland, Texas 79705
(432)684-6724
http://midlandpaintball.com

Splatter Madness
Paintball & Pro-Shop
4310 NCR 1135
Midland, Texas 79705
(432) 684-1111
casey@splattermadnesspaintball.com
http://www.splattermadnesspaintball.com

Mountasia Splatter Park
8851Grapevine Highway
North Richland Hills, Texas 76180
817-503-8833
info@mountasiafamilyfuncenter.com
http://www.mountasiafamilyfuncenter.com/splatterpark_index.html

Just 4 Fun Paintball
410 East 8th Street
Odessa, Texas 79761
(432)580-0200

Outlaw Paintball
1436 Grand Ave Parkway
Pflugerville, Texas 78660
512-252-1664
OutlawPaintballField@yahoo.com
http://www.outlawpaintballfield.com/indexx.html

Point Blank Paintball Games
10390 US Hwy 190
Point Blank, Texas 77364
936-377-2866
andy@pointblankpaintballgames.com
http://www.pointblankpaintball-games.com

Splatter Action (Lufkin)
10342 Hwy 69 North
Pollok, Texas 75969
936-853-4098
http://www.playxtremesports.com

Dry Creek Paintball
6061 CR 2297
Quinlan, Texas 75474
903-883-0190
info@drycreekpaintball.com
http://www.drycreekpaintball.com

Petty's Paintball
550 Bateman Rd
Red Rock, Texas 78662
512-601-3235
info@pettypb.com
http://www.pettypb.com/

Paintball Paradise
3523 E Hwy 114
Rhome, Texas 76078
940-433-5447
http://www.paintballinparadise.com

Brazos Splat Games
22011 S.W. Freeway.
Richmond, Texas 77469
keith@bsgpaintball.com
http://www.bsgpaintball.com

DFW Adventure Park
13055 Cleveland-Gibbs Road
Roanoke, Texas 76262
paintball@dfwap.com
http://www.dfwap.com/DFWAP/index.html

Paintball Challenge Park
301 Chisholm Trail
Round Rock, Texas 78681
512-255-3866
http://paintballchallenge.puttn-funn.com

Angelo Paintball
Knickerbocker Rd.
San Angelo, Texas 76904
325-223-8082
angelopaintball@hotmail.com
http://www.angelopaintball.com

Lackland Outdoor
Adventure Center Paintball
Lackland AFB
San Antonio, Texas 78236
210-925-5532
http://www.lacklandservices.com/OutRec/Paintball-Course-Grand-Open.jpg

Predator Paintball Park
20590 Bandera Rd.
San Antonio / Helotes, Texas 78023
predatorpbpark@aol.com
http://www.predatorpaintball-park.com

Paintballerz
32944 Fm 1577
San Benito, Texas 78586
Razamed@aol.com

The Realm Paintball
5840 South IH 35
San Marcos, Texas 78666
830-214-4680
http://www.realmpaintball.com

#1 Paintball - Quinn Rd Park
31233 Quinn Rd
Tomball, Texas 77375
281-255-3500
Quinn@1pb.com
http://www.1pb.com

Extreme Paintball
6611 S. Broadway, Suite #1
Tyler, Texas 75703
903-534-9003

Mission Valley Paintball
573 Albright Rd. W.
Victoria, Texas 77904
http://www.mvpball.com/

Paintball of Victoria
6560 Hanselman Rd.
Victoria, Texas 77905

Xtreme Paintball of Victoria
1000 Raab Rd.
Victoria, Texas 77905
361-574-9720
franknpete@xtremepaintballvicto-ria.com
http://www.xtremepaintballofvic-toria.com

Guru Paintball Park
2234 E. Tinsley
Waco, Texas 76706
gguru@hot.rr.com
http://www.gurupaintball.com

Powerplay Paintball
4301 Meyers Lane
Waco, Texas 76705
254-867-0047
powerplay@powerplaypaintball.com
http://www.powerplaypaintball.com

Madd Dogz Paintball Park
410 Mushroom Road
Waxahachie, Texas 75165
214-228-9598
MaddDogzPB@aol.com
http://www.madddogz.com

Pure Action Paintball
1567 N. Bend Road
Weatherford, Texas 76085
817-598-1122
Mhemby@airmal.net
http://www.pureactionpaintball.com

UTAH

Splatter Zone
3492 N Minersville Hwy
Cedar City, Utah 84720
(435) 586-1820
splatterzone@peoplepc.com

Battlegrounds Paintball
Grantsville, Utah 84029
801-759-4064
jonesderekt@comcast.net
http://battlegrounds-paintball.com

J&J Speedball
Hyrum, Utah 84325
johncarter@jandjspeedball.com
http://www.jandjspeedball.com

Action Center Paintball
4129 Cottonwood Canyon Rd
Morgan, Utah 84050
801-876-3132
jeff@actioncenterpaintball.com
http://www.actioncenterpaint-ball.com

Urban Warfare Center
897 West 100 North, Unit H
North Salt Lake, Utah 84054
(801) 936-1028
info@urbanwarfarecenter.com
http://www.urbanwarfarecenter.com

Pick-Up Paintball
810 S 3110 W
Provo, Utah 84606
pickuppaintball@gmail.com
http://www.pickuppaintball.tk

Paintball Addicts
999 West 2610 South
Salt Lake City, Utah 84119
801-886-8899
travis@pb-addicts.com
http://www.pb-addicts.com

Paintball Planet
8700 S Sandy Pkwy
Sandy, Utah 84070
http://www.peglegpaintball.com/planet.html

Velocity Paintball
3105 W. Pioneer Rd.
Slaterville, Utah 84404
801-529-0276
info@playatvelocity.com
http://www.playatvelocity.com

Red Cliffs Paintball Park
St. George, Utah 84770
redcliffspc@hotmail.com
http://www.freewebs.com/red-cliffspaintballclub

Splat
535 South 4500 W
West Point, Utah 84041

VERMONT

Colchester Paintball
1751 East Road
Colchester, Vermont 05446
802-878-2905
vtpaintball@hotmail.com
http://www.vtpaintball.com

Hidden Sights Paintball
U.S. Route 2
Middlesex, Vermont 05602
MailBag@Hiddensights.com
http://www.Hiddensights.com

Champlain Valley Paintball
Wooster Road
Shoreham, Vermont 05770
cvpb@sover.net
http://www.champlainvalleypaint-ball.bizhosting.com/

VIRGINIA

Master Blasters Paintball
701 N. Battlefield Blvd.
Chesapeake, Virginia 23320
masterblasters@paintball.hrcox-mail.com
http://www.masterblasterspaint-ball.com/

X-Zone Paintball
6851 Courthouse Road
Chesterfield, Virginia 23832
804-745-3232
xzone@lifespringfoundation.org
http://www.xzonepaintball.com/

Wolf's Ridge Paintball
Christiansburg, Virginia 24073
wolfsridgep8ball@aol.com
http://www.wolfsridgepaintball.com/

All American Paintball
1521 Oakland dr.
Danville, Virginia 24540
434-685-2790
allamericanpaintball@sitestar.net
http://www.allamericanpaintball.net

Paintball Plus
Fishersville, Virginia 22939
webmaster@paintball-plus.net
http://www.paintball-plus.net

Action Town Sports
876 Lee Blvd.
Fort Eustis, Virginia 23606
axntwn@aol.com
http://www.actiontownsports.com

Big Pearl Paintball
Glasgow, Virginia 24555
434-258-1200
admin@bigpearlpaintball.com
http://www.bigpearlpaintball.com

The Swamp Fun Park
Gloucester, Virginia 23061
804-642-8778
paintmaster@theswampfunpark.com
http://www.theswampfunpark.com

Bethel Park Battlefield
Access from Saunders Road
Hampton, Virginia 23666
kissmy10inbass@aol.com

The Paintball Store
604 Aberdeen Rd.
Hampton, Virginia 23661
757-826-5806
http://www.thep8ntballstore.com

Captain Tee's Paintball
1594 S Main St
Harrisonburg, Virginia 22801
540-442-9200

Rudy's Paintball
1084 Virginia Ave
Harrisonburg, Virginia 22802
540-564-0002
http://www.rudyspaintball.com

Cross Creek Paintball
Rt. 637 (Drill Rd.)
Honaker, Virginia 24260
bubba_rowe@hotmail.com
http://www.fortunecity.com/olympia/brucelee/44/index.htm

Splat Brothers Paintball
13908 James River Drive
Hopewell, Virginia 23860
804-452-1150
splatbrothers@comcast.net
http://www.splatbrotherspaint-ball.com

New Kent Paintball Games
14375 Marine Corps Drive
Lanexa, Virginia 23089
8049665104
http://www.newkentpaintball-games.com

Hogback Mountain Paintball
20261 Hogback Mountain Rd.
Leesburg, Virginia 20175
question@hogback.net
http://www.hogback.net

Pev's @ AG Paintball
20136 Gant Lane
Leesburg, Virginia 20175
http://www.pevs.com/

DarkSide Paintball
31164 Zoar Rd
Locust Grove, Virginia 22508
(540) 364-0293
darksidepaintball@mac.com
http://www.darkside-paintball.com/

Soggie Bottom Paintball
Locust Grove, Virginia 22407
evan@soggiebottompaintball.com
http://www.soggiebottompaint-ball.com

Warplay Paintball
Rt. 20
Locust Grove, Virginia 22508
703.727.0271
http://www.warplaypaintball.com

Painted Forest Adventure Games
14307 Wards Rd.
Lynchburg, Virginia 24501
http://www.painted-forest.com

Splatter Mountain
Candler's Mountain Road
Lynchburg, Virginia 24501

Old Church Paintball
7089 Cobbs Farm Road
Mechanicsville, Virginia 23111
804-916-0701
crj2203@email.vccs.edu
http://www.freewebs.com/crj2203/index.htm

Rockwood Paintball
10239 Hull Street Road
Midlothian, Virginia 23112
804-301-6824
rockwoodpaintball@msn.com
http://www.rockwoodpaintball.com

Hot Shots Paintball
520 Industrial Park Drive
Newport News, Virginia 23608
(757) 872-4130
http://www.hotshots-
paintball.com

Paintball Authority
1945 Urbine Rd (RT.676)
Powhatan, Virginia 23139
Reyz@aol.com
http://www.pbauthority.com

Savage Paintball
Richmond, Virginia 23059
(804) 798-2147
http://www.savagepaint.com

High Velocity Adventure Park
1002 Columbia Street
Roanoke, Virginia 24015
540-366-2020
http://www.hvpaintball.com

Accusplat Paintball
1832 Apperson Dr
Salem, Virginia 24153
(540) 387-0995
accusplat@netzero.net
http://www.accusplat.com/

Pink Painter Paintball
5920 Courthouse Road
Spotsylvania, Virginia 22553

Powerline Paintball
2698 Poplar Rd
Stafford, Virginia 22406
(540)-286-0404
powerlinejon@aol.com
http://www.powerlinep.fitzde-
signs.com/

Mad Dog Paintball
2010 Madison Road
Stanardsville, Virginia 22973

Skyline Paintball
363 Radio Station Road
Strasburg, Virginia 22657
540-465-9537
sue@skylinepaintball.com
http://www.skylinepaintball.com

FOX Paintball Park
2968 Holland Road
Virginia Beach, Virginia 23454
(757)737-3699
http://www.foxpaintballpark.com

VB Splat Zone
700 S. Birdneck Rd.
Virginia Beach, Virginia 23451
757-422-6419
motorworldkb@aol.com
http://www.vbmotorworld.com

Star Paintball
Wise, Virginia 24293

Total Eclipse Paintball
5401 Mudd Tavern Rd.
Woodford, Virginia 22580
540-582-7400
http://www.totaleclipsehasairball
.com/

Lake Paintball
Zion Cross Roads, Virginia 22942
(434) 990-0010
http://www.rudycustoms.com/rud
y%20customs/index.php

WASHINGTON

Splat Attack Airball Field
6224 114th Ave
Puyallup, Washington 98372
(253) 852-7105
http://www.shopsplatattack.com/

100 Degrees Northwest
27032 Meridian Ave N
Arlington, Washington 98223
425-299-1449
Mister.dude@verizon.net
http://www.100degreesnw.com

Skinny Joes Paintball
17022 Burn Road
Arlington, Washington 98223
(866) 784-5100
skinnyjoe@skinnyjoespaintball.com
http://skinnyjoespaintball.com

Splat Attack Outdoor Field
148th Way SE & SE Auburn Black
Diamond RD
Auburn, Washington 98092
253-852-7602
info@splatattackonline.com
http://www.splatattackonline.com/

Spoolz Paintball Club
28400 NE 91 Ave
Battle Ground, Washington 98604
360-798-6803
webmaster@spoolz.net
http://www.spoolz.net/

NW Paintball Park
Bremerton, Washington 98311
360-377-0398
http://www.northwestpaintball-
park.org

Powerline Paintball Inc.
1605 Delameter Rd.
Castle Rock, Washington 98611
(360) 425-1131
powerlinepaintball@yahoo.com
http://www.geocities.com/power-
linepaintball/index.htm

NeverWood Paintball
East 11220 Hartley Lane
Chattaroy, Washington 99003
Neverwood@icehouse.net
http://www.neverwoodpaintball.com

Dragon Wars Paintball
463 Autoview Dr.
Colville, Washington 99114
509-684-2848
dragonwarspaintballfield@msn.com
http://www.dragonwarspaintball-
field.com

East Side Paintball
21500 Lake Fontel Rd.
Duvall, Washington 98019
425-760-8252
info@splatemsports.com
http://www.eastsidepaintball.net

TPS (The Paintball Field)
South Union Rd.
Elma, Washington 98541
360-482-5091
paintballstore@msn.com
http://www.tpspaintball.com

DoodleBug Sportz Indoor
Paintball Arena
3326 Paine Ave
Everett, Washington 98201
doodlebugsportz@aol.com
http://www.doodlebugsportz.com

Paranoid Paintball
37222 28th Ave S. Federal Way
Federal Way, Washington 98003
inquiries@paranoidpb.com
http://www.paranoidpb.com

Friday Harbor Paintball
276 Salmonberry Lane
Friday Harbor, Washington 98250
http://www.fhpb.net/
Danger Zone Paintball
4535 Vancouver Rd.
Ft. Lewis, Washington 98433
dzpaintball@hotmail.com
http://www.dzpaintball.com

Ace's High Paintball
Graham, Washington 98338
youngahps@netscape.net
http://www.ahppaintball.com

Operation Paintball
20819 Jansky Road E.
Graham, Washington 98338
(360)893-3440
jeffcartel@hotmail.com
http://www.operationpaintballwa.com

Adrenaline Sports NW
5300 Menzel Lake Rd
Granite Falls, Washington 98252
425-328-6561
pureadrenaline@verizon.net
http://www.adrenalinesportsnw.com

Crave It Paintball
13222 Jordan Rd.
Granite Falls, Washington 98252
craveit@att.net
http://www.craveitpaintball.com/

Black N Blue
Chinook Valley
Ilwaco, Washington 98624
360-642-4986
bgchvy98@yahoo.com
http://www.blacknbluepb.com/

Splat Attack Indoor Field
1600 Central Ave South Suite 107
Kent, Washington 98032
(253) 852-7105
http://www.splatattackonline.com

ForestFire Paintball
5410 123rd Ave NE
Lake Stevens, Washington 98258
425-879-2102
Ezra@ForestFirePB.com
http://ForestFirePB.com

Semper Fi Paintball
2149 E. Badger Rd.
Lynden, Washington 98264
field@semperfipaintball.com
http://www.semperfipaintball.com/

Hole in the Wall Paintball Park
18019 Renton Maple Valley Rd. SE
Maple Valley, Washington 98092
(253) 735-1989
http://www.holeinthewallpaint-
ball.com

Splat'em Sports Paintball
18600 HWY2
Monroe, Washington 98272
info@splatemsports.com
http://www.splatemsports.com/

CDR Park
19027 Milltown Rd
Mount Vernon, Washington 98273
360-424-9440
cedar@cdrsports.com
http://www.cdrsports.com

Paint A Mania
2464 E Blackburn Road
Mount Vernon, Washington 98274
360-848-7617
info@paintamania.com
http://www.paintamania.com

General Quarters Paintball
NAS Whidbey Island
Oak Harbor, Washington 98278
360-257-2074
GQPaintball@yahoogroups.com
http://www.navylifepnw.com/site/
221/default.aspx

Paradise Paintball
Jackson and Lund Avenues
Port Orchard, Washington 98366
darkeninc@aol.com
http://www.paradisepaintball.com

Urban Myth Paintball
Port Orchard, Washington 98366
(360) 362-3962
u_m_pjst4you@yahoo.com
http://www.Urbanmythpaintball.com

Paranoid Paintball
12413 Meridian E, Suite B
Puyallup, Washington 98373
253 446 0199
http://www.paranoidpaintball.net/

NiteHawk Paintball
Reardan, Washington 99029
dale@nitehawkpaintball.com
http://www.nitehawkpaintball.com

Tri-City Paintball
288 Williams Blvd.
Richland, Washington 99352
sales@tricitypaintball.com
http://www.tricitypaintball.com/

Cadillac Paintball
18025 Sargent Rd SW
Rochester, Washington 98579
360-273-1363
http://www.freewebs.com/cadil-
lacpaintball/

Thunder Paintball
6118 Seabeck Holly RD NW
Seabeck, Washington 98380
360.710.1992
LAN@THUNDERPAINTBALL.COM
http://THUNDERPAINTBALL.COM

Family Paintball and Rentals
1146 SE Hwy 3
Shelton, Washington 98584
360-426-8503
paintballsales@aol.com
http://www.familypaintballan-
drentals.com

KC Crusaders
South Prairie, Washington 98385
(360)-897-6267
http://www.kccrusaders.net

Virtual Assault Paintball
4103 E. Mission Ave.
Spokane, Washington 99202
509-535-6620
krc@va-paintball.com
http://www.va-paintball.com

Tacoma Paintball Indoor
2610 Bay Street East
Tacoma
Washington 98421
253-460-4600
http://www.tacomapaintball.com/

Xtremez Indoor Paintball
1212 W Fourth Plain Blvd
Vancouver
Washington 98660
(360) 567-2520
tbalfe@xtremez.com
http://www.xtremez.com/field/in
dex.html

Paintball Sports
5110 Lackey Road
Vaughn
Washington 98394
1-253-884-5293
robyranger@aol.com
http://www.tournamentpaint.com

Tour Fairways Paintball Course
Walla Walla
Washington 99362

Battle Ground Paintball
6920 Green Mountain Rd
Woodland
Washington 98674
360-667-0181
Gary@battlegroundpaintball.com
http://www.battlegroundpaint-
ball.com

Woodland Paintball Outdoor
303 Lewis River Rd.
Woodland
Washington 98674

WEST VIRGINIA

West Virginia Paintball
Coalton, West Virginia 26257
(304) 636-0456
scott@wvpaintball.com
http://www.wvpaintball.com

Tri-County Paintball
500 Straight Street
Evans, West Virginia 25241
(304)372-7377
rgarnes@citynet.net
http://www.tricountypaintballwv.com

Flat Top Paintball
Flat Top, West Virginia 25841

North Mountain Paintball
Gerrardstown, West Virginia 25420
(304) 229-1412
http://www.northmountainpaint-
ball.com/

Teays Valley Indoor Paintball
3548 Teays Valley Rd.
Hurricane, West Virginia 25526
304-421-5517
teaysvalleypaintball@yahoo.com

Knobley Farms
Cut Off Rd
Keyser, West Virginia 26726
304 788 6304

Greensburg Paintball
3162 Greensburg Rd
Martinsburg, West Virginia 25401
304-263-5171
http://www.greensburgpaintball-
park.com

Big L's Paintball Plus
100 Lemon Rd
Ranson, West Virginia 25438
http://www.biglspaintball.com

Scary Creek Paintball
434 Scary Creek Road
Scott Depot, West Virginia 25560
information@scarycreek.com
http://www.scarycreek.com

WISCONSIN

Commando Paintball Sports
3247 Pagel Ln.
Abrams, Wisconsin 54101
Commando@bayland.net
http://www.commandopaintball-
sports.com
Matt's House Indoor Adventures
2145 S. Memorial Dr.
Appleton, Wisconsin 54915
920.882.6618
http://www.mattshousepaintball.co
m

Crossfire Paintball
135 Lincoln Dr.
Athens, Wisconsin 54411
(715) 443-3898

St. Croix Paintball
Baldwin, Wisconsin 54002
(715) 337-0441
info@stcroixpaintball.com
http://www.stcroixpaintball.com

The Wargame Field
7200 W Hwy SS
Batavia, Wisconsin 53001
414-546-0337
wargameroom@aol.com

Terminal Velocity Paintball
16314 Cavern Ln
Blue River, Wisconsin 53818
608-537-2327
richs@tvp4u.com
http://www.tvp4u.com

Splat Tag
Burkhardt, Wisconsin 54016
651-488-7700
info@splattag.com
http://www.splattag.com/

Patriot Paintball
1166 30th St
Chetek, Wisconsin 54728
(715) 651-0456
patriot_paintball@yahoo.com
http://www.patriotpaintball.cjb.net

First Strike Paintball Games
10327 Highway 29
Chippewa Falls, Wisconsin 54729
info@firststrike-paintball.com
http://www.firststrike-
paintball.com

Combat Paintball
2125 Hwy 63
Deer Park, Wisconsin 54007
888-494-8511
combatpaintball@bww.com
http://www.combatpaintball.biz

Bubba's Paintball
E7525 County Road J
Elk Mound, Wisconsin 54739
todd@bubbaspaintball.com
http://www.bubbaspaintball.com

Hidden Valley Paintball
N24125 Wayside Lane
Ettrick, Wisconsin 54627
(608)525-3931
contact@hiddenvalleypaintbal-
landmx.com
http://www.paintballmx.com

Do-It-All Paintball
N7799 Hwy 151
Fond Du Lac, Wisconsin 54935
info@doitallsports.com
http://www.doitallsports.com

Frederic Paintball
150 th st & hwy 35
Frederic, Wisconsin 54837
715-205-9775
fredericpaintball@hotmail.com
http://www.fredericpaintball.com

Outdoor Adventures Paintball
N600 County Road U
Fremont, Wisconsin 54940
920-729-4419
http://www.outdooradventurespb.c
om/index.php?action=home

BFG Paintball
N113 W18750 Carnegie Dr.
Germantown, Wisconsin 53022
parkranger@bfgpaintball.com
http://www.bfgpaintball.com/

Jack Pine Paintball
25440 Spaulding Rd
Grantsburg, Wisconsin 54840
715-463-5788
jackpinepaintball@yahoo.com
http://www.jackpinepaintball.com

Arrows in the Square
Holmen, Wisconsin 54601
(608) 526-2609
information@arrowsinthesquare.com
http://www.arrowsinthesquare.com

Edge Paintball
5946 S Highway 51
Janesville, Wisconsin 53546
608-743-0533
Ishoot@charter.net
http://www.discoverpaintball.com

Jungle Cat Paintball
N3075 HWY 26
Juneau, Wisconsin 53039
junglecat@junglecatpaintball.com
http://www.junglecatpaintball.com

Hillcrest Paintball
N5605 Woodlawn Road
Kennan, Wisconsin 54537
hillcrest@centurytel.net
http://www.hillcrestpaintball.com

Action Territory
Kenosha, Wisconsin 53158
262-857-7000
http://www.actionterritory.com

Stinger Paintball / Ke-West Sports
7865 Sandy Ridge Road
Kewaskum, Wisconsin 53040
262-334-9760
http://www.ke-westsports.com

Paintball Thunder
Ladysmith, Wisconsin 54848
1-888-532-6623
paintballbcd@webtv.net
http://community-
2.webtv.net/paintballbcd/Paintbal-
lViewsand/

Stalker Paintball Games
W1923 Bass Lake Lane
Lyndon Station, Wisconsin 53944
info@stalkerpaintball.com
http://www.stalkerpaintball.com/st
alker.htm

Dedicated Paintball
2642 Rimrock Road
Madison, Wisconsin 53713
(608) 441-1501
dedicatedpaintball@hotmail.com
http://www.dedicatedpaintball.com

Paintball Dave's
203 N. Broadway
Milwaukee
Wisconsin 53202
Webmaster@paintballdaves.com
http://www.paintballdaves.com

The Siege Paintball
S108 W28220 Maple. Ave
Mukwonago
Wisconsin 53149
thesiegepaintball@yahoo.com
http://www.thesiegepaintball.com

Adventure Paintball
New Franken
Wisconsin 54217
http://www.Adventurepaintball.info

Fox Valley Paintball
Oshkosh, Wisconsin 54901
920-426-5566

Battlefield Paintball
W12151 Vold Road
Osseo, Wisconsin 54758
715-597-6644
Jason@bfpaintball.com
http://www.bfpaintball.com

Xtreme Paintball
511 Bruener Ave.
Port Edwards, Wisconsin 54469
715-213-4272
info@cwrapidfire.com
http://www.cwxtreme.com

Apocalypse Paintball
W9496 County Road Cs
Poynette, Wisconsin 53955
apocinc1@aol.com
http://www.apocalypsepaintball.com

Black Rain Paintball
Racine, Wisconsin 53402
262-752-0077
staff@blackrainpaintball.net
http://www.blackrainpaintball.net

Paintball Sam's
Racine, Wisconsin 53406
(262) 895-3070
samswis@aol.com
http://www.paintballsams.com

Top Guns Paintball
Covered Bridge Rd.
Richland Center, Wisconsin 53581
http://www.geocities.com/top-gunspb

Superior Firepower
4105 S. Shallermeir Road
Superior, Wisconsin 54880
http://www.superiorfirepower.com

Zinger's Paintball
W5594 Muskellunge Lake Road
Tomahawk, Wisconsin 54487
715-453-6144
dave@zingerspaintball.com
http://www.zingerspaintball.com

Promised Land Paintball
29039 Wilmot Rd.
Trevor, Wisconsin 53179
paintball@promisedland.com
http://www.promisedland.com

Full Hopper Paintball
N8910 Lakeshore Drive
Van Dyne, Wisconsin 54979
viau@thesurf.com
http://www.fullhopper.com

Action Packed Paintball
Lenius Lane
Waterloo, Wisconsin 53594
info@appaintball.com
http://www.appaintball.com
Ambush Alley Paintball Sports
5540 Hwy. G
West Bend, Wisconsin 53095
262-335-1838
info@ambushalleypaintball.com
http://www.ambushalleypaintball.com

SPLAT Camp
McCabe Road
Whitewater, Wisconsin 53190
http://www.paintballdaves.com

Shawack Field
311 14th Ave. North
Wisc. Rapids, Wisconsin 54495
715-423-6986
shawack@charter.net
http://www.shawack.com

WYOMING

WASP Paintball
13250 W Garbut Rd
Casper, Wyoming 82604
307-232-8479
http://www.wasppaintball.us

Gillette Primetime Paintball
350 State Highway 50
Gillette, Wyoming 82718
(307) 685-3752

Shadow Walker Paintball Fields
2480 Highway 20
Greybull, Wyoming 82426
307-765-4455
shadow_walker_paintball@yahoo.com
http://www.shadowwalkerpaintball.com

Raging Bull Paintball
1198 Lower Prairie Dog Rd.
Sheridan, Wyoming 82801
307-752-7003
info@ragingbullpaintball.com
http://ragingbullpaintball.com

Maximus Paintball
315 N 4th ST
Worland, Wyoming 82401
(307) 347-4578
air@maximuspaintball.com
http://www.maximuspaintball.com

YUKON

Paintball Yukon
Mile 5.5 Klondike Highway
Whitehorse, Yukon Y1A 3M1
info@paintballyukon.com
http://www.paintballyukon.com

Other Resources

Here are just a handful of the many great publications and web destinations out there for paintball enthusiasts. Happy hunting!

U.S. MAGAZINES

Action Pursuit Games
Apprise Enthusiast Media, LLC
265 S. Anita Drive, Suite 120
Orange, CA 92868
(714) 939-9991
http://www.actionpursuitgames.com
editor@actionpursuitgames.com

Paintball 2Xtremes Magazine
570 Mantua Blvd
Sewell, NJ 08080
(888) 834-6026
www.paintball2xtremes.com

Paintball News
Paintball News, Inc.
PO Box 1608
Hillsboro, NH, USA 03244
(603) 464-6080
www.paintballnews.com
pbninformation@paintballnews.com

Paintball Sports Magazine
2090 Fifth Ave. Suite 2
Ronkonkoma, NY 11779
(631) 580-7772
www.paintballsportsmag.com
dawn@paintballsportsmag.com

INTERNATIONAL MAGAZINES

Paintball Games International
Maze Media
21/23 Phoenix Court
Colchester, Essex,
CO2 0NH, ENGLAND
www.p8ntballer.com
P8@p8ntballer.com

PBUK
PO Box 702
Stockton on Tees
TS20 2WS
England
+44 7970 065628
www.pbuk.biz
gillie@pbuk.biz

Facefull
1 Rue Borda Paris
75003 France
+33 (0)1 42 78 19 49
www.Face-Full.com
info@face-full.com

XPaint Magazine
Frost Publications
32, Boulevard Paul Vaillant Couturier
93100 MONTREUIL
FRANCE
+33-(0)1-42-87-09-69
www.info-paintball.com
xtremepaint@wanadoo.fr

Paintball7
Continent7 GmbH
Eufinger Str. 17
65597 Hünfelden-Dauborn
Deutschland
06438-836 470
www.paintball7.com

Portal Paintball
Portal Paintball S.L
C/ Francisca Calonge 1
Madrid 28029
+34 91 733 30 92
www.portalpaintball.com
info@portalpaintball.com

WEBSITES

(Usenet group) rec.sport.paintball
forceofnature.com
paintball.com
paintballnation.com
pbnation.com
pbreview.com
pbstar.com
p8ntballer.com
specialopspaintball.com
warpig.com
68caliber.com

Index